DATE DUE

NBD 4-20-86			
GAYLORD			PRINTED IN U.S.A.

Coping with Abundance

Energy and Environment in Industrial America

Coping with Abundance
Energy and Environment in
Industrial America

Martin V. Melosi, 1947-
University of Houston

Temple University Press
Philadelphia

Temple University Press
Philadelphia 19122

First Edition
987654321
Copyright © 1985 by Newbery Award Records, Inc.

Library of Congress Cataloging in Publication Data
Melosi, Martin V., 1947-
    Coping with abundance.

    Bibliography: p.
    Includes index.
    1. Power resources—United States—History.
2. Energy consumption—United States—History.
I. Title.
HD9502.U52M44   1985   333.79'0973   84-29693
ISBN 0-87722-372-6

Manufactured in the United States of America

59.404

To my daughters, Gina and Adria, who give energy a new meaning

PREFACE

"DOE," "ERDA," "AEC," "OPEC," "ARAMCO," "PEMEX." These acronyms added to the popular lexicon in recent years recall an earlier crisis in American history—the Great Depression of the 1930s. Just as the "alphabet soup" of the New Deal calls to mind an era in which belief in the promise of American life was shaken, so the new acronyms call into question fundamental beliefs about economic growth, the abundance of our natural resources, and the quality of life in the 1970s and beyond.

The theme of the 1970s was energy. The "energy crisis" was on everyone's mind: Will we run out of gasoline? How much will it cost to heat and cool our homes? Who is to blame for the shortages? While no one could answer the first two questions with any certainty, almost everyone had a theory about the latter: Big Oil. Big Government. The Arabs. Wasteful Consumers. Developed Nations. Developing Nations. The Communists . . . If Americans were short on fuel in the 1970s, they were long on opinions. A veritable explosion of books, articles, reports, and research studies speculated about the causes of the crisis and offered myriad projections, prophecies, and policies. While experts failed to agree upon the solution to the nation's energy woes, most concluded that the era of American bountifulness was ebbing; cheap and abundant fuel was a thing of the past.

In the early 1980s the pessimism of the previous decade was momentarily quelled. The cost of heating and cooling homes continued to rise, but more energy-efficient appliances appeared on the market. As oil consumption declined, gasoline prices began to drop—to the delight of motorists. Indeed, there was much talk about an "oil glut" and the imminent collapse of OPEC. Energy experts and political leaders announced that fears of a *real*, longterm energy crisis were perhaps premature or even wrongheaded.

Whatever its limits, the "energy crisis" of the 1970s has proved to be as much a crisis of ideas and policies as a crisis of diminishing resources. However, the books and articles that have sought to explain the current energy scene or to uncover the immediate roots of the crisis failed to examine the nation's energy past effectively. The intimate relationship between the growth and development of the United States and the use of its energy resources is a major story which transcends the details of the "energy crisis" of the 1970s. That the United States, with 5 percent of the world's population, uses 33 percent of the world's energy production is reason enough to study energy history in America.

Coping with Abundance: Energy and Environment in Industrial America examines the United States as a producer and consumer of energy from the beginnings of the nation's industrial revolution in the 1820s through the early years of the 1980s. The book does not suggest solutions to current problems. Describing and evaluating America's energy history primarily from a national perspective, it seeks to answer the question: What has been the place of energy in the nation's life? An understanding of energy development, energy policies, and energy use as part of the process of American life must precede any speculation about the future.

Coping with Abundance is the first broad overview of United States energy history in the industrial age. It is essentially a synthesis of scholarship on energy history, relying on the most up-to-date literature available. It treats the development and use of coal, petroleum, natural gas, and electrical and nuclear power, while also focusing on the economic, political, social, diplomatic, and environmental implications of energy development and use. There was a conscious effort to link energy and environmental themes—normally treated separately in other studies—because the exploitation of energy is an environmentally intensive enterprise. The book also emphasizes the significance of American energy abundance as a guiding force in our use of energy and in the development of national energy policies. It is America's range of energy choices that has made the establishment of a comprehensive energy policy most difficult.

Martin V. Melosi

ACKNOWLEDGMENTS

For me, there are three pleasurable events in the writing of a book. The first is the initial outline, when the overall project takes shape. The second is the galleys, when scrawl is magically transformed into print. And the third is the acknowledgments, when I get to recall all those people who made the work possible.

This book grew out of a course I taught at Texas A & M called "Energy and Environment in Industrial America." I was able to prepare such a novel course through the financial assistance of the Center for Energy and Mineral Resources, and I was able to teach it through the aid of my former department heads, Henry Dethloff and Keith Bryant.

Robert Divine, Littlefield Professor of History at the University of Texas and my mentor in graduate school, read the whole manuscript, and as always, he has been a strong source of support and has contributed sound editorial advice.

Several others read all or parts of the manuscript. Two of my colleagues at Texas A & M, Joseph Pratt and Bruce Seely, read the earlier draft of the manuscript, providing immeasurable help in conceptualizing it. David Shi and Lance Stell of Davidson College—and colleagues at the National Humanities Center—nudged my introduction toward clarity. And Joel Tarr of Carnegie-Mellon University and John Clark of the University of Kansas gave me fits with their rigorous evaluations of the whole manuscript, but, as usual, kept me from making many errors of fact and interpretation.

Participation in two energy conferences—one sponsored by Mark Rose and George Daniels at Michigan Tech University and the other by Arthur Donovan at Mountain Lake, Virginia—exposed me to much of the current historical research on energy history. I certainly gained more at these meetings than I contributed.

I received important financial assistance from the Department of History and the Mini-grant Committee at Texas A & M. The crucial element in the success of the project, however, came as a result of a year's fellowship at the National Humanities Center in North Carolina in 1982–1983. Without the time to finish the last crucial chapters and reflect on the whole project, I would still be chained to my word processor. The intellectual environment and the congeniality at the center were marvelous, but the staff was the real gem of the place. Special gratitude must be given to Karen Carroll who saw this book through three drafts. She not only typed the manuscript with flawless precision, but also introduced me to the wonders of word processing.

To my wife Carolyn and my two girls, Gina and Adria, I can only say that without them there would be no reason to work so hard on any project.

Martin V. Melosi
Houston, Texas

CONTENTS

Coping with Abundance
Energy and Environment in Industrial America

INTRODUCTION

Energy in American Life

The United States was blessed with abundant energy sources throughout its history. Whether immediately exploitable or only potentially so, these sources were vital to the developing nation in the nineteenth century and the developed nation in the twentieth. Abundance affected the way Americans used energy, how businesses developed and marketed it, and how government established policies about it. While bestowing many benefits, the array of energy sources posed problems of choice. The *luxury of choice* was preferable to the *necessity to choose*, but it often proved a curse when policy makers tried to arrive at coherent and comprehensive energy policies or strategies. The energy history of the United States, therefore, has been an ongoing effort to cope with abundance.

This book examines the United States as a producer and consumer of energy—primarily from a national perspective—from the beginnings of the nation's Industrial Revolution in the 1820s through the "energy crisis" of the 1970s. *Coping with Abundance* does not suggest solutions to current problems. Describing and evaluating America's energy history from several vantage points—political, economic, social, diplomatic, and environmental—it seeks to answer the question: What has been the place of energy in the nation's life? An understanding of energy development, policy, and use as part of the process of American life must precede any speculation about the future of energy.

ENERGY DEFINED

"Energy" has many meanings. Some are ambiguous, others quite precise. Energy can be an end in itself, but it can also be a means to an end. In the most conventional sense, energy is the capacity to do work. From the perspective of human well-being, chemical, thermal, mechanical, and electrical energies are most vital in the modern world. Food contains an important form of chemical energy for the human body. Thermal energy provides warmth and heat for cooking. Mechanical energy runs machines. And electrical energy is at once a source of power and an "end-use" with wide-ranging applications.[1]

[1]See J. H. Harker and J. R. Backhurst, *Fuel and Energy* (London, 1981).

For the purposes of this book, the concept of energy is limited to major energy sources and several important end-uses—especially electricity, gasoline, and illuminants—derived from those sources. Energy is evaluated in terms of its connection to the development of the nation; its economy; its political, social, and cultural influence; and its impact on the physical environment. Wood and the principal fossil fuels—coal, petroleum, and natural gas—are given substantial attention because they have had major roles in the evolution of industrial America. Nuclear power (primarily fission) is discussed because of its technical and political ramifications. Other sources—wind, water, solar heat, biomass, geothermal deposits—receive less attention because they remain largely untapped, have limited regional use, or have been traditionally less important in industrializing the nation. (A major exception is waterpower, which is discussed at some length.)

PERIODIZATION: A NATION IN TRANSITION

The periodization of the book—1820 to 1980—reflects the emergence of the United States as a modern nation. During those years, an overwhelmingly rural people with a primarily local agricultural/commercial economy made way for a large, polyglot population, sprawling cities, mechanized factories, and national transportation and communication networks. A wave of territorial and economic expansion transformed a relatively insular society into a hemispheric power and then into a global power.

By almost any statistical measure, the history of the United States in the nineteenth and twentieth centuries is the story of relentless growth. A large country in 1820, more than 1.7 million square miles, the United States exceeds 3.6 million square miles today. By the mid-nineteenth century, the nation spanned from the Atlantic to the Pacific oceans and had acquired Florida, Texas, the Southwest, the Oregon territory, and California by treaty or conquest. Beyond the continent, Alaska, Hawaii, Puerto Rico, the Philippine Islands, and others came under American sway. A population of about 9 million in 1820 now exceeds 226 million. By 1920, more Americans lived in cities than in the countryside; in 1980, almost 80 percent of the population was urbanized.

The transformation of the United States into a modern, industrialized society could not have occurred without the convergence of several factors: investment capital, an expanding labor force, technological innovation, sufficient markets at home and abroad, an accommodating geographic location, and plentiful natural resources—including abundant energy supplies. The nation's phenomenal economic growth is reflected in the rise of the Gross National Product (GNP) from approximately \$7.4 billion[2] in the mid-nineteenth century, to \$2,626 billion in 1980. It is also mirrored in the steady rise in energy production and consumption. (See Figures I.1 and I.2 and Table I.1 for the major uses of energy in recent years.)

---

[2]Not adjusted to current dollar value.

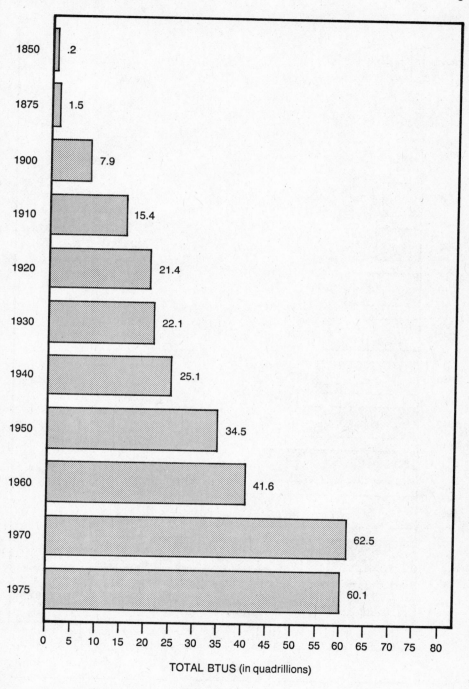

Figure I.1.   Gross Energy Production, 1850–1975
Source: Henry C. Dethloff, *Americans and Free Enterprise* (Englewood Cliffs, N.J., 1979), p. 4.

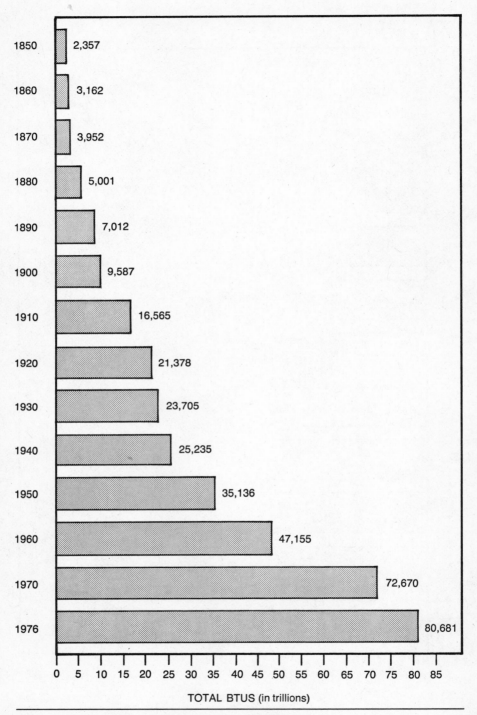

Figure I.2   Gross Energy Consumption, 1850–1976

Source: Adapted from Sam H. Schurr and Bruce C. Netschert. *Energy in the American Economy, 1850–1975* (Baltimore, 1960), pp. 36, 145; Craufurd D. Goodwin (ed.), *Energy Policy in Perspective* (Washington, D.C., 1981), pp. 686–687.

Table I.1. *Major Uses of Energy, 1973*

Sector	Percentage Distribution
Residential (total)	20.5
Space heat	10.4
Water heat	3.1
Air conditioning	1.5
Refrigeration	1.7
Cooking	0.9
Lighting	1.2
Clothes drying	0.5
Other	1.1
Commercial (total)	14.4
Space heat	5.1
Water heat	0.7
Air conditioning	2.0
Refrigeration	1.1
Cooling	0.1
Lighting	3.9
Road surfacing	1.5
Industrial (total)	39.7
Process steam	14.1
Direct heat	9.5
Electric drive	8.7
Electrolysis	1.3
Feedstocks	5.3
Other	0.8
Transportation (total)	25.4
Automobiles	13.1
Trucks	5.2
Aircraft	1.7
Rail	0.8
Pipelines	2.4
Ships	0.3
Buses	0.2
Other	1.5

Source: Adapted from Sam H. Schurr, *et al.*, *Energy in America's Future* (Baltimore, 1979), p. 75.

The growth and development of the nation, which energy sources helped to achieve, yielded major qualitative changes in the lives of Americans. Economic growth brought national power and national abundance. But few shared in wielding that power and not everyone benefited from the general affluence. Growth also took a heavy toll on the physical environment.

In order to understand better the various impacts of energy use and development on modernizing America, *Coping with Abundance* is divided into four chronological periods. The first period (1820–1914) traces the transition to an industrialized society. Wood- and coal-use were essential to the

Industrial Revolution; petroleum emerged as the leading illuminant; and electrical power systems were developed. The role of government began to shift from promoter of economic growth to regulator of energy industries.

The second period (1914–1945) treats the United States as the world's leading economic power. Oil emerged as the nation's most important fuel, and the production and use of electrical power increased dramatically. Government had a central role in establishing national energy policy.

In the third period (1945–1970), the United States became a global power with far-reaching strategic and economic interests. The economy was becoming "postindustrial," since services and high technology were as important as manufacturing and the extraction of natural resources. The participation of government in the energy economy continued to be significant. And Americans' demand for energy began to outstrip the nation's capacity to produce it.

The fourth period (1970s) is a major turning point in the energy history of the country. The United States, despite its superpower status, was forced to operate in a multipolar world, where it no longer produced nor controlled the majority of petroleum. The rise of the environmental movement, converging with the energy crisis, created difficult problems and policy choices. Energy scarcity became a national issue on a larger scale than ever before.

A brief epilogue assesses the role of the United States as a producer and consumer of energy in the early 1980s. Special attention is given to the impact of the energy crisis and national affairs on the establishment of the energy policies of President Ronald Reagan.

MAJOR THEMES

While the text follows a chronological format, several major themes emphasizing the cultural, historical, institutional, and physical impacts of energy over the last 160 years are interwoven into the discussion.

Energy Abundance

The idea of "energy abundance" tells a great deal about the cultural impact of energy use and development in the United States. In his often-quoted book, *People of Plenty: Economic Abundance and the American Character* (1954), David M. Potter maintained that abundance "is partly a physical and partly a cultural manifestation" (p. 164). It influences "all aspects of American life in a fundamental way" (p. 141). Endowed with an abundance of domestic sources of energy and having access to foreign sources, Americans expected supplies to be never-ending and cheap. Energy was often a counterweight to traditional scarcities, especially through much of the nineteenth century—labor, capital, manufactured goods, land (in New England), water (in the

West), and bullion for specie.[3] Abundant energy turned labor-intensive jobs into capital-intensive ones. It also provided sources of commercial wealth and aided in increasing agricultural and manufacturing efficiencies.

More generally, abundant energy altered American material life, influenced the formation of energy policy, and distinguished the United States as a rising world power. Other consequences of abundance were equally dramatic. Energy resources were squandered or inefficiently extracted. Since profit was the prime mover, other factors in the exploitation of wood, waterpower, coal, and petroleum were often superceded. In fact, the notion of "America the Abundant" was built largely on the belief that energy resources were inexhaustible. The "energy crisis" of the 1970s severely challenged that notion, but it remains to be seen if "scarcity" replaces "abundance" as a central theme in America's energy future.

Not only have Americans believed that their energy supplies were abundant, but they also considered the change from one major source to another as an obvious improvement—more energy, better energy, cheaper energy. One historian argued that energy myths are perpetuated because "any newly discovered source of energy is assumed to be without faults, infinitely abundant, and to have the potential to affect utopian changes in society."[4] This assessment is overly sweeping, but Americans have developed a kind of "single-source mentality" over the years. It is generally accepted that the United States has witnessed two major shifts in energy sources: from wood and waterpower to coal (or from renewable to nonrenewable sources) in the mid-nineteenth century; and from coal to petroleum and natural gas in the early twentieth century.

However, in the wake of the "energy crisis" of the 1970s these shifts have promoted a mind-set that convinced many Americans that they have always been, and will continue to be, dependent on a single source (or a few major sources) until overwhelming circumstances force a change. Moreover, energy sources usually have been regarded as competitive rather than complementary. The "one best way" will prevail until it is replaced by a new "one best way."

An examination of the nation's energy past suggests that the change from one source to another has been neither immediate nor absolute. Older sources are not replaced totally by newer ones; nor are new sources necessarily interchangeable with older ones without significant modifications or adaptions. Instead, older sources are supplemented, complemented, or slowly displaced according to location and use. Energy eras, therefore, can best be viewed as an accumulation of several smaller eras. Furthermore, transitions are not necessarily due to energy scarcities. Price, technology, transportation, accessibility to sources, consumer preference, environmental impact, and

[3]Michael Kammen, "From Scarcity to Abundance—to Scarcity?" in Kenneth E. Boulding, ed., *From Abundance to Scarcity* (Columbus, Ohio, 1978), p. 43.

[4]George Basalla, "Some Persistent Energy Myths," in George H. Daniels and Mark H. Rose (eds.), *Energy and Transport* (Beverly Hills, Calif., 1982), p. 27.

several other economic and noneconomic factors can influence a transition. Still, the single-source mind-set has influenced energy policy despite historical trends.

Energy, the Economy, and Government

To understand the economic and political impact of energy requires close scrutiny of the existing economic and political institutions. A great deal has been written and said about energy industries, cartels, the energy market, and energy policy. Popular rhetoric often assumes that there is a monolithic world of business in constant struggle with a monolithic world of government. Extreme views do little to clarify the place of energy in the American economy, the relationship between energy industries and government, and the nature of American energy policies.

For the energy historian, nothing is more difficult to grasp and to explain than the interaction of energy, the economy, and government. A few generalizations will help guide the reader through this institutional maze:

(1) *Business enterprise* underwent a major change in the nineteenth century. In many industries—including energy industries—the traditional American business firm (small, personally owned and managed) lost ground to the modern corporation (large, multiunit enterprise). "Big business" first began to appear in the 1840s with the emergence of the railroad and telegraph industries. These industries established patterns of administrative structure while stimulating a revolution in transportation, communications, and production and distribution of goods. The technological innovation that provided the large-scale manufacturing capability also stimulated the development of new managerial structures. The mass-production system built on these technical and organizational changes, along with mass marketing, played an important role in creating a truly national economy. Integrated firms with salaried managers and centralized administrative structures acquired a powerful advantage in the marketplace, especially in the industrializing East. By the 1880s, some companies, especially in manufacturing industries, chose another route to bigness—the merger. By the twentieth century, many businesses became multinational enterprises.[5]

The rise of big business strongly affected the development and control of energy resources in the United States. Indeed, among the pioneers in building large firms were energy companies, such as Standard Oil. While great variation existed among the energy industries, the trend toward bigness meant less competition (with the exception of bituminous coal) and greater dominance of resources and markets by the largest integrated companies. However, competition between energy industries often occurred through attempts to capture common markets.

(2) The *role of government* also began to change in the nineteenth century—although not as rapidly as the role of business. The idea of "big govern-

---

[5]See Alfred D. Chandler, Jr., *The Visible Hand* (Cambridge, Mass., 1977).

ment" owed much to progressive reforms in the late nineteenth and early twentieth centuries. Before then, the primary function of government with respect to energy was the promotion of economic growth. Initially through an accommodating political and social climate, and then through direct subsidies, loans, and favorable legislation, state and federal governments encouraged economic activity and the exploitation of natural resources. Only since the 1880s have the questions of antitrust, regulation, and conservation complemented (or competed with) the promotional role of government.

By World War I, the need to increase energy production resulted in the first major efforts at energy planning. However, wartime programs were quickly dismantled after the armistice, and a systematic planning program did not emerge, not even during the New Deal years of expanding governmental activities. Much of what the federal government attempted to do from World War II to the present could legitimately be referred to as "crisis management," that is, planning with only short-term objectives. Governmental involvement in the energy field, which was substantial by the 1970s, focused on maintaining adequate energy supplies at low prices within the domestic market. Government policy toward American multinationals abroad was primarily promotional.

The notion that federal policy often interfered with the "natural" workings of the marketplace is accurate. But the question often raised is: In whose interest was the intervention made? consumers? producers? both? neither? Governmental intervention in the energy market had varying, and sometimes contradictory, motives—to restore competition, to promote or discourage production, to control price. On some occasions, government entered the market as a producer of energy, as in the case of the Tennessee Valley Authority. The federal government, however, never achieved a planned energy economy—no nationalization of resources, no permanent mandatory allocation programs, no effective pricing policy. Yet few would deny that changing business-government relations are a matter of increasing significance in dealing with energy questions throughout the twentieth century.

(3) What about the nature of the *energy market* itself? Those who argue that the United States abandoned the free market in energy in the twentieth century assume that a free market existed. The market in energy, however, has always been a hybrid. Free enterprise—the absence of external control or direction on the negotiations in the marketplace—only existed in theory. While never reaching the status of a command economy,[6] the energy economy shifted from limited external constraints to several diverse and more stringent constraints, including governmental intervention, the lack of competition, and environmental "costs." Noneconomic factors have been as influential as have economic factors in determining the nature of the energy market.

---

[6]A "command economy" is a planned economy in which all necessary choices among alternates come from a single authority. In a "market economy," supply and demand determine price and other factors.

(4) Various economic and political interests have worked against the development of a coherent *national energy policy*. Since there are so many vested interests in energy, the lack of a uniform national energy policy has been construed as a sign of a truly democratic society. More accurately, the lack of a coherent national policy is largely a function of American faith in the capitalist system and the free market—unless those institutions work against vested interests.

The perception of energy as a commodity, rather than as a means to an end, worked against significant energy planning. Individual fuels presented specific problems, but "energy" was too broad a concept to be dealt with accurately through legislation. In the 1970s, when the environmental movement and the energy crisis converged, policy makers and energy specialists began to articulate a holistic view of energy. Several sources shared the capacity to provide motive and stationary power, heat and light, and so forth. Policies governing fuels would do little to help solve the larger problems of adequate supplies, allocation and distribution, and a variety of end-uses. Furthermore, a comprehensive energy policy failed to emerge because energy was most often viewed in terms of domestic demand. In the 1970s, a global perspective was forced on policy makers when they began to realize that domestic demand was not simply dependent on domestic supply.

In large measure, national energy policy failed to move beyond a policy of abundance at a cheap price. Few people took account of the noneconomic impacts of energy. Rural electrification did more than provide farmers with a means to light their chicken coops. Hydroelectric dams and nuclear power plants have had a direct impact on the people who live near them. The lack of a coherent national energy policy, however, speaks not only to the diversity and complexity of the nation but also to the limited definition of energy accepted by Americans.

Energy and Environment

Viewing energy as a commodity has also obscured its impact on the physical environment. Until recently, scant attention was given to the relationship between energy and environment. Throughout the history of the United States, the environmental implications of a particular source of energy played only a small role in the decision to exploit that source. Only after a new source of energy achieved wide usage were its environmental repercussions taken into account. (Smoke pollution from bituminous coal is a good example.) In addition, energy abundance has always had a counterpart in the squandering and inefficient use of energy. The United States has been one of the most wasteful societies precisely because it has been one of the most affluent.

Despite the important physical implications of energy use, the environmental issue only recently reached national proportions. In the late nineteenth and early twentieth centuries, conservationism, the efficiency movement, and various antipollution efforts were a direct response to specific threats posed by wasteful or destructive energy practices. However, in the late 1960s, the confluence of the modern environmental movement and the emerging energy crisis provoked a clash of interests over the question of the environmental costs of energy.

The environmental implications of energy use and development help to explain the physical impact of energy on the nation. They also help to bring into sharper focus several other issues that have already been raised: abundance, the nature of the energy market, and the limits of energy policy.

FURTHER READING

Ian G. Barbour. *Technology, Environment, and Human Values*. New York, 1980.
──────────, Harvey Brooks, Sanford Lakoff, and John Opie. *Energy and American Values*. New York, 1982.
Alfred D. Chandler, Jr. *The Visible Hand*. Cambridge, Mass., 1977.
Earl Cook. *Man, Energy, Society*. San Francisco, 1976.
David H. Davis. *Energy Politics*. 3rd ed. New York, 1982.
Melvin Kranzberg, Timothy A. Hall, and Jane L. Scheiber (eds.). *Energy and the Way We Live*. San Francisco, 1980.
Hans H. Landsberg and Sam H. Schurr. *Energy in the United States: Sources, Uses, and Policy Issues*. New York, 1968.
Lewis J. Perelman, August W. Giebelhuas, and Michael D. Yokell (eds.). *Energy Transitions: Long-Term Perspectives*. Boulder, Co., 1981.
Joseph M. Petulla. *American Environmentalism*. College Station, Tex., 1980.
──────────. *American Environmental History*. San Francisco, 1977.

(Note: Some books and articles may apply to topics in several chapters, but they will be listed only once. Check "Further Reading" sections for additional titles.)

PART ONE

Coal-Age America, 1820–1914

CHAPTER 1

Wood, Coal, and the Industrial Revolution

Coal-age America emerged from the nation's first major energy transition—a transition that occurred in an era of energy abundance. The dominance of coal was due less to the depletion of wood resources than to the transformation of the United States from a rural, agrarian, decentralized society into an urban, industrial, national culture. While it did not bring about that transformation, coal adapted more successfully to it than did the more territorially bound and less versatile sources.

This first energy transition was a slow but steady shift from wood, waterpower, and windpower to anthracite and bituminous coal; from an array of "renewable" resources to two quite unique fossil fuels. While wood, windpower, and waterpower retained a portion of the domestic and industrial energy market, the increasingly urban-based industrial economies of the East Coast and the Midwest came to depend on coal.

INDUSTRIAL REVOLUTION IN THE UNITED STATES

Beginning as early as 1820, the Industrial Revolution ushered in a period of unprecedented economic growth for the United States. Steampower and waterpower supplanted human and animal sources of energy. Manufacturing challenged agriculture as the nation's leading economic enterprise.

As a whole, the United States was overwhelmingly agricultural throughout the nineteenth century. However, starting in the Middle Atlantic and North Central states, several factors contributed to the rise of large-scale industrialization: the advent of power-driven machinery, the centering of production in large factories, major changes in transportation and communications, a growing labor force, the development of corporations, the influx of foreign capital, an array of technical and organizational innovations, the extension of a market economy, growth-oriented state and federal governments, and accelerated urbanization. In addition, westward expansion provided staple crops for export and gold for increasing the money supply.

While agriculture was responsible for the largest single share of production income before the Civil War, the growth and importance of manufacturing rose rapidly during the decades that followed the war. In 1859, there were 140,000 industrial establishments in the United States—many of them hand or neighborhood industries. Just forty years later, there were 207,000 industrial plants, excluding hand and neighborhood industries. Between those years, the value of commodities produced increased from less than $2 billion to more than $11 billion. By the turn of the century, the United States was the world's leading manufacturing nation.

The textile industry provided much of the experience for handling high-volume production by specialized firms selling in national markets. But by World War I, textiles had slipped into second place; food and related products were the leading industrial group in the United States. Iron and steel production and lumber were the other major industrial groups. In 1914, food manufacturing and processing accounted for $4.8 billion in production; textiles, $3.4 billion; iron and steel, $1.2 billion; lumber and other wood products, $1.5 billion. These four groups constituted 54 percent of the value of manufactured goods and contributed 55 percent of the workforce.

The glowing picture of a vibrant industrial economy tends to overshadow the instability in the rate of expansion and growth of manufacturing in the late nineteenth and early twentieth centuries. The most rapid rates occurred just prior to and immediately following the Civil War. Recurring business cycles after the war marked an economy rife with instability. While the Industrial Revolution ultimately transformed the United States into a modern nation, it exacted a heavy toll from workers unable to adjust to the shifts in the economy, and it contributed mightily to the deterioration of the natural environment and urban living conditions. There was no turning back to the Jeffersonian dream of a society dominated by contented yeomen farmers and agrarian simplicity.

THE AGE OF WOOD IN AMERICA

Until the late nineteenth century, wood was "a basic foundation of the economy."[1] Europeans marveled at the forests in America, since their own landscape had been denuded by centuries of exploitation. Wood was the primary construction material for houses and other buildings, for furniture, for ships and boats, for carts and wagons, for tools and toys. It was a source of potash, tannin, charcoal, and other chemical products. Moreover, it was the most important fuel of its time.

Wood has always been regarded as "the fuel of civilization." Its use elevated humans above the rest of the animal world. In America, fuelwood has the longest history of any energy source. Important as a heating and cooking fuel, wood played an important role in the nineteenth century: it was crucial to the development of locomotives, steamboats, stationary steam en-

[1]Brooke Hindle, "The Artisan During America's Wooden Age," in Carroll W. Pursell, Jr. (ed.), *Technology in America* (Cambridge, Mass., 1981), p. 9.

gines, and iron production. Its abundance and versatility made wood the un-qualified choice of Americans well after the English and other Europeans turned to fossil fuels.

Wood and Home Heating

Blessed with dense forests, North America seemed to offer an unending source of cheap fuel for the average citizen (except on the relatively barren Great Plains). Bountiful supplies of timber encouraged extravagant and waste-ful heating practices, especially on the frontier of the thirteen original colo-nies. Many Americans built enormous fireplaces where the "cheerful blazes" burned day and night. Poor American farmers could boast of burning bigger fires than could most European nobles. It was unthinkable to spend good money on blankets, when it was cheaper and easier to throw another log into the fireplace.

A hearty fire also had social significance. It offered a central focus in the room, a place to cook, to converse, or just to daydream. "Your whiskey is as good as your fire," stated a guest in a Kentucky cabin, "and that is saying a good deal, for you are the severest old beaver to tote wood that I've seen for many a long day." "I like to warm my friends inside as well as out, when they call on me," the host replied. "The nights are getting powerful cold, and they say it's not good for a man to lie down with a chill in his blood."[2]

More efficient means of home heating, such as the famous Franklin stove (1740s), had little appeal for people living within walking distance of the great forests. Until wood became scarce or expensive east of the Missis-sippi River, fireplaces burned the bulk of an estimated 100 million cords a year. As late as the 1850s, the average American family burned approximately 18 cords of wood annually, which was roughly equivalent to 2.5 tons of coal per person.

Eastern cities, however, were first to discover that fuelwood was not inexhaustible. As urban centers grew along the Atlantic Seaboard, the forests steadily receded. A cruel price of urban growth and expansion was recurrent shortages, higher fuel costs, and exploitation by predatory vendors. Snow, ice, and unnavigable waterways cut off the flow of fuelwood to several cities. Boston routinely experienced shortages and grew to depend on sleds rather than the traditional "wood boats" to haul logs in winter. In the bleak winter of 1726, 500 loads a day came across Boston Neck into town, and still there was not enough wood to go around. The poor were hardest hit and often had to go without. The general wave of reform that swept the country in the 1820s and 1830s offered some hope. For example, the Fuel Saving Society in Philadelphia and the Widow's Wood Society in Portland, Maine, gave wood to the disadvantaged. Wealthy citizens, on the other hand, turned increas-ingly to imported coal.

The concern over fuel scarcity was one reason for municipal regulations

[2]Cited in Richard G. Lillard, *The Great Forest* (New York, 1947), pp. 85–86.

governing the acquisition ànd sale of wood. Some towns hired "official corders" to insure against vendors selling short faggots. In 1757, the *New York Mercury* began publishing the current wood prices to deter gouging. These were at best stopgap measures. Ultimately, eastern towns and cities turned to more plentiful or cheaper sources for home heating. Blacksmiths and blaziers sought alternatives to charcoal. Coal offered such an alternative by the mid-nineteenth century. In the meantime, cities braced themselves for the perpetual winter shortages. In an article calling for a reforestation law, a writer for the *Rhode Island Gazette* (early 1730s) concluded: "When I consider how much the Price of Wood for Firing has advanced in [Providence] for thirty Years past, it puts me to some Apprehensions for Prosperity." How ironic that while urbanites in the East dreaded the onset of winter, settlers on the frontier merely threw open the doors of their cabins when the blaze in the fireplace got too hot.

Transportation

Next to home heating, wood was most important as a transportation fuel. In fact, the development of motive steam power in the United States would have been delayed without an abundant and accessible supply of wood. By the Civil War, steamboats consumed three million cords annually while railroads consumed six million. Coal did not begin to replace wood as a transportation fuel until the 1870s.

Interlaced with vast navigable waterways, the United States first turned to river transportation as the primary means of inland travel and transport. In the formative years of the nation, river boats depended on sails, oars, or poles to move upstream. The cordelle, a large rope tied to trees or rocks, was used to tow boats forward. But it was the application of steam power that created the heyday for river transportation in the early to mid-nineteenth century. Building upon the work of English steam-engine pioneers Thomas Savery, Thomas Newcomen, and James Watt and the French steam-vessel builder Marquis de Jouffroy d'Abbans, American inventors produced commercially viable steamboats by 1812.

European countries with their numerous roads and canals and slow-paced rivers had little need for the steamboat—but the United States certainly had that need. William Henry, James Rumsey, and John Fitch effectively applied steam power to river boats, while Robert Fulton, on the Hudson River, and John Stevens, on the Delaware, promoted the use of the steamboat as early as 1807. An eccentric inventor from Windsor, Connecticut, John Fitch is credited with building the first operational steamboat in 1786, but his second effort, in 1790, was more practical. It was driven by a single paddlewheel and reached the breakneck speed of 8 miles per hour. Robert Fulton's "Clermont"—which completed a round trip between New York City and Albany (300 miles) in sixty-two hours running time—first demonstrated that steamboat traffic was economically profitable.

After the War of 1812, the economic climate improved, and the steamboat came of age. By 1830, it dominated internal transportation throughout the country. The New York to Philadelphia route was the most important traffic lane in the East. Steamboats, while not indispensable there, provided important passenger service. In the West, the steamboat was vital to commerce and travel. Only 17 steamboats operated on western rivers in 1817, but there were no less than 727 by 1855.

The abundance of wood was a major factor in the distribution of steamboats. These vessels burned as much as one cord of wood per hour, and thus required vast and ready supplies. Wood bulk meant that most steamboats could only carry enough fuel for a fifty-mile trip. In the 1840s, steamboats in the East began to turn to coal because of the diminishing supply of wood, while sailing ships prevailed for many years on the Great Lakes and on the Atlantic, largely because of the fuel problem.

But in the West, the steamboat was king. After adapting riverboat technology to the hazards of western river navigation—fluctuations in water levels, snags and other obstructions, and rapidly varying weather conditions—the steamboat became a necessity. The western steamboat rarely had the glamour of the southern "showboat," but in an unpretentious way, it promoted the growth of the frontier.

As crucial as it was to the economy of the American West, the steamboat was limited to navigable rivers. On the other hand, land transportation offered greater flexibility. The advent of the railroad provided a relatively inexpensive and rapid form of transportation to meet the diverse needs of farmers, manufacturers, retailers, merchants, and travelers. By the 1870s, trains were the last word in American transportation. Like the steamboat, the locomotive was the product of the Age of Wood. Railroads considered a rule-of-thumb formula for consumption of fuel wood as 140 cords per mile per year. In 1857, the Pennsylvania Railroad alone used over 25,000 cords.

Railroad development, like steamboat development, had its origins in Europe. In England, trains proved to be commercially feasible by 1829. But like the steamboat, railroads had their most dramatic growth in the United States. By 1840, there were only 1,818 miles of track in all of Europe, while there were more than 3,000 miles in the United States—twenty-nine years before the completion of the first transcontinental line.

The combination of improved track building and the perfection of motive steam power gave the railroads their competitive advantage. Before effective steam engines were developed, horses, mules, and stationary engines were sometimes attached to cables that pulled cars over steep inclines. At first, American railroad companies relied on British locomotives, which were too heavy for the lighter American rails and trestles. Engines suited to American needs were developed by John B. Jervis and others in the 1830s. With the major technical problems resolved, questions of financing, new markets, labor, and cut-throat competition occupied the time of railroad executives. By the 1850s, with almost 9,000 miles of track, the United States had established an effective land transportation system.

The use of steamboats declined steadily in the late nineteenth century, but railroads continued to thrive as the dominant transportation medium until the advent of the automobile. Trains also outlived their dependence on wood. The tenderbox of the pre-Civil War locomotive rarely carried more than three or four cords, and it had to stop frequently to replenish supplies of wood and water. By 1870, coal replaced wood in all but those regions rich in timber, such as Maine and the Far West. Nonetheless, wood and the steam engine pioneered the earliest large-scale transportation systems in the United States.

WOOD, WATERPOWER, AND GRASSROOTS INDUSTRIALIZATION

Few people question the crucial role of fuelwood in home heating and transportation in eighteenth- and nineteenth-century America. But the origins of large-scale manufacturing, factory production, and resource extraction also depended on fuelwood and waterpower.

Charcoal and Iron

Before the coking process revolutionized the production of iron in the United States, charcoal was an essential ingredient. Charcoal was produced by slowly burning wood with a restricted air supply, which essentially left pure carbon. Since the mid-eighteenth century, charcoal was one of the most versatile by-products of wood. It was a fuel in glassmaking and ironmaking, and an ingredient in gunpowder, printer's ink, and black paint. Charcoal was also used as a filter to purify liquids and as insulation for ice storage. In the home, some people used it as a toothpowder or even ingested it to "settle the stomach."

Charcoal had a long history in American ironmaking. The charcoal industry even expanded during the early nineteenth century, when producers learned the basics of tree-crop rotation to insure constant supplies of wood. Large wood-producing areas were necessary because it took 6,000 cords of wood to produce 1,000 tons of iron. In Pennsylvania, several furnaces were supported by over 8,000 acres of company-owned forests.

The use of charcoal for iron production points to one of the ironies of abundance. As long as there were adequate supplies of wood, there was little inclination to experiment with coking. Only when charcoal became prohibitively expensive and difficult to obtain, during the 1840s, did Americans turn to coke. Since the iron industry began in areas where wood depletion occurred earliest, and since almost 62 percent of the cost of making iron resulted from converting wood to charcoal, the transition to coking was swiftest in the East. However, charcoal-smelted iron was tough, malleable, and had a high capacity for welding, which made it especially popular in the West where it was used for many agricultural purposes. At mid-century, half of all iron produced in the United States was still smelted with charcoal.

Waterpower versus Steam Power

The importance of wood and steam power have obscured the role that water-power played in industrializing America. Grist mills or textile mills nestled in a tranquil rural setting come to mind when we think of waterpower. In many traditional interpretations of the first major energy transition, waterpower was considered a local energy source that rapidly declined in importance in the early Industrial Revolution as more modern sources came to the fore. That assumption has been discredited in recent years. Improvements in stationary waterpower in the nineteenth century were unfairly overshadowed by the better-known applications of steam power as an energy source for riverboats and locomotives.

The successful adaptation of steam power to transportation, however, did not lead to its universal adoption as an energy source. Not until the 1880s did steam exceed waterpower as an energy source for industrial expansion in the United States. Furthermore, the use of steam power was highly concentrated in only a few industries, such as saw-milling. Since the cost of steam power was higher than was that of waterpower, industries used it only when they needed freedom of location—away from waterways. Stationary steam power was above all an urban phenomenon, where ready access to water-power was absent but interest in manufacturing great.

Conversely, the newer watermills situated in predominantly rural areas were not the old country watermills depicted in nostalgic paintings. Water-mills began to take on more than local roles; in particular, they were used to power large commercial mills and factories. As a waterpower expert stated: "Although the basic elements remained much the same—dams, millponds, races, wheels—the scale, complexity, and refinement of detail in design and operation found in such major hydropower installations as those of the New England textile centers bore slight resemblance to the water mills in which they had their origin."[3]

The growing demand for power in the early Industrial Revolution set off a "turbine revolution," that is, a revolution in waterpower.[4] The Merrimack River, which runs 110 miles through New Hampshire and Massachusetts, is one of the best illustrations of the importance of waterpower to burgeoning industry. The "hardest working river in the world" provided approximately 80,000 horsepower to 900 mills and factories in 1880, and it was largely responsible for the success of its three leading textile centers, Lowell, Lawrence, and Manchester.

The dramatic shift of manufacturing to major urban areas by mid-century clearly undercut the importance of waterpower. In the late nineteenth

---

[3]Louis C. Hunter, *Waterpower in the Century of the Steam Engine* (Charlottesville, Va., 1979), p. 113.

[4]The French coined the term "turbine" to describe an ideal water motor. The traditional water motors were transformed into "more efficient, more powerful, more adaptable and more compact devices." Edwin T. Layton, Jr., "The Industrial Evolution in America," *Materials and Society*, vol. 7 (1983), p. 254.

century, it remained important only in New England and the Middle Atlantic states, which accounted for 67 percent of developed waterpower nationwide. By 1870 it accounted for slightly less than half of the total power used in manufacturing. But the early vitality of waterpower and wood suggests the importance of a range of viable energy choices in the early years of the Industrial Revolution.

THE TRANSITION TO COAL

Fuelwood dominated the home-heating market until the late nineteenth century. While important as an early industrial fuel, wood was unable to sustain a broad, national manufacturing economy. In an industrial economy, wood was too valuable for other purposes to be used as fuel. The timber industry, which emerged in the nineteenth century, made its profits in finished lumber products, not fuelwood. In 1850 only 10 percent of wood used as fuel was converted into mechanical energy; in 1870 only 20 percent went for industrial purposes. Furthermore, while timber is a renewable resource, it was utilized inefficiently, wasted indiscriminately, and not renewed. Instead of replanting trees in the East, Americans opened new forest tracts westward until they reached the Pacific Ocean. (See Fig. 1.1.)

The actual dependence on coal in America took many years, but after certain barriers were overcome, coal use grew quickly though selectively. Opportunities to exploit coal go back to the colonial period. Early settlers to North America had knowledge of European coal-mining techniques, but they rarely chose to apply them on the new continent. With few exceptions, American Indians had not used coal and, therefore, stimulated little interest among the white settlers to exploit the resource.

The nature of fossil fuels provides a partial answer for why coal remained a relatively obscure energy source until the nineteenth century. Simply put, in most parts of the country it was more difficult to locate, mine, and transport coal than it was to chop down trees. In an agriculturally based society, clearing the land of trees offered a double bonus: space for building a home and planting a crop as well as fuel for the fireplace. Prejudice against the use of coal also grew out of an ignorance or a disregard for its commendable properties: high heat content, relative compactness, exceptional versatility, and, in the case of anthracite, burning cleanly.

From a broader perspective, Americans had established an intricate wood-based energy system by the nineteenth century: fireplaces made for wood-burning, a charcoal-based iron industry, steam boilers adapted for wood, and supporting institutions within the economy that acquired and marketed fuelwood. Many jobs—woodcutting, cording, operating wood depots—depended on the commodity. The reluctance to abandon wood, therefore, was built upon a practical foundation. Not only would vested interests be threatened, but new techniques for mining, transporting, marketing, and uti-

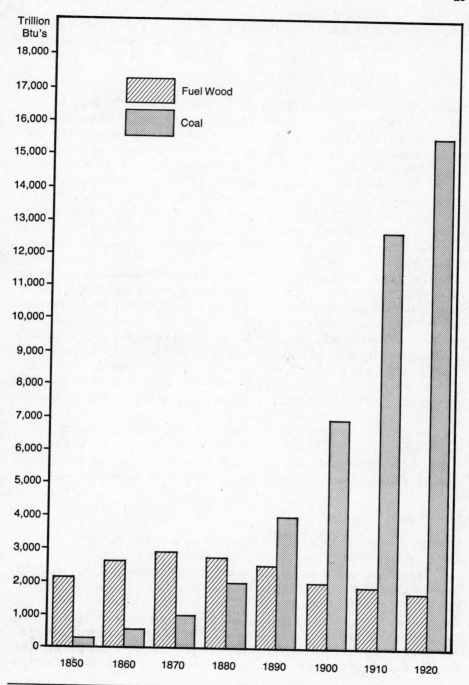

Figure I.1 Consumption of Fuel Wood and Coal, 1850–1920

Source: Adapted from Sam H. Schurr and Bruce C. Netschert, *Energy in the American Economy, 1850–1975* (Baltimore, 1960), p.47.

lizing coal would have to be developed. Forces of change had to be formidable or, at a minimum, they required an environment receptive to change.

The Chandler Thesis

Some authorities argue that the conditions were right in the early to mid-nineteenth century to affect a major change in power source. Prominent business historian Alfred D. Chandler, Jr. contended that anthracite coal from eastern Pennsylvania provided the basic fuel used for power and heat in the large-scale urban factories. The availability of anthracite, advances in steampower, and increasing supplies of iron led to the extension of major enterprises in many industries. The factory system was essential to the process of industrialization, but, Chandler queried, "Why did factories, which had become significant in British manufacturing by the end of the eighteenth century, not become a major form of production, except in the textile industry, in the United States until the 1840s?"[5]

The answer, he argued, lay in the revolution in iron-making during the 1830s, that is, the use of coal in making wrought iron and cast iron. The availability of more and better iron through the use of coal, in combination with the increasing use of steampower, changed the very nature of manufacturing. Early textile mills, powered by water and equipped with machinery constructed of wood and leather belting, were supplanted by factories powered by steam, equipped with metal machinery, and located in major cities. The demand for anthracite, Chandler concluded, did not grow out of an energy scarcity but rather out of a need for an improved technology to increase the supply of good quality, inexpensive iron.

An alternative view is that changes in iron production, essential to the industrialization process in the United States, grew out of the labor scarcity of the era. In other words, improved methods of iron production were developed to offset the lack of adequate labor for large-scale production.

The Philadelphia Fuel Crisis

Changes in iron production—like depletion of fuelwood supplies—provides only a partial answer to the question: Why the transition to coal?

The emergence of a domestic market for anthracite (or hard) coal—at least on a local or regional basis—began with a fuel crisis in Philadelphia. When war broke out between Great Britain and the United States in 1812, the city faced a critical fuel shortage. Residents in the anthracite region of northeastern Pennsylvania had used local hard coal before the war, but Philadelphia depended on bituminous coal from Virginia and Great Britain. The British blockade of the East Coast reduced supplies of trans-Atlantic coal to

[5]Alfred D. Chandler, Jr., "Anthracite Coal and the Beginnings of the Industrial Revolution in the United States," *Business History Review*, vol. 46 (Summer 1972), p. 142.

a trickle. Coal prices soared from $.30 a bushel in March 1813, to more than $1.00 by April.

Artisans and craftsmen in the city responded to the impending shortage by establishing the Mutual Assistance Coal Company of Philadelphia to seek other sources of coal. Seizing the opportunity, local and regional merchants hauled in anthracite from fields 100 miles northeast of the city. The best-known anthracite pioneer was Jacob Cist, a Philadelphia-born merchant based in Wilkes-Barre. A leading figure in the development of the Pennsylvania anthracite trade, he encouraged consumers, merchants, scientists, and local financiers to take an interest in Pennsylvania hard coal. Other promoters and merchants underwrote the cost of "anthracite canals" (six in Pennsylvania) to transport coal to Philadelphia and other cities in the region. These efforts generated the initial domestic and industrial markets for anthracite in the United States. Until the 1830s, production was small in absolute terms, and restricted to Pennsylvania and its environs. Between 1830 and 1850, however, production of anthracite increased 1,000 percent.

ANTHRACITE AND INDUSTRIAL DEVELOPMENT

Anthracite, Canals, and Railroads

The success of anthracite coal as an industrial fuel and then as a heating fuel was dependent upon effective transportation from mine to market. In the earliest years of its mining, anthracite was loaded on flatboats and poled downriver. Eventually, specially designed coal boats were operated. The canals were the first large-capacity, inexpensive transport system for moving coal. Pennsylvania's dominance in the coal industry rested largely on its ability to exploit the "anthracite canals" which tied her deposits to the New York-Philadelphia market. Between 1826 and 1842, Pennsylvania constructed 772 miles of canals. The canals also made the bituminous coal fields near Pittsburgh accessible to the eastern markets. Furthermore, Pennsylvania coal shippers exploited the Atlantic coastal route so that they could extend markets from New Haven, Connecticut, to Wilmington, North Carolina.

The adaption of coal to the steam engine made the relationship between coal and transportation essential. Anthracite was used in steam engines as early as the mid-1820s, and it became a practical source of steampower by 1830. By 1835, steam-driven factory machinery, steamboats, and locomotives were using anthracite. The mutual dependence of anthracite and the railroads changed the very nature of the coal industry in the United States.

The railroads helped to make coal preeminent as an energy source, rather than coal helping to make railroads preeminent as a transportation system. Direct demand for coal by the railroads was slight before 1860, largely because effective technologies to burn coal were not previously available, many railroads had improved their access to timber. But railroads dominated the anthracite coal industry even before they relied on coal as an energy source. By 1911, eleven railroads served the anthracite regions of Pennsylvania. Several lines carried anthracite to New York, Philadelphia, and Baltimore; from tidewater installations, sailing vessels distributed coal to New England and other markets. Similar experiences can be found in Virginia, where "coalers" dominated the rails in bringing coal to markets in the East.

Within a short time, the "anthracite railroads" controlled the transportation of anthracite from the mines and, ultimately, owned the mines themselves. For example, Franklin B. Gowen, president of the Philadelphia and Reading Railroad, acquired the Philadelphia and Reading Coal and Iron Company in 1871 and incorporated it into the railroad company. The railroad company owned 100,000 acres of coal lands and subsidized the building of iron furnaces along the railroad's route. The anthracite railroads, by consolidating mining, transportation, and even smelting operations, brought stability to the coal industry at the cost of being virtual monopolies in some areas. Pooling, interlocking stock ownership, and buying up competing smaller lines became standard practice. By 1917, four railroads mined approximately 50 percent of the total hard-coal output in Pennsylvania.

Hard Coal and Iron Production

The use of coal for industrial purposes propelled it to the front rank among energy sources by 1885. The impact of anthracite coal on the iron industry set the standard, which not only transformed that industry in less than fifty years but also changed the energy base for almost every industrial venture until World War I. The cost of transporting anthracite from the coalfields of northeastern Pennsylvania was the most immediate hindrance in the proliferation of this clean, long-burning fuel. By the 1820s, many blacksmiths abandoned charcoal for anthracite as an ingredient in the processing of iron. The major impact of anthracite, however, did not occur until the 1830s when it was used for smelting. Lehigh Coal and Navigation Company tried but failed to construct an effective anthracite iron furnace in 1820, but several companies entered the field after a patent was filed in 1830 for making pig iron using anthracite. By 1839, an anthracite pig-iron industry was well established in Pennsylvania.

Anthracite also helped to stimulate the modernization of the iron industry. The production of wrought and cast iron stagnated badly after the American Revolution, when cheap imported English iron drove many large domestic producers out of business. After the War of 1812, two major British innovations were introduced into the United States: "rolling"—a process that mechanized the refining and shaping of iron—and "puddling"—a process that heated the iron without bringing it into contact with the fuel. The use of anthracite in the 1820s and 1830s improved these processes markedly. A third major British improvement—using coal in blast furnaces—was developed in the 1840s and 1850s. It was especially important in the manufacture of rails for train tracks in the United States.

The greater demand for iron led to a major relocation of the industry at mid-century, from the center of Pennsylvania to two major locations: Pittsburgh (for the production of wrought iron), and Allentown, Wilkes-Barre, and Philadelphia (sites of many rolling mills). In addition, new pig iron-producing furnaces in eastern Pennsylvania replaced the charcoal furnaces of the central counties. Little by little the migration of the iron industry separated iron mining from iron production.

In the West, the situation was quite different. It was out of the question to ship anthracite westward, especially since wood and, to a lesser extent, bituminous coal dominated the energy system of that region. The use of bituminous coal as an industrial fuel, however, proceeded slowly in the trans-Appalachian region. Not until the eve of the Civil War were bituminous coal and coke well established as blast furnace fuels in the major pig-iron districts of the West.

Home Heating and Illumination

While coal had its most immediate impact on industry and transportation, it soon vied for the domestic market dominated by wood. Coal had been used occasionally as a heating fuel during wood shortages or in the homes of the wealthy. Wider acceptance of coal as a home-heating fuel required several preconditions. Promoters of anthracite deluged consumers with information— or propaganda—extolling the virtues of the fossil fuel. Inventions such as coal-burning stoves, furnaces, and grates made the use of anthracite feasible. Scientific fuel analyses added to the general understanding of the properties and capabilities of hard coal.

Anthracite first became a standard home-heating and cooking fuel in areas bordering the northeastern fields or in cities serviced by them in the 1820s and 1830s. Before the Civil War, most coal was burned in open grates, although heating stoves had penetrated urban markets before that time. By the 1850s, most public buildings were using mineral coal as a fuel, since air furnaces were adapted into central heating systems.

Aside from heating, promoters insisted on anthracite's value as a cooking fuel. The Franklin Institute in Philadelphia offered a $100 cash prize (donated by mine operators) and a silver medal to anyone who could invent an inexpensive anthracite cooking stove. A fuel committee in New York offered a $50 prize for the invention of a cheap cooking grate to be used with anthracite.

Coal also challenged animal fats, tallows, and other animal by-products as a major illuminant. Coal-gas and coal-oil found some important uses in the nineteenth century. Relying on British technology, Baltimore became the first city in the United States to build a gasworks (using bituminous), which was profitable by the 1830s. Gasworks in New York and Boston soon followed. (Philadelphia used rosin from turpentine instead of coal as its source for gas.) Companies on the Eastern seaboard imported cannel coal from England and, by the 1850s, Albert bitumen from New Brunswick; inland companies turned to cannel coal from West Virginia, Kentucky, Illinois, and Pennsylvania. In 1856, Abraham Gesner established New York Kerosene Company, which was the first firm to manufacture coal-oil illuminants.

THE RISE OF BITUMINOUS COAL

Anthracite coal effectively challenged the dominance of wood as an industrial fuel. Its greatest period of growth was between 1820 and 1850—during which time output increased from 365 tons to more than 4 million tons. As late as 1860, anthracite accounted for approximately 55 percent of all coal mined in the United States, but, on the other hand, as early as 1870 its importance had ebbed, except as a heating fuel in the Northeast. By 1910, only 2 percent of pig iron was made with hard coal.

The use of bituminous coal increased dramatically in the late nineteenth century. Like anthracite, bituminous coal initially was most successful as a local fuel. But there was a key difference. Whereas the region for mining anthracite was geographically limited, bituminous deposits were found throughout the nation. In the mid-nineteenth century, bituminous was mined in at least twenty-two states. Five states—Pennsylvania, Ohio, Illinois, Virginia, and Maryland—mined 90 percent of the total production. Pennsylvania alone accounted for 45 percent of the national output.

Accessibility was a major reason for the success of bituminous, although its versatility and other special properties also made it an attractive fuel. Coking of bituminous made it preferable for iron smelting,[6] while the coal itself could be converted with relative ease to gas for lighting and heating. Railroads also found it convenient for stoking boilers. By 1880, coal—mostly bituminous—was used for about 90 percent of locomotive fuel. Coal also constituted the largest simple item of revenue tonnage for the railroads. By 1920, more than five times as much bituminous coal (498.1 million net tons) was being consumed as anthracite coal (85.8 million net tons).

The pattern of control in the bituminous industry was substantially different from that of anthracite. The wide distribution of bituminous fields made monopolization of the resource impossible. One historian has noted that the bituminous coal-mining industry more closely resembled the development of agriculture, insofar as local coal was mined to satisfy local demand. As a result, bituminous mining represented "an unconnected set of individual enterprises located in many different regions."[7] A small group of railroads, therefore, could not control the mines directly. Instead, promoters or officers in railroads—especially with interests in Virginia and West Virginia—first established coal companies that bought large holdings of coal lands and then entered into transit agreements with railroads.

---

[6]Coke is largely the carbon residue of dry distillation of bituminous coal. It is used primarily in blast furnaces to supply heat and gases for reducing iron ore.

[7]Arthur L. Donovan, "Carboniferous Capitalism," *Materials and Society*, vol. 7 (1983), p. 271.

In the early twentieth century, large corporations, such as United States Steel, Bethlehem Steel, and Ford Motor Company, bought and operated mines to fill their own needs—"captive mines." A few large consolidations, such as Consolidation Coal Company and Pittsburgh Coal Company, dominated some important bituminous coal fields. Yet, until the 1960s, the bituminous coal industry was never systematically organized, consolidated, nor controlled by railroads or any other industrial entity.

The Production of Steel

The rise of bituminous coal as an industrial fuel evolved side by side with the development of large-scale steel production in the second half of the nineteenth century. In 1856, the Englishman Henry Bessemer announced that hot pig iron could be cleansed of its carbon and silica impurities if a blast of air were forced through it (since oxygen consumed the impurities). Experiments by others reinforced Bessemer's claim. William Kelly, a Kentucky ironmaster, came to the same conclusion even before Bessemer. Litigation over the patent rights to the idea resulted in the consolidation of Kelly's and Bessemer's patents in the United States. By 1864, steel was being produced by the Kelly-Bessemer process, and it was used widely in the 1870s.

An alternative method, the open hearth—or Siemens-Martin—process was introduced into the United States in 1868. In this method the iron was cooked by heat coming from outside the molten mass, resulting in the removal of sulfur and phosphorus. Proponents of the Siemens-Martin process claimed that it was easier to control than was the Kelly-Bessemer method, and it produced steel that did not fracture under sudden shock.

Both methods dramatically vitalized the American steel industry. Kelly-Bessemer steel adapted well to rail production, while Siemens-Martin steel found an important market as a structural material—particularly to steel-frame buildings. The latter also opened up a larger portion of the ore reserve of the United States, especially scrap metal. The United States surpassed Great Britain in the production of Kelly-Bessemer steel by 1880 and in open-hearth steel by 1900.

Soft Coal and the Smoke Problem

The widespread use of bituminous coal had one serious drawback—highly toxic smoke. In fact, the increased consumption of bituminous coal from the 1870s through World War I contributed greatly to pervasive pollution problems in industrial cities. The smoke problem combined with unprecedented population densities, traffic congestion, tainted water supplies, inadequate sewerage systems, mounds of refuse, unbearable noise levels and increased incidence of communicable diseases produced America's first major environmental crisis, with repercussions still felt today.

The use of any energy source poses environmental problems of one sort or another. The vast exploitation of wood as a fuel led to serious problems of deforestation and accompanying erosion in several locations. The mining of anthracite scarred northeastern Pennsylvania. Many citizens were concerned about the effects of anthracite fires upon health. Periodically, stories appeared in local newspapers describing the debilitating effects of escaped coal gas from improperly installed stoves. An irate New Yorker called for the abolition of anthracite furnaces because they "will hourly destroy the health of our women and children." In a letter to Henry C. Carey, a promoter of anthracite coal, a friend wrote: "You ought to hear our Cousin Charlotte talk against the hard coal fires, and tell of the injury thereby done to Eye-sight, hair, complexion and nerves."[8]

The effects of smoke pollution from soft coal posed a much more serious threat than did any from wood, anthracite, or coal-gas. Unlike modern air pollution problems, coal smoke was not a national issue. It was restricted to areas where bituminous was a primary fuel for industry, transportation, and domestic purposes, and where temperature inversions were common. Particularly hard hit were Pittsburgh, Cincinnati, St. Louis, and Chicago. Methods of burning were so primitive that great amounts of heat and various pollutants (especially sulfur) went up the smokestacks and chimneys.

The smoke problem was marginal in cities like New York, Boston, and Philadelphia, which relied on anthracite (or in San Francisco which utilized natural gas). However, when anthracite was unavailable, New York, for instance, turned to bituminous. The Edison Company, which generated electricity for the city, periodically used soft coal to fire its boilers and was cited repeatedly by smoke inspectors. In order to escape the citations, the company placed scouts on the roof to warn the engineers to stop feeding coal into the furnaces when inspectors were photographing the plant.

The negative effects of smoke became quite obvious by the 1890s. There were few scientific measures for smoke pollution, but the annoyances to the senses were enough to set off protests. A physician writing in 1915 stated:

> The old idea that black smoke is indicative of a prosperous community is still too prevalent. It is not sufficiently known that smoke spells waste and inefficiency, wear and tear of everything about a city, including man. What we look upon as normal may be wholly abnormal; conditions need correcting.

Citizens in Pittsburgh and St. Louis complained about frequent nasal, throat, and bronchial problems. Some observers argued that fatalities from pneumonia, diphtheria, typhoid, and tuberculosis could be traced to smoke pollution, as could psychological trauma. The sooty walls of buildings, corroding marble statues, ash flakes on hanging laundry, and excessive grime on light-colored clothes were further reminders of the ubiquitous smoke.

[8]Cited in Frederick M. Binder, "Anthracite Enters the American Home," *Pennsylvania Magazine of History and Biography*, vol. 82 (1958), pp. 96–97.

Although the smoke problem became a real menace, it initially attracted little more than derogatory comments or irritable behavior from the citizenry. A widespread environmental consciousness did not develop in the cities until the late 1890s, when pollution problems became so severe and criticism so widespread that they could no longer be endured.

The difficulty in confronting the smoke problem went beyond its detrimental effects: smoke was a visible sign of economic prosperity and material progress. Contemporary art and photographs show the degree to which billowing smokestacks were a sign of life and vitality for a city. Smoke was a nuisance to be endured—no smoke, no economic activity, no livelihood.

The dilemma for citizen groups and others interested in smoke abatement was delicate—how to reduce the debilitating and noisome effects of smoke without undermining economic growth. Despite this conflict, several antismoke groups appeared throughout the country in the 1890s. Women and women's organizations were especially attracted to the cause. In their socially established roles as mothers and homemakers, middle-class women reformers assumed the duty of caring for their communities and cleaning their cities as they had done for their families and homes. Engineers involved themselves in the antismoke campaign from the vantage point of industrial efficiency. Less smoke meant more efficient use of resources and, thus, financial savings to the businessman.

The courts initially offered little support to the smoke-abatement groups. Judges were reluctant to impose heavy fines on violators for fear of hampering economic activity or unduly burdening industry with damage suits. By the early twentieth century, however, the courts began to acknowledge the existence of social costs through pollution and began to apply nuisance laws more aggressively. These actions helped to constrain the most egregious polluters.

The most tangible success of the smoke-abatement leagues was the initiation of tougher antismoke laws in almost every city by 1912. But city officials were unwilling to rebutt industrial development and selectively enforced the ordinances. By World War I, when production of goods became a patriotic duty, smoke abatement fell on hard times. Only when coal use diminished in the 1920s did smoke pollution likewise subside.

THE DOMINANCE OF COAL

The transition from wood to fossil fuels, especially coal, marked a monumental turning point in the history and development of energy use in the United States. At its peak in 1920, more than 658 million tons of coal were mined in the United States. Consumption increased seventy-seven times between 1850 and 1918. In fact, the growth of coal consumption outstripped energy consumption as a whole through the early twentieth century. In the 1910s, coal represented more than 75 percent of the total energy consumption in the country, and exports exceeded 929,000 tons a year.

The change from renewable sources—wood and waterpower—to non-renewable fossil fuels occurred gradually over decades, but its general impact was truly revolutionary. Wood and waterpower helped to set in motion the Industrial Revolution, but coal proved to be the most appropriate fuel for the times. Market forces—price, technical innovation, access, and consumer preference—led to the use of coal, first, as a specialized and regionally bound fuel and, then, as a general, national energy source. (Other than promoting general economic growth, however, the impact of government on the transition to coal was limited.)

The United States emerged as a leading industrial power by the early twentieth century, but there were costs. Few people viewed the smoky skies of Pittsburgh and St. Louis as more than a necessary accommodation to the modern world. Yet coal as an urban-industrial fuel contributed to the rise of congested cities, the concentration of polluting factories, and the large-scale exploitation of natural resources. Coal-age America was "modern America"—with all its benefits and detriments.

FURTHER READING

Frederick Moore Binder. *Coal Age Empire: Pennsylvania Coal and Its Utilization to 1860*. Harrisburg, Pa., 1974.

Asa Briggs. *The Power of Steam*. Chicago, 1982.

Alfred D. Chandler, Jr. "Anthracite Coal and the Beginning of the Industrial Revolution in the United States," *Business History Review*, vol. 46 (Summer 1972).

Thomas C. Cochran. *Frontiers of Change: Early Industrialism in America*. New York, 1981.

George H. Daniels and Mark H. Rose (eds.). *Energy and Transport*. Beverly Hills, Calif., 1982.

Dolores Greenberg. "Reassessing the Power Patterns of the Industrial Revolution," *American Historical Review*, vol. 87 (December 1982), pp. 1237–1261.

Brooke Hindle (ed.). *America's Wooden Age*. Tarrytown, N.Y., 1975.

Louis C. Hunter. *Waterpower in the Century of the Steam Engine*. Charlottesville, Va., 1979.

Martin V. Melosi (ed.). *Pollution and Reform in American Cities, 1870–1920*. Austin, Tex., 1980.

Sherry H. Olson. *The Depletion Myth: A History of Railroad Use of Timber*. Cambridge, Mass., 1971.

H. Benjamin Powell. *Philadelphia's First Fuel Crisis*. University Park, Pa., 1978.

Sam H. Schurr and Bruce C. Netschert. *Energy in the American Economy, 1850–1975*. Baltimore, 1960.

George Rogers Taylor. *The Transportation Revolution, 1815–1860*. New York, 1951.

CHAPTER 2

Oil Strike! The Birth of the Petroleum Industry

The petroleum industry was born in coal-age America. While coal was the mainstay of the industrializing nation in the nineteenth century, oil was to become the energy source of the twentieth century. Since the petroleum industry grew so rapidly, it took much less time for oil to rival coal's dominance than it took for coal to rival wood and waterpower. Like its fossil fuel counterpart, petroleum began as a specialized form of energy. It first emerged as an important source of artificial light, then as a superior lubricant, and finally as the leading transportation fuel.

The oil industry had its roots in the heart of Pennsylvania coal country. But its most dramatic impact grew out of oil strikes in the Southwest and West at the turn of the century. While the oil boom began as a regional phenomenon, it ultimately had a major impact on the entire nation. The expanded supplies of oil undercut the economic dominance of the Northeast and Midwest, as modernization and mechanization crossed the Mississippi River.

The rise of the oil industry was central to the development of the modern corporation. The Standard Oil Trust—integrated, organizationally sophisticated, and large in size—became the model for American big business. The abundance of oil and private access to it meant that the industry would not develop in an orderly fashion nor without casualties. Abundance of oil, like abundance of coal, also meant wasteful acquisition and use of the resource. The rise of a new and versatile fossil fuel was an important occurence. How to acquire it, how to process it, how to sell it, and how to use it were the major concerns of the era. The United States' second energy transition was underway well before Americans got accustomed to the first.

THE EARLY USES OF OIL

While human exploitation of oil goes back at least 5,000 years, the United States fostered the first modern petroleum industry. Prior to 1850, the only commercial role that petroleum had in America was as a medicine. Under a host of names—Seneca oil, rock oil, fossil oil, Genesee bank oil, British oil,

American oil—petroleum was recognized as having numerous therapeutic properties. Settlers acquired their knowledge of the medicinal value of rock oil from local Indians. Often purified by boiling, Indians used the oil for toothaches, headaches, swelling, rheumatism, sprains, and as a salve for wounds and burns. Sometimes they even ingested it.

White settlers in northwest Pennsylvania traded with the Seneca Indians, who lived in the vicinity of Oil Creek, a tributary of the Allegheny River, for "Seneca oil." By the early 1800s, petroleum was a well-known item in apothecaries throughout the East. The white settlers used it to treat virtually everything that humans and their animals suffered or contracted.

PRECONDITIONS FOR OIL EXPLOITATION

The search for an efficient and inexpensive illuminant in the nineteenth century led to petroleum. The exploitation of petroleum on a commercial scale, however, depended on several preconditions. Foremost, a vast market already existed for illuminants. Beeswax, tallow, and whale oil were becoming increasingly costly and scarce. The once thriving whaling industry peaked in 1848; by the 1860s, the whale herds in nearby waters were depleted.

Abraham Gesner and Kerosene

Experimentation with camphene (a mixture of alcohol and turpentine) and coal oil as new sources of artificial light was a second precondition to the development of the petroleum industry. In 1830, Isaiah Jennings took out a patent for camphene, the first synthetic oil lamp illuminant used in America. Although it was quite volatile, camphene was the dominant lamp illuminant during the 1840s. Jennings' distillation techniques eventually were applied to coal and then petroleum. In Europe, French and Scottish chemists succeeded in producing coal oils on a commercial basis in the late 1830s and early 1840s. Coal oil had the advantage of combining safety with high-burning qualities.

Coal-oil production in the United States was short-lived (1850s–1860s), but it provided the basis for petroleum distillation, refining, and marketing. A Nova Scotian, Dr. Abraham Gesner, was instrumental in producing coal oil commercially in the United States. In 1854, he established the New York Kerosene Oil Works, which was the nation's largest and most influential manufacturer of hydrocarbon illuminating oils. Gesner coined the term "kerosene" which he used to describe a liquid product of asphaltum pitch that had qualities similar to paraffin oils. It soon became the generic term for several illuminating oils. Gesner's work was so successful that by 1859 there were at least thirty-three "coal-oil" refineries in the country. To a great extent the success of the hydrocarbon oil business inspired others to consider the value of petroleum as an illuminant. The refining techniques for coal oil were easily transferable to petroleum, and many coal-oil refineries were converted to crude petroleum usage.

Samuel Kier and Rock Oil

A third precondition for the rise of the petroleum industry was the development of exploration and drilling techniques. While the collection of petroleum from seepages offered little promise for developing a large-scale energy industry, the experience of salt-well drillers provided the necessary technology for getting crude oil out of the ground.

Samuel Kier, a former canal boat operator in Pennsylvania, popularized the use of oil produced from salt wells. In 1839 or 1840, Kier and his father drilled for salt near the Pennsylvania Canal. The well produced a small quantity of petroleum, but the Kiers drained it off and dumped the crude into the canal. According to a popular story, the illness of Samuel Kier's wife linked the petroleum from the salt wells with commercial development of petroleum for medicinal purposes. The "American oil" prescribed by his wife's doctor looked and smelled like the crude waste from the salt well. After further evaluation, Kier decided to bottle and market his "Rock Oil." Eventually, his product gained national attention, but Kier's claims were bold, if not outrageous:

> The healthful balm, from nature's secret spring,
> The bloom of health and life to man will bring;
> As from her depths the magic liquid flows,
> To calm our sufferings and assuage our woes.[1]

THE FIRST AMERICAN OIL CRAZE

Drake's Folly

It was just a matter of time before someone merged the disparate elements that led to a full-fledged commercial oil industry—drilling, refining, and marketing. Given the history of petroleum exploitation, it is not surprising that the modern oil industry was born out of the efforts of amateurs and speculators.

In the 1850s, Titusville, Pennsylvania, became the focal point of the coming oil boom. The lumber firm of Brewer, Watson and Company, situated in Titusville, leased an old oil spring and was bottling a modest amount of crude in the fashion of Samuel Kier. An outgrowth of this venture was the establishment of the Pennsylvania Rock Oil Company of New York in 1854, which held approximately 1,200 acres of land in the Titusville area. Pharmaceutics manufacturer Luther Atwood and Yale professor Benjamin Silliman, Jr. were hired to determine the potential commercial value of the crude in the area. In their 1855 report, Silliman announced that "your Company have

[1]Cited in John Ise, *The United States Oil Policy* (New Haven, Conn., 1926), p. 7.

in their possession a raw material from which, by simple and not expensive process they may manufacture very valuable products."

Armed with the Silliman report, the Pennsylvania Rock Oil Company appeared to have a bright future. But the road to success had several detours. Plagued with financial troubles, the company was re-incorporated in Connecticut in September 1855, and barely survived the panic of 1857. The new company president, New Haven banker James M. Townsend, commissioned E. L. Drake to begin operations in the Titusville area. A more unlikely candidate for the job could not have been found. Drake—later dubbed "Colonel" as a way of raising his esteem among the locals in Titusville—was a conductor on the New York and New Haven Railroad line. Townsend met Drake in New Haven where the recently widowed conductor was recovering from a case of neuralgia. Townsend liked and trusted Drake, concluding that he was available, cheap, and had his own railroad pass—even though he had no experience with mining or drilling.

The Colonel went to Titusville in December 1857. Townsend and others of the parent company established the Seneca Oil Company, with Drake as chairman and general agent. At first Drake dug near seepages, but his arcane techniques and his constant financial troubles made him little more than a curiosity in the area. In the spring of 1859, he hired W. A. "Uncle Billy" Smith to drill a well. To accommodate the drill Drake constructed a wooden derrick and eventually used steam power and cast-iron piping to streamline the work.

Persistent but inexperienced, he spent two years drilling less than one-tenth the depth that an average salt-well driller achieved in six to eight months. Luckily for Drake, the Titusville strike occurred relatively close to the surface. On August 28, 1859, while inspecting the drilling site, Uncle Billy caught sight of a dark film floating on the water around the rig. Oil had been hit at sixty-nine feet. The commercial oil boom in the United States was underway.

The reaction in Titusville was little short of pandemonium. "The excitement attendant on the discovery of this vast source of oil," one observer noted, "was fully equal to what I ever saw in California, when a large lump of gold was turned out." Another quipped: "The news spread like a Dakota cyclone."[2] Every oil-witcher, oil-smeller, doodlebug man, promoter, and speculator poured into this little corner of Pennsylvania. Soon more than 800 wells were producing. Although the Civil War temporarily stunted the boom, by the mid-1860s it was roaring again. Pithole became the wildest of the boomtowns in the area, boasting fifty hotels and attracting all manner of bawdiness, opportunism, greed, and revelry. In a pattern that became familiar in this erratic industry, Colonel Drake did not share in the rewards of his labors. Pushed aside by his business partners, he died in poverty, leaving the profits to those who trampled him.

[2]Cited in Richard O'Connor, *The Oil Barons* (Boston, 1971), p. 15; J. Stanley Clark, *The Oil Century* (Norman, Okla., 1958), p. 29.

An Industry Emerges

Like the drinker who wakes up Sunday morning with fuzzy memories of the night before, the budding oil industry had to face many practical problems after the euphoria of the early strikes. There were few industries that grew so fast with such limited expertise in directing its growth. Production figures demonstrate almost uninterrupted increases from the mid-nineteenth century into the twentieth. Within a decade of the Drake strike, oil production increased tenfold. From 1872 to 1882, the average daily yield in Pennsylvania and nearby New York increased from 17,000 barrels to 82,000 barrels. By 1900, *total* production of oil in the United States exceeded 1 billion barrels; by 1929, *annual* production exceeded 1 billion barrels.

Pennsylvania was at the heart of the industry in the nineteenth century. By 1881, the Pennsylvania fields were producing 95 percent of the nation's total. Shortly thereafter, drilling extended to West Virginia, Ohio, and Indiana. And as early as the 1860s, California experienced its first oil craze.

Rapid and indiscriminant exploitation of oil led to several problems: unrelenting production, the discovery of new fields, and the drying up of others contributed to wild price fluctuations. In 1860, a barrel of oil sold for $19.25; two years later, it sold for $.10 a barrel; and in another three years, the price rose to $11.00. Prior to 1900, supplies consistently outstripped demand, which exacerbated price fluctuations.

The rapid growth of the industry also forced oilmen to confront a range of technical issues, such as drilling, storing, refining, and transporting crude. The most nagging problem was transportation. At first crude was shipped as if it were coal or wood. Wagons delivered barrels or tanks of oil to barges and later to railroads. Water became the first important source of transportation because of the available technology and also because of the location of the wells in Pennsylvania. The barges generally floated on "pond freshets" (a temporary rise in the river or creek caused by opening several dams simultaneously). However, waterways were not a satisfactory means of transportation. Because few barges could be floated at one time costs were high. Barges often crashed into bridges, spilled oil, or caught on fire. In December 1862, ice at the mouth of a creek pounded against 350 boats, resulting in a loss of 150 and 30,000 barrels of oil.

Railroads, which bordered on the oil region, became a more popular form of transportation, once lines were pushed close to the fields. By 1866, railroads were substituting tank cars for barrels, making shipment more effective. By 1871, horizontal iron-boiler cars were added.

The liquid state of crude, the excessive amount of human handling, and other difficulties of shipping by barge or rail eventually led to the use of pipelines. That innovation revolutionized crude transportation and distinguished the oil industry as a reliable supplier of energy. Oil was first pumped through wooden pipes in 1862, but not until three years later did pipeline builders successfully combat the problem of leakage. Samuel Van Syckel, a pioneer refiner, in 1865 successfully piped oil on a commercial basis from

Pithole to a railroad loading point several miles away. The pipe was only two inches in diameter (compared to modern pipes which are in excess of thirty inches) and pumped only eighty barrels an hour. Despite the precedent, pipelines only supplemented other forms of transportation for many years. The railroads remained unchallenged for long-distance oil movement. And some pipelines faced sabotage or threats of sabotage from displaced teamsters or others fearing the competition. By 1900, however, there were more than 18,000 miles of pipeline in the United States as well as several pipeline-gathering systems (dominated by Standard Oil).

JOHN D. ROCKEFELLER AND THE STANDARD

The dramatic impact of the Titusville strike set off a chain of events leading to the rise of the petroleum industry. However, the establishment of a petroleum industry with a national (and international) scope awaited the formation of the Standard Oil Trust. The significance of the Standard Oil Trust rested on its complete dominance of the industry and its leadership in the organizational revolution, of which big business was the most immediate beneficiary.

John D. Rockefeller seemed to be an unlikely spearhead of one of America's great corporations. Hardly an individual out of the rags-to-riches mold, Rockefeller acquired wealth before venturing into oil. Unimpressive physically, he was reserved, almost colorless, with a relentless zeal for precision and an eye for detail. Biographer John T. Flynn observed that Rockefeller "in his soul was a bookkeeper."

In the world of business, Rockefeller was nothing if he was not shrewd. As his sister Lucy noted: "When it's raining porridge, you'll find John's dish right side up."[3] At the time of the discovery of oil in Titusville, Rockefeller and his partner, Maurice Clark, were merchandizing produce in Cleveland. In 1863, Rockefeller, Clark, and Sam Andrews, a young engineer, decided to bring order and stability to the oil industry, but at the price of weakening the competitive system. Standard came as close as any company to establishing a true monopoly, especially in the area of oil refining.

Rockefeller had a different perspective. In his memoir, *Random Reminiscences of Men and Events* (1909), he defended the Standard against charges of unfair practices. On the issue of eliminating competition, he stated:

> It is a common thing to hear people say that this company has crushed out its competitors. Only the uninformed could make such an assertion. It has and always has had, and always will have, hundreds of active competitors; it has lived only because it has managed its affairs well and economically and with great vigour.

[3]Cited in Robert L. Heilbroner, "The Grand Acquisitor," *American Heritage*, vol. 16 (December 1974), p. 22.

Standard's success and its ability to dominate the early oil business grew out of several important circumstances. First, Standard maintained a strong cash position throughout its years of development, and its financial solvency allowed it to cut costs and stay in business. Rockefeller and his partners realized that the oil business was so risky that access to cash resources was necessary to avoid incurring large debts or being controlled by financial institutions. By 1870, Standard was its own banker.

A second key to Standard's success—and where it drew the greatest criticism—was its ability to eliminate competition. Standard bought out smaller refineries, often resorting to freight rate discrimination, abuse of pipeline control, and unfair sales practices. Yet Rockefeller was no fool. He wanted both to thwart combinations against the Standard and to tap the available talent in the oil industry. He often permitted former refinery owners to operate their plants—under Standard control—and allowed them to do the purchasing, transporting, and marketing of the oil. Cooption and paternalism were effective ways of heading off the kind of cutthroat competition that Rockefeller had seen in the railroad industry.

The most significant measure of Standard's success, beyond dominance in refining, was its control of petroleum transportation—first by rail and then by pipeline. Aided by railroad lines, such as the Erie, the New York Central, and the Pennsylvania, Standard was able to secure cheap shipping rates for its product, especially through rebates (a rate reduction that was often part of a secret deal). By 1879, a government agency estimated that in a period of five months Standard had shipped about eighteen million barrels of oil for which it received rebates ranging from 11 percent to 47 percent of the total shipping costs.

Standard also made substantial returns on the "drawback," a device that forced the railroads under its influence to pay Standard a rebate on the oil it shipped and a portion of the freight charge paid by other refiners. The most notorious example of this practice was the creation of the South Improvement Company, a cartel organized in 1871 by Standard and several railroads. In an effort to keep prices high, and also increase the revenue of the participating railroads, the company arranged rebates for members and higher rates for nonmembers. The South Improvement Company raised such a furor that its charter was revoked in three months.

While Standard began as a side venture for the partners, it soon became a very profitable company. The cautious Clark was not as willing as Rockefeller and Andrews to devote major attention to the oil business. In 1865, the partners put the firm up for auction among themselves, with Rockefeller getting the refining business and Clark the produce business. The new firm, Rockefeller and Andrews, was the first step toward the establishment of the Standard Oil Company of Ohio (1870), initially capitalized at $1 million.

Cleveland, by virtue of Rockefeller's consolidations, became the chief competitor of the Oil Creek refineries and ultimately wrested the leadership from Pittsburgh. Cleveland's favorable location allowed Rockefeller to exploit cheap water transportation on Lake Erie and the Erie Canal, as well as to utilize available railroad trunk lines. The transportation advantage offset Cleveland's distance from the producing wells. Soon Rockefeller controlled the country's largest refinery, but Standard only captured 10 percent of the market due to competition from approximately 250 smaller firms. Within eight years, however, Standard did almost 95 percent of the refining in the country.

Standard's rise to unquestioned leadership in the oil industry rested on its ability to take advantage of the chaos in the oil fields and the decentralization of the refining business, as well as to cultivate important allies in transportation. The manipulation of producers, refiners, and shippers came as a result of business acumen and ruthless and unfair practices. Standard's style of business prompted severe criticism, especially from the enthusiastic reformer-turned-socialist, Henry Demarest Lloyd. In an 1881 issue of *Atlantic Monthly* he concluded: "America has the proud satisfaction of having furnished the world with the greatest, wisest, and meanest monopoly known to history."[4]

Standard's practices were leading to a major vertical integration within the oil industry. Standard became a self-contained corporation with control of its oil from well-head to market. By 1882, it became apparent to company officials that Standard's continued growth required a new, more sophisticated business structure. Samuel T. C. Dodd, the astute counsel of the firm, recommended the development of a "trust," an old device but in a new setting. Through reorganization, nine trustees would hold all the certificates of Standard's companies "in trust." In 1882, the Standard Oil Trust was formed, providing the firm with clear tax advantages and more flexibility in controlling the pricing of oil and other features of the industry. Standard paved the way for trusts in several other industries, especially sugar, steel, tobacco, and whiskey. (See Chapter 4 for more details.)

The Ohio courts nullified the trust agreement in 1892, but the company reorganized in New Jersey. The new arrangement was much more congenial to Standard's goals and practices. Under New Jersey's holding company laws, taxes levied on the corporation were reduced, more extensive issuance of stock was permitted, and the liability of stockholders was limited. By 1904, Standard once again controlled about 90 percent of the country's kerosene production; the rest of the market was shared by about seventy-five companies. Standard also moved in some new directions. It began to emphasize production—uncharacteristic of its early practices—especially in Latin America. In 1888, Anglo-American Oil Company became the first of Standard's foreign affiliates.

Standard achieved a remarkable place in American business and completely altered the oil industry. However, the 1890s brought glimmers of what was soon to come. Oil was struck in Ohio and, soon thereafter, in Indiana, Illinois, Kentucky, and Virginia. The emergence of the Pure Oil Trust in 1895—the most successful challenger to Standard in the nineteenth century—raised hopes for the return of competition. In 1897, John D. Rockefeller severed his ties with Standard. His turn toward family life and philanthropy in the waning years of the old century punctuated, in a symbolic way at least, an end of an era in the oil industry.

THE SUNBELT OIL BOOM

Gigantic oil strikes in the Southwest and California in 1900 and 1901 changed the nation west of the Mississippi and also had a major impact on the oil industry. Beginning as a regional phenomenon, the discovery of vast oil fields in Texas, Oklahoma, and California created a new form of wealth in what would become the American "Sunbelt," and it accelerated the process of industrialization in the area.

The ultimate impact of the strikes was national, however. First, the supply of crude available on the market soared. Second, since these new sources of oil were not the most suitable for kerosene production, the new companies promoted their oil as domestic fuel oil and to be used for locomotives, ships, and, eventually, automobiles. In this way, oil became more directly competitive with coal. Finally, the rise of several new oil companies undermined the dominant position of the Standard. A new era of competition did not undo the process of "bigness" and consolidation in the business world, but it did make the oil industry more heterogenous and certainly more complex.

Spindletop

When a top official of Standard Oil boasted that he could drink all the oil found west of the Mississippi, he had no idea what a colossally foolish statement that was. The discovery of the Gulf of Mexico, midcontinent, and California oil fields signaled a major turning point in the production of crude in the United States, and it brought repercussions throughout the world. A dramatic symbol of this historic watershed was the 1901 strike at Spindletop in south Texas.

As in the Pennsylvania oil region, the history of exploration and discovery of oil in Texas predated a dramatic strike by many years. The Spanish made the first discovery in 1543, and similar to the situation in Pennsylvania, Indians exploited some of the "medicine springs" through the nineteenth century. By 1890, evidence of petroleum had been noted in eighteen counties in the state.

The production of petroleum on a commercial basis dates from 1894 when a company drilling an artesian well accidentally struck oil in Corsicana. A local real-estate firm became interested in the prospect of leasing the land for oil exploration and persuaded Pittsburgh wildcatters, James M. Guffey and John H. Galey, to participate in the venture. By 1900, the wells in Corsicana were producing 836,000 barrels. In the midst of the chaotic development in the area and a glut in the oil market, J. S. Cullinan of Pennsylvania constructed a pipeline and storage facilities and built the first refinery in the region. By the turn of the century, Texas had a modern oil-refining facility, helping to reestablish the fledgling industry on a firmer and less chaotic footing.

While Texas was only one of several states to challenge Pennsylvania's dominance (others included California, Oklahoma, and Kansas), Spindletop became synonymous with the birth of the twentieth-century oil industry in the United States. The *Year Book of Texas* reported how the famous well in south Texas "blew in" on January 10, 1901:

> At exactly 10:30 a.m., the well that made Beaumont famous burst upon the astonished view of those engaged in boring it, with a volume of water, sand, rocks, gas and oil that sped upward with such tremendous force as to tear the crossbars of the derrick to pieces, and scattered the mixed properties from its bowels, together with timbers, pieces of well casing, etc., for hundreds of feet in all directions.

The world's largest producing well, outside of the Baku field in Russia, was the result of eight frustrating years of effort by Pattillo Higgins, a Beaumont local who insisted that oil lay under a swamp near the Neches River, and Captain Anthony F. Lucas, an Austrian mining engineer who Higgins took as a partner in 1899. The venture's financial woes brought in Guffey and Galey of Corsicana fame. And with replenished backing—and a new rotary rig—Lucas struck oil at 1,160 feet, almost exactly where Higgins predicted that there would be oil.

Newspapers everywhere announced the Lucas strike, and the little town of Beaumont was soon overrun with promoters, speculators, swindlers, low-lifes, and the simply curious. Beaumont became the "Queen of the Neches," where you could see "a gusher gushing." In three months the population tripled to 30,000, as six trains daily pulled in from Houston. Shacks and shanties dotted the town, saloons and bawdyhouses provided the entertainment. It was a time for legendary fortunes to be made, for even grander talltales to be circulated. One commentator claimed that half the whiskey sold in Texas between 1901 and 1902 was consumed in Beaumont. Others tell of the vast sums of money changing hands, as much as $100,000 per acre, in order to take advantage of the boom. Some recall the hucksters who gave the area the name "Swindletop" because of all the bogus deals that were made.

The field itself was the most extraordinary story. By the end of 1902, almost 400 wells were bunched together on Spindletop; by 1904, about 1,200. In one 7 1/2-acre section alone, 200 derricks were erected with legs overlapping. The first six wells drilled at Spindletop accounted for more oil than all the world's other wells. Storage facilities were not built quickly enough to accommodate the volume, and fire and spillage accounted for great waste. This much drilling on a field only 170 acres in size quickly led to depletion. By 1904, only 95 wells were producing, and total production dropped to about 6,000 barrels a day. As Captain Lucas concluded: "The cow was milked too hard and she was not milked intelligently."[5]

Gulf, Texaco, and Shell

The strike at Spindletop produced a variety of results. It meant new financial resources for the state of Texas. It led to the exploitation of other salt-dome fields near the coast, including Sour Lake, Goose Creek, Humble, Jennings, Batson. The boom ultimately spread across the state, from the Gulf of Mexico to the Panhandle, and throughout the Southwest. Businesses servicing the oil industry, such as Hughes Tool Company, brought an industrial capacity to Texas. Oil's effect on the development of major cities was no less significant: first Beaumont, then Houston, then Dallas and Fort Worth—all benefited from oil wealth.

On a broader scale, Spindletop signaled the permanent establishment of the oil industry in the Southwest, which provided important precedents for technique and growth. Most important, it produced a new group of rivals to challenge Standard's control of the industry—Gulf, Texas (Texaco), Shell, Sun, and others.

The origins of Gulf Oil can be traced to the J. M. Guffey Petroleum Company. Guffey Petroleum was formed in Pennsylvania, with backing from the Mellon family, for the purpose of developing oil interests in the Spindletop area. John H. Galey, a wildcatter with a nose for oil, and James F. Guffey, who one writer called "a W. C. Fields type, who always seemed about to break into a patent-medicine spiel,"[6] had backed Lucas' venture in the latter stages of the drilling, but were slowly losing control over the venture. The Mellons, especially William Larimer Mellon, saw production of oil as the foundation for a new, integrated oil firm and saw Texas as a good place to become involved (later, he saw the same opportunity in Indiana). He bought out Lucas' and Galey's interests in the original Guffey company, and kept Guffey on only as titular head. In 1907, Guffey was removed as president for some alleged mismanagement and was replaced by W. L. Mellon. The company was subsequently renamed Gulf Oil, with several subsidiaries in Mexico, Venezuela, and the Netherlands.

Texas (later Texaco) was formed by a group who had connections with the development of Texas oil going back to the Corsicana fields. Joseph S. Cullinan, a pioneer in Corsicana refining, organized the Texas Fuel Company shortly after the Spindletop strike. He combined his resources with former governor of Texas James Hogg, who had a lease from Guffey at Spindletop and land for a refinery at Port Arthur. Cullinan first formed Producers Oil Company and then reorganized his holdings in 1902 as the Texas Company. In the early 1900s, Texas Company devoted substantial attention to refining

[5]Cited in James C. Simmons, "The Great Spindletop Oil Rush," *American West*, vol. 17 (January/February 1980), p. 61.

[6]O'Connor, *The Oil Barons*, p. 71.

Oklahoma crude. By 1909, both Texas and Gulf were in direct competition with Standard.

A third new giant, Shell Oil, also had tangential connections with Guffey. Guffey had signed a twenty-year contract with Shell Transport and Trading Company of London to deliver fuel oil to the British navy at $.25 a barrel. When the automobile market raised the price of crude, this arrangement almost ruined Gulf, which had assumed responsibility for fulfilling Shell's original contract with the British navy. Shell, however, flourished with such a price advantage, bought more tankers, and eventually merged with Royal Dutch.

In the early days of the Texas boom, Standard was not a major factor in the development of the fields. It was little impressed with Texas crude, which was asphaltic, sulfurous-based, and thus ill-suited to the production of illuminants. The leadership at Standard, however, had not considered the potential market for Texas oil as a fuel.

Despite the efforts of local companies to keep the eastern giant out of the state, Standard remained in Texas one way or another. Hostility toward Standard's marketing affiliates in the state and support of local companies by the state government discouraged the company from doing business there using its own name. Waters-Pierce, a Standard affiliate based in Missouri but doing business in Texas, was indicted for violating the state's antitrust law in 1889; it was forced out in 1897. Standard was persistent and Waters-Pierce— not even bothering to change its name—obtained a new license. Again the company was ousted when it was discovered that Standard held controlling interest.

Standard Oil of New Jersey was driven out in a similar manner. But local hostility rarely flustered the oil giant, and it eventually bought a half interest in Humble Oil Company, thus entering the state on a more permanent basis. However, Standard was never able to dominate the Texas fields or the refineries. Spindletop, having spawned three major oil companies and several smaller ones, irreparably altered the oil industry in the twentieth century.

The California Fields

Spindletop was as much an indication of things to come as it was an immediate turning point in the industry. Within a short time the whole Southwest was engulfed in the boom, especially with the gigantic strikes in Oklahoma. (Oklahoma was at the heart of the great midcontinent field that spanned northern Texas, Kansas, Oklahoma, and parts of Arkansas.) Between 1907 and 1931, Oklahoma's cumulative production exceeded that of any other state.

Because of the dramatic impact of the Texas strike and then the exploitation of the midcontinent field, the earlier rise of California as a leading oil producer is often relegated to a footnote. California, however, was one of the richest oil territories in the United States. Although an oil craze swept the state as early as 1865, the California wells did not come into their own until the 1890s. Several speculative ventures collapsed largely because California was too distant from its potential oil markets. High freight rates in particular kept California crude from competing effectively. Despite some respectable strikes, Californians themselves continued to depend on illuminants and lubricants from the East. As in Texas, the California industry eventually built its strength on fuel oil, especially because of the difficulty of getting coal to the Pacific Coast.

The turning point for the California oil industry came in 1892, when Edward L. Doheny discovered high-quality oil in the Los Angeles area. Within two years, hundreds of wells were sunk and the scene was reminiscent of earlier booms. By 1913, an estimated 1,300 wells had been drilled in Los Angeles, but only about 300 were long-term producers.

The potential of the California fields drew Standard into the state in 1906 and led to the establishment of Standard Oil of California. Union Oil Company, organized in 1890, became the second largest firm. Both Standard and Union were far ahead of the competition in marketing fuel oil and refined products. While Standard led in the domestic sale of these products, Union was the leading exporter of fuel oil.

By 1900, California successfully rose from sixth to fifth in oil production in the United States. In 1903 it was the leading producer, and reached its peak in 1923. (In 1927, Oklahoma became the leading producer followed by Texas in 1928.) As in Texas, the oil boom in California stimulated industrial development. Oil, combined with its agricultural prowess, put California in the forefront of economic growth and production in the United States.

By the late 1910s, the automobile and the demands of war vastly changed the oil industry. But the dramatic strikes in Texas, Oklahoma, and California had already forced Standard of New Jersey—the nation's third largest industrial corporation in 1917—to share the market with several new rivals. The oil industry became more competitive, in a relative sense at least, and spanned the continent. In time, competition would be international as well as regional and national, and the preponderance of the petroleum industry in the economic and social life of the nation would be greater than ever.

THE RULE OF CAPTURE AND THE WASTE OF OIL

The euphoria over striking oil was not matched by foresight and restraint in producing and marketing it. The abundance of "black gold" appeared to be a permanent blessing; conservation was for the overly cautious or the cynical. The waste and overproduction of the age was due to several factors: poor drilling and storing techniques, natural disasters, the competitive market, simple disregard, and greed. Some of the trial-and-error methods of discovery took effective conservation out of the hands of the oilmen, but others did not. In almost all cases, the ends seemed to justify the means.

Many of the problems oilmen encountered in fields across the continent were first experienced in Pennsylvania. The use of salt-dome techniques overcame some of the difficulties of drilling. Rarely, however, was storage of oil provided for before drilling began. Part of the reason for this was in the nature of early oil exploration: the search for oil was so expensive and so unscientific that it was impossible to finance storage facilities before the certainty of a strike. But even after a strike, adequate storage was rare. Seepage from wells was common because reliable casings were not employed. Often earthen pits or wooden tanks were used to store oil, which resulted in substantial loss from evaporation or calamities such as fire.

In June 1892, Oil City experienced one of the worst fire and flood disasters in oil history. A dam burst on Oil Creek, knocking over a huge tank of naphtha which covered the water and filled the air with flammable gas. A spark from a passing train ignited the fumes, engulfing tanks of crude in flames. About 300 people were killed in the conflagration.

Inefficient transportation also contributed to the substantial loss of oil. Poorly constructed barrels carted over bumpy roads led to spillage, and barge accidents on pond freshets were frequent. Less noticeable problems, such as the infiltration of water into oil strata, plagued the Pennsylvania fields. A local newspaper poignantly noted in 1861:

> So much oil is produced it is impossible to care for it, and thousands of barrels are running into the creek; the surface of the river is covered with oil for miles below Franklin. Some wells are being plugged to save the production. Fears are being entertained that the supply will soon be exhausted if something is not done to prevent the waste.[7]

The pattern of waste and the disregard for conservation measures were remarkably similar at Spindletop, despite the years of experience in drilling for oil. Great fires periodically spread across the fields. One fire burned 62 derricks and sent flames 1,000 feet into the air. Safety measures were eventually employed, but only after heavy losses were incurred.

The general squandering of oil at Spindletop was legendary. In 1902, the *Oil Investors' Journal* estimated that 10 million barrels of oil had been wasted since the Lucas strike. To impress investors, oil promoters in the area opened up the wells, sending gushers of 125 feet into the air. In September 1901, 12 gushers were opened simultaneously for the benefit of 15,000 onlookers. Gamblers placed bets on which well would gush the highest. In little time, the Spindletop field was ruined by such flagrant disregard.

Overproduction of oil and squandering of supplies were not due simply to shortsightedness or recreational wastefulness; they were linked to the competitive economic system of the day. Several geologists in the 1870s warned about the dangers of extracting oil too rapidly, but few oilmen heeded the warnings. The traditional rights of landowners to exploit their real property encouraged immediate drilling. Unlike other minerals, oil flowed. Unless a producer pumped as much of the resource as he was able, competitors could

[7]Ise, *The United States Oil Policy*, p. 25.

drain the oil on adjacent property. In some cases, "slant wells" were used, that is, wells drilled on one piece of land but aimed at pools under another.

Producers often faced the prospect of losing their leases unless they were actually drilling. The so-called "Rule of Capture" dominated the production of oil until the 1930s. It stated that those who owned the surface property over a common pool could take and keep all the oil and gas that they took from the wells—regardless of the possible drainage from adjoining property. The Rule of Capture was based on the sanctity of private property and the right of individuals to own natural resources through control of the land. However, it encouraged rampant drilling and pumping, which in turn led to severe overproduction.

The overproduction and squandering of oil was but one dimension, albeit an important one, of the environmental impact of oil production in the early twentieth century. Drilling and refining polluted the land, air, and water where oil was taken from the ground and where it was processed for marketing. This "localized pollution," especially in refining areas such as Beaumont-Port Arthur, was serious, but it rarely attracted much attention from oil companies or state government before World War I.

In the fields, drain-offs of crude soaked the ground immediately around the wells. Rapid pumping of oil led to the introduction of salt water in the underground pools as well as in the local water supply. Among the wells, the pumping stations, and the tankers, spillage was common. In these preautomobile days, oil even contributed to air pollution. Several days after the Lucas well blew, a thick, yellow fog laden with sulfur engulfed the houses of Beaumont and continued to do so periodically until production slowed down. As a petroleum historian argued: "At least as much oil probably found its way into the region's ground water and air in this period as found its way to market."[8]

Early refineries were built with little regard for environmental concerns. Often unrecovered petroleum was simply discarded in the most convenient location; open (sulfurous) flames from burning crude were noticeable everywhere. Floods along the coastal region washed oil into the rivers, streams, lakes, and even the Gulf of Mexico.

With immediate profits in mind and industrial growth virtually a religion during this period, pollution control was a luxury at best or, more often, a nuisance to be ignored. Despite the fact that in the early twentieth century several major cities were beginning to cope with pollution problems, such as sewerage, solid waste, smoke, and noise, the equation of oil with progress precluded serious attempts to deal with its various environmental impacts. Ironically, one of the few conscious efforts at dealing with waste was the burning off of billions of cubic feet of natural gas—then considered a useless by-product of drilling for oil. Rising demand for energy in general and oil in

[8]Joseph A. Pratt, "Growth or a Clean Environment?" *Business History Review*, vol. 52 (Spring 1978), p. 4.

particular, meant that oilmen concentrated on expanding their markets rather than on eliminating waste.

OIL VERSUS COAL

Until World War I, the rise in demand for oil did not appreciably undercut the dominant position of coal as the nation's leading energy source. In 1915, coal represented 74.8 percent of the total aggregate consumption; oil represented only 7.9 percent. Yet the importance of oil as an illuminant, lubricant, and then as a fuel grew steadily. While electricity eliminated the kerosene market in the twentieth century, the automobile turned petroleum refining toward gasoline. Since total energy consumption more than doubled between 1900 and 1920, oil became a significant energy source in absolute terms, if not as a percentage of overall consumption.

In the short run, at least, coal appeared to have a competitive advantage over petroleum. This was true until oil found its market as a fuel. Beginning as a regional fuel in the Southwest and West, oil was used by railroads, steamships, various industries, and urban centers. Local experimentation with oil provided the necessary impetus for acquiring a much larger market and led to improved methods of transportation, efficient conversion of coal-burning equipment, and more sophisticated marketing techniques. In 1889, fuel oils amounted to only 6.4 million barrels; in 1920, consumption jumped to 300 million.

Building on its regional base, oil as fuel had some long-term advantages in its competition with coal on a national basis. Foremost was price—oil was a bargain at less than $1.00 a barrel. Even when prices rose, the relatively low cost of equipment conversion and shipping gave oil an advantage over the more cumbersome coal. Furthermore, compared to the fragmented, financially weak, labor-intensive coal industry, the well-financed and effectively managed major oil companies were efficient forms of business enterprise.

As competition between oil and coal became more intense in the 1920s, the United States began to pass into a new energy era. Coal-age America faded into an era of oil power. The rising competition between these major fuels most profoundly speaks to the vast energy abundance of the nation. Competing for markets took precedence over conserving resources; unrestrained economic growth was the credo of the day.

FURTHER READING

Kendall Beaton. "Dr. Gesner's Kerosene: The Start of American Oil Refining," *Business History Review*, vol. 29 (March 1955), pp. 28–53.
J. Stanley Clark. *The Oil Century*. Norman, Okla., 1958.

David Freeman Hawke. *John D: The Founding Father of the Rockefellers*. New York, 1980.

John Ise. *The United States Oil Policy*. New Haven, Conn., 1926.

Arthur M. Johnson. *The Development of American Petroleum Pipelines . . . 1802–1906*. Ithaca, N.Y., 1956.

Roger M. Olien and Diana Davids Olien. *Oil Booms*. Lincoln, Neb., 1982.

Joseph A. Pratt. "The Ascent of Oil," in Lewis J. Perelman, August W. Giebelhaus, and Michael D. Yokell (eds.). *Energy Transitions*. Boulder, Colo., 1981.

————. *Growth of a Refining Region*. Greenwich, Conn., 1980.

Carl Coke Rister. *Oil! Titan of the Southwest*. Norman, Okla., 1949.

Harold F. Williamson and Arnold R. Daum. *The American Petroleum Industry: The Age of Illumination, 1859–1899*. Evanston, Ill., 1959.

CHAPTER 3

Harnessing Electrical Power

Electrical energy bears little resemblance to fuels such as coal or oil. It is at once a marvelous source of power and a versatile end-use. As a source of power, electricity often relies on coal or oil to generate it; but electricity also is a competitor of fossil fuels. As a product, or end-use, electricity is converted into heat, light, and mechanical power. It can run the greatest machinery as well as the smallest, most precise motor, and it can be regulated quickly and accurately.

The first attempts at harnessing electrical power took place in coal-age America. By the early twentieth century, the uses of electricity multiplied rapidly and its cost dropped significantly. The process of transforming electricity into heat, light, and motive power for wide-scale use was extremely difficult. Within a relatively short time, however, electricity revolutionized communications, displaced other sources of illumination (especially in urban areas), and brought new sources of power to industry.

More than any previous energy source, the utilization of electricity depended on the design and construction of sophisticated systems of transmission and conversion to other types of power. Thus the impact of electrical power on the lives of Americans, their economy, and their physical environment was pervasive and profound. To some people, electricity was magic, a wonder, a genie; to others, it was an unknown to be feared. Its mystical qualities were bound up in its unique properties and in the sophisticated technologies required to unleash it.

In spawning technical wonders indispensable to the modern world such as the incandescent light bulb and the telephone, electricity changed the material life of the nation. In a tangible sense, it changed the nature of energy services, that is, what people use energy for. In a more abstract way, electrical power gave Americans a new vision of the world, creating a society less bound by nature and more dependent on human imagination and technical innovation. The process of modernization stimulated by the Industrial Revolution found its most sublime expression in electrical power.

PRECONDITIONS

Electrical power was commonplace by 1900, but its development, application, and implementation required decades of experimentation. An array of legendary figures contributed to its ultimate use—Gilbert, Volta, Franklin, Faraday, Oersted, Edison, Ampere, Tesla. Yet individual inquiry and investigation was only one aspect of the birth of the electrical age. The advent of electric power systems demanded an incredibly complex technology; it was not the product of the lone inventor. Rather, it was the result of an international community of scientists, inventors, engineers, and businessmen participating in a collaborative, and often intensely competitive, field.

The development of the battery in the late eighteenth century provided the first continuous flow of electrical current. A practical invention with several potential applications, the battery also opened the way for further experimentation with electricity, the most significant of which was the study of electromagnetism. The work in electromagnetism led to two major lines of development: communications and broadcasting and the generation of electric voltages by mechanical rotative and motive power.

TELEGRAPHY AND TELEPHONY

Telegraphy was a logical application of electromagnetism. From a technical standpoint, a device for transmitting electrical impulses over a wire was not difficult to accomplish. Since the telegraph only required low voltage, current from a battery was sufficient to operate it. But the practical application of the telegraph was another matter. In England, William F. Cooke and Charles Wheatstone completed a working model in 1838. While it was used throughout Europe in the 1840s, it ultimately proved too costly for universal application. Samuel F. B. Morse developed the first commercial telegraph system in the United States, which became a standard for more sophisticated systems.

Like William Cooke, Morse began with little knowledge of electricity. An artist and professor of painting and sculpture at the University of the City of New York, the idea of inventing captured Morse's imagination almost as much as art did. While on an ocean voyage to Europe in 1832, he developed the general concept of his telegraph system. Through collaboration with men like Joseph Henry, the New York pioneer in electromagnetic induction, Morse was able to perfect his device by the late 1830s. After several delays, Congress, in 1843, allocated funds for a test of Morse's electric telegraph. Over lines strung from Baltimore to Washington, DC, Morse transmitted the famous message, "What hath God wrought."

Morse had synthesized the ideas of many others into a workable device. His code—which was the most unique aspect of the invention—provided a new way to relay messages over long distances. However, the test line from Baltimore to Washington was not economically profitable, and Morse was constantly plagued with patent infringement litigation. He even sought governmental ownership of the system, but to no avail. Morse's problems were endemic to this new communications system in the early nineteenth century. Technical shortcomings, such as noninsulated wires and poor line-stringing practices, made the system vulnerable to changing weather conditions. Chaotic expansion of lines, with more regard for profit than performance, also tarnished the burgeoning industry.

Despite impulsive building practices and the gargantuan task of devising a new communications network for a whole continent, the telegraph became an essential feature of American life. By 1847, lines extended from the East Coast westward to Pittsburgh, Cincinnati, and Louisville. By the end of 1848, every state east of the Mississippi except Florida was part of the telegraph network. After the Civil War, more than 200,000 miles of line were in service. But instead of becoming a public utility, the telegraph was quickly monopolized by a powerful company. Beginning modestly in 1856, Western Union Telegraph Company was aggressively consolidating the industry. By 1866, Western Union bought up its two chief rivals, making competition insignificant. Although there were 214 telegraph companies in the United States in 1886, all but 4 were tiny. Consolidation solved many of the problems of earlier overexpansion, but it gave a single company great influence over communications.[1]

The most dramatic aspect of the new telegraph industry was its impact on news gathering, social communications, and the commercial life of the nation. News of the war with Mexico in the late 1840s and the Civil War in the 1860s was flashed over the telegraph lines. During the Civil War alone, more than six million messages were transmitted by telegraphers. Westward expansion and the extension of transcontinental railroad lines contributed to the further development of the telegraph network. And, in turn, the telegraph made it possible to manage the railroad system and link the agricultural ventures and mining operations of the West with eastern markets. Along crowded trunk lines in the East, railroad officials used the telegraph to control traffic. The telegraph had conquered distance and time—an idea that had not yet become a cliché.

The practical application of the telegraph not only produced the first national communications system but also the first international system. In the late 1860s, communications by ocean voyage was replaced with the operation of the Atlantic Cable. Several successful efforts in submarine telegraphy in Europe and Canada, however, predated the Atlantic Cable.

Like telegraphy, the idea of a transatlantic cable was simple, but the implementation was enormously difficult. A truly international venture, the project depended upon the cooperation of the British and Americans in a costly and audacious project. The British pioneered much of the technology for submarine telegraphy. On the American side, Cyrus W. Field, a wealthy paper manufacturer from Massachusetts, provided the organization and much of the financing. After several failures, the cable was successfully laid in July 1866. This triumph of man over the elements provided great nationalistic

---

[1]An additional result of monopoly was low wages for employees, especially for women since they were used widely as operators.

pride for the participating countries, not to mention the impact on worldwide communications.

In the broadest sense, the invention of the telephone grew out of experimentation with telegraphy. However, while the invention of the telegraph depended on hundreds of experiments throughout the world, the development of the telephone was the work of a relatively few inventors. Charles Wheatstone is credited with coining the word "telephone" in the 1820s in connection with the transmission of sound through wooden rods for short distances through the air. Philip Reis of Frankfurt, Germany, invented a musical telephone in 1860. Reis' transmitter used musical sound to create spurts of current that a receiver produced as notes.

Reis' efforts were most closely linked to the work of Elisha Gray, chief electrician of Western Electric Company of Chicago, who invented a liquid form of transmitter in 1874. Unfortunately, he filed a patent for the basic telephone mechanism only a few hours after Alexander Graham Bell filed his—and lost an enviable place in history. Despite poor timing, Gray is now also credited with inventing the telephone.

Their differences in approach to invention—not luck—separated Gray from Bell. A professional inventor and telegraphy expert, Gray was apparently close to completing his invention on two occasions before filing for a patent. But only after Bell demonstrated the practicality of the telephone did Gray believe that a market existed. By then it was too late.

Bell, on the other hand, was not burdened with "the prejudice of the experts."[2] His tenacity, rather than his professional experience, led him to the invention of the marvel of the age. Bell, a native of Edinburgh, Scotland, was primarily known as a teacher of the hearing-impaired. In 1871, he accepted an appointment at the Boston School for Deaf Mutes, and in 1873, he was named professor in the field of Vocal Physiology and Elocution at the newly opened Boston University.

Bell's experiments with the harmonic telegraph led him almost by accident to basic telephone principles. Through trial and error, he produced undulating currents, employing several devices. On March 10, while testing a variable resistance device, Bell accidentally spilled battery acid on his clothes. He called out to his assistant: "Mr. Watson, come here. I want to see you." From the next room Watson heard the now famous command and a practical telephone was close to reality.

Public acceptance of the invention did not come immediately, however. Demonstrations of the liquid-resistance and magneto transmitters were conducted at the Centennial Exhibition in Philadelphia in 1876. Bell amazed many people; but he left many more skeptical of the telephone's practical application. Exhibition judges nonetheless awarded Bell a prize for his telephone.

[2]David A. Hounshell, "Elisha Gray and the Telephone," *Technology and Culture*, vol. 16 (April 1975), p. 159.

Bell had won but the first round in the commercialization of the telephone. A celebrated patent battle with Elisha Gray was part of an intense tug of war for what Bell's biographer called "perhaps the single most valuable patent in history." Bell retained the patent, but he faced stiff competition in setting up a telephone network. Western Union, which had rejected Bell's telephone rights in 1876, subsequently purchased Gray's rights and enlisted Thomas Edison to improve the commercial viability of the telephone. Edison's transmitter was superior to Bell's, but Bell was able to retain control over the establishment of a telephone system in the United States. In a formal settlement, Western Union relinquished its telephone rights (including the Edison transmitter) for 20 percent of the telephone rentals for the remaining seventeen years of the patents. Bell, therefore, secured a monopoly for about twenty years, despite approximately 600 legal challenges.

As one historian of electricity noted: "From the very start, Bell officials had in mind a national system of telephones controlled by one company."[3] Bell controlled the manufacture of telephone equipment through Western Electric Company. In 1880, American Bell Telephone Company was organized, and it formed the basis for control of a national telephone system. The parent company in turn formed American Telephone and Telegraph Company to handle its long-line operations. After the expiration of the Bell patents, flocks of independents rushed into the telephone business. They received strong local support in many cities because of poor customer relations on the part of Bell licensees. Bell reacted by cutting rates, which drove scores of independents out of business, but also expanded the number of telephones in service. "Ma Bell" was well on the road to dominance of the industry.

The invention of the telephone was only one link—albeit the key link—in the development of a practical telephonic network. Not before the twentieth century did the telephone compete successfully with the telegraph for long-distance communication. The first line to be used exclusively for the telephone was completed in 1877. The strongest selling point for the telephone was that it could be operated without a skilled attendant, that is, a method of communication for the ordinary individual.

By the turn of the century, the communication device "for the masses" was still an expensive toy. There were only two telephones for every one hundred people, and most of them serviced limited geographical areas. Not until 1892, was New York connected to Chicago; not until 1915, were lines extended to San Francisco. After an early lead in installing telephones, the United States briefly fell behind Europe in the 1890s. However, by 1900, there were more than 1.3 million telephones in this country, clearly the United States was outstripping Europe. The "conquest of solitude" became a national phenomenon.[4]

---

[3]Harold I. Sharlin, *The Making of the Electrical Age* (London, 1963), p. 53.
[4]Robert V. Bruce, *Bell: Alexander Graham Bell and the Conquest of Solitude* (Boston, 1973).

MICHAEL FARADAY, JOSEPH HENRY, AND MOTIVE POWER

The application of electromagnetism to communications was dramatic, but it did little to capture the full potential of electrical power. The work of Michael Faraday and others led to the development of the electric motor and the generator which provided the means to employ electrical power on a large scale in industry and in the home.

In 1821, Michael Faraday, a laboratory assistant at the Royal Institution in London, gave the first recorded illustration of "electromagnetic rotation." Ten years later, he produced a primitive electrical generator.[5] He accomplished this by moving an electric conductor in a magnetic field which generated electric current. This simple device evolved into the modern alternator, and his other experiments strongly influenced the development of the electric motor.

Joseph Henry—almost simultaneously with Faraday—discovered the phenomenon of electromagnetic induction. He devoted more attention to converting electrical energy into mechanical energy, however. His "reciprocating engine" produced motion, he stated, "in a little machine by a power, which, I believe, has never before been applied in mechanics—by magnetic attraction and repulsion."

By the late 1830s, electricity was being applied on a small scale for actual industrial work. Early motors were run by batteries, which meant that they offered few practical applications for large-scale industrial or home use. Further development of the generator led to alternatives to the battery-operated motor. Parisian Hippolyte Pixii first described a mechanism to produce direct current (DC) in 1832, and experiments were conducted with some success in England, France, Germany, and Italy.

ARC LIGHTS, LIGHT BULBS, AND THOMAS EDISON

Electric lighting experiments proved crucial in perfecting generators, especially dynamos.[6] They also stimulated the development of whole electrical systems, an accomplishment essential to the most effective application of electrical power.

Arc lighting was the first successful form of electric lighting. In 1808, Sir Humphrey Davy of England gave a public demonstration of his electric light, which was composed of pieces of charcoal connected to electric current. The commercial application of the arc light did not succeed until the 1870s, however. A Belgian, Zénobe-Théophile Gramme, used hand-operated gen-

---

[5] A generator converts mechanical rotative energy into electrical energy.

[6] Dynamo, short for dynamoelectric machine, is a generator that supplies current needed to excite the magnets in the device, rather than using an auxiliary source of electricity to excite the magnets.

erators to demonstrate potential commercial uses of direct current generators. He influenced the application of the generator to electroplating and arc lighting in the 1870s. Gramme also designed a high-voltage generator, which was connected to an arc light. The resulting system was used widely throughout Europe until the 1880s.

In 1875, two Cornell University professors built the first practical dynamo constructed in the Western Hemisphere. The dynamo was used to furnish light for the Cornell campus. The change in the application of the dynamo from a device that ran as an electric motor to a central source of power for several motors, provided the impetus for what some have called "an electrically based technological revolution."

By the mid-1870s, conditions were right for practical application of arc lighting. A market was available because many large cities already had gas lighting systems. The first American city to have gas lighting was Baltimore (1816–1817); during the next thirty years, gas lighting was installed in New York, Boston, New Orleans, Louisville, Philadelphia, and Washington, DC. With many of the technical and organizational problems resolved by the late nineteenth century, gas lighting was a successful competitor with electric lighting through the turn of the century. As in the case of telephone operations, traction, and other utilities, promoters of gas lighting struggled for city franchises, and prospects for large profits attracted individuals or groups interested in monopolistic control of the systems.

An Ohio inventor, Charles F. Brush, was instrumental in developing a technologically advanced and economically feasible arc lighting system. His first public lighting system was constructed in Cleveland in 1879. Since neither his arc lamp nor his dynamo were patentable, the new industry that Brush fostered became extremely competitive. His most serious competition came from the American Electric Company (later called the Thomson-Houston Company), which dominated the market by 1890.

Arc lighting of city streets, a marvel in itself, demonstrated the possibility of extending electrical lighting into the home. Rapid population growth and urban concentration in the late nineteenth century offered a vast potential market for indoor electric lighting. Arc lamps were too brilliant and too harsh to adapt to indoor use, and the cost was prohibitive. Available illuminants, such as kerosene, had serious shortcomings. Open flames produced soot, dirt, and heat and posed a serious fire danger. Oil lamps had to be used in certain locations and under proper atmospheric conditions. The answer to these problems was an incandescent lamp.

In 1802, Humphrey Davy produced "incandescence"—passing current through a wire or filament to heat it and make it glow. Hundreds of experiments in the following fifty years or so, however, failed to produce a long-lasting filament. Many discouraged scientists and inventors abandoned the search as too impractical and too expensive.

In 1877, Thomas Alva Edison turned his attention to the tantalizing problem of indoor lighting. By that time, the invention of the vacuum tube and further experiments with dynamos opened the door for someone to combine the necessary elements into a workable, inexpensive, incandescent lighting system. Herein lay Edison's accomplishment and his genius.

To understand the contributions of Edison fully is to cut away the myth and lore surrounding a great man. In a characteristic American way, Edison is remembered as a brilliant, lone inventor who turned vague scientific abstractions into practical devices. Movie portrayals especially reinforced this image. Mickey Rooney as the boy Edison lived in a world where eccentric behavior branded him as "addled." In the end, however, young Tom's curiosity and tenacity forced the community to recognize his genius. Then there was "Edison the Man"—portrayed by Spencer Tracy—working alone in his dingy laboratory, unlocking the secret of the electric light bulb.

Myth-making aside, Edison was uniquely qualified—by his natural abilities, by his training, and by his cultivated pragmatism—to develop a practical light bulb. He turned his attention to invention in the late 1860s. As an employee of Western Union in Boston he invented an automatic vote recorder, but could not sell it. This experience convinced him that the professional inventor had to find his market before sallying forth to produce any device. He never violated that lesson in pragmatism again.

In the telegraph business, Edison acquired skills and experience that eventually proved invaluable in the development of his light bulb. In 1870, he left the telegraphy business to set up his own manufacturing shop and laboratory in Newark, New Jersey. By mid-decade he obtained the necessary financial support to establish, what historian Thomas P. Hughes calls, his "invention factory" at Menlo Park, New Jersey. At this isolated spot on a railroad line between New York and Philadelphia, Edison and his colleagues were free from distractions without being cut off from the large cities. At Menlo Park, Edison pursued various projects that interested him and also encouraged his talented staff to develop and implement projects through team research and cooperation.

Edison's Menlo Park experiment was a model of modern research technique; it offered a working atmosphere conducive to achievement. Edison—the "inventor-entrepreneur"[7]—acquired financial backing, selected good personnel, and coordinated and directed the activities toward marketable products.

The development of the incandescent bulb is the best example of Edison as "inventor-entrepreneur," and the result of good timing. By the late 1870s, Edison had acquired a substantial expertise in electricity and electrical applications; he had an impressive research facility at Menlo Park; and the demand for artificial lighting was strong. Edison also had a good reputation as an inventor. His successful stock ticker and his multiplex telegraph gave

[7]Thomas P. Hughes, "The Electrification of America: The System Builders," *Technology and Culture*, vol. 20 (January 1979), pp. 125–126.

him the prestige to attract research funds, and his notoriety aroused public confidence in his ventures.

Popular lore ends the story of Edison's triumph with the light bulb in 1879. In that year, he discovered that a carbonized thread used as a filament would glow successfully for about forty hours. This was merely a first step in his conquest of electric lighting. The real success came with the development of the electrical lighting system in 1882. Solid financial backing and promotion of his project came primarily through the establishment of the Edison Electric Light Company in 1878. The company became the touchstone for several subsidiary companies which either produced components for his lighting system or offered some necessary function, such as machine works, lamp works, tube manufacturing, and so forth.

The discovery of the ideal filament—which had a resistance sufficient to sustain a high current—was a commercial rather than a technical requirement in Edison's system. The light bulb would have to produce long-term, consistent lighting in order to compete with gas or kerosene. In addition, an elaborate power and delivery system had to be devised, including steam engines, dynamos, a cable system, house wiring, meters, and even lamp bases. Edison based the technology of the central generating station and the distributing system on those worked out by gas companies.

The establishment of the Pearl Street Station—the first central station for public supply of power for incandescent lighting—was the visible symbol of the completed Edison system. Within one year of its successful demonstration on Wall Street, in 1882, 8,000 Edison lamps were being supplied with electricity. In 1884, Pearl Street Station lighted more than 11,000 lamps in 500 homes. The Edison Company also installed more than 59,000 lamps in homes with their own generating capability. By 1885, the Edison Electric Light Company had a virtual monopoly in the electric lighting field, selling 200,000 of the 250,000 lamps in use.

AC VERSUS DC: A BATTLE OVER SYSTEMS

Edison's dominance of the electric lighting field was short-lived. The most immediate and serious competition came from Westinghouse Electric Company. Competition, however, went beyond attempts to dominate a lucrative new market. At the base was a controversy over the best and most effective means of generating and distributing electrical power. The debate centered on the merits of direct current (DC) versus alternating current (AC) power generation.

George Westinghouse, who became Edison's foremost professional antagonist, was also self-taught in the field of electricity. His formal education virtually ceased at age fourteen, and he worked in his father's machine shop for several years. In 1867, he invented a device for returning derailed railroad cars to the track and, in 1869, he invented an air brake for railroad trains. The

Westinghouse Air Brake Company gave him status as an important inventor and effective entrepreneur.

Westinghouse's years as an inventor, and his venture into the natural gas business, gave him practical experience useful in electrical manufacturing. He began to study the commercial applications of electricity in the early 1880s, but by 1885 he was disenchanted with the commercial possibilities of the DC system. Despite opposition from several of his staff members, Westinghouse pursued the development of an alternating-current system. The major advantage of an AC system was its efficiency in the transmission of electricity. Electrical impulses could be transmitted at high voltages over long distances without a substantial loss of energy along the transmission lines. Furthermore, through the use of a transformer, voltages at high transmission levels could be easily reduced to lower levels necessary for lighting incandescent bulbs. His first commercial incandescent light system was tested near Pittsburgh in 1886.

Westinghouse's goal was to produce a system that was more economical than was Edison's. The DC system was well-entrenched in densely populated urban areas. Westinghouse's plan was first to capture markets where Edison was weak—places where transmission distance was great, and where customers were far apart. Westinghouse also faced competition from another AC company, Thomson-Houston Electric Company.

Aside from developing new markets suited to his system, Westinghouse found himself in a patent battle with the Edison Company and in a debate over the advantages of AC as compared to DC current. The Edison Company tried to demonstrate that the Westinghouse system was inefficient and unreliable. It also claimed that the AC system was unsafe. In 1887, Edison and his assistants staged grizzly experiments for the press in the West Orange lab, notably electrocuting stray cats and dogs with high-tension currents. In 1888, the Edison group issued a red-bound pamphlet entitled "A Warning" that enumerated the dangers of AC and attacked Westinghouse and Thomson-Houston as "patent pirates." When it was announced that New York was turning to electrocution as capital punishment—using AC current—some critics coined the term "to Westinghouse a prisoner."

The debate over AC and the assault on Westinghouse had several dimensions. It was a commercial rivalry fought with the weapons of the "dog-eat-dog" world of business. While not a party to all the outrageous publicity stunts, Edison remained skeptical of AC as a replacement for his DC system. Some of his reservations were justifiable, since each system had its strengths and weaknesses. But Edison was also defending the status quo, committed to a system he had spent so long to develop and market.

Edison's criticisms, however, did not halt new invention and application. Westinghouse and his company prospered and, in time, more than 95 percent of the electrical energy generated in the United States was AC. The merger of the Edison Company and Thomson-Houston to form General Electric Company (GE) in 1892 ended the public controversy over AC and DC: the new company produced both AC and DC power.

PRACTICAL APPLICATION OF THE ELECTRIC MOTOR

The Electric Streetcar

Electric lighting was instrumental in translating the theory of electricity into practice. The same can be said for the commercial development of the electric motor. The work of Faraday, Henry, and others demonstrated the principles of motive power, but it took a long time for a practical electric motor to compete successfully with the steam engine. Experiments with traction were essential to the commercial development of the electric motor. The invention of the electric streetcar was not only crucial to the rise of the industrial city and the evolution of transportation but also to the development of electric power systems. Traction systems provided more effective means of generating, distributing, and utilizing electrical power. The DC motor, in particular, was perfected through the development of the streetcar.

The electric motor is based on the same fundamental principle as is the dynamo—only run in reverse. The impetus to develop the electric motor grew out of its great market potential, especially in transportation. While steam power came to dominate intra-urban, regional, and intercontinental transportation, it had not penetrated urban transportation markets effectively. Trains were too expensive, too bulky, too noisy, and too heavily polluting to be an attractive form of mass transit in the cities. Consequently, other means of transportation dominated the cities.

In the 1830s, individual means of transportation were replaced by omnibuses and then, in the 1850s by horsecars or horse-drawn streetcars. Relatively safe and comfortable, the horsecars could transport many passengers along tracks at a relatively rapid speed (7 miles per hour). By 1880, there were 18,000 to 19,000 horsecars using more than 3,000 miles of track. The dependence on the horse was the weakness of the system, however. Urban horses had a life-span of about two years; they were ineffective under poor weather conditions, required constant care and attention, and were a major source of urban pollution. Cable cars were an alternative to horsecars, and they had some success in the 1870s and 1880s, particularly in high-density inner cities. The first cable railway opened in San Francisco in 1873. But the system never had universal appeal because it was prone to breakdown, posed extensive construction problems, and was very expensive.

With a built-in market, the electric streetcar offered an alternative to the horse and the cable car. With the application of the dynamo as a power source, a practical traction system became workable by the 1870s. In 1879, German inventor Werner Siemens gave a demonstration of the streetcar at the Berlin Industrial Exhibition. In the United States, the irrepressible Thomas Edison conducted some of the earliest experiments. In 1880 and 1881, he built an electric railway, using his generating system during the day when there was a low demand for lighting.

Edison eventually lost interest in electric traction, but others pursued its development. As early as 1884, sections of the East Cleveland Railway were electrified. John C. Henry, a Kansas farmer and telegraph operator, overcame the dangers and inconvenience of electrified rail transmission with the development of the "troller," a wheeled carriage (later a rigid pole) attached to a wire that in turn was connected to electrified lines running alongside the track. Charles Van Depoele built the first citywide "trolley" system in Montgomery, Alabama (1886).

The best-known and most successful pioneer in the traction field was Frank J. Sprague. In 1884, he established Sprague Electric Railway and Motor Company. His most important contribution was a well-designed electric motor. He was audacious enough to accept a contract to install an elaborate streetcar system in Richmond, Virginia. Despite several problems in roadbed construction, power transmission, and motor performance, the system went into operation in 1888. Although Sprague lost money on the construction of the system, he acquired valuable experience which led to several improvements in urban traction.

By the turn of the century, there were almost 22,000 miles of streetcar track in the United States. Electric streetcars replaced virtually all horsecars. The electric streetcar contributed significantly to the growth and development of American cities. The physical layout of modern American cities— dense central business districts surrounded by expanding suburbs—was due in large part to the electric streetcar. This new technology had a triple effect: it advanced the development of transportation, it furthered the practical application of electrical power, and it helped to transform the city physically.

Streetcars were often the focus of major franchise battles. Unlike water and waste-water systems, street railways were typically built and operated by private companies. A city franchise was valuable because it conferred a monopoly, or semimonopoly, on the favored company. To encourage private firms to assume the high capital costs of these systems, city officials tried to make the franchises as attractive as possible. Often they were drawn up quickly and carelessly, extending over long periods and providing low taxation on the companies' property. Most early franchises were extended over periods of 50 to 100 years, but Albany, New York, granted a 1,000-year franchise to its traction company. Over time, the franchises incurred criticism from reform groups who protested the quality of service, the raising of rates, or the granting of special privileges to the traction companies. However, few cities in the late nineteenth and early twentieth centuries moved toward municipal systems of transportation.

Tesla's AC Motor

By the 1890s, the electric motor was used for several industrial purposes. However, where steam engines were the preferred power source, the DC motor was not adaptable to perform those functions. Low transmission voltages meant high costs, and the inability to transmit electricity over long distances hampered the application of electrical motors. To be fully competitive with steam engines, electrical motors had to exhibit greater versatility. Recognizing the potential advantages of a commercial AC motor, Westinghouse sought the patent rights to AC motors currently under development. It was primarily the motor of Serbian-born electrical engineer Nikola Tesla that Westinghouse began to rework for his AC system.

Tesla, the "eccentric genius," had come to the United States in 1884 to work with Edison. But he soon established his own company, Tesla Electric Company, to develop electrical inventions. He is best known for the discovery of the rotating magnetic field, which led him to develop the polyphase induction motor. This motor used multiple AC currents to produce rotation. The subsequent motor built on this design was rugged and turned at a relatively constant speed regardless of the load. Although DC motors were easier to adjust and could run at varying speeds, the induction motor and its electrical system allowed for long-distance application of electrical power.

Westinghouse had a great opportunity to showcase the AC motor and power system when he acquired the lighting contract for the Chicago World's Fair (1893). His system illuminated the "White City" at the Centennial and ran its machinery in a dramatic display of AC's potential. Popular acceptance of alternating current followed, and the rugged competition between AC and DC began to end. With over 300 patent suits pending, Westinghouse and GE agreed to pool their patents and standardize equipment.

Niagara Falls and Hydropower

The real victory for alternating current came at Niagara Falls, New York. Since the mid-nineteenth century, there had been strong interest in utilizing the water of Niagara Falls for power production. The falls were an excellent choice because of their steady flow and their proximity to large populations. Until the advent of AC and efficient dynamos, however, the project was impractical. The local community could not support the high cost of development or absorb the vast power to be generated.

As the technology changed and the market for electricity expanded, the development of the falls became more practical. In 1895, the first of three 5,000-horsepower AC generators was completed. George Forbes, designer of the Niagara plant, described it as "one of the greatest engineering works in the world." The completion of the plant marked the beginning of large-scale hydroelectricity in the United States. By World War I, the new energy industry produced more than 4 million horsepower.

Electricity and Manufacturing

About the time hydropower developed, electrical power from steam turbines became practical. In 1884, Charles Parsons of England invented a steam turbine (compound reaction steam engine), and Westinghouse purchased the

American rights in 1896. Soon after, 100,000 horsepower, steam-turbine electric generators were in operation. This new source of low-cost electricity competed with and then replaced nonelectric equipment. With the steam turbine and hydroelectric power, electricity had come of age as an industrial energy source.

The project at Niagara Falls demonstrated that central-power generation was feasible on a large scale, but effective electrical utilities did not mature until the turn of the century. The improvements in steam turbines led to the proliferation of electrical power generation, since thermal stations were more versatile than were hydropower ones.

Manufacturing companies were a major beneficiary of the new electrical generation systems. A cotton mill was the first factory in the United States to be completely electrified (1894). A dramatic shift from steam to electricity was underway. For instance, in 1899, only 22.5 percent (or 36,000 of 160,000) of motors manufactured were used for industrial purposes; in 1909, 48.2 percent (or 243,000 of 504,000) were for industrial use. During the same period the number of industrial motors multiplied by 580 percent. Horsepower also increased dramatically. By 1920, manufacturing had become the largest user of electricity in the American economy.

The adaption of electricity to manufacturing not only led to a change in power source but also to physical changes in the factories themselves. Factories no longer required large water supplies for their steam boilers. This enhanced the versatility of factories and allowed many industries to migrate from the countryside to major cities. It also facilitated decentralizaton of industry within metropolitan areas and spurred the development of industrial parks. Electric motors also took up less space than did more cumbersome steam engines. Thus factories could be smaller (and less costly to build) or they could use available space for other functions. As one commentator aptly noted: "The electric motor is the muscle of the age of electricity. The electric light and electric communications give spirit to the age but the electric motor animates it."[8]

Electricity on the Farm

Agriculture was less willing and less able to adopt electrical power as quickly, or on the same scale, as could manufacturers. The widest use for electrical power on the farm was for house lighting. As late as the 1940s, however, many farms had no electric power. Although European and American experiments demonstrated that electrical power was feasible for several farm tasks, it proved impractical for field work. Some success was achieved in adapting electrical power to stationary belt work and even irrigation, but the promotional literature often promised more than it delivered. Even if electric smudge pots, electrified fences, and other farm equipment operated effec-

[8]Harold I. Sharlin, "Applications of Electricity," in Melvin Kranzberg and Carroll Pursell (eds.), *Technology in Western Civilization*, vol. I (New York, 1967), p. 278.

tively, most farmers could ill afford the cost, let alone tap into convenient power sources—if they existed. The farmers themselves, generally conservative and skeptical, had to be convinced that electrical power was versatile and practical. As a writer stated in a 1911 issue of *Scientific American:* "To the average farmer electricity is a mysterious agent, to be gingerly dealt with."[9]

Municipal Power

Aside from manufacturing, the most dramatic impact of electrical power production came in the lighting and powering of American cities. Cities were the logical place to establish electrical systems because of size and population. Yet more than the feasibility of a system or its uses affected the development of municipal power. A major issue focused over control of the systems.

As the technology of lighting systems was refined, many cities believed that they could save money by purchasing their own street-lighting plants. Serving home and commercial customers, however, could remain in the hands of private utilities. In 1882, there were only four municipally owned electrical systems for street lighting; by 1892, there were 235, with some expansion into residential lighting. In most cases, municipal systems were found in small cities where private utility companies did not expect sufficient profits. The major exceptions were Chicago, Allegheny, and Detroit.

From the mid-1890s through 1910, the municipal-ownership debate intensified, spilling over into residential lighting and traction. The issues broadened as well. During this period, municipal governments—in the throes of dramatic urban growth and expansion—sought to extend "municipal home rule," that is, to control their own affairs more than they had in the past. (Most cities had been under the influence of state legislatures and were demanding a greater share of local responsibility.) As electrical power became as much a necessity as water or sewers, several city authorities recognized the need to gain greater control over electric utilities. By 1902, there were 851 municipally owned electrical systems in the United States, and, by 1924, the number peaked at more than 3,000.

This was a fleeting phenomenon in the United States. After 1924, the number of municipally owned systems declined. Investor-owned utilities eventually constructed large generating units and established interconnected transmission lines leading to more efficient and larger-scale electrical networks. One of the earliest and best-known pioneers of the elaborate electrical network was Samuel Insull. Edison's secretary and personal representative from 1880 to 1892, Insull left the General Electric Company to become president of Chicago Edison Company. At the age of thirty-two, Insull had made a major career change from the electrical manufacturing business to the utility field. His objective was to create a comprehensive system of electric light and

[9]Cited in Clark Spence, "Early Uses of Electricity in American Agriculture," *Technology and Culture,* vol. 3 (Spring 1962), p. 142.

power in Chicago. He eventually reached beyond the city to establish a system that interconnected the inner city with its suburbs.

Insull became a leader in the utility field and mapped out the direction that utility development was to follow. From the modest city system of Edison, Insull established an impressive regional system which, by 1923, supplied an area of 6,000 square miles and 195 communities. This became the foundation for an incredible national utility system, Insull's Middle West Utility Company, with subsidiaries operating in nineteen states. The modest beginnings at Pearl Street and Niagara Falls had come a long way.

Insull's system was symbolic of the pervasiveness of electrical power by the early twentieth century. Electrical power had not touched all Americans' lives by that time, but a revolutionary communications system, new forms of transportation, electrified factories, and the light bulb were staggering technical changes for a single generation. Historian Edwin Layton claimed that the coal-powered steam engine became "the beating heart of industrialism." If that is true, then electrical power was surely the nervous system of the nation.

FURTHER READING

John Brooks. *Telephone*. New York, 1975.

Robert V. Bruce. *Bell: Alexander Graham Bell and the Conquest of Solitude*. Boston, 1973.

Thomas P. Hughes. *Networks of Power*. Baltimore, 1983.

Matthew Josephson. *Edison: A Biography*. New York, 1959.

Malcolm MacLaren. *The Rise of the Electrical Industry During the Nineteenth Century*. Princeton, N.J., 1943.

Harold C. Passer. *The Electrical Manufacturers, 1875–1900*. Cambridge, Mass., 1953.

Ithiel deSola Pool (ed.), *The Social Impact of the Telephone*. Cambridge, Mass., 1977.

Harold I. Sharlin. *The Making of the Electrical Age*. London, 1963.

Robert L. Thompson. *Wiring a Continent: The History of the Telegraph Industry in the United States, 1832–1866*. Princeton, N.J., 1947.

Martha Moore Trescott. *The Rise of the American Electrochemicals Industry, 1880–1910*. Westport, Conn., 1981.

Wyn Wachhorst. *Thomas Alva Edison: An American Myth*. Cambridge, Mass., 1981.

CHAPTER 4

Government and Energy: Antitrust, Regulation, and Conservation

Four major energy industries emerged by the late nineteenth century: anthracite coal, bituminous coal, petroleum, and electrical power. Essential to the industrialization and urbanization of the nation, these industries became large and influential. They were also part of the trend toward "big business." As historian Samuel P. Hays argued: "The business community took the initiative in the organizational revolution. Business commanded enormous resources of capital, technical and managerial skills, and public influence, the groups which it formed became the most powerful in the country."[1]

While coal, petroleum, and electrical power held vast economic influence in industrial America, they were also unique industries. Anthracite coal was regionally bound and closely linked to railroad interests. Bituminous coal was more diffuse and much more competitive. Petroleum was dominated by Standard Oil, which controlled the industry until the early twentieth century. Electrical power was newly emerging as a local and then regional enterprise with numerous facilities and several functions.

In the late nineteenth century, the federal government began to change its role in response to the rise of big business. For most of the century, its response to the business world, including the new energy industries, had been benign and often promotional. The federal government encouraged economic growth by providing a favorable legal climate in which to conduct business (including opposition to labor organization), protective tariffs, the disposition of natural resources on public lands, and sometimes direct subsidies (for example, landgrants to railroads).

Like business enterprise, the federal government grew in scale during these years. Much of the power for influencing economic activity shifted from the states to the federal government, and sometimes from the private sector to Washington. The trend toward large corporations led government officials to fear a threat to competition, an increase in unfair business practices, and the potential squandering of natural resources.

[1]Samuel P. Hays, *The Response to Industrialism* (Chicago, 1957), p. 49.

Beginning in the 1880s, the federal government began to regulate business enterprise while still promoting economic growth. This eventually led to antitrust legislation, the creation of regulatory bodies, and resource conservation.

THE TRUST AND ANTIMONOPOLY

By the late nineteenth century, concern over concentration of economic power through pools, cartels, and other combinations made antimonopoly a lively national issue. The emergence of a new type of business combination—the trust—in the 1880s led to direct governmental intervention in an attempt to restore competition. Standard Oil pioneered the development of the modern trust in 1879. The trust agreement of 1882 was particularly important. The constituent companies of Standard were no longer arranged in a loose combination: rather, they were under direct control of the new board of nine trustees. Each company transferred its properties and stocks, that is, its control, to the board and received trust certificates in return. The trust achieved a much greater degree of concentration than under previous combinations.

The formation of trusts insured the rise of a new antimonopoly movement. Between 1888 and 1890 alone, fifteen states passed laws to allow prosecution and dissolution of combinations involved in restraint of trade. But state action could only protect local competition, and soon the cry went out for national legislation. In 1890, Congress passed the first national antimonopoly law, the Sherman Antitrust Act.

The Sherman Act declared illegal all contracts, combinations, and conspiracies "in restraint of interstate and foreign trade" as well as monopolies in, or attempted monopolies in, such trade. But the law provided no bureaucratic structure for maintaining competition and no special prosecution agency to handle antitrust suits. Prosecution was not energetic, save in cases against labor groups charged with restraint of trade, which initially accounted for most of the government's early victories.

Nevertheless, the Sherman Act and other efforts at restoring competition gave momentum to more stringent governmental intervention after 1900. During the presidency of Theodore Roosevelt, a new antimonopoly movement took shape. In the famous Northern Securities case (1904), the government sought and achieved the dissolution of a railroad holding company charged with restraint of interstate commerce. Besides reviving the Sherman Act, it also established the Bureau of Corporations, which was responsible for conducting on-going corporate investigations, and the Antitrust Division within the Justice Department, for prosecuting violators. Under William Howard Taft, Roosevelt's hand-picked protégé, antitrust actions led to forty-eight cases between 1910 and 1912.

The federal government's role in the economy was a central theme of the 1912 presidential election. Theodore Roosevelt reentered politics as the standard bearer of the Bullmoose party. With respect to the economy, his

"New Nationalism" purported that consolidation and concentration of power were inevitable and constructive. Government's role should be to supervise economic activity and protect the interests of nonbusiness groups. The Democratic candidate, Woodrow Wilson, argued the "New Freedom" line. He called for "regulated competition," that is, stopping the spread of monopoly through antitrust agencies and by ending special government privileges.

A badly split Republican party (between Taft and Roosevelt) assured a victory for Wilson and his "New Freedom." The Clayton Antitrust Act (1914) expanded the Sherman Act by defining unfair business practices more clearly and forbidding interlocking directorates. A companion bill established the Federal Trade Commission (FTC) in 1914, a body given power to prevent unlawful suppression of competition. The FTC was closer to the New Nationalist formula than to the New Freedom one, indicating a deemphasis of antitrust and a move toward business regulation.

The Dissolution of the Standard Trust

It should come as no surprise that the Standard Trust was the focus of antimonopoly prosecution. Its relentless efforts at concentration, its aggressive and sometimes illegal business practices, and its unchallenged success made Standard a natural target as well as a symbol of monopolistic practices. The outcry against Standard came from diverse quarters—the public, the muckraking press, aggrieved businessmen, and government officials. In particular, Standard had incurred intense antagonism from small independents and other competitors in the oil business.

Ida Tarbell's *History of the Standard Oil Company* (1904) captured the spirit of the attack on Standard. A reluctant muckraker, Tarbell grew up in Titusville. Her father and brother were oilmen, and she acquired an appreciation for the organizational skills of Rockefeller but a resentment for his combine:

> While there can be no doubt that the determining factor in the success of the Standard Oil Company in securing a practical monopoly of the oil industry has been the special privileges it has enjoyed since the beginning of its career, it is equally true that those privileges alone will not account for its success. Something besides illegal advantages had gone into the making of the Standard Oil Trust. . . . But this huge bulk, blackened by commercial sin, has always been strong in all great business qualities—in energy, in intelligence, in dauntlessness. It has always been rich in youth as well as greed, in brains as well as unscrupulousness. (p. 196)

The case against Standard received publicity because of people like Ida Tarbell, but it entered the courtroom because of antimonopolists in state government. In 1892, a common law suit led to the dissolution of Standard of Ohio and the reestablishment of the trust in New Jersey (1899). Following the Ohio suit, no less than ten states (and the Oklahoma Territory) filed antitrust actions against affiliates of the combination.

Standard's operations, however, were not disrupted. Moreover, competition did not return to the oil industry. In Kansas, attempts to undercut Standard's alleged monopolistic practices included efforts to establish a state-owned refinery in 1905. The Kansas Supreme Court declared against the refinery law, and after a lengthy antitrust campaign, Standard's influence in the state remained intact. In 1907, Texas authorities succeeded in ousting Waters-Pierce Oil Company, an affiliate of Standard of New Jersey, only to see it readmitted through the efforts of Senator Joseph A. Bailey. The pattern of parry-and-thrust was similar in Tennessee, Missouri, and the Oklahoma Territory.

Actions at the state level, however, played a major role in stimulating interest in a national investigation. In the wake of the Kansas case, the Bureau of Corporations investigated the industry and charged Standard with monopolistic practices. The bureau's report led President Roosevelt and the Justice Department to begin dissolution proceedings against Standard, under the provisions of the Sherman Act.

Hearings on the suit began in September 1907, and testimony was taken from approximately 400 people in the ensuing fifteen months. In the 1911 decision of the Supreme Court, the Standard Trust was dissolved and was broken into thirty-four independent companies. In terms of future antitrust proceedings, the most significant aspect of the suit was Chief Justice Edward D. White's invocation of the famous "rule of reason," which held that reasonable restraints that have no undue effect on competition were legal. This left the door open for a broad interpretation of restraint of trade.

Did the dissolution of Standard accomplish what antimonopolists had hoped—a competitive market for oil? Many scholars and commentators say "no." There was a transition from monopoly (or near monopoly) to oligopoly, not because of antitrust action, but because of the emergence of Gulf, Texas, Shell, and other vertically integrated companies. In addition, the faltering kerosene market and the rising demand for fuel oil and gasoline did more to undermine Standard's leadership of the industry than did antimonopoly. Nevertheless, the case against Standard brought the problem of restraint of trade to public attention and helped to institutionalize the antitrust process within the structure of government.

Western Union, Bell Telephone, and "Natural Monopoly"

The effects of the antimonopoly movement on other energy-producing industries had less dramatic or immediate impact than did the case of Standard. However, they do suggest a change in government-business relations with future implications.

Antitrust measures were taken in the field of electrical communications, but they often proved to be inappropriate. In time, the major companies, Bell Telephone and Western Union, came to be treated as "natural monopolies." The rationale behind this was based on an alternative view of competition: since the transmission and distribution costs of service were high and quite inflexible, competition would be duplicative and inefficient. In this sense, some form of regulation rather than antitrust was called for to insure reasonable prices and better service.

Until 1920, however, the notion of natural monopoly was not clearly articulated or fully accepted in the field of electrical communications. The case of Western Union is a good example. By 1866, Western Union had bought out its chief competitors resulting in greater stability for the industry and improved service. By 1916, there were twenty-six companies in the business, but Western Union, its affiliates, and Postal Telegraph handled 98 percent of the commercial service.

Western Union's success, however, coincided with the growing interest in antimonopoly. Moreover, since the first telegraph line was constructed by the federal government, there had always been a possibility of public ownership. Between 1845 and 1900, there were no less than nineteen congressional committees investigating telegraph monopoly. Of these committees, seventeen favored government ownership. By the turn of the century, the illusion of renewed competition with the rise of Postal Telegraph—and the appearance of the United Press as a news-gathering competitor to Western Union's Associated Press—deflated the interest in public ownership and temporarily ended talk of antitrust action.

Through patent control, Bell Telephone maintained its strict monopolistic hold on the telephone through the early 1890s. Renewed competition in 1893–1894 was the result of the expiration of those patents and the temporary loss of some markets. Bell was not idle while the wolves approached the door. It had the advantage of establishing markets early and accruing valuable business and technical experience over the years. Because of its size, Bell was able to cut rates without undermining financial stability, thus, driving competitors out of the market. Bell also had help from within the Patent Office, which granted it a patent on an improved transmitter that had previously been delayed for fourteen years.

Bell responded to the competitive challenge in another way—through a major reorganization of its business. American Telephone and Telegraph Company (AT&T), a subsidiary of American Bell established in 1885, acquired the assets of the parent company and incorporated several competing companies. With additional mergers, Bell made its operations more efficient while further weakening its competitors. It also avoided governmental intervention through this reorganization by maintaining the illusion of a competitive market.

The government did object to an alliance between Bell and Western Union in 1913. As a result, Bell agreed to dispose of its holdings, promised to acquire no additional competing companies, and offered to cooperate with independents in long-distance service. On the eve of World War I, nonetheless, Bell controlled 7,326,000 of the country's 11,716,000 telephones. Rather than taking antitrust action, attempts by state agencies to control rates were the only means of policing the industry.

Electrical Power and Antitrust

In the electrical light and power industry, companies tended to have natural monopolies in limited geographic areas. While competition continued in the production end of the business, General Electric (GE) and Westinghouse were moving the industry closer to oligopoly. By the 1890s, these two companies controlled a substantial portion of the electrical manufacturing industry through patent control, similar to the experience of Bell Telephone. Not only did they maintain control of original patents, but they constantly acquired patents from competing firms and individual inventors, through research and development, and by the merger process.

As GE and Westinghouse eliminated competitors, their own rivalry got fiercer. In 1896, more than 300 patent suits were pending between them. To avoid the ravages of competition, GE and Westinghouse ultimately pooled their patents, further consolidating the electric manufacturing business and making them the only full-line producers in the nation.

Because of GE's growing dominance in the electric lamp industry, the Justice Department brought equity proceedings against the company in 1911. Price-fixing and market-sharing agreements with Westinghouse and other companies came under attack. The Justice Department action also questioned GE's pyramiding of patents on machinery improvements, production processes, lamp design, and filament improvements, which allegedly gave it a monopoly on the carbon-filament lamp even after the basic patents had expired. Although GE first intended to fight the charges, it finally accepted a consent decree in October. In the end, the antitrust action did little to change the nature of the electric lamp industry.

The Anthracite Combination

In the anthracite industry, pooling agreements were made to regulate production and shipping throughout the 1870s and 1880s. Pennsylvania hard-coal companies had become vertically integrated corporations. Even though the anthracite railroads owned less track than major trunk and transcontinental lines, they were among the most heavily capitalized railroads in the nation. Independent mine operators were "squeezed" by high freight rates. The independents mined 45 percent of the total output by the end of the century, but they were powerless against the growing "anthracite combination." For example, in 1898, independents planned to build their own rail line, but anthracite carriers blocked it. By 1901, the anthracite combination was able to buy much of the independents' coal at the mines, relieving them of transportation expense while keeping them under control.

Between 1902 and the early 1920s, there were fifteen investigations of the anthracite combination. In 1908, the Justice Department filed a suit against six coal railroads under the "Commodities Clause" of the Interstate Commerce Act, which forbade railroads from transporting goods manufac-

tured or mined under their authority. The trial court found the clause unconstitutional. But the U.S. Supreme Court sustained the ruling as it applied to
the Delaware and Hudson, on the grounds that it merely owned stock in a
coal company. In the *Lehigh Valley* case, the trial court stated that the law
did not apply, but the Supreme Court overruled, asserting that the mine was
under the railroad's direct control. In other actions through 1920 the courts
forced some dissolutions, and a few railroads voluntarily disposed of their
holdings. While these decisions freed specific mines from railroad control, a
"community of interest" between the large coal companies sometimes replaced railroad control. Complex relationships with the railroads supplanted
the more open and less confusing relationships. The anthracite combination
remained intact.

Bituminous and Excessive Competition

By contrast, the bituminous coal industry was excessively competitive, inefficient, and economically volatile. The industry failed to stabilize production,
marketing, and prices prior to World War I. As early as 1880, various operators attempted to establish marketing groups, sales agencies, and trade associations—but without success.

Part of the problem was the nature of the commodity itself. While coal
was the major energy source of the period, short-term demand became
relatively fixed and inflexible. In the 1880s, production began to outstrip
demand. Lower prices had a limited effect because the primary users—
railroads, public utilities, and steel mills—utilized energy on the basis of their
rate of activity, not price. Production control was difficult because coal deposits were widely dispersed geographically. Despite the realities of the chaotic industry, charges of "coal trust" surfaced when prices rose.

The first merger movement in the industry, from 1898 to the 1910s, did
not produce the desired results of price stability and substantially less competition. It did, however, draw the ire of government officials. Although Roosevelt and Taft did not bring cases against the mergers, they did not accept
the operators' analysis of the economic woes of the industry.

When the growth of the industry ceased in the 1910s, and an experimental trade association failed, operators looked to the government for a stabilization plan. They wanted regulatory functions to be removed from the
Department of Justice to a commission where antitrust would not be the primary goal. One suggestion called for a National Mining Commission to restrict the opening of new mines and equalize supply and demand. Instead,
the government created the Federal Trade Commission, which was designed
to look into unfair methods of competition rather than to establish stabilization. Aside from the periodic FTC investigation, the bituminous industry received little attention from the federal government and no direct assistance
in alleviating its problems.

REGULATION: AN ALTERNATIVE TO ANTITRUST

While antimonopoly had a mixed record in dealing with problems of concentration and competition in energy industries, governmental regulation offered a different approach—sometimes complementary, often contrary.

Historian Thomas McCraw argued that the onset of regulation usually occurred in response to "identifiable crisis" in particular industries. In other words, regulation was a threat-reaction, rather than the result of long-range evaluation of economic growth or concentration.[2] This assessment applies to energy industries, especially in those areas akin to the general economic problems of the era: railroad rates, price-fixing, quality of service. But in many ways, energy industries were only regulated because of these connections, with little attention to their unique qualities or to energy issues such as resource depletion, pollution, and private control of raw materials.

Most crises leading to regulation first occurred between 1870 and 1930. During those years, the market failed to regulate itself because competition was undercut by the rise of big business. Natural monopolies quickly came under the purview of regulation, especially those in the railroad and utilities industries. State and local authorities attempted to encourage competition through issuance of franchises or charters to an array of companies. However, this approach was too simplistic and often failed to regulate business operations or provide stable, effective service to the people.

The existence of natural monopolies also helped to establish the legal basis for regulation. Since these industries were so intimately associated with "the public interest" or "the public welfare," they stood apart from most enterprises in their responsibility to the collective well-being of the citizenry. The courts wrestled with concepts such as "public good," "public interest," and "public welfare" to determine to what extent these industries should or could come under government regulation.

Railroads and Regulation

The first modern regulatory agencies in the United States dealt with the railroad industry. Initially, state commissions were established to deal with the nation's first big business. Although their concern was limited to the the railroad charters and operation within their boundaries. Massachusetts established the first railroad commission in 1869. It was a "weak" commission in the sense that it regulated railroad practices without taking responsibility for setting rates or fares. In the Midwest, "strong" commissions regulated rates within their boundaries. However, these were less effective than were the so-called weak commissions, because economic conditions or railroad pres-

[2]Thomas K. McCraw, "Regulatory Agencies," in Glenn Porter (ed.), *Encyclopedia of American Economic History* (New York, 1980), p. 788.

sure could force a fluctuation in rate-setting practices. Nonetheless, both types contributed to legitimizing regulation as a government function.

Eventually, state regulation was extended to other businesses—most notably public utilities—first in Massachusetts (1880s) and then in New York and Wisconsin. The most important aspect of regulating public utilities was establishing rates.

Federal regulation was urged when a state proved incapable of dealing with interstate or national problems. In the case of railroads, the federal government had to deal with several issues dictated by geography and economic circumstance. For example, in the East, the presence of many lines led to rampant, cutthroat competition. In the West and South, the few existing lines established regional monopolies. These differences made the passage of national regulation difficult, for the issue was further complicated by insurmountable political overtones. In the famous case of *Munn* v. *Illinois* (1877), the Supreme Court declared that since no federal law existed, the state could regulate interstate commerce. Nine years later, in *Wabash, St. Louis, and Pacific Railway Company* v. *Illinois*, the Supreme Court reversed itself. It declared that an Illinois statute prohibiting certain railroad hauling practices was unconstitutional because only Congress had power over interstate commerce. The *Wabash* case virtually insured some sort of federal regulation of interstate trade.

A bill presented by Senator Shelby M. Cullom (Rep., Ill.) in 1883 called for a federal railroad commission. The bill resulted in the Interstate Commerce Act (1877), which forbade pooling, rebates, and rate discrimination, and established the Interstate Commerce Commission (ICC). The act became the standard by which all federal regulatory power was measured.

Despite its precedent-setting role, the ICC proved ineffective. The federal judiciary restricted its power, deciding in favor of the carrier in fifteen of the sixteen cases brought before it by the commission between 1887 and 1905. Eventually, Congress gave the ICC additional authority and other regulatory acts were passed that increased the prohibition over rebating, enhanced rate-setting authority, and extended regulation to pipelines.

Outside of the transportation field, the most important regulatory authority of the period was the FTC (1914). Replacing the Bureau of Corporations, the FTC had power to investigate corporations (except banks and common carriers), receive reports, and issue "cease and desist" orders to prevent unfair business practices.

The Regulation of Electric Utilities

Electrical power, which was prone to natural monopoly, was a logical candidate for government regulation. Until the 1920s and 1930s, the federal government stayed out of the picture, and regulation remained primarily a local and state matter. The competitive franchises made way for exclusive franchises, but there was a continual debate over what was considered "reasonable profitability." Especially after 1880, municipal ownership gained a substantial following in the wake of greater demand for "home rule." Debates continued, nonetheless, over whether public or private systems were more efficient, less corruptible, and least costly.

Because of the expansion of electrical systems and the mixed record of local regulation, state governments increasingly were called upon to regulate electrical power companies. In many cases, local support was achieved by turning over regulation to commissions rather than to state legislatures. New York and Wisconsin led the way in 1907, and by 1922 forty-seven states and the District of Columbia had public utility commissions. In several cases, telephone companies also came under state regulatory power.

As with the railroad commissions, the effectiveness of the utility commissions varied greatly; some were controlled outright by power companies. In what seemed to many a surprising move, Samuel Insull publicly favored the state regulatory approach, but for very self-serving reasons: he preferred it to the less appealing alternative of municipal ownership. Despite vigorous interest in local utilities, government focused little attention on the trend toward regional systems.

Regulating Coal

Those advocating the regulation of the coal industry called for the establishment of a specialized regulatory agency similar to the ICC, to deal with coal in particular and mining in general. In 1903, the Pennsylvania legislature created a department of mines, which assumed more responsibility for mine safety in the region and established some branch offices for more efficient surveillance. On the federal level, the United States Bureau of Mines and the United States Coal Commission were useful during and after World War I in the dissemination of literature about mining and in the production of investigative reports. In the bituminous industry, however, FTC action did little to help stabilize the industry.

Coal Miners and the Government

In large measure, labor relations and strikes triggered government responses to the coal industry. Coal was a labor-intensive industry, and as such, labor and the organization of labor posed a major problem to government regulation. Traditionally, the federal government held cool-to-hostile feelings toward labor. The courts, especially, helped break up labor strikes through injunctions. However, coal miners were among the first labor groups to garner at least paternalistic attention from state and federal governments during the early twentieth century, setting the stage for more substantive changes in government-labor relations in the 1930s.

The most successful effort to organize miners was achieved by the United Mine Workers (UMW), which was formed in 1890. In the beginning, its major concern was survival. An 1897 strike paralyzed the northern bituminous fields and led to a labor agreement (1898) with operators in the Central Competitive Field (Pennsylvania, Ohio, Indiana, and Illinois). The UMW, however, failed to achieve an agreement with southern operators and had yet to break through in the anthracite fields.

The 1898 agreement provided some wage stabilization in the northern fields as well as an eight-hour day, a standard wage, and a standard tonnage. However, the absence of unions in the South allowed southern coal to be more competitive, and it helped to create a schism between North-South elements in the industry. Failing to organize the entire industry also seriously weakened the collective-bargaining ability of the UMW.

Unionization proved particularly difficult in the anthracite industry, but the 1902 anthracite coal strike had a significant impact. In May 1902, more than 50,000 anthracite coal miners in the UMW went on strike, demanding increased pay, union recognition, and the eight-hour day. Through the able leadership of John F. Mitchell, the miners maintained solidarity during the ordeal of the strike and the protracted negotiations. The arrogance of the operator's spokesman, George F. Baer (president of the Reading Railroad), reinforced the feeling that management was unwilling to cooperate. Baer stated that the interests of the miners would be protected "not by labor agitators but by the Christian men to whom God in His Infinite Wisdom, has given control of the property interests of the country."[3]

As the winter arrived, public sympathy with the strikers ebbed and patience with the negotiations wore thin. Government intervention in the strike gained wide support. In October, President Roosevelt had called operators and union leaders to Washington, hoping to settle the strike on a voluntary basis. Little was accomplished other than more acrimony between the sides. Outraged with the operators' unwillingness to accept arbitration, Roosevelt threatened to send federal troops into the mines to produce coal under government control. Aroused by the threat, powerful Republicans and business leaders tried to help break the impasse. After much debate and continued resistance by the operators, a compromise was worked out, establishing a seven-member commission authorized to arbitrate the strike. In the final awards, workers received a 10 percent pay increase and a nine-hour work day. Union recognition, however, was ignored.

In his campaign for reelection, Roosevelt stated that his role in the coal strike gave the operators and miners a "square deal," a phrase that soon became identified with his administration. Although the agreement itself was modest, Roosevelt established an important precedent in the use of presidential and federal authority. Although he would be recognized as the first president to aid the cause of American labor, he proved to be no champion of unionism. In fact, he later used federal troops to restore order during a mine strike in the Arizona territory; he also refused to intervene in a violent strike in Colorado.

[3]Cited in William H. Harbaugh, *Power and Responsibility* (New York, 1975; orig. pub., 1963), p. 172.

In an industry where as much as 75 percent of the cost went for wages, miner participation in decision making was an explosive issue. In many cases, miners simply wanted adequate wages and safe working conditions. Few jobs were more dangerous than coal mining, especially when precautions in the mines were haphazard. Mine safety, therefore, was a crucial issue in the early twentieth century.

Until 1910, the role of the federal government in mine safety was negligible; it clearly played a subservient role to that of the states. As a result of lobbying by miners, inspectors, operators, conservationists, and government officials, the U.S. Bureau of Mines was finally established in 1910. Among other things, it took the first steps toward a national policy on mine safety, followed by a campaign on the state level for uniform legislation.

The impetus for reform was the growing number of disastrous mine explosions. Increased demand for coal in the late nineteenth century created more mine activity and drew miners deeper below ground. Fatalities mounted like never before. By 1890, fourteen states had suffered at least one major explosion. Between 1906 and 1910, almost 2,500 miners died in accidents. Supported by inspectors, miners called for new safety laws, and several states responded.

At first, operators resisted demands for safety reform. They feared that coal mined in regulated states would not be competitive with coal from non-regulated states. But they were forced to accept the fact that some type of safety regulation was beneficial to their interests—and inevitable in any event. They viewed national standards as less stringent than state standards and thus lobbied for federal legislation.

The agitation over mine safety produced few tangible results by World War I. No national regulatory legislation was enacted. Without clear authority, the Bureau of Mines simply operated as an educational and scientific data-gathering agency. Regulation and inspection remained a state responsibility, but uniformity in the laws was not achieved. Southern mine operators in particular resisted any form of regulation.

Despite its severe limitations, governmental labor policy was being shaped by the coal industry. As in the case of antitrust and business regulation, energy production and energy use played important roles in the evolution of business-government relations.

ENERGY AND THE CONSERVATION MOVEMENT

Antimonopoly and business regulation were directed at corporate growth and competition within the American economic system. In this sense, the development of an energy policy was subordinated to a broader interest in defining the relationship between business and government. Similarly, government interest in energy resources, in the early twentieth century at least, was subordinated to broader issues of conservation and preservation. Nonetheless, the relationship between energy sources and the rise of the conservation movement hints at government concern over the ownership of resources, resource exploitation, and waste.

Origins of the Conservation Movement

As business reform was meant to bring order to the American economy, so conservation was meant to rationalize the use of natural resources. What came to be known as "the conservation movement" in the United States had its intellectual antecedents in eighteenth-century Europe and its American origins in the nineteenth century.

By the late nineteenth century, several milestones marked the coming of the movement: from the publication of George Perkins Marsh's *Man and Nature* (1864) to the implementation of the "national park" concept; from the establishment of the U.S. Geological Survey (1879) to the founding of the Sierra Club (1892). By the turn of the century, the conservation movement achieved national status, especially with the presidency of Theodore Roosevelt.

Public policy on resource questions after 1900 were guided by those who wished to prevent waste through efficient use—resource conservationists—as opposed to those more interested in saving what remained of the wilderness—preservationists. A central figure in public-policy formation was Gifford Pinchot, Roosevelt's chief forester and the major proponent of the notion that resources should be rationally and efficiently developed for use, not withheld. As Pinchot stated in *The Fight for Conservation* (1910):

> We are prosperous because our forefathers bequeathed to us a land of marvellous resources still unexhausted. Shall we conserve those resources, and in our own turn transmit them, still unexhausted, to our descendants? Unless we do, those who come after us will have to pay the price of misery, degradation, and failure for the progress and prosperity of our day. . . . Therefore the conservation of natural resources is the basis, and the only permanent basis, of national success.

To some historians, the conservationists of the Progressive Era were combatting the greed and wastefulness of the business world. As J. Leonard Bates stated: "The organized conservationists were concerned more with economic justice and democracy in the handling of resources than with mere prevention of waste." Their task was to make sure that "the common heritage" did not pass into the hands of "vested interests."[4]

Samuel P. Hays was the first historian to counter that perspective: "Conservation neither arose from a broad popular outcry, nor centered its fire primarily upon the private corporation. Moreover, corporations often supported conservation policies, while the 'people' just as frequently opposed

---

[4]J. Leonard Bates, "Fulfilling American Democracy: The Conservation Movement," in Carroll Pursell (ed.), *From Conservation to Ecology* (New York, 1973), p. 21.

them." He went on to suggest that conservation history cannot be understood as part of the struggle against corporations, or, at least, monopolistic practices. "Conservation, above all," he asserted, "was a scientific movement, and its role in history arises from the implications of science and technology in modern society." Conservation leaders were experts from the fields of hydrology, forestry, agrostology, geology, and anthropology, who brought their ideas to bear on the establishment of federal resource policy.[5] In other words, professionals and scientists from the East, acting from within the federal bureaucracy, employed centralized policy-making powers to curtail the waste of resources and establish programs of "wise use," especially in the West. This meant that western interests were often at loggerheads with federal conservationists, since they wanted local control and the ability to exploit the resources for their own economic ends.

Waterpower and the West

Hays' perspective is most valuable in assessing the impact of the conservation movement on energy resources. The controversy over waterpower, especially, went to the heart of the issue of "wise use." America's waterways came to be viewed as a multipurpose resource, for navigation, flood control, irrigation, municipal and industrial uses, and hydroelectric power. Conservationists' interest in the development of hydroelectric power focused in the West, where private access to water on public lands and along navigable rivers was greatest.

Hydroelectric power was generated in Oregon as early as 1889, followed by similar ventures in Montana, California, and Washington. Before 1901, waterpower sites in the public domain were gobbled up by private companies, without any effort by the federal government to reserve those sites or regulate their use. The reason for this, in part, was ambiguity over the extent of federal jurisdiction and regulatory authority.

The first step toward waterpower conservation occurred in 1901, with the passage of the Right of Way Act. This law codified congressional acts going back to the 1890s. Although primarily intended as a way of facilitating reclamation and irrigation programs adjacent to public lands, it was broadened to cover many utility functions. The secretary of the interior could grant rights-of-way over public lands for dams, reservoirs, waterpower plants, and transmission lines. The act, however, made no attempt at public regulation or control. Congress eventually transferred the reserves to the Department of Agriculture. The Forest Service granted temporary permits, while the Department of the Interior remained responsible for permanent easements. Through this charge, the Forest Service acquired extensive authority for the regulation of waterpower, at least within the national forests.

Private power companies were opposed to any permit system, proposing as an alternative the granting of perpetual leases. Through loopholes in

[5]Samuel P. Hays, *Conservation and the Gospel of Efficiency* (New York, 1959), pp. 1–2.

the new law, private companies sometimes evaded the permit system and entered power sites nonetheless. Chief Forester Pinchot, with the aid of Secretary of the Interior James R. Garfield, attempted to counter these actions. One method used was the withdrawing of certain lands from any form of entry under the pretext that they were valuable locations for ranger stations. Eventually, Roosevelt adopted the doctrine of "executive supervisory power," which meant that he could withdraw land for any purpose that would aid in the execution of the laws.

The Forest Service permit system did little to retard the growth of waterpower. Private companies continued to fight for more favorable legislation, but they accepted the permit system. By 1916, power facilities in the national forests represented 42 percent of the total developed power in the western states.

President Taft's appointment of Richard Ballinger as secretary of the interior in 1909 weakened the new regulatory system. Ballinger refused to apply the Forest Service permit system to waterpower sites on public domain. In 1911, Walter L. Fisher succeeded Ballinger and decided to follow Garfield's policy. He had to contend with the General Land Office, which regarded the permit system as illegal and thus he gave the Geological Survey the responsibility for administering it. The revised permits included a fifty-year limited grant and imposed a waterpower fee ("conservation charge"). Not until the Water Power Act of 1920 was the principle of public regulation of hydroelectric power more firmly established.

These machinations did not resolve the problem of waterpower development on navigable streams. An important issue was the relationship between the multiple-purpose development of waterways and the question of financing such development. In the 1903 veto of private use of Muscle Shoals, Alabama, Roosevelt protected the site for later government development, but he also helped to establish the principle of national ownership of resources previously considered only of local value. In this particular case, Roosevelt recommended using revenue from power production to finance navigation improvements. Within five years, the administration worked out a plan for federal development and lease of waterpower on navigable streams.

The Taft administration was unwilling to follow Roosevelt's lead, viewing power dams as obstructions to expanding navigation. However, the Water Power Act of 1920 permitted federal supervision of hydroelectric facilities on both public lands and navigable streams, and it established the Federal Power Commission (FPC). Yet it did not provide for multiple-purpose development as a public goal, an the FPC activity was generally limited to licensing and site location. Flood control and irrigation were not included, power revenues were not linked with construction of multiple-purpose dam construction, and federal revenues from hydroelectric facilities would be paltry.

Not all waterpower debates during the period were limited to varying "wise-use" concepts. The battle over a dam project in the beautiful Hetch-Hetchy Valley in Yosemite National Park stands as the most dramatic example of a conflict between preservation and conservation.

The controversy arose over San Francisco's attempt to build a reservoir in Hetch-Hetchy Valley for use as a water supply. Eventually the plan was expanded to include the possible development of an electricity-producing dam. John Muir and his Sierra Club objected strenuously, bent on saving the Toulumne River and the Hetch-Hetchy Valley from development. Interior Secretary Garfield and Gifford Pinchot lined up against Muir, other preservationists, and, curiously, Pacific Gas and Electric Company (PG&E). PG&E's motives were fairly obvious—to challenge the development of a municipally run power facility.

The Hetch-Hetchy debate pitted conservationists against preservationists, and public power advocates against private power advocates. Self-interest dictated how the sides formed. Nonetheless, Congress passed a bill in 1913 settling the issue in favor of development and private power. Hetch-Hetchy became the first major multipurpose water project authorized by Congress.

Coal, Oil, and Conservation

The disposition of mineral rights on public lands was also an important question for conservationists. The right to exploit coal deposits generated some heated debate in 1906. The Roosevelt administration learned that coal claims had been filed on national forest land in order to obtain the timber on the surface; some individuals had acquired valuable coal deposits by fraud under the Homestead Act. Because of these and other misuses of land laws, the Roosevelt administration temporarily withdrew some 50 million acres in order to determine the value of their coal deposits. Withdrawals continued until 1916, when more than 140 million acres had been withdrawn. Some lands were restored to entry as early as 1907, and, in 1908, the newly formed Land Classification Board began to examine the other withdrawn land. By 1916, about 21 million acres were classified as coal lands.

The Roosevelt administration was unable to establish an effective coal-leasing system, largely because of opposition from two divergent sources: Westerners, who did not want public lands removed from exploitation, and Senator Robert La Follette (Rep., Wisc.), who wanted more rigorous withdrawals and stricter mineral land laws. The administration, however, favored raising the price of coal lands to frustrate exploitation. The plan met with some success, but conservationists still pushed for a leasing system. The first conservationist victory came in 1914 with the passage of a coal-leasing measure for Alaska. This approach, however, was not applied to all minerals on the public domain until 1920. Conservationists' interest in western coal lands was not matched by concern over the extensive waste of coal in existing fields in the East. In some cases, 60 percent of the coal was not recovered in the mining process.

The Roosevelt administration treated oil lands similarly to coal lands. Prospectors themselves requested better federal regulation. Traditionally, they had to find oil deposits before filing entry, and thus they had little protection from land sharks who claimed the land for other purposes under the agricultural laws. Secretary Garfield was sympathetic to these requests and withdrew from agricultural entry a large area of oil deposits in California. The oil lands reopened to entry under mineral law only. Secretary Ballinger continued the withdrawal program for oil lands, with some limitations, despite his usual opposition to Rooseveltian policies.[6] By 1916, fifty oil reserves were created. With respect to the broader question of leasing mineral rights, Congress passed a bill in 1920 allowing the federal government to retain ownership of the land while leasing mineral rights to private firms and returning revenue to the West for various purposes, including irrigation.

Oil Pollution and Waste

Oil-field waste and pollution were not effectively addressed by government before World War I. Careless drilling and refining practices, however, produced great waste and aroused a serious concern over exhaustion of oil supplies. Some predictions in the mid-1910s suggested that exhaustion of the nation's reserves could occur in twenty years, although later studies recognized that these predictions were too severe. In any case, the issue inspired little more than debate over the problem of waste.

State and federal governments explored some remedies for potential oil depletion. In the late 1870s and early 1880s, New York and Pennsylvania established regulations for plugging wells to reduce waste. Soon thereafter, Indiana tried to regulate waste by creating the Department of Geology and Natural Resources and, later, the office of the State Natural Gas Supervisor. Kansas (1891) and West Virginia (1892) regulated drilling and operation of wells. Texas, California, and Oklahoma also inaugurated some regulation programs. Oklahoma's program was the most comprehensive; it included the first state law to control production (1915). Yet wasteful practices, such as flaring wells, continued without much abatement.

In the cases of air and water pollution due to drilling oil, the oil companies, the states, and the federal government were equally silent. The American Petroleum Institute—the lobbying body of the major producers—ignored self-regulation until it sensed the possibility of federal action. Oil-producing states placed economic growth—not antipollution—as their highest priority. And it was not until the passage of the Oil Pollution Control Act (1924) that the federal government established a precedent for combatting oil pollution.

ECONOMIC GROWTH VERSUS REGULATION

Government encouragement of economic growth did not disappear in the era of antitrust, regulation, and conservation. Indeed, the federal government

[6]Under Ballinger, oil lands were reserved as future fuel supplies for the Navy, and these lands Ballinger closed even to mineral entry.

sought new ways of stimulating competition, encouraging production, and exploiting natural resources. Energy policy *per se* was simply an extension of a broader economic policy. In the most elementary sense, the several pieces of legislation, court decisions, and policies that impinged on energy sources added up to the nation's energy policy. More accurately, the United States did not have a comprehensive energy policy during this period. Energy remained a commodity, a means to an end, a component of the larger economic interests of the nation. The uniqueness of the new energy industries was not understood or taken into account in the establishment of fuel policies.

Faith in energy abundance contributed to the piecemeal approach to energy policy in coal-age America. The late nineteenth and early twentieth centuries were a time of economic optimism. Abundant energy supplies helped to assure the faith in the economic future of the nation. The response of the federal government, especially, was a reflection of that optimism.

FURTHER READING

J. Leonard Bates. *The Origins of Teapot Dome*. Urbana, Ill., 1963.

Bruce Bringhurst. *Antitrust and the Oil Monopoly*. Westport, Conn., 1979.

William Graebner. *Coal-Mining Safety in the Progressive Period*. Lexington, Ky., 1976.

Samuel P. Hays. *Conservation and the Gospel of Efficiency*. New York, 1959.

James P. Johnson. *The Politics of Soft Coal*. Urbana, Ill., 1979.

John G. McLean and Robert W. Haigh. *The Growth of Integrated Oil Companies*. Boston, 1954.

Gerald D. Nash. *United States Oil Policy, 1890–1964*. Pittsburgh, 1968.

Joseph A. Pratt. "The Petroleum Industry in Transition," *Journal of Economic History*, vol. 40 (December 1980), pp. 815–837.

PART TWO

Oil Power and World Power, 1914–1945

CHAPTER 5

Fueling the Great War

World War I virtually obliterated a whole generation of Europeans, changed the map of the European continent, and gave rise to what became the Third World. For the United States, the impact of the war was strikingly different. By 1919, it was the leading economic power in the world with a diversified economy and growing strategic interests. The carnage of the war was less severe for Americans than for Europeans, and the Western Hemisphere was spared the physical scars of battle that were left at the Somme, Verdun, and along the Eastern Front. While Europe faced the grim task of rebuilding, Americans looked to a future of economic prosperity and growing international prestige.

The institutions of the United States, especially the federal government, were transformed by the war nonetheless. The demands of war production inspired more governmental participation in the economic affairs of the nation. The rise of "big government" began to match the rise of "big business" of previous decades. The centralization of governmental and corporate power moved toward subordinating local and regional interests to "the national interest." Clearer lines of national energy policy emerged, which favored greater productivity of major fuels and offered stable prices. The war also encouraged the transition from coal to petroleum—especially in transportation and in industry—as demand for gasoline and fuel oils grew dramatically.

Huge governmental expenditures for wartime production promoted industrial expansion and contributed to a rising demand for energy. Between 1900 and 1920, for example, total energy use increased by almost three times while population increased 1.4 times. Furthermore, wartime industries directly influenced the conversion to electrical power. The production of electricity increased approximately 40 percent between 1916 and 1917 alone, and nearly doubled by 1921.

Energy use during the war demonstrated the utter dependence of an industrialized society on abundant sources of power. The diversion of energy to wartime needs and resulting domestic shortages reenforced that notion. While the shortages were brief in duration, they were national in scope. A faith in energy abundance survived the war, but questions of the allocation, distribution, and control of energy resources lingered into the 1920s and beyond.

WORLD WAR I AND THE EXPANSION OF GOVERNMENT

As historian Robert D. Cuff stated: "The Great War produced an unparalleled expansion of the state in the United States, as it did in every country under arms. An administrative army marched into Washington before a military force sailed overseas."[1] The stimulus for an organizational revolution in government grew out of the way in which the nation fought the war. First, industrial production was stepped up to meet the needs of the Allies. Second, an American expeditionary force was raised. Once reluctant to see the United States break its "strict neutrality," President Woodrow Wilson brought the nation into war in April 1917 (the war began in Europe in 1914). He did so with the hope of quickly ending the conflict and establishing a lasting peace settlement. With these goals, the nation underwent a crash program of industrial production, a major change in consumption patterns, and a shift to compulsory military service.

Efforts to enlarge the federal bureaucracy for the sake of preparedness failed until the eve of American entry into the war. In 1910, President Taft had called for a Council of National Defense (CND) to coordinate the activities of pertinent government agencies. Congress refused to oblige until 1916, when it passed the National Defense Act and the Military Appropriations Act. Because of President Wilson's reluctance to participate in the war, the CND played a limited role in establishing a preparedness program. However, it examined a wide range of issues and created state equivalents of the national council in the event of an emergency. As war approached, the council gave serious consideration to manpower needs, while the Federal Reserve Board and other agencies concentrated on financial policy.

When the United States entered the war, an array of boards and agencies were established to oversee various aspects of the war effort, including the War Finance Corporation, National War Labor Board, the Food and Fuel Administrations, the Committee on Public Information, the Allied Purchasing Commission, the U.S. Railroad Administration, and the War Industries Board.

The War Industries Board (WIB), established in 1917, was the major civilian agency for industrial mobilization. It acted as a clearinghouse for war industries and was the principle agency responsible for increasing production and eliminating waste. The WIB wielded much influence within the Wilson administration. However, major decisions over fuel supply, price, and allocation came from other agencies, especially the Fuel Administration. Under crisis-management conditions, the establishment of energy policy was diffuse and often subordinated to the demands of production. Nonetheless, the dramatic increase in governmental influence over the economy began to change the way government officials viewed the energy needs of the nation.

[1]Robert D. Cuff, *The War Industries Board* (Baltimore, 1973), p. 1.

COAL AND INDUSTRIAL PRODUCTION

Coal was the central ingredient in industrial production, the heart of any program to deliver the goods of war. Adequate supplies of bituminous coal were crucial, especially because of the demand for munitions and other materiel essential to an Allied victory. There was little need to mine more anthracite, since a record surplus was available and hard coal functioned chiefly as a domestic fuel.

The demand for bituminous was critical because production had fallen off drastically in war-torn Europe. Mine workers were in short supply. German troops overran coal-producing areas in France and Russia. Rail lines and other land transportation were disrupted; German U-boats challenged Allied freighters. The Allies attempted to adjust to war conditions by using inland waterways rather than rail to deliver coal, stepped up conscription to put more miners on the job, and invoked conservation programs. Still, they were obliged to place their confidence in the industrial capacity of the United States.

Increasing coal production was not as difficult in the United States as it was in Europe, but it still posed problems. Demand outstripped supply through much of the war, with delivery of coal the major stumbling block. The American railroad system had inadequate numbers of cars and locomotives to deliver coal to industrial sites or to ports already congested with goods. With the institution of the draft, labor for mining, shipping, and manufacturing was in short supply. Even if large quantities of coal could be amassed, it was too bulky to store effectively and deteriorated once exposed to the elements. As one observer noted in 1919: "The whole problem of coal supply was like a chain, the breakage of a single link of which meant disaster."

After years of instability and uncertainty in the bituminous industry, the wartime demand in 1916 resulted in a dramatic rise in price—from $1 a ton to as high as $5 a ton. Industry leaders hoped that the increase marked a new period of stability and prosperity for the coal business. The reaction in Washington was quite different. Congressmen and government officials viewed the rise in price as threatening to industrial production. Antitrusters believed that the coal industry was greedily taking advantage of the war. Responding to severe coal shortages in 1916, the Federal Trade Commission (FTC) investigated both the hard and soft coal industries. In a report issued in May 1917, the FTC recommended that the government consider setting prices and regulating distribution as a way of encouraging higher production of war material. As an historian of the coal industry concluded: "In 1917 government officials were condemning an essentially fragmented and leaderless industry as if it were a monopoly."[2]

---

[2]James P. Johnson, *The Politics of Soft Coal* (Urbana, Ill., 1979), p. 34.

The question of prices for all war-related supplies had become a major government concern before the FTC action. In February 1917, the CND created the General Munitions Board, which was responsible for establishing an informal price arrangement with the vital munitions industry. To deal with coal, the CND created the Committee on Coal Production (CCP), a group dominated by leading operators but also including former UMW President John Mitchell and government representatives; Francis S. Peabody, a Chicago coal operator, was named chairman. The CCP's job was to stimulate production and insure the delivery of coal to its markets. It organized state committees of coal operators, formed consumer groups, set up an exchange to expedite shipments to the Allies, and appointed miners' committees to defuse strikes.

In June, the FTC issued a second report on coal, calling for the pooling of production under government control. This stunned coal operators and scuttled the work of the CCP. Additional pressure on the Peabody Committee and the coal interests came from Secretary of the Navy Josephus Daniels. Daniels wanted to purchase coal virtually at prewar prices; he viewed any attempt at raising prices as unpatriotic.

Confronting these challenges, operators meeting with members of the CND and the FTC reached an agreement on June 30, fixing the price of bituminous at $3 a ton. The secretary of war, who acted as chairman of the CND, repudiated the agreement, arguing that the council could not fix prices. Several officials, including the President, believed that the price was too high. Outraged consumers and antitrusters shared this feeling. At this point the CCP's voluntary program lost credibility, and further governmental control was a foregone conclusion.

UNITED STATES FUEL ADMINISTRATION

The Food and Fuel Control (or Lever) Act of August 10, 1917, gave the government extensive power over the production, distribution, and consumption of coal on the grounds that national security required adequate supplies of fuel (also food, fertilizer, and equipment necessary to produce them). The Lever Act also gave the President the power to fix coal prices, an option he exercised a few days after the passage of the act. Based on an FTC study of coal-production costs, Wilson cut the price to $2 a ton. The industry was confused and incensed by the action: Why did the government want to threaten the coal companies' new-found economic health?

To administer the new powers over energy sources, Wilson created the United States Fuel Administration (USFA) on August 23, 1917. This was a less drastic step than was pooling coal production under government control. However, it would require the cooperation of the coal, petroleum, and railroad industries. The USFA ultimately was divided into three divisions: Administrative, Distribution, and Oil, with subordinate agencies on the state level. As a body it was concerned with stimulating production, adjusting disputes between operators and employees, fixing prices, controlling distribution and apportionment, and conserving fuels.

To administer this new agency, Wilson chose an old friend and academic colleague, Harry A. Garfield. The son of President James Garfield, the new fuel czar was president-on-leave from Williams College, currently serving under Herbert Hoover in the Food Administration. Wilson passed over several other candidates in choosing Garfield, who had no connection with the coal industry or any other energy-related industry. But it was for exactly that reason—as well as Garfield's background in law, education, and government—that Wilson believed his fuel administrator would be able to put the nation's interest above special interests.

Wilson and Garfield shared a faith in public solutions to the country's problems. Garfield, especially, placed great stock in the need for cooperation between government and business. A follower of the socialist engineer Charles Steinmetz, Garfield believed that democracy needed to be balanced with an orderly process of corporate consolidation. Given his background, it would appear that energy producers would be troubled by Garfield's appointment, but in the long run it was well received. Coalmen preferred someone willing to cooperate with the private sector rather than an antibusiness "radical."

Garfield's task as fuel administrator was not an enviable one. After setting up the administrative structure of the USFA and establishing a system of state fuel administrators and local coal committees, he turned to the most pressing problem in 1917—the production and distribution of coal. At first, the coal industry was confused and incensed over government price-setting. However, Garfield's relationship with operators and miners was positive, because he strove to make the cooperative idea work.

Detractors accused Garfield of being a tool of the coal operators, but his office devoted substantial attention to labor relations as well as to the interests of operators. This is not to say that Garfield did not develop strong ties with the industry. The USFA hired several coal-industry executives, and the operators recognized the agency as an island of security within the federal bureaucracy. Operators found Garfield and the USFA willing to promote price increases and to encourage the stabilization of the industry, without relying on production controls. Coal operators also used the USFA in dealings with buyers, as a buffer against public criticism, and as a sympathetic spokesman within government circles.

The working relationship between the USFA and the coal industry was aided by the generally favorable wartime economic conditions. These were golden days for the coal industry in the sense that rising prices for coal meant more profits, and increased demand meant more employment. For the first time, the coal industry was able to establish a workable trade association— the National Coal Association—which worked closely with the USFA. The issues that divided coal operators in the past did not disappear overnight, but prevailing conditions gave the NCA an opportunity for industry-wide cooperation.

The labor policy of the Fuel Administration was uncharacteristically middle of the road, particularly as compared to the hostility previously exhibited by the federal government. In spirit, Garfield adopted Theodore Roosevelt's paternalism, that is, favoring higher wages and better working conditions while dismissing union recognition. But also like Roosevelt, Garfield's major concern was production. A first general agreement with coal miners was struck in August 1917. The emphasis was on avoiding the disruption of mining operations. In exchange for higher wages, a mechanism for grievances, and recognition of collective bargaining in areas where locals existed, the UMW agreed to tone down its campaign for unionizing southern fields and to avoid the use of strikes. Union recognition, on a national scale at least, was not included in any agreement supported by the USFA.

Garfield did confront potentially explosive labor disputes on a case by case basis, however. For instance, when anthracite miners became restive in 1918, negotiations over wages were instituted. The agency also worked with local draft boards, persuading them to defer "essential" mineworkers and to arrange furloughs for those drafted but not sent overseas.

Fuel Crisis: 1917–1918

In the winter of 1917–1918, the nation experienced a major fuel crisis. Some charged that the Wilson administration's short-sightedness in estimating coal demand during the summer of 1917 was a contributing factor. Bernard Baruch, head of the War Industries Board, had warned the President about possible shortages, but Garfield announced that coal production would be sufficient for the winter. When production increased by November, Garfield's projection appeared sound.

The lack of railroad cars for shipping coal—not production—was the primary reason for the crisis. A battle raged within the administration for priority shipments of various commodities. Food Administrator Herbert Hoover argued that food rather than fuel had to have the highest priority; Garfield thought otherwise. However, Priority Commissioner Robert S. Lovett issued an order placing most commodities ahead of coal. This meant immediate fuel shortages in factories and homes.

Not only was coal in short supply, but the United States experienced one of the worst winters in history. People began to panic even before the bitter cold hit the East and Midwest. Coal hoarding was chronic, and there were incidents of violence and vigilante action to acquire coal. In Ohio, shipments of coal to Great Lake ports were stalled when angry citizens tore up railroad track to prevent the trains from by-passing their towns.

In December, Boston and Philadelphia faced record lows, − 14 degrees and − 4 degrees, respectively. Transportation routes were snarled as trains were bottled up and harbors frozen over. Coal supplies were frozen in dealers' lots, making them difficult to ship even if transportation was available. Water needed to supply steam for locomotives was also depleted because so many people ran water in their homes to avoid cracked pipes.

The impact of the scarcity on individuals was most critical. The lengthening of Christmas vacation for children, extended hours for saloons and theaters, and work layoffs produced a carnival atmosphere for a few days in some cities. But the grim realities of the shortage set in when layoffs continued into January, as people were forced to burn furniture or wooden toys, as cities curtailed outside lighting and established other conservation programs. Rioting broke out in Brooklyn. People stormed coal wagons in Manhattan. In Detroit, some residents abandoned their homes, while one person who did not froze to death. During one week in New York, 263 people died of pneumonia. Exploiting the tragedy of the situation, developers in Lakeland, Florida, advertised: "COME TO FLORIDA, The Permanent Solution to the Coal Problem."

Voluntary programs of fuel conservation were inadequate. Many cities tried to restrict the use of coal; they urged churches to consolidate their services, allowed office buildings to operate only during daylight hours, and even issued rationing cards. In the hardest hit areas, such as Chicago, consideration was given to shutting down factories and other industrial establishments. In Cleveland, two-thirds of the factories were closed for several days to save power for homes and streetcars.

In January, the Fuel Administration finally decided to intervene; it would coordinate conservation plans and curtailments. On January 16, Garfield met secretly with President Wilson, Secretary of War Newton Baker, and Secretary of the Navy Daniels. Garfield explained what seemed to be an audacious plan for temporarily shutting down industry and establishing fuel holidays. Gaining Wilson's support and the crucial backing of Railroad Administrator William G. McAdoo, he announced the USFA's plan that would go into effect January 17: every industrial plant east of the Mississippi—where 85 percent of the steam plants were located—would be shut down from January 18 to January 22, with very few exceptions. For ten consecutive Mondays (beginning January 28 and ending March 25), no fuel could be utilized by any business except for essential needs and services. Garfield hoped that the plan would save thirty million tons of coal.

Opposition to the plan was fierce. Congress protested the action. The *New York World*—usually sympathetic to the Wilson administration—called the order the "greatest disaster that has befallen the United States in this war," an action "worthy of a Bolshevik Government."[3] Americans who lost wages as a result of the curtailments cursed the "Garfieldays." Debate also raged over what kind of savings, if any, the program produced. With the support of government propagandist George Creel and his Committee on Public Information, Garfield announced that the order helped to move 480 ships—369 of which carried munitions and war supplies. Critics claimed that the order was an overreaction, with costs unnecessarily high for the given results. Yet President Wilson publicly backed his fuel administrator. Patriotism and the war effort were on Garfield's side.

[3]Johnson, *The Politics of Soft Coal*, p. 67.

Implementing the plan was more difficult than riding out the immediate criticisms. Garfield permitted approximately 1,000 exemptions for a variety of reasons, but denied thousands more. His major concern was getting Railroad Administrator McAdoo to rush cars to the mines. While McAdoo agreed to give coal top priority, he was unwilling to order an embargo on other commodities.

On February 13, Garfield lifted the Monday holidays; the crisis seemed to have passed. What lingered were memories of a nightmarish crisis and uncertainty about the government response to it. Garfield had done what he felt was necessary, but the inconclusiveness of the action pointed to the complexity of the fuel situation.

Conservation and Production

The fuel crisis pointed to the need to conserve fuel and to educate the public about conservation. The Fuel Administration created several conservation programs. In March 1918, it also established a rationing system for domestic consumers and carried out a presidential proclamation for licensing those engaged in distributing coal. The USFA estimated that 32 million tons of coal were saved between October 1917, and February 1919, as a result of various conservation programs: shortening the work week in several industries, restricting outdoor lighting, reducing temperatures in passenger trains, and, in some cases, substituting wood for coal. The USFA's Bureau of Conservation encouraged coal saving by increasing steam-production efficiency. Garfield urged President Wilson to support daylight-saving legislation. On the state level, directors of conservation promoted various educational programs.

The USFA, along with the Railroad Administration, set up another important program: the establishment of producing districts and consuming regions throughout the United States. Coal industry and railroad experts proposed a zoning plan to increase production and reduce railroad crosshauls, and it was announced in late January. The plan divided the nation into twenty consuming and eleven producing regions. It outlined how much coal each consuming region required and determined which producing districts most effectively could provide the coal. A product of government-business cooperation, the zone system increased the coal operators' and shippers' confidence in the USFA and Garfield.

Coal and Reconversion

The various USFA programs were directed toward a single end—production. By the close of the war, production was booming, because of both the demands of the war itself and the cooperation of the USFA with the coal industry. Between 1916 and 1920, the annual output of bituminous coal increased from 502.5 million tons to 568.7 million tons. The number of mines, during the same period, increased from 5,726 to almost 9,000 (although most new ones were of small capacity).

The wartime surge in production, higher prices, and better wages for miners were only temporary relief for the industry. When the Fuel Administration was dismantled in 1919, practically all restrictions on price, distribution, and production were lifted. With the exception of Garfield, there were few who saw the government's involvement with the coal industry as anything more than an emergency effort. Garfield's hope for some kind of major governmental reorganization was dashed with the termination of the USFA. The bituminous coal industry slipped back into its normal pattern of instability. The operators' honeymoon with labor proved short-lived. The UMW struck in November 1919, in order to maintain its wartime wage levels. With some exceptions, demand for coal began a decline until World War II.

What had the relationship between the industry and government accomplished? Certainly it had produced the necessary production requirements to fight the war, but little else. Into the 1920s, it seemed as if the government had learned little about this sick industry.

PETROLEUM AND THE WAR

The only similarity between the government's coal and petroleum policies was the desire for increased production. The federal government temporarily abandoned interest in antitrust, and, in fact, encouraged greater integration within the oil industry. The only restrictive actions focused on the regulation of certain business practices, on conservation, and on the elimination of waste.

Unlike bituminous coal, petroleum had a bright future. By World War I, oil was an essential fuel. Demand for petroleum was rising incredibly fast—from 63.6 million gallons in 1900 to 335.3 million by 1917. Prices had not accelerated as rapidly because of the myriad discoveries of oil, especially in the midcontinent fields. But when the United States entered the war, demand accelerated even more quickly and prices rose by about 50 percent.

The petroleum industry's position of strength in the energy economy gave it an effective bargaining lever with the government, and limited the kinds of restrictions placed on coal. Whereas coal was primarily an industrial and domestic fuel, oil was a military-naval fuel. Oil played a key role in affecting the daily outcome of an increasingly mechanized war, and therefore it gave producers some advantage in dealing with government officials. The unique properties of petroleum—especially its ease of transport—created fewer bottlenecks in delivering the vital resource to its users. Furthermore, since petroleum was not a primary fuel for domestic or industrial usage, it could more easily be diverted to the battlefield without creating controversies on the homefront.

As Lord George Nathaniel Curzon of the British War Cabinet remarked in 1918: "The Allies floated to victory on a wave of oil." World War I was the first major conflict in which belligerents were heavily dependent on motorized transportation on the sea, on land, and in the air. Before the war, the major naval powers adapted their vessels to use fuel oil rather than coal. Submarines employed diesel engines. Gasoline-powered land vehicles moved personnel and equipment. Tanks and aircraft were fitted with internal-combustion engines. Efforts by both the Allies and Central Powers to control oil supplies became standard war strategy.

The American oil industry was crucial in providing Europe with adequate supplies prior to 1917. Along with Mexico, the United States was the principal supplier. The major problem was getting the oil to Europe, since very few of the world's tankers were under American registry. The oil industry's primary interest was continuing its trade in illuminants, but new refining techniques allowed American oil companies to adapt their outputs to the demand for gasoline and fuel oils. Thus, losses in markets for kerosene were offset by demands for fuel oils and lubricants.

Europeans were importing the lion's share of exported lubricating oils, fuel oils, and gasoline during the early years of the war. And despite initial fears, the supply of available tankers was adequate. Attack on American shipping—due to Germany's announcement of unrestricted submarine warfare in January 1917—seriously jeopardized trade and was an important factor in the breakdown of German-American relations.

The PAC and the NPWSC

Along with coal, the Wilson administration considered petroleum as an essential part of the preparedness program in 1916. And government's initial overture to the industry was also through a program of cooperation and voluntary action. In March 1917, one month before the United States entered the war, Bernard Baruch, a prominent member of CND's Advisory Committee, approached leaders in the oil industry to form the Petroleum Advisory Committee (PAC). Alfred C. Bedford, president of Standard Oil of New Jersey, headed the committee and he enlisted other prominent industrial leaders in the effort. PAC had broad functions and substantial freedom to insure the delivery of oil to the armed services and recommend allocation of supplies. The administration, therefore, was more willing to recognize the need for oil-industry expertise in establishing oil policy, than it was in making similar arrangements with the coal companies.

When the war began, the Wilson administration replaced PAC with the National Petroleum War Services Committee (NPWSC). Despite fears of additional federal encroachment, the NPWSC was a simple reconstitution of PAC under the Fuel Administration, with virtually the same personnel and functions.

As in all cases of business-government cooperation, questions of conflict of interest were significant. NPWSC advised the government on purchases and allocations and provided the best source of statistical information available. At the same time, the members represented the companies from which the government acquired its supplies. Without a major trade association, the oil industry depended on NPWSC to protect its interests, and the federal government depended on NPWSC as a link to private energy suppliers.

The Oil Division

Full production was the goal of Wilson's oil policy. NPWSC was only one tool in meeting that goal. At Garfield's urging, the President issued an executive order in January 1918, establishing an Oil Division (OD) within the Fuel Administration. In a subsequent presidential proclamation, Wilson announced federal control over the distribution of fuel oil through a licensing system. A priority arrangement was authorized under the same proclamation. (The Lever Act did not authorize price-fixing for oil.) In August, the President transferred to the USFA the responsibility for preparing and adopting standardized specifications for supply of petroleum products to all government departments and agencies. Because of the importance of oil in national affairs, the OD did not assert much direct governmental authority over the industry. Instead, with the assistance and influence of NPWSC it set out to stimulate production, improve transportation, and regulate price and distribution without rigid standards or controls.

On January 10, 1918, Garfield chose Mark Requa to head the OD. Requa came from a different background than did Garfield, but he shared many of his boss's beliefs. A protégé of Herbert Hoover, Requa was an important petroleum engineer, who began his career in Nevada mining and railroad enterprises. The oil boom in California drew ıim farther west, where he formed his own oil company. He came to Washington as Hoover's assistant in the Food Administration. As oil administrator, he demonstrated such a strong preference for business-government cooperation that some observers believed he was merely an industry spokesman. Although Requa was convinced that the oil industry could govern itself in many areas, he was not afraid to set policy in what he believed to be the national interest.

While not confronting an emergency like the 1917–1918 coal crisis, Requa faced several difficulties: the need for uninterrupted production, consistent and sufficient transportation, and domestic conservation of fuel were all important. In particular, Requa found the OD involved in several intergovernmental squabbles. For example, the FTC issued a report in April 1918, charging oil producers and refiners with profiteering, and specifically cited Standard Oil of Indiana for violations of the Clayton Act. The report intimated that nationalization of the industry might be necessary in order for the United States to meet its oil requirements. Requa was able to prevent formal proceeding in exchange for a face-saving prosecution of Standard of Indiana on some lesser charges. The FTC also agreed to abide by future rulings of USFA and to keep them informed of antitrust matters in peacetime.

On the question of price, Requa did not play the pliant industry spokesman to the extent his critics charged. By spring 1918, Requa believed that the rise in prices no longer was acting as a stimulus to production. Earlier in 1918, he had moved on an idea to control production through local initiatives and pooling of fuel oil by the industry. In this way, for better or for worse, he was encouraging further integration and consolidation of the oil industry.

Beyond the immediate interest in production, Requa concentrated on price stabilization as a necessary adjunct to federal oil policy. As long as production lagged behind the increasing demand for oil, rising prices would be an important issue. Although he sought voluntary measures to keep prices down, Requa did warn the industry that prices had to be stabilized. The industry responded by attempting to arrive at "voluntary control" to avoid further governmental intervention. Relying on a plan originating with PAC, the 600 or more midcontinent producers and refiners stabilized at July prices. In addition, the USFA set a scale of prices that applied to government contracts. These and other measures brought about price stabilization; it did not require a pricing scheme similar to the one used in the coal industry.

Limiting waste and establishing a system of oil conservation had a more immediate impact on production than on price. At least fifteen boards were created to observe or monitor all phases of the industry. Several approaches were employed to reduce waste and increase efficiency. Scientists in the Bureau of Mines encouraged oilmen to improve their methods of drilling, producing, and refining. Within OD, Requa promoted scientific research and threatened to close inefficient refineries (which led to charges that he favored large refiners). The Bureau of Conservation sent inspectors to advise manufacturers on eliminating waste. Programs in public education instructed consumers on how to conserve natural gas. And city governments were encouraged to reduce the use of street lights.

Despite the various conservation measures, domestic consumption increased and the Allies demanded more supplies. Rather than establish a rationing system, Requa and the OD appealed to patriotism and requested that motorists and pleasure-craft operators reduce their use of gasoline and oil. Over the objections of the National Automobile Dealers Association, "gasless Sundays" were instituted for almost two months, beginning in September, until stocks increased.

The Oil Depletion Allowance

A significant aspect of the production and conservation programs, and the policy with important implications for the future, was the oil depletion allowance. In 1913, oil producers induced Congress to provide tax relief. The Revenue Act of 1913 allowed producers to deduct 5 percent of the gross value of their annual oil and gas production. An act in 1916 replaced the percentage deduction with a "reasonable" allowance that could not exceed the annual cost of discovery of oil. The war allowed producers to exert additional pressure on Congress for an even more generous allowance. Moreover, Requa viewed tax reductions as a way to increase supplies. After Senate Finance Committee hearings in April 1918, a new bill was passed, liberalizing the allowance based on producers' "reasonable" deduction of either the cost of discovery or the fair market value of their properties. Since the market value of mineral properties greatly exceeded direct discovery costs, the oil industry acquired a major tax advantage that accrued benefits to the industry for years to come. However, the first depletion allowances were not political issues; they were simply meant to increase production.

Oil and Reconversion

The cooperative efforts of the oil industry and the Oil Division kept supplies flowing during the war. Unlike coal, the production of adequate supplies was never a truly critical issue. It was estimated that direct shipments of petroleum to the Allies reached 133 million barrels, of which 63 million were shipped between June 30, 1914, and December 31, 1916, and 70 million during 1917–1918. Such activity harkened a strong export market for the industry after the war.

The reconversion program, however, muddied the waters of government-business cooperation for the future. The role of the federal government in the nation's economic affairs would grow, especially during the 1930s, but efforts at cooperative planning or assessment of energy needs ended for the time being. Wilson's dismantling of the Fuel Administration and other, similar bodies was not looked upon with unbridled enthusiasm by the oil industry—for good reason. The end of the USFA meant the end of the NPWSC's influence over oil policy.

The NPWSC was not abandoned, however. In 1919, it was transformed into the American Petroleum Institute (API), the most important trade association and lobbying body in the industry. (Mark Requa and NPWSC members became key members of the API.). With the background and experience of the NPWSC, the API also became the leading source of petroleum statistics, and API continued its efforts of conservation and efficiency as a way to control supply and increase profits.

The almost immediate dismantling of the government's wartime bureaucracy resulted in much confusion. The lack of direction for the reconversion, coupled with dire predictions of exhaustion of American oil reserves, contributed to a postwar oil shortage. The secretary of the navy and others in the military establishment viewed the shortage as a threat to American security. The immediate reaction to these postwar stresses was general support for overseas exploitation of petroleum supplies. In the years after 1920, overseas operations became a central activity of the major oil companies, and it also pitted small domestic producers and refiners against the importers.

From the vantage point of 1919, few contemporaries grasped the impact of World War I on the enhancement of federal power in the American economy. After the war, Woodrow Wilson turned a deaf ear to Harry Garfield's vision of a major governmental reorganization. For the President and many of his top officials, governmental actions in World War I were simply emergency measures to meet the crisis. They did not recognize that important precedents had been established through such agencies as the War Industries Board and the Fuel Administration. During the New Deal and World

War II, the growth of the federal buraucracy would come to depend heavily on the models of governmental organization established during 1916–1919.

World War I also changed the relationship between energy industries and the government. There was no turning back to a laissez-faire economy— if it ever existed. Theodore Roosevelt's New Nationalism provided the blueprint for sustained governmental involvement in the American economy. While continuing to promote general economic growth and to monitor business practices, the federal government had begun to play a role in the production and price mechanisms of the energy economy.

The era of oil power began with World War I. Oil not only mobilized the war, but it would also mobilize the peace. The rise of the automobile, the expansion of cities, the powering of all manner of machines, and even the development of an array of synthetic products came to depend on petroleum. The second American energy transition had been achieved.

FURTHER READING

John G. Clark. "The Energy Crises of 1919–1924 and 1973–1975," *Energy Systems and Policy*, vol. 4 (1980), pp. 239–271.

Robert D. Cuff. "Harry Garfield, the Fuel Administration, and the Search for a Cooperative Order during World War I," *American Quarterly*, vol. 30 (Spring 1978), pp. 39–53.

————. *The War Industries Board*. Baltimore, 1973.

David Davis. *Energy Politics*. 3rd ed. New York, 1982.

William Graebner. "Great Expectations: The Search for Order in Bituminous Coal, 1890–1917," *Business History Review*, vol. 48 (Spring 1974), pp. 49–72.

Ellis W. Hawley. *The Great War and the Search for a Modern Order*. New York, 1979.

James P. Johnson. "The Wilsonians as War Managers: Coal and the 1917–1918 Winter Crisis," *Prologue*, vol. 9 (Winter 1977), pp. 193–208.

Richard L. Watson, Jr. *The Development of National Power.* Boston, 1976.

Harold F. Williamson, *et al*. *The American Petroleum Industry: The Age of Energy 1899–1959*. Evanston, Ill., 1963.

CHAPTER 6

Energy and Consumerism

If energy production was the by-word of the war, energy consumerism was at the heart of the 1920s. The role of energy was crucial to this change, especially in the form of myriad new end-uses. Oil and electricity not only powered American factories, heated and lighted American homes, but they also spawned a cornucopia of appliances, revolutionary communications, individualized transportation, and a vibrant mass culture. Monickers such as the "Jazz Age," the "Roaring Twenties," and the "Era of Excess" tend to oversimplify the complex society of the postwar years. However, these descriptions capture the spirit of an age of prosperity and acquisitiveness.

PROSPERITY DECADE

Productivity and Prosperity

The ill-conceived demobilization and the rapid return to a peacetime economy gave the impression that America was plunging headlong into a depression that matched the one in war-torn Europe. But by 1922, the economy began to surge. The "boom" mentality of the era, to be sure, ran ahead of economic growth, but the 1920s experienced unmatched prosperity.

World War I was the underpinning of what was to become the modern American service economy. Built on war-generated investment capital, industrial planning, technical innovation, and rising demand, the 1920s saw the development of several consumer-oriented industries, dramatic metropolitan growth, and the expansion of the middle class and the white-collar work force.

The application of Frederick W. Taylor's theory of scientific management, as well as technical research, cost evaluation, production planning, and market surveys led to a rise in efficiency in industry. Technical innovations such as interchangeable parts, machines to make glass tubing, and techniques to produce continuous strip-sheets of steel and tin also contributed to the impressive record of production in the postwar years. In fact, productivity in the 1920s rose twice as fast as did population.

Productivity is but one measure of the economic activity of the decade. The Gross National Product (GNP) leaped from about $73 billion in 1920 to about $104 billion in 1929 (in 1929 dollars). The per capita GNP increased from $719 during the 1917–1921 period to $875 in 1929. There was also growth in real wages. Poverty was not eliminated, and the few still controlled much of the nation's wealth, but the middle class was indeed expanding. Workers in many industries were being paid the highest wages in American history. National income rose from $480 per capita in 1900 to $681 in 1929. Real wages rose by 11 to 13 percent for industrial workers, and some fringe benefits were added. These were modest increases, however, when compared with corporate profits which grew by 62 percent. Few workers were likely to earn more than $600 a year.

The trend toward bigness and business consolidation continued during the 1920s. In the automobile industry, Ford, General Motors, and Chrysler sold 83 percent of all cars in 1930. Of the nation's 25,000 banks, 1 percent possessed 46 percent of the assets. In broadcasting, CBS and NBC dominated the airways. By 1929, the 200 largest corporations controlled about 20 percent of the nation's wealth and about 40 percent of business wealth.

An Era of Consumerism

Businesses that catered to the consumer market became the most successful of the era. Industrial uses of mass production techniques, an emphasis on high-pressure advertising, and easy consumer credit tended to produce "democratized materialism."

Middle-class Americans—if not the working class as a whole—were in a good position to purchase the wide range of consumer items made available after the war. Not only had real wages increased in the 1920s, but a larger portion of the work force gained more leisure time. In 1923, U.S. Steel abandoned the twelve-hour day, with the Gary plant going on eight-hour shifts. In 1926, Ford Motor Company instituted a five-day work week. Companies such as International Harvester began increasing fringe benefits by adding a two-week vacation. Between 1920 and 1930, the hours for manufacturing workers decreased from 47.4 to 42.1 per week.

The attractiveness of American consumer goods in the 1920s derived from variety and price. The chemical industry produced an array of new fabrics, kitchen utensils, floor coverings, and cosmetics. DuPont, which had grown dramatically as a result of wartime production, moved quickly into the consumer market. With access to confiscated German dye patents and expertise from a team of innovative chemists, it introduced rayon and cellophane. Other synthetics—plastics, Bakelite, Celanese—were produced; items as wide-ranging as Pyrex cooking utensils, linoleum, lacquers, and antifreeze captured the attention and the dollars of the American public. The maturation of the electrical power industry brought wider uses for electrical power in the home and a whole range of new appliances. The granddaddy of all consumer goods, the automobile, made private transportation widespread. By 1930, nine of the twenty leading corporations in the United States specialized in consumer goods, as compared with one of twenty in 1919.

Traditional enterprises, however, suffered in the wake of the consumer revolution. Agriculture failed to respond to the postwar recovery because of overproduction on world markets and falling demand at home. Bituminous coal lost its preeminence as a result of effective competitors, such as petroleum, and chronic instability. Textiles had a difficult time competing with the new synthetic fabrics.

While the demand for consumer goods was in some ways a response to wartime austerity, it was shaped by new methods of advertising and salesmanship. Advertising made the ranks of big business in the 1920s, with major campaigns directed at the larger, more concentrated urban markets. Even religion was merchandised. Madison Avenue ad-man Bruce Barton wrote *The Man Nobody Knows*, a best-seller that depicted Jesus Christ as the greatest salesman of all time. Barton's "Americanization" of Christ as a supersalesman epitomized the consumer orientation of the age.

Easy financing made the purchase of consumer goods even more attractive. Financial institutions offered consumers the opportunity for "a little bit down" and "small monthly payments" throughout the decade. Between 1919 and 1929, the amount of nonfarm consumer credit rose from $32 billion to $60 billion. During this period, about 15 percent of all goods were sold on installment plans.

THE AUTOMOBILE

As historian Roderick Nash observed: "Much of the roar of the twenties came from the internal combustion engine."[1] The automobile became an essential part of the American way of life, achieving the status of a social, if not an economic, necessity.

The Internal Combustion Engine

The first gasoline-fueled, four-stroke cycle engine was built in Germany in 1876. By the 1890s, motor cars reached their modern stage of development. In fact, the models of that decade were so successful that there has been no fundamental change in the basic principles of the ordinary automobile engine since that time.

It took several more years for the internal combustion engine to sweep the American market. General conditions—the expansiveness of the nation, the lack of decent roads, and the relatively well-developed urban transit systems—worked against adoption of the motor car. Furthermore, gasoline-fueled vehicles had stiff competition from steam-driven and electric cars. In

[1]Roderick Nash, *The Nervous Generation* (Chicago, 1970), p. 153.

fact, of the 4,200 cars built in the United States in 1900, only one-fourth employed internal combustion engines.

With the increased availability of gasoline and oil lubricants after the Spindletop strike and favorable publicity from automobile race results, the gasoline-powered car claimed performance superiority over its competitors. In 1900, Ransom E. Olds switched from producing steam-driven cars to producing gasoline-fueled vehicles, and, in 1903, Henry Ford founded a motor-car company specializing in automobiles with internal combustion engines.

The Model T and Mass Production

When Henry Ford put his mass-produced Model T on the market in 1908, the car ceased to be a toy for the rich. Ford did not originate the idea of the assembly line nor was he the first automobile producer to employ it. In 1901, Ransom Olds attempted volume production of a curved-dash Oldsmobile which sold for $650. But Ford, adapting Olds' idea and combining it with Henry Leland's utilization of interchangeable parts, perfected the assembly line for automobile production and made it a vast financial success. His Model N, produced in 1906, was well-designed, well-built, and competitively priced at $600. Its success led to the development of the prototype for all low-priced cars of the day, the Model T (the Flivver). The four-cylinder, twenty-horsepower vehicle was available in a runabout model ($825) and a touring car ($850). As his advertising claimed: "No car under $2,000 offers more, and no car over $2,000 offers more except the trimmings."[2] By 1925, the price of the Model T had dropped to $290.

Ford's moving assembly line accomplished its goal of increasing production dramatically; on the other hand, it sacrificed individual craftsmanship and converted workers into little more than robots. The technique reduced the time to make a car from twelve hours to two hours. By 1925, Ford was turning out a Model T every ten seconds. The production of Model Ts increased from about 32,000 in 1910 to almost 735,000 in 1916, which represented about half of the output of new cars in the United States at the time. The total for 1921 reached the 1 million mark, and by 1924, Ford Motor Company had produced more than 13 million cars. The admiring Germans coined the revolutionary mass production techniques "Fordismus."[3]

Henry Ford as "Symbol for an Age"

No one epitomized the contradictions of the automobile age better than Henry Ford. In a poll of college students conducted during the period, Ford

[2]Cited in James J. Flink, "Henry Ford and the Triumph of the Automobile," in Carroll W. Pursell, Jr. (ed.), *Technology in America* (Cambridge, Mass., 1981), p. 169.

[3]The development of transmissions, rubber tires, and suspension systems complemented the assembly-line technique in the production of a mass-market automobile.

rated behind Jesus Christ and Napoleon as the greatest figure in history. Born in Michigan in 1863, he was a farmboy who would rather fool with machinery than break his back in the fields. Ford built his first automobile in 1896 in order to gain a reputation as a racecar designer and driver. He founded Ford Motor Company at age forty and soon came to dominate the competitive industry.

Ford was a folk hero with a genius for machinery, a sense of order, a faith in technology, and an unswerving adherence to national advancement. Sometimes these traits were inverted, however, and the unattractive side of the "Flivver King" prevailed. A man of simple tastes, his habits of denial and his sense of morality made him an opponent of personal indulgences and a critic of urban life. In business, he was antiunion and paternalistic. Petty and often obtuse, he was intolerant of those who failed to share his vision of the future or his interpretation of the past. Notoriously anti-Semitic, Ford blamed the "International Jewish Conspiracy" for many of the world's ills.

What appear as paradoxes in Henry Ford's character may be no more than characteristics of the self-made man who achieved wealth and power before wisdom and education. What made Ford a symbol of his age—if he was one—was not only his exceptional deeds but his commonality. Ford promoted the American faith in progress, while revelling in the past accomplishments of his countrymen—despite the often misquoted comment that "History is bunk." America's history was rich in the frontier traditions of individualism and self-reliance that he so admired. Little wonder that many rural people identified with Ford, his values, and his vision.

Much of what made Ford a central figure of the age was embodied in the Model T: its simplicity, plainness, and dependability. There was also its resistance to changing styles, its unimaginative sameness over the years, its mechanical and performance limitations. Whatever the Model T's shortcomings, however, America would never be the same after Henry Ford. As Sinclair Lewis stated in *Babbitt*, the motor car was "poetry and tragedy, love and heroism." After the 1920s, one could no longer think of America and not think of the automobile.

The Auto Industry

Henry Ford irrevocably changed the American automobile industry, not to mention the very lifestyle of the nation. By the 1920s, only those companies that could afford the cost of mass production could expect to continue in the automobile industry. Of the more than 180 companies in the business between 1903 and 1926, only a handful survived the decade. By 1925, Ford, General Motors, and Chrysler dominated the industry.

Even Ford discovered that the techniques he pioneered could not assure his company's dominance for long. Where production methods and substantial financing had been critical to Ford's success, by the mid-1920s, management expertise and marketing skills became preeminent. By that point a saturated market meant increased competition among auto makers—a competition designed to woo consumers seeking to buy newer or more prestigious vehicles. Price was not so much the competitive weapon as product differentiation, easy financing, and mass advertising. The automobile that offered sleeker styling, more comfort, ease of performance was winning over the consumers.

General Motors surpassed Ford Motor Company as the premier American auto maker by the end of the 1920s, largely because GM's new president, Alfred P. Sloan, Jr., realized the changing nature of competition in the industry before the stubborn Ford did. In 1921, Ford made three-fifths of all U.S. vehicles, but these Tin Lizzies were essentially the 1908 model unchanged. The methodical Sloan did not share Ford's view of a "homogenous America" and designed a range of cars for different strata of society.[4] By the late 1920s, Chevrolet took first place among American cars, and remained largely unchallenged for many years. By the time Ford abandoned the Model T (1927) and produced the Model A (1928), the industry had changed too drastically for it to recapture control of the market.

The automobile industry was the leading manufacturing enterprise in the nation in the 1920s, and certainly the leading consumer-oriented industry. Automobile sales represented one-eighth of the total value of all manufactured goods. Production soared from merely 4,200 cars in 1900 to 5.6 million cars and trucks by 1929. This represented nearly five-sixths of the world's production. There was 1 car for every 5 people in the United States, compared with 1 out of 43 in Great Britain, 1 out of 325 in Italy, and 1 out of 7,000 in Russia.

To produce this many vehicles meant a large work force. Employment in automobile factories rose to a staggering 400,000 by 1929. In fact, 7 percent of all wage earners in manufacturing—one-tenth of all nonagricultural labor—worked in the auto industry.

Industrial output of automobiles in the 1920s was matched by impressive sales for most of the decade. Between 1919 and 1929, automobile sales increased from 1.6 million to 4.5 million, and for trucks and buses, from 225,000 to 882,000. In 1925, 68 percent of automobile purchases were on installment plans. The effect of high production and high demand meant an amazing increase in the automobile-owning population of the United States. In 1915, only 2.5 million cars were registered in the country; by 1930, that figure increased more than ten times to 26.5 million.

The economic impact of the automobile was not limited to sales. As a major consumer itself, the industry sustained and stimulated other economic development. It purchased 20 percent of American steel, 80 percent of the rubber, 75 percent of plate glass, 25 percent of the machine tools, and many other items. It also stimulated the growth of numerous roadside businesses, from "motels" to fruit stands, from trailer courts to curio shops.

[4]Robert Sobel, *The Age of Giant Corporations* (Westport, Conn., 1972), pp. 33–35.

Roads and Highways

The growth of automobile travel was particularly beneficial to highway and road construction companies. In fact, during the 1920s the construction industry (including highway and building construction) employed more workers and spent more money than did any single private industry. The construction of streets and highways alone was the second largest governmental expenditure during the 1920s.

Early demand for better roads had come from bicyclists, from city authorities wanting to remove their wastes efficiently from inner cities, and from the early purchasers of automobiles. Agitation over Rural Free Delivery of the mails in the 1890s was also crucial.

The Federal Aid Road Act of 1916 established the concept of a national highway system. It authorized expenditure of $75 million for road construction by 1921, under the proviso that states that organized highway departments and matched federal grants would receive aid. However, the funds could only be spent on rural toll free roads, not interurban systems. It was hoped that federal impetus to road construction would produce a better farm-to-market road system and a system of connecting trunk highways. At the time, only 11.5 percent of the nation's 2.45 million miles of rural roads were paved.

While World War I temporarily stalled the road projects, it made clear the need for a better highway system. With heavier vehicles, more volume of traffic, and higher speeds, postwar planners faced additional problems. The Federal Aid Act of 1921 created the Federal Aid Highway System, which was meant to establish a coherent highway network of interstates and intercounty roads. A minimum of 60 percent of the aid was to be spent on primary roads.

Not surprisingly, the 1920s became boom years for construction. Annual expenditures for roads increased from $1.4 billion in 1921 to $2.85 billion in 1930. The number of miles of surfaced highways reached 407,000. By 1928, a motorist could travel on paved roads from New York City to St. Mary's, Kansas. Federal aid to road construction spurred states to participate more fully than in the past. Legislatures passed gasoline taxes to finance road construction. Oregon was the first in 1919; but by 1929, every state had a similar law. Federal aid also helped to standardize the sign system of highway numbering and markings.

In cities, however, financial aid came exclusively from within, because federal law and state action did not provide for local development of roads. Out of necessity, many cities poured substantial funds into street construction, demonstrating the increased importance of the automobile and the diminishing influence of public transit. The fact that cities were essential to the nation's economy eventually gave local business leaders more clout in influencing federal highway policy. The automobile industry also may have played a key role in promoting interstate highways that ran through cities, as a way of increasing urban demand for automobiles. But it was not until the 1930s, that federal funds were designated for road construction within cities.

In any event, the rise in automobile purchasing and the construction boom led to the decline of streetcars, trains, and other forms of mass transit. Railroads initially solicited business from the auto industry in the form of hauling vehicles and parts. Ultimately, they faced head-on competition from trucks, which could carry light loads and make local hauls. Since the railroad industry was much more highly regulated than was the automobile industry, it never had a chance to recoup its losses. The United States was moving in the direction of a one-dimensional transportation system, which came to full blossom after World War II.

The Auto and the Petroleum Industry

Demand for gasoline was the major impetus to the petroleum industry in the twentieth century. Gasoline consumption soared from less than three billion gallons in 1919 to more than fifteen billion in 1929. Refineries shifted their production to meet the new demand. In 1900, a forty-two-gallon barrel of crude yielded only five gallons (or 13 percent) of gasoline. With rising demand and the introduction of new refining techniques (especially thermal pressure cracking), gasoline represented 42 percent of a refined barrel of crude in 1930.

Quality of gasoline—not simply quantity—was crucial to automobile performance. The discovery and commercialization of tetraethyl lead as an antiknock agent was a major breakthrough. Before Charles F. Kettering and Thomas H. Midgley perfected the additive in 1922, they were criticized for blaming poor performance on the fuel rather than on engine design. Their achievement was soon praised throughout the automobile industry. In 1926, an octane scale for gasoline was introduced. The Ethyl Corporation which devised the octane scale was a joint venture between Jersey Standard and General Motors. This indicated how the auto and petroleum industries operated a mutually beneficial system of increasing gasoline sales and selling more cars. With higher octane antiknock fuels, higher compression engines could be produced. The economic benefit of such a venture overshadowed questions of safety in the production of tetraethyl lead and questions of health through the use of leaded gasoline.

Autos and the City

As anyone living today will attest, the impact of the automobile has not just been economic. The rise of new communities and the physical transformation of others have been strongly influenced by the automobile. By the 1920s, the car was ending rural isolation: the general store and mail-order houses were fading into the past. Rural education was revolutionized—consolidated, graded schools serviced by school buses were replacing the one-room schoolhouse. Further mechanization of agriculture even contributed to the decline of the family farm.

The automobile was also central to the growth of suburbs, recreational areas, and vacation retreats. California and Florida, especially, were in the throes of a real-estate boom, previewing the explosion of the Sunbelt that took place after World War II. Miami, a typical beneficiary (or casualty) of the automobile boom, grew from 30,000 in 1920 to 75,000 by 1925.

The automobile's most dramatic impact was transforming industrial cities into modern metropolises. By 1930, 8 million more people lived in places with 250,000 than in 1920. Cities continued to grow upward as well as outward, but clearly defined central business districts and uniform residential patterns were challenged by the ubiquity of the automobile. In determining where they wished to live and shop, urbanites were no longer limited by streetcar lines. Roads and highways extended into the suburbs and linked cities together rather than merely servicing the downtown areas.

While the impact of the automobile on cities took years to develop, certain patterns appeared immediately. Home builders began construction into areas between streetcar routes, and land speculators promoted suburban expansion in previously neglected tracts. By the mid-1920s, 800,000 houses were built annually, mostly along the urban fringe. The automobile united the city and the countryside—or obliterated the countryside altogether—by engulfing the hinterland through annexations or by invading it with fun-seeking tourists.

Even city design was influenced by the automobile. The new suburbs were scaled to the car, not the pedestrian. Shops and other services catered to automobile drivers and passengers. Roadside advertising was car level, not human level. And gasoline stations were everywhere. Los Angeles, Houston, Atlanta, Phoenix, and Miami became the clearest expressions of the automobile age. Their downtown areas were small or inconsequential; they were dominated by suburban sprawl; and their miles of highways interconnected random residential and commercial enclaves.

The Automobile Environment

The reliance on the automobile did not evolve without costs. Intricately woven into the economy of the nation, the fate of the automobile industry affected the pocketbook of all Americans. In the late 1920s, for instance, the saturation of the automobile market contributed in a direct way to the depression. In part at least, urban growth and rural penetration stimulated by the automobile brought the "machine into the garden," reduced places of natural beauty, and broke rural seclusion. Auto emissions, such as hydrocarbons and waste heat, were just beginning to be perceived as a source of pollution. The car contributed to congestion in major cities, especially where streets were not designed for motorized traffic. While cities passed speed limits and tried to prevent illegal parking and standing along major thoroughfares, the accident rate mounted. In 1924 alone, there were 23,600 auto deaths, 700,000 injuries, and more than $1 billion in property damage.

The most important impact of the automobile may have been on American values. Many people viewed the automobile as a great boon to the freedom and liberty that is the nation's tradition. A car within the financial means of many Americans provided the opportunity to come and go as one pleased. But some people feared that the car—as a stimulus to individual action— would weaken family bonds, undermine church attendance, inspire crime, and lead to moral laxity. The approbation and the fear were at once overly simplistic and not sufficiently profound. The automobile was not totally responsible for the social achievements nor malaise of the nation, but its long-term influence on the American lifestyle and economy was nothing short of revolutionary.

ELECTRICITY AND CONSUMERISM

Electrical Appliances

In the 1920s, electrical power and electrical appliances became as essential to middle-class life as did the automobile. Few industries grew as rapidly as the electric light and power industry. Between 1902 and 1929, output of electrical power increased more than nineteen times (from 6 billion kilowatt hours to 117 billion kilowatt hours). Vast regional, electrical networks (grids) grew out of hundreds and thousands of smaller facilities. Most of the power was generated by steam (two-thirds by steam, one-third by waterpower), which suggests the lingering value of coal. The primary reason for the phenomenal growth was increased industrial use. In 1914, only one-third of all industrial plants were electrified; by 1929, three-fourths were electrified. Technical advances and lower prices were essential to this expansion. While rates to retail customers did not fall rapidly, access to electrical power made home hookups more convenient and more desirable. In 1912, only one-sixth of all American families had electricity in their homes, but by 1927 about two-thirds had electrical power.

The increased electrical consumption was concentrated in the cities. Consequently, the growth of the electrical appliance industry was dependent on urban markets. With vastly wider access to electrical power, homes were invaded by all manner of gadgets. By 1925, 80 percent of the homes with electricity had electric irons, 37 percent had vacuum cleaners, and 25 percent had washing machines. However, throughout the 1920s and 1930s, most homes continued to depend on ice for food storage. Sales of home appliances amounted to $178 million in 1922; five years later sales soared to $361 million.

Purchase of electric appliances was made more convenient by the spate of chain stores and the advent of easy credit. In 1929, 90 percent of all sewing machines and washing machines, and more than 80 percent of all vacuum cleaners, radios, and refrigerators were purchased on installment plans. A vacuum cleaner costing $28.95 could be purchased for $2 down and $4 a month; a $97.50 washing machine, $5 down and $8 a month. Credit buying increased in good years, but decreased sharply in poor ones. Instead of cutting back production in slack years, many appliance manufacturers worked to maximize sales in order to create a steady demand. This meant heavy investment in advertising.

As one historian noted, most appliances were "sold" rather than "bought," as advertisers turned with a vengeance to the new consumer market.[5] In 1927 alone, $1.5 billion was spent on advertising. An ad for GE refrigerators showed couples in evening wear standing around the new appliance. Inscribed below the picture was the following testimonial: ". . . the thing that appeals to me most is the way it has cut my housekeeping job." The "Premier Duplex" vacuum cleaner brought "a light touch to heavy work." Toastmaster claimed that its electric toaster was "the world's ONLY completely automatic toaster!"

Utility companies themselves had a direct hand in peddling all kinds of electrical appliances to consumers. Some utilities initiated electric appliance campaigns or established "home economy bureaus" to demonstrate appliances and even assist in social events. Others conducted home inspections to make repairs or to explain the use of various electrical devices. Several companies funded their own laboratories to test and advertise new appliances. "Load building," or the use of sales promotions and rapid extension of service, was a common way to attract customers and create demand for electricity. Since many houses used gas for heating and cooking in the 1920s, electric utilities often became distributors—and even producers—of natural gas. (Electric ranges did not have the technical capability to compete effectively with gas until the 1920s.)

While it is customary to think of the new electrical appliances as labor-saving devices, their impact on the life of the American middle-class housewife was not so obvious. Certainly, several products reduced the drudgery of housework. The electric iron was inexpensive and quickly replaced the old flatiron. It not only eased the physical labor required to maneuver the heavy flatiron but significantly reduced kitchen heat, since the stove did not have to remain on to reheat the new electric iron. Electric washing machines, while not yet equipped with automatic cycles, still made the chore less back-breaking. But these changes for the better did not mean that housewives necessarily had more leisure time. Childcare, cooking, and shopping, sewing, and hauling children from home to school fell more heavily on women than ever before. Some experts claimed that the standards of household care became more stringent with better appliances, and the greater consumption of goods required the acquisition of new skills by housewives. Somewhat surprisingly, as a historian of technology noted, housewives with conveniences were spending just as much time on household duties as housewives without

[5]Sobel, *The Age of Giant Corporations*, p. 56.

those conveniences. The housewife of the 1920s had become "a veritable jane-of-all-trades."[6]

In his role as observer of American life and social critic, dramatist Eugene O'Neill wrote *Dynamo* (1929), one of his lesser plays but no less strong in its indictment of the American compulsion for material well-being. Reuben—the protagonist—felt betrayed by the women in his life, and he leaves home. When he returns he has abandoned Christianity and has taken up a new god, "electricity." Devoted to the dynamo, he rejects the love of human women, commits murder, and electrocutes himself in the coils of his new mistress. Dehumanized by his infatuation or compulsion, Reuben is uncontrollably drawn to this power: "It's so mysterious . . . and grand . . . it makes you feel things . . . you don't need to think . . . you almost get the secret . . . what electricity is . . . what life is . . . what God is . . . it's all the same thing. . . ." Electricity is for Reuben "a great dark idol . . . a great dark mother!"

Mass Communications: Radio and the Movies

If O'Neill bemoaned that humanity was being lost in the technical age, many Americans marveled at the spectacle of change. The revolution in electric communications was a powerful nationalizing force, largely responsible for a new mass culture and dependent on the electrification of homes, business establishments, and theaters.

Radio was a very personal form of communications, but one that linked the nation in a new and far-reaching way. Transmitting tubes of increased power and better receivers made way for the commercial development of radio broadcasting in the 1910s. Westinghouse Electric Company constructed the first commercial radio station, KDKA, in East Pittsburgh in 1920. Interestingly, the station was established in order to sell receiving equipment. Westinghouse faced strong competition from the Radio Corporation of America (RCA), formed by General Electric, and decided to promote its receivers through regularly scheduled evening programs. By the end of the decade, there were more than 600 radio stations in the United States.

With the expansion of broadcasting, there came a dramatic rise in the purchase of receivers. As early as 1922, three million homes had radios; by 1929, one-third to two-fifths of all American families owned radio sets. Radio quickly became big business, as an extensive industry grew up around the new toy. Soon radio stations were consolidated into radio "networks." David Sarnoff of RCA led his company's "Radio Group" to create a subsidiary, the National Broadcasting Company, which established a network of twenty-five stations by the end of 1926. The following year, cigar magnate William Paley established the Columbia Broadcasting System.

[6]See Ruth Schwartz Cowan, "The 'Industrial Revolution' in the Home: Household Technology and Social Change in the Twentieth Century," *Technology and Culture,"* vol. 17 (January 1976), pp. 1–23.

Radio as a private enterprise hardly grew as a form of "public service" entertainment. Whether the fathers of the medium liked it or not, radio became a major commercial venture. Dr. Lee DeForest, who invented the three-element vacuum tube, bemoaned:

> What have you done with my child? You have sent him out on the street in rags of ragtime to collect money from all and sundry. You have made of him a laughing stock of intelligence, surely a stench in the nostrils of the gods of the ionosphere.

Sarnoff and others fought the trend, fearing that the commercialization of radio would trivialize the art of the medium. However, the potential for acquiring revenue and covering costs was too great an enticement for even the Sarnoffs of the industry to resist. Soon advertisers were paying $10,000 an hour for a national hookup. In 1929, NBC's gross income reached $150 million, most of it from advertising revenue.

The federal government had legitimate interests in radio, not simply with respect to defense, but because the industry was inherently national. The Radio Act of 1912 made the secretary of commerce responsible for monitoring the activities of broadcasting, but little more. The Radio Act of 1927 authorized the establishment of the Federal Radio Commission (FRC; later the Federal Communications Commission), which was charged with controlling the use of the airwaves. This authority did not imply abridging the right to free speech; rather, the FRC's primary functions were to issue licenses and enforce laws concerning fair use of the air waves. Although clashes arose over governmental regulations, the FRC set a precedent for relatively sound protection of the rights of the public and the legitimate uses of radio.

"In a sense, radio told the masses what to do, and movies showed them how to do it. . . ."[7] Motion pictures as a mass medium began in the late 1890s; they were an attraction on vaudeville programs and at nickelodeons and storefront theaters. But the cinema came of age in the 1920s. The movies not only became a popular art form but also one of the nation's ten largest industries. In 1929, revenues from motion pictures topped $720 million—three times the amount spent on books and ten times the amount spent on spectator sports. Like so many other industries, motion pictures quickly became concentrated in a few leading studios (Universal, Twentieth-Century Fox, Paramount, MGM, Warner Bros.), with production companies dominating the field. Businessmen from various other enterprises invested and speculated on the potential goldmine. One very important development—but clearly an exception rather than the rule—was the organization of United Artists, a production and distribution firm organized in 1919 by Charlie Chaplin, Mary Pickford, Douglas Fairbanks, and D. W. Griffith.

---

[7]Donald R. McCoy, *Coming of Age: The United States During the 1920s and 1930s* (Baltimore, 1973), p. 128.

The 1920s was the era of the mature silent film, although the first "talkie," *The Jazz Singer*, was released in 1927. Americans in the 1920s wanted to be entertained, and they voted for the movies with their feet and their pocketbooks. By 1929, the average weekly attendance at movies reached about 90 to 100 million, up from 40 million in 1922. In 1931, there were almost 23,000 theaters in the United States. Movie houses—"the temples of a secular society"—all but replaced political rallies and camp meetings as places for mass entertainment. The "electric age" was changing the face of the country. Movies, radio, and phonographs were making over popular tastes and popular perceptions.

Cheap and abundant energy in the postwar years contributed directly to the era of consumerism. The new and refined technologies in transportation and communication, and the myriad electrical appliances, were made available for mass consumption because of the favorable market in energy. In turn, the petroleum and electrical power industries were transformed by the rising demands for energy. An economy dependent on the production of agricultural goods and primary industrial products was evolving into a sophisticated service, or postindustrial, economy. Mass communications, mass culture, and the automobile transformed American society as well. Without a doubt, energy was an integral part of the process of modernization.

FURTHER READING

Hugh A. J. Aitken. *Syntony and Spark: The Origins of Radio*. New York, 1976.

Daniel J. Boorstin. *The Americans: The Democratic Experience*. New York, 1974.

Alfred D. Chandler, Jr. *Giant Enterprise: Ford, General Motors, and the Automobile Industry*. New York, 1964.

James F. Flink. *The Car Culture*. Cambridge, Mass., 1975.

George N. Gordon. *The Communications Revolution*. New York, 1977.

William E. Leuchtenburg. *The Perils of Prosperity*. Chicago, 1958.

John B. Rae. *The American Automobile*. Chicago, 1965.

Robert Sklar, *Movie-Made America*. New York, 1975.

Reynold M. Wik. *Henry Ford and Grass-Roots America*. Ann Arbor, Mich., 1972.

CHAPTER 7

Private Power versus Public Utility

The bonanza in electrical appliances in the 1920s pointed to the growing presence of electrical power in the lives of Americans. The accompanying rise in consumption and production of electricity seemed to fulfill the nineteenth-century prophecy of abundant "white gold" too cheap to meter and easily accessible to everyone. However, the ubiquity of electrical power in the postwar years obscured the vast changes taking place in the utility industry and government's response to those changes.

Technical achievements, such as high-voltage transmission, and power shortages during the war stimulated the interconnection of electric utilities, which, in turn, encouraged the development of regional electrification systems. State and federal government, along with individual champions of conservation and business reform, responded to the transformation of the industry in several ways. First, regulation of private power underwent deep scrutiny. Second, advocates of public power gained their first national forum. Finally, a clash between advocates of public and private power introduced a whole new set of issues.

GIANT POWER

The scale and nature of growth in the electrical power industry spawned the idea of "giant power" (or "superpower") in the 1920s. Giant power entailed the linking of small, independent electrical systems into regional, integrated networks. Giant power was to be more than the interconnection of technical systems; it was to go beyond efficiency into economic, political, and social planning. Although the idea failed to materialize, it provided the basis for a debate over energy centralization and public power.

Electrical engineers began to discuss the concept of giant power during World War I. The unplanned growth of the industry and the loss of efficiency stimulated an interest in a national power development policy and an interconnected network operated by private enterprise. William Spencer Murray, a consulting engineer from New York, especially gained support from the

American Institute of Electrical Engineers, the Department of the Interior, and the U.S. Geological Survey.

Congress appropriated money for a superpower survey, completed in 1921. Specifically, the survey offered a plan for power supply in the North Atlantic region to serve a market consisting primarily of railroads, manufacturers, and utility companies. More broadly, the report gave wide publicity to blanketing the nation with large interconnected systems, with power generated in central stations—preferably built at mouths of coal mines—and transported along high-voltage lines. Murray believed that the system could efficiently supply all central-station requirements plus nearly three-fourths of the power for electric railways, manufacturing, and mining operations. He also believed the system could guarantee the generating capacity necessary for demand at any time of the day or night, as well as reduce the need for substantial reserve power.

The Impact of World War I

Power shortages during the war were an important stimulus to the idea of giant power. Limited manufacturing of generators, transformers, and other equipment produced serious shortages in industrial regions by 1917. Yet the more effective use of existing equipment led to the interconnection of several utilities. Material shortages also encouraged engineers to take up the idea of superpower, which coincided with their interest in large-scale planning. Among other things, long-distance transmission meant that previously untapped waterpower sites could be connected to urban and industrial centers.

Electric Utilities: A "Go-Ahead" Enterprise

Another factor favoring giant power was the general state of the electric power industry in the 1920s. As historian Thomas Park Hughes stated: "The utility industry was, in the American tradition, a 'go-ahead' enterprise."[1] In other words, it had already demonstrated its potential for large-scale growth. Between 1917 and 1930, the number of residences served from central stations increased from 6 million to 20 million; kilowatt-hours increased from 21 billion to 75 billion. By 1929, the United States was producing more electrical power than the rest of the world combined.

Samuel Insull was a pioneer in the development of electrical networks, and his Chicago system was an important beginning. Insull effectively blended financial management and entrepreneurial skill with technical expertise. His experiment with rural electrification in Lake County, Illinois (1910–1913) was the first attempt at extensive market development outside an urban area. It demonstrated the feasibility of rural electrification through the interconnection of twenty-two towns.

---

[1]Thomas Park Hughes, "Technology and Public Policy: The Failure of Giant Power," *Proceedings of the IEEE,* vol. 64 (September 1976), p. 1361.

In the 1920s, men like S. Z. Mitchell elaborated on the work of Insull by developing regional systems. Mitchell, a product of the Edison Company in New York, had peculiar skills in finance and organization. His Electric Bond and Share Company, and the array of holding companies it controlled, was the center of an expanding utility empire. Established in 1905, E. B. and S. acquired stock from companies held by General Electric (which was its principal owner until the 1920s) and provided the same companies with financing and management and engineering expertise. Acquired companies in the same geographic area were linked into a single system, and frequently were merged into larger operating companies.

The Rise of Utility Holding Companies

The rise of utility holding companies gave an additional boost to giant power by providing an organizational structure conducive to regional development. Increased production and consumption of electricity played a major role in the consolidation of the industry. Between 1919 and 1930, the actual number of central stations decreased from 4,300 to 1,600, but the number of electrical operating systems (4,000 plus) grew. The largest operating systems began to acquire regional dominance.

The utility holding company revolutionized the industry, not by producing or distributing commodities or services, but by acquiring many smaller operating companies through control of their stock. In strict terms, Electric Bond and Share was not a holding company, but it began the trend toward utility holding companies in the 1920s.

The financial and organizational advantages of the holding company were substantial. Those interested in establishing a large network found the holding company an easy way to acquire capital and an efficient means to manage large-scale operations. For smaller local companies, participation in a sound holding company often provided the means to secure capital, to achieve better transmission of power, and to attract effective engineering and technical talent. In 1926 alone, there were more than 1,000 mergers involving utility companies. In many cases, consolidations involved municipally owned plants selling out to private companies, which weakened efforts at public ownership on the local level during the 1920s.

The chance to abuse such an organizational device was great. Holding companies were used for blatant profiteering, through stock manipulation and "pyramiding," that is, building companies on top of companies. This suggests their fragile nature in an era of business speculation and overconfidence in the boom cycle. As a financial tool, the holding company had little regard for the nature of the system it was building. It often controlled properties, not within a clearly defined region, but anywhere opportunity knocked.

In seeking to make profits from financial deals, and buying up properties at excessive prices in an intensely competitive environment, rates could be set very high. In cases where combination was geared toward developing a system, there could still be rate inequity, with the lowest rates to the biggest users—industry—and higher rates to the consuming public. Holding companies also took advantage of their own subsidiaries by performing services at inflated costs.

The major result of holding companies in the electric utility industry was a high degree of financial concentration. Interconnection and the delivery of service was immense. In some ways, these results justified the claim that electric utilities were prone to be natural monopolies, that is, competition is sacrificed for decent service. Profiteering, however, was often more important than was developing efficient systems. During the 1920s, holding companies controlled two-thirds of the privately owned electric utilities. In 1930, ten holding company groups controlled about 72 percent of the industry. The Insull group—the best known but not the largest (11 percent)—consisted of five systems with about 4.5 million customers and extended over 23 states from North Carolina to Maine. Insull himself chaired sixty-five firms and was involved in business operations in every conceivable field.

Power Progressives and Giant Power

Conservationists and business reformers looked upon giant power as a way to circumvent the dangers of the "power trust." As Gifford Pinchot stated: "Either we must control electric power [by means like giant power], or its masters and owners will control us."[2] With the utility industry moving ahead with little direction or planning, with the rise of holding companies, and with the popularization of the superpower idea, reform of the utility industry gained the attention of "power progressives."[3]

The link to the conservation movement and the antimonopoly movement was very strong. Power progressives might be advocates of regulation by commission or agency, proponents of public power, or a combination of both. In general, these reformers sought to weaken the grip of the so-called power trust, reduce the influence of holding companies, and, in some cases, establish public power projects. Among the best known of this loosely organized group were conservationist Gifford Pinchot; Senator George W. Norris (Rep., Neb.); Governor Franklin D. Roosevelt (Dem., New York); and mechanical engineer Morris L. Cooke. This group digressed from the private power approach of Murray and his colleagues.

While many of the power progressives became best known for their role in the New Deal, in the 1920s they operated on the state level. Two general approaches were most typical: an effort to expand the regulatory authority of commissions and agencies, led by Pinchot, Cooke, and Roosevelt; and promotion of public power projects, as exemplified by Norris' battle for Muscle Shoals.

[2]Cited in Hughes, "Technology and Public Policy." p. 1363.

[3]Reformers of New Freedom and New Nationalism background, who were interested in control of energy and the utilization of natural resources. See Jean Christie, "Giant Power," *Pennsylvania Magazine of History and Biography*, vol. 96 (October 1972), pp. 480–507.

The regulatory battles were most dramatic in Pennsylvania and New York. As the governor-elect in Pennsylvania, Pinchot teamed up with Cooke, a renegade engineer and disciple of Frederick Taylor's scientific management. Together they sought to redirect the efforts of private utilities in Pennsylvania. Upon election in 1922, Pinchot sought Cooke's advice on the utility question. Cook proposed, then directed, the Giant Power Survey Board, established in 1923. The board examined water and fuel sources in the state, and in 1925 issued *Giant Power*. The report outlined a plan to reorganize the power industry with emphasis on "mine-mouth" plants—power-generating plants located at the coal mines in western Pennsylvania—that would transmit power to industry and rural communities.

Giant Power hedged on the question of public ownership, and therefore it was not as radical as some feared. The response of the electric power industry was predictable, nonetheless. Other business groups and state legislators also criticized the plan. Even organized farm and rural groups turned away from it when the private companies coopted them through various concessions. Soon Cooke and Pinchot found themselves isolated within the state, and the enthusiasm for the plan ebbed, withered, and then died.

The giant power plan in Pennsylvania was doomed not simply because Pinchot and Cooke were proposing a radical technical system, but because they were challenging the political and economic status quo. As power progressives, they threatened to shift control from utility owners and managers to administrators of the plan, and possibly into the government. Murray's superpower plan also failed. While less threatening to the existing power structure, engineers began to question the technical and economic problems associated with it; later, they feared its effects on the utility industry as a private enterprise. Giant power/superpower nevertheless provided a significant forum for discussing regional and national planning in a major growth industry.

PUBLIC POWER IN THE 1920s

Debate over utility regulation often led to the question of public power. Prior to the 1920s, many cities grappled with the issue of municipal power as part of the general trend toward "home rule." But electrical power as a municipal utility was a far cry from public power projects on the state and national level. The rapid growth of the electrical power industry and the trend toward interconnections of systems brought the issue of public power into the open in the 1920s.

Utility Regulation in New York

Efforts at greater public control of electrical utilities fared better in New York than in Pennsylvania. Hydroelectric power—couched in terms of public versus private power—was an issue in the 1928 gubernatorial election, which

Franklin Roosevelt won. Although Al Smith, Roosevelt's predecessor, had preserved state waterpower sites, dissatisfaction with the state's regulatory commission was strong during the early 1920s. Moreover, an on-going battle persisted over granting upstate utility interests the right to develop power facilities on the St. Lawrence River.

In 1929, a Commission on the Revision of the Public Service Commissions Law investigated the activities of the regulatory body and assessed alternatives. A minority report—supported by Roosevelt—stated that commmission regulation had failed, and in 1931, a substantial revision in the system was made by the creation of the New York State Power Authority. This change included a decision to substitute regulation by contract and government competition for previous regulatory practices. In his message proposing the authority, Roosevelt stated that the alternative policies would provide "the whiphand, the trump cards, with which the state can treat with the power trusts."[4]

Morris Cooke played a role in this reform, touting his convictions that had been thwarted in Pennsylvania. His counsel led to an appointment on the power authority. The program in New York ultimately influenced New Deal power policy, although it did not cause any major shift in regulatory activity on the state level at the time. Nevertheless, the question of public power was gaining attention.

The Muscle Shoals Controversy

The battles over western hydroelectric power development in the early twentieth century touch lightly on the issue of public power. However, federal ownership and operation of hydroelectric facilities in the rural South, especially Muscle Shoals, led to more vigorous interest in public power.

Muscle Shoals is located in an area of rapids and swift currents along the Tennessee River in northern Alabama. The river cuts a valley through six states and drains seven others: Tennessee, Virginia, North Carolina, Alabama, Georgia, Mississippi, and Kentucky. The Tennessee Valley was notorious for recurrent flooding, depleted soil, and serious erosion. In 1920, the primitive rural area was inhabited by two million people, most of whom lived in chronic poverty.

At one time, Muscle Shoals posed a severe navigation problem, but early in the nineteenth century it was regarded as a strategic site along the 650-mile river. From time to time it gained attention as a location crucial to navigation, hydroelectric exploitation, and agricultural development.

World War I was primarily responsible for turning Muscle Shoals into a national controversy over the issue of public power and economic development. With the prospect of American participation in the war, Congress ap-

---

[4]Cited in Richard Hellman, *Government Competition in the Electric Utility Industry* (New York, 1972), p. 23.

propriated $20 million in 1916 for the construction of nitrate plants (nitrate was a necessary ingredient in explosives). President Wilson chose Muscle Shoals as the site because of the area's potential for producing abundant, inexpensive hydroelectric power—an essential factor in extracting nitrogen from the atmosphere. In 1918, two nitrate plants were built and work began on what later was named Wilson Dam (completed in 1925). The total government investment for the project was approximately $145 million.

The development of Muscle Shoals raised many questions about the government's role in such varied projects as navigation, flood control, economic rehabilitation, conservation of agricultural lands, regional planning, development of natural resources, and the generation of power. The last issue, however, took priority in the postwar years because of the passage of the Federal Water Power Act of 1920 and the agitation of midwestern progressives who sought stricter regulation of waterpower.

Immediately after the war, Secretary of War Newton D. Baker attempted to turn the plants over to private companies for production of fertilizers. Attracting no takers, a bill was introduced in Congress to create a government corporation for that purpose, but it failed. In March 1921, the new Republican Secretary of War John W. Weeks announced that the government would accept bids for the facility which it would be willing to sell for a reasonable price.

A bid from Henry Ford set off a major dispute over Muscle Shoals. In July, Ford offered to buy the nitrate plants and accompanying steam plants for $5 million and to lease the dams for a period of 100 years. Ford also agreed to produce fertilizers on a limited profit basis. The bid attracted wide support from Secretary of Commerce Herbert Hoover, Thomas Edison, the Farm Bureau, several key southern politicos, and local developers in the Tennessee Valley. Power progressives fought the bid vigorously; so did southern power companies who feared the competition, and southern manufacturers who were skeptical of Ford's motives.

Locally, the distaste for land speculators reinforced the notion that the Ford offer was exploitative. Some opponents simply held a grudge against the Flivver King. His anti-Semitism and other crude opinions may have weighed into the equation. As a result of the groundswell of opposition and desertion of support, especially among southern political leaders and manufacturers, Ford withdrew his offer in 1924 saying: "A single affair of business which should have been decided by anyone within a week has become a complicated political affair."[5]

The key figure in the withdrawal of the Ford offer was George Norris, who was emerging as the leading proponent of public power. Born in Ohio in 1861, Norris studied law and served as a prosecuting attorney and a district judge in Nebraska. In 1902, he was elected to the House of Representatives and quickly became the leader of insurgent Republicans. He was elected to

---

[5]Cited in Preston J. Hubbard, *Origins of the TVA* (New York, 1968; orig., 1961), p. 138.

the Senate in 1913 and, for thirty years, championed an array of causes. A maverick in his party, he supported the Progressive ticket in 1912 and 1924 and supported Democrats from 1928 onward.

Norris first developed his interest in public power during the Hetch-Hetchy controversy in California in 1913 (see Chapter IV). Although he was not a preservationist, he supported the concept of "wise use" of resources. In time, Norris came to advocate complete government ownership of the electric utility industry.

When Ford submitted his bid, Norris was serving as chairman of the Senate Agriculture and Forestry Committee and thus was in a central position to influence the outcome. Before the Ford deal fell through, Norris introduced a bill, in 1922, calling for a government corporation to control and operate the Muscle Shoals facilities, although it had little chance of passing while optimism still ran high over the Ford offer.

In the meantime, President Calvin Coolidge appointed a Muscle Shoals Inquiry Commission, which recommended in 1925 that the properties be leased to a private operator for fertilizer production and only incidentally for power production. Lukewarm interest in the recommendation resulted in no lessee being secured. Norris pushed through Congress a bill for public operation of Muscle Shoals, but Coolidge vetoed it in 1928. President Hoover vetoed a similar Norris bill in 1930. The time was not propitious for public power.

The Boulder Canyon Project

Norris failed to get his bill by the Republican presidents, but he kept the public power issue alive through the debate over Muscle Shoals. The Boulder Canyon Project, established in 1928, proved to be "the first halting step" toward the public power movement of the 1920s.[6]

The Boulder Canyon Project Act (1928) allocated lands in California, Arizona, and Nevada for the development of the Colorado River. The first multiple-purpose project undertaken by the Bureau of Reclamation (in the Department of the Interior), it originally consisted of the construction of a dam and a canal to connect the Imperial and Coachella valleys. The production and sale of electrical power was authorized simply as a way of recovering costs from the massive financing ($165 million) of the project—but it was a small step toward public power.

President Hoover fought every attempt to include efforts at government competition with private utilities. In the 1928 presidential election, he defended the principle of federal regulation, but he also supported private development of power sites and state and local regulation of utilities. During the debate over the Boulder project, Hoover's Secretary of the Interior, Ray Lyman Wilbur, declared that power generated at the dam could be sold to private parties. This angered proponents of public power, who believed that

[6]Linda J. Lear, "The Boulder Canyon Project," *Materials and Society*, vol. 7 (1983), pp. 329–337.

electricity generated with public funds should not be returned to the "power trust."

Far from ending the controversy over public power, the Boulder project intensified it. During the New Deal, the project devolved to a strong advocate of public power, Secretary of the Interior Harold L. Ickes. Ickes' strategic position in the Interior Department and his leadership of the Public Works Administration allowed him to elevate power production at the Boulder project to a much higher priority than had existed under Hoover. The Boulder Canyon Project was another prelude to the development of national public power policy in the 1930s.

UTILITY REGULATION IN THE 1920s

The debate over public power did not diminish interest in federal regulation of business practices, rates, and distribution of electricity. On the contrary, the relentless growth of holding companies caused rumblings and tremors within the federal bureaucracy and within the electrical power industry itself. Other than setting the stage for New Deal reforms, the 1920s produced few tangible changes in federal regulatory power. Advocates of antimonopoly and regulation were keenly aware of the limits of state authority and efforts to determine "fair value" or "fair return" to the utility companies. But they were unable to act in the probusiness climate of the day.

Congress initiated the only significant effort to confront the utility holding companies, but this came in the wake of the Great Depression. In 1928, the Senate instructed the Federal Trade Commission (FTC) to conduct a full-scale investigation of holding companies. As the depression unfolded, the House Commerce Committee followed with a second investigation. In 1934–1935, the FTC completed its study, which spanned ninety-six volumes. The findings were dramatic. The FTC reported that state regulation was ineffective in dealing with such abuses as watering of stock, propaganda techniques, control of newspapers, and opposition to municipal ownership. Many abuses flourished "not in spite of law but with the aid of law." Despite the strong language, the report fell short of declaring that a "power trust" existed. The findings, nonetheless, were used by New Dealers to extend the federal regulatory powers in the late 1930s.

The Fall of Insull

Public dissatisfaction with state commissions and renewed support for regulatory reform came only after the onset of the Great Depression and the stock market crash in autumn 1929. As the dramatic bank failures and the plummeting stock market demonstrated the structural weakness of American financial institutions, the fall of the house of Insull confirmed the instability of the holding companies.

The collapse of the Insull empire in 1932 cost investors an estimated $1 billion—the largest corporate failure in American history. Many of Insull's individual companies survived, but the pyramid of holding companies came tumbling down. Lacking the momentum of constant growth in the economy, the whole structure fell into disarray. In an act of supreme irony, Samuel Insull—the archetype for the successful business executive of the 1920s—stood trial for fraud in 1934 and 1935. The trial ended in acquittal, but Insull's reputation as a shrewd and effective business leader crumbled along with the country's faith in the private sector in general (at least temporarily).

At the same time, New Dealers, by rejecting probusiness Republican 1938. His demise is a poignant dividing line between the rising star of the private utility industry in the twenties and the challenge from public power in the thirties. New Dealers pointed to Insull as an object lesson and as a rationale for deeper governmental involvement in the utility industry. In one sense, the collapse of the Insull empire accomplished what power progressives had failed to produce in the 1920s—a *cause célèbre* for governmental action.

FDR'S NATIONAL POWER POLICY

The context for debating private versus public power changed markedly in the 1930s. Franklin Roosevelt's administration could afford to break with the past because the 1932 election, if nothing else, was a mandate to bring the country out of the depression. Much of what was done in changing federal regulatory policy and implementing public power was done in the name of business recovery and economic reform to facilitate that recovery. The advocacy of public power was often rationalized as a way to invigorate the economy by providing more jobs, promoting construction and related economic activity, and producing cheaper energy.

At the same time, New Dealers, by rejecting probusiness Republican leadership and even traditional Democratic leadership, had the opportunity to test alternative responses to the electric power question. Roosevelt himself set the tone for reform, through both his campaign rhetoric and his actions while governor of New York. He publicly supported control of holding companies, regulation of power-company financing, and revision of rate making. In a campaign speech on electric power delivered in Portland, Oregon, he emphasized the notion of governmental competition as an alternative to regulatory commissions. Private ownership of utilities was the normal approach, he argued, but every community should have the right to convert to municipal ownership or at least use that right as a bargaining weapon against the private company.

In addition to this "birchrod in the cupboard" principle, FDR supported the establishment of a "national power policy" based on more effective regulation of private utilities and the adoption of public power projects. For New Dealers, private and public power were not mutually exclusive concepts. The 1930s would not usher in an era of public power, rather, it would be a new era of private *and* public power.

The proposed national power policy was a reflection of the New Deal itself, that is, it emphasized pragmatic solutions to the depression through a wide range of approaches. There was a commitment, in the broadest sense, to preserve the strongest features of the American capitalist system, while reducing its abuses and experimenting with new ideas. There was also a strong commitment to increase the role of government as a force within the economy. World War I provided examples of central planning—production controls, fair business practices, and balances between management and labor. New Dealers also emphasized social welfare and, in some cases, social engineering.

The national power policy was a product of the New Deal spirit; it contained inventiveness as well as inconsistency and even incoherence. It reflected the nation's commitment to private power sprinkled with the reformers' zeal for experiments in public power. The New Deal programs fell into three broad categories: regulatory reform, public power, and rural electrification. As a whole, these constituted the most thorough-going reevaluation of the electrical power industry in American history.

The staff that Roosevelt assembled had broad experience in power questions and strong ideas on what was to be done. For instance, he enlisted Frank Walsh, James C. Bonbright, and Morris Cooke from the NYPA, David Lilienthal from the Wisconsin power commission, and Harold Ickes. Public power advocates, especially George Norris, had the President's ear too. These men agreed little beyond their commitment to some sort of reform. Consequently, the power program produced internal conflicts as well as public controversies.

Regulating the Holding Companies

The fall of Insull and the disarray among holding companies gave momentum to stronger regulation of the electric utilities industry. The question was: How far should regulation go? Few expected FDR to nationalize the industry. He was too much a child of New Nationalism and New Freedom to take such an extreme course. New Dealers, nonetheless, moved on several fronts to revamp utility regulation.

The revision of the Federal Power Act in 1935 gave the FPC partial control over the interstate business of electric utilities. The Roosevelt administration also attempted to modify the "fair value" rule that was instrumental in determining rates and profits in the utilities industry. The FPC and other federal agencies cooperated with state commissions in requesting that the

Supreme Court reconsider its rulings. FDR's court appointments, however, were more effective in changing the approach to the "fair value" doctrine than was any political pressure.

The FPC used its influence by initiating an electric-rate survey and by publishing "typical" bills paid by consumers in various communities. The dramatic impact of the discrepancies was meant to generate local interest in the rate question. This tactic attracted vigorous criticism from the industry and from commissions who regulated the rates. They charged that comparing rates without taking the local variables into account presented an unfair picture of rate-setting.

Of all the New Deal approaches to utility regulation, none was more explosive than the assault on the holding companies, which began in 1934. Critics charged that "pyramiding" enabled holding companies with minimum investment to maintain control over myriad operating facilities, thus encouraging several abuses. For instance, holding companies entered agreements with subsidiaries to record arbitrary profits. Executives manipulated security markets, paid dividends from capital, and drained subsidiaries through excessive service charges and loans.

The FTC and the House Committee on Commerce reports simply reinforced the gut feelings of Roosevelt, antitrusters, and the power progressives who were bent on curbing private concentration of power in the utilities field. The assault on the holding companies was not directed at the generation and distribution of power, per se, but with business organization and the manipulation of profits and rates. The New Deal attack on the holding companies was a final act in the story of private utilities regulation; it was not the initial step in a new direction.

The first stage in regulating holding companies began with FDR's appointment of a National Power Policy Committee (NPPC), chaired by Harold Ickes. The committee was composed of representatives from eight federal agencies. Its major goal was to consider legislation to regulate holding companies, not to develop a plan for a public power alternative. Characteristic of FDR's administrative style, the structure of the committee encouraged infighting among the participating agencies as a means of fleshing out an array of solutions. A major issue was whether holding companies should be more carefully regulated or simply abolished—although members of the committee clearly leaned to the former.

The NPPC produced a bill that, as originally conceived, prohibited several specific abuses and gave the newly formed Securities and Exchange Commission (SEC) extensive power to regulate the financing of holding companies and to force a simplification of their corporate structure.

Representatives from the FTC, ICC, and FPC also presented various schemes for regulating the holding companies. These were referred to Attorney General Homer Cummings, who chaired an interdepartmental committee. A new draft bill was written that incorporated much of the work of the NPPC and—at the insistence of FDR—a mandatory "death sentence" for utility holding companies. Accordingly, utility holding companies would be dissolved within five years unless the FPC certified that they were necessary for the operation of a system in a clearly defined region. The proposal was submitted to Congress, in February 1935, as a bill cosponsored by Senator Burton K. Wheeler (Dem., Mont.) and Representative Sam Rayburn (Dem., Tex.).

The industry did not stand still under such an assault and mounted one of the most intense lobbying efforts Washington had ever seen. Protests came not only from utility officials but from investment bankers and leaders in the American Bar Association. Some lawyers declared that the bill ignored the obvious advantages of the holding companies, especially their ability to diversify risk, to raise capital, and to provide better and cheaper service. Power companies strongly encouraged stockholders to protest the destruction of the holding companies, charging that the Wheeler-Rayburn bill was not regulation in the conventional sense. Operating through the Committee of Public Utility Executives, the American Federation of Utility Investors, and a public relations firm, the power companies collected vast sums of money to lobby against the bill.

In the midst of the protracted battle, Congress launched investigations into lobbying, and it found that the power companies had spent more than $1 million to fight the legislation. The Senate investigation, directed by Hugo Black, claimed that power companies mass-produced protest letters and telegrams. In a few cases, names were forged and a Texas congressman may have been bribed.

The Black committee revelations and the general disillusionment with utilities aided the passage of the bill in 1935. The compromise Wheeler-Rayburn Act—or the Public Utility Holding Company Act—included a modified "death sentence." Systems with more than three tiers of companies (or more than twice removed from operation) were abolished. In other cases, the SEC was to limit the smaller holding companies to a single, integrated utility system of one tier. The act also required utility holding companies to register with the SEC, to furnish detailed financial information, and to secure approval before completing most financial transactions. (As stated earlier, the FPC had the authority to regulate the rates, security issues, and financial transactions of operating companies engaged in interstate transmission of electricity.) Although not as stringent as some reformers hoped, the modified Wheeler-Rayburn Act, according to the *Boston Globe*, substituted "only a chance for life imprisonment in the place of capital punishment."

The major victory for the administration took place in the courts, not in Congress. Among other things, utility executives believed that SEC regulations would interfere with operations, retard the flow of capital, and ultimately stunt the growth of the industry. But in 1938, the Supreme Court upheld the right of the SEC to intervene into the utility business. The SEC, nevertheless, moved slowly, since the regulation of business had gone about as far as the collective interests of the nation would allow in the late 1930s. However, the New Deal had changed the rationale of utility reform to reflect not only a faith in open competition but also the interest of consumers.

TVA: The Victory of the Public Power Concept

On May 18, 1933, President Roosevelt signed into law the Tennessee Valley Authority Act, establishing a major governmental commitment to public power. George Norris had his fondest dream come true—a rare occurrence in the pragmatic world of politics. In the broadest sense, the Tennessee Valley Authority (TVA) was more a triumph for the multiuse concept and the idea of regionalism than it was a turn toward public power. Private power would continue to dominate the industry.

TVA was a multipurpose river project involved in flood control, fertilizer production, soil conservation and reforestation, inland waterway construction, promotion of regional economic growth, *and* the generation of hydroelectric power. As part of the New Deal recovery program, TVA was also meant to serve as a source of unemployment relief. Multipurpose meant multiinterest as well: farmers wanted cheap fertilizers; conservationists envisioned effective resource management; regional planners glowed at the prospect of social experimentation; local businessmen saw an opportunity to tap new markets; public power advocates wanted to test new rate mechanisms and to provide electricity to rural families; and politicians chirped about an era of new prosperity in the valley.

TVA was at once an experiment in federal ownership and decentralized, regional control. Only the private utility companies reeled in horror at the thought of this kind of competition. By serving so many interests, however, the successes and failures of TVA had to be measured in the specific as well as the general, in the present as well as the future. The power question was but one element, albeit an important one.

TVA was meant to fulfill Norris' dream for Muscle Shoals. Believing that FDR would champion his cause, he and other midwestern Republican Progressives campaigned for the Democrats in 1932. Roosevelt lived up to expectations when he formally pledged himself to Norris' plan in January 1933. In fact, before the inauguration, Roosevelt invited Norris to tour the Tennessee Valley with him—an emotional high point in the senator's long political career.

Norris realized that Roosevelt desired to go well beyond his vision of power- and water-resource development. FDR indicated a stronger interest in planning, with Muscle Shoals as a small part of the useful development of the valley. What made the project special—and potentially revolutionary as American governmental activity went—was that the act established a public corporation with the flexibility and initiative of private enterprise.

While the power issue was the major focus during the congressional debate over the bill, after the passage of the act, the scope of TVA as embodied in the appointment of the commissioners took center stage. Arthur E. Morgan, the first chairman of the TVA board, was a renowned hydraulic engineer-turned-college president (Antioch College, Ohio), who was an "impressive man of fifty-five, a Yankee moralist and mystic, honest and righteous, given to ethical meditations of a somewhat jejune but uplifting kind, a social thinker touched with utopianism."[7] The engineer-prophet shared not only FDR's interest in planning but his moderate views, as compared to Norris, on public power. Destroying the "power trust" and committing the nation to a nationalized utility was of less consequence to Morgan than was the larger goal of social reordering.

Morgan was given the opportunity to select his two colleagues on the TVA board, with the stipulation that one be familiar with agriculture and one with electric power. As his agricultural expert he chose Harcourt A. Morgan. The sixty-year-old president of the University of Tennessee was an agricultural scientist with vast experience. He had developed a close relationship with the Tennessee Extension Service, inspired confidence in the farmers of the area, and was endorsed by several land-grant colleges and the Department of Agriculture. His major goal on the board was to educate the people of the valley to the value of TVA. On the power question, his interests predictably lay in the development of rural electrification. Morgan was to be cast time and again as swing man among the directors.

The third director would become Arthur Morgan's antagonist in the battle over the power issue. Thirty-four-year-old David Lilienthal of Wisconsin was a formidable figure. The Harvard Law School graduate was intense and ambitious. He practiced law in Chicago and had been appointed to the Wisconsin Railroad Commission. Lilienthal gave up a lucrative law practice for a chance to battle utility magnates and to protect the public interest, as he saw it. Youthful enthusiasm accounted for a great deal in this stage of his life. Upon FDR's election, Lilienthal looked longingly to Washington for a role in the new administration. After some speculation about other possible assignments, he was snatched up for the TVA board.

The power issue involving TVA was enmeshed in a triangular conflict between Lilienthal and Arthur Morgan, and the TVA board and the private utilities. The major industrial opponent of TVA was the Commonwealth and Southern Corporation (CSC), a holding company with extensive properties in the valley. The major battle focused on power markets. What gave CSC formidable standing was its president, Wendell L. Willkie, who would become the Republican standard-bearer in the 1940 presidential election. Willkie, in his early forties, was the youngest head of a large utility system in the nation. Unlike most executives of the industry, Willkie was a Wilsonian Democrat— in many ways indistinguishable from FDR. He proved to be an articulate spokesman for his company and for private power in general.

Unlike Arthur Morgan, Lilienthal wanted to confront the utilities openly if it became necessary. In 1934, the initial contact between TVA and the CSC resulted in a contract providing for cooperation between the two. TVA hoped to secure a practical "yardstick," that is, a measure that would provide a guideline for setting reasonable rates. The agreement was doomed to fail because of the inevitable clash in goals between public and private

[7]Arthur M. Schlesinger, Jr., *The Coming of the New Deal* (Boston, 1958), p. 327.

power, and also because the terms of the contract were never met. In practical terms, a public power project could not establish a "yardstick" that would be valid nationally in a competitive market.

Complicating the negotiations with CSC was Lilienthal and Arthur Morgan's disagreement over the goals of TVA. Much to Lilienthal's frustration, Morgan supported a policy of cooperation with CSC. Lilienthal found Morgan's amorphous interests in planning and his enthusiasm for folk industry out of touch with the present. "I am against 'basket-weaving' and all that implies," Lilienthal stated. "We cannot prepare for the 'second coming of Daniel Boone' in a simple handicraft economy."[8]

Rather than use the concepts of overhead planning and control, Lilienthal borrowed the idea of "grassroots democracy" from Harcourt Morgan, which emphasized "decentralized administration of centralized authority." Recognizing the inevitability of centralization in government and industry, it still would attempt to give more authority to the regional agency as well as to seek the active participation of the local community in the processes of decision making.

Arthur Morgan, on the other hand, was convinced that his fellow directors wanted to depose him, and was suspicious of what he believed to be Lilienthal's political deviousness and his limited goals.

In 1936 the feud became public, which complicated the negotiations with CSC. Yet the real battle over the legitimacy of TVA was decided in 1939, when the courts established TVA's right to participate in the power business. Arthur Morgan was a casualty of the battle. FDR removed him from the board in 1938, after Morgan took his case to the press, severely criticizing his codirectors, especially Lilienthal.

In retrospect, TVA achieved some outright successes, some qualified successes, and some failures in the 1930s. Various components of the multipurpose system were in place and operating well. Gains were made in flood control, navigation, fertilizer production, the development of recreation areas, disease control, and the production of cheap electricity. Broader goals of social planning and grassroots democracy faded in importance by the end of the decade. The ultimate achievement—the establishment of similar projects in other parts of the country—did not materialize. The enemies of massive government spending, social planning, and public power held greater sway as the depression eased and as the world moved toward war in 1939. Denunciations of TVA and public power continued from all quarters of the business community, including the U.S. Chamber of Commerce, the National Association of Manufacturers, and even the National Coal Association (which feared increased competition from hydropower).

With respect to the development of public power, the record of TVA is instructive. The valley evolved from one of the least electrified regions to one of the most electrified, and with the lowest rates in the country. The residential rates in 1933 ranged from \$.1 to \$.3 per kwh, as compared to \$.55 nation-

[8]Schlesinger, *The Coming of the New Deal*, p. 331.

ally. To sustain such low rates, TVA encouraged greater consumption. In every community that sold TVA electricity, usage rose sharply as prices fell. TVA even sponsored campaigns to sell electrical appliances door to door on installment plans and guaranteed credit purchases. In addition, it encouraged the establishment of cooperatives and developed an elaborate publicity campaign. In the long run, the pressure to increase consumption moved TVA beyond hydroelectric power into more capital-intensive and more polluting steam and nuclear power generation.

In the strictest sense, the idea of using TVA as a "yardstick" failed. But TVA demonstrated that electric rates were not inelastic. This placed indirect pressure on private power rates in various parts of the country. However, efforts to extend TVA-type programs throughout the country never materialized. In 1937, FDR appointed a new National Power Policy Committee to study a proposal to establish eight regional authorities. Unlike TVA, they were to be limited primarily to regional planning, with the possibility of expansion into power authorities. An alternative presented by Senator Norris and Representative John Rankin (Dem., Miss.), would have set up "little TVAs" in six areas of the country. Neither proposal received much support, largely because of other pressing political battles and the onset of a recession in 1937.

In 1938, the Supreme Court clarified the legal standing of public power. It upheld the right of the Public Works Administration (PWA), a New Deal unemployment relief agency, to make grants for municipal power plants. The PWA was set up to stimulate employment through various construction projects. Under its mandate, PWA was instructed to aid municipal power plants, and thus extended the New Deal's public power interest into several local arenas. The total expenditure for this program was not great, however. Of the $647 million allotted for power, only 16 percent went to municipal power systems. Moreover, PWA was simply providing funds; it was not purchasing municipal systems. Private power interests were alarmed, nevertheless, and several began to dispose of their properties to public agencies. The director of the PWA, Harold Ickes, used the threat of competing public systems to reduce rates of the private firms, but he did not have unlimited authority over local projects.

PWA efforts in the public power area were nonetheless important to the development of the public power concept. In addition to municipal grants, PWA money eventually funded several important federal dam projects, most notably Boulder Dam (Colorado), Bonneville Dam (Oregon), Grand Coulee Dam (Washington), and Fort Peck Dam (Montana). PWA also worked closely with TVA to the point where litigation against either hurt both. The Boulder Canyon Project, in particular, played a significant role in establishing precedents in natural resource management, federal river basin development, and maximum development of hydroelectric power as part of each reclamation project.

Other efforts at public power had some regional significance, but they did not lead to a network of TVA-type projects. Responsibility for developing federal hydroelectric projects was divided among several agencies, making a unified policy difficult if not impossible. The independent TVA had jurisdiction in its region, while various Department of the Interior agencies had influence over about three-fourths of the nation. The Bonneville Power Administration, undertaken in 1937, covered the Pacific Northwest. Other authorities were eventually added.

TVA did not inspire a public power revolution, but it was the most visible achievement of public power in the United States. A victory of finite limits, TVA was the product of timing and luck: the immediate needs of a depression society converged with the persistence of social planners and public power advocates.

RURAL ELECTRIFICATION AND THE NEW DEAL

The federal decision to participate in the electrification of rural America superficially seemed to be another step in the direction of centralized public power. The emphasis on electric cooperatives, however, signaled a step in the direction of a decentralized, grassroots approach to energy.

Extending electricity to rural areas was slow in coming, not because farmers chose to utilize other sources of power, but because they were almost forced to do so. From the point of view of electric utilities, the cost of furnishing service to rural customers was so high as to be unprofitable. Studies indicated that there were fewer than five farmers per mile of electric-distribution farm lines in most rural areas (See Table 7.1). Furthermore, utility companies rationalized that farmers were not equipped to use electricity fully because of the lack of electrically driven equipment.

This view, however, was short-sighted. Many farmers and public power advocates criticized the electric industry for refusing to serve the rural market or for charging exorbitant rates for service. In the 1920s, the electric utility industry—in cooperation with the Department of Agriculture, various agricultural colleges, and the American Farm Bureau Federation—made a half-hearted attempt to reduce costs and extend services through the initiation of the unsuccessful Committee on the Relation of Electricity to Agriculture.[9]

While ignoring the needs of rural America, the utility companies simultaneously fought public power. The result was that by 1930 only one farm in ten had electricity, and most of them were concentrated in California, Oregon, and Washington. Most European countries had a much higher proportion of electric service for rural populations, but villages in Europe were not as widely dispersed as were American farms.

Rural electrification became a public issue largely because of the lack of commitment from private utilities to provide service. The 1930s were a propitious time for a change, especially because of the public power commitment

---

[9]Established in 1923, the committee grew out of the National Electric Light Association (NELA), a powerful trade and lobbying organization.

Table 7.1 *Growth of Dwelling Units with Electricity (Residential service in percentages)*

	All Dwellings	Farm	Urban and Rural Nonfarm
1920	34.7%	1.6%	47.4%
1925	53.2	3.9	69.4
1930	68.2	10.4	84.8
1935	68.0	12.6	83.9
1940	78.7	32.6	90.8
1945	85.0	48.0	93.0

Source: Bureau of the Census, U.S. Department of Commerce, *Historical Statistics of the United States* (Washington, DC, 1975), p. 827.

of the New Deal. But additional pressure came from various agricultural groups and public power advocates, who pressed their case more successfully in a time when new transmission lines and rural electricity meant jobs. At least initially, the Roosevelt administration itself saw rural electrification as part of the relief program. Moreover, a few rural states planned programs of rural electrification and brought pressure on the government for federal funds.

Initially, New Deal rural electrification grew out of some scattered projects under the auspices of the Emergency Relief Appropriation Act (1935). In 1935, FDR created the Rural Electrification Administration (REA). To those who doubted the wisdom of the program, the argument that it would provide work relief was persuasive.

To head REA, the President appointed Morris L. Cooke. At the time, Cooke was serving as a consultant for PWA and as a Roosevelt advisor on conservation and power matters. His initial approach to REA was to press private electric companies to extend their lines into rural areas, offering low-interest federal loans as an incentive. When private utility companies balked, Cooke turned to the formation of nonprofit electric cooperatives.

Few cooperatives existed prior to World War I, but the idea was a central feature of agricultural life since the nineteenth century. Cooke's change in approach attracted strong opposition from private utilities, but it broadened the appeal of rural electrification in the administration. No longer a program in work relief, the promotion of cooperatives extended the New Deal's commitment to public approaches to electric power.

Under the sponsorship of George Norris and Sam Rayburn, Congress passed the Rural Electrification Act of 1936, establishing REA as a lending agency that would give preference to nonprofit cooperatives rather than to private utility companies. Unlike the central role of the federal government in the construction, maintenance, and operation of TVA, the rural cooperatives placed authority in the community, with REA acting as a source of funding and a stimulator of electrical development.

REA was not without its troubles, but under the direction of Cooke's hand-picked successor, John Carmody, REA proved a smashing success. By 1941, four out of ten farms had electricity; by 1950, nine out of ten. REA also stimulated new industrial growth in areas previously dominated by small farming ventures.

The greatest impact was on the life of the farm family itself. Rural electrification virtually brought American farmers out of the preindustrial era and into the age of power. While it is impossible to gauge the psychological effects, the material effects were enormous. The drudgery of farm life was alleviated in many ways by the introduction of power-driven machinery and the internal combustion engine. The farmer's home and community underwent massive changes. Running water, refrigeration, electric lighting utterly destroyed old habits and old routines. Radios brought news from the outside world. Schools could operate without the impediments of weather and darkness or the lack of heat.

The REA underwent some tumultuous times during World War II, but cooperatives became a permanent feature in many communities: Almost 1,000 are in operation today, serving more than 7.5 million people. The cooperatives proved economically successful as well. REA suffered less than 1 percent default on its loans since 1935. Moderate in approach but revolutionary in results, REA might very well be the most significant aspect of the New Deal power program.

The New Deal response to the electric power industry was modest in light of the rapid, unchecked growth of holding companies, the dislocations of the depression, and the disillusionment with business leaders. The most radical response—nationalization of the industry—was a faint dream of a few die-hards at best. FDR had no intention of making over the capitalist system, only curbing its abuses and seeing that government was a countervailing force in the economy.

In confronting the issues of holding company abuse, regional power development, and rural electrification, the New Dealers drew heavily on proposals advanced in the 1920s. They also dealt with these issues as specific, finite problems. What constituted the national power policy was a collection of decisions without a common thread. The random nature of the New Deal is expressed in the various aspects of the power policy. Holding company abuse was dealt with through conventional regulatory channels. Regional power development—specifically TVA—was built upon the concept of "decentralized administration of centralized authority." And REA was the purest expression of the grassroots approach. In large measure, the parts of the so-called national power policy were greater than the whole, and they grew out of diverse interests of which electrical power was only one aspect.

Going into World War II, the nation was committed to a mixed electrical power system, with a large private component and an important accumulation of public projects. If nationalization was not a real choice in the 1930s, neither was the electrical power system operating in a free market. The debate over public versus private power was settled temporarily at least. The principle of public power was legitimized in the 1930s but not as an alternative to private power—only as a supplement to it.

Electrical power had become too significant a part of American life to operate beyond the gaze of many competing interests. Few believed that electricity would flow as freely as did water, but almost everyone believed that access to electrical power had become as essential to well-being as was any other necessity.

FURTHER READING

Douglas D. Anderson. *Regulatory Politics and Electric Utilities*. Boston, 1981.

James C. Bonbright. *Public Utilities and the National Power Policies*. New York, 1972; orig. 1940.

D. Clayton Brown. *Electricity for Rural America*. Westport, Conn., 1980.

Philip J. Funigiello. *Toward a National Power Policy*. Pittsburgh, 1973.

Richard Hellman. *Government Competition in the Electric Utility Industry*. New York, 1972.

Victor C. Hobday. *Sparks at the Grassroots*. Knoxville, Tenn., 1969.

Preston J. Hubbard. *Origins of the TVA*. New York, 1968; orig. 1961.

Richard Lowitt. *George W. Norris*, 2 vols. Urbana, Ill., 1971, 1978.

Thomas McCraw. *The TVA and the Power Fight*. Philadelphia, 1971.

Forrest McDonald. *Insull*. Chicago, 1962.

CHAPTER 8

Through Boom and Bust—
Waning Coal, Rising Oil

The diversity of the major energy industries was never more apparent than in the interwar years. Utility holding companies were hard hit by the boom and bust cycle of the 1920s and 1930s, but the structure of the industry survived the depression and New Deal. Coal's good fortune in World War I turned to serious decline in the 1920s as the industry's age-old problems reasserted themselves. Petroleum entered the 1920s on a firmer footing than did coal. Demand for gasoline, especially, allowed the industry to survive a period of overproduction and competition from electrical power.

For coal and oil the interwar years were a major period of readjustment. After 1920, coal consumption ceased to grow; by 1940, coal was no longer the dominant fuel (in terms of aggregate energy consumption). In 1920, coal represented 72.5 percent of all energy consumed in the United States, while oil and natural gas represented only 16.3 percent. Twenty years later, coal had dropped to 48.7 percent, and oil and natural gas had climbed to 41.2 percent.

Coal was supplanted as the energy king in the 1920s for many reasons. Operators, miners, and government officials urged cooperation, but the problems of the industry transcended the ability of any one party to solve them. Traditional markets were being lost. While increases in coal consumption by electrical utilities temporarily restored a portion of the coal market, newer competitors, in some cases hydropower, offered attractive alternatives. Ironically, greater thermal efficiency of coal utilization meant a reduction in demand. Coal was also expensive to transport and dirty to burn. Opportunities to reduce costs through technical innovations—such as strip mining—and improved methods of transportation did not emerge until after World War II.

The coal industry was sinking by its own weight, but it was also being sunk by its major competitor—oil. Coal's intense competition with fuel oil (including diesel fuels) tended to expose the industry's major weaknesses. In addition, as historian Joseph Pratt stated: "The twentieth-century decline of coal resulted from more than simply its internal weaknesses, for the strengths of the petroleum industry made it a formidable competitor."[1] While over-

[1]Joseph A. Pratt, "Natural Resources and Energy," in Glenn Porter (ed.), *Encyclopedia of American Economic History*, vol. 1 (New York, 1980), p. 208.

production had a disastrous effect on the stability of the industry in the 1930s, it survived the calamity due to its business techniques, its growing markets, and its favorable treatment from state and federal government in the form of beneficial tax policies, conservation laws, and, later, import quotas. After World War I, especially, the largest companies in the industry were active in developing foreign supplies and foreign markets. While the international ventures created serious conflicts between "majors" and "independents," they strengthened the role of the American oil industry on a global basis. The industry's advantages meant that oil was not on a collision course with the future, as was the case with coal.

THE SICK ENERGY INDUSTRY—COAL IN THE 1920s

The highs and lows of the coal industry in the early twentieth century were a prelude to a serious decline soon after World War I. Most experts agreed that the industry suffered most from overcapacity. During the Great Depression, coal consumption plunged to 55 percent of what it had been in 1918. However, the market opportunities of the war encouraged new mining ventures, which led to unnecessary expansion. In 1922, the secretary of commerce recommended that 2,500 of the 8,000 mines should be closed; this meant that 200,000 miners would lose their jobs.

Overdevelopment of mines produced intense competition for declining markets. The loss of railroad customers to diesel fuel was most debilitating. Passenger traffic and freight tonnage declined dramatically by mid-decade. Maritime usage of coal dropped by a whopping 95 percent between 1920 and the mid-1950s. Only in heavy industries and utilities did coal hold its own during that period.

The problems of the coal industry must be measured in human, as well as economic, terms. Many of the industry's severest problems revolved around its work force. The irregularity of mine work, the unsafe conditions, and the perpetual labor turmoil sapped the strength of the once-dominant energy industry. In 1923, the industry employed 700,000 workers in the bituminous coal fields, but work for these people was sporadic. Although the average hourly wage ($.71) was higher than for all industries ($.66), the average miner worked only 210 of 308 work days a year.

Labor unionism responded to these problems in the 1920s. The United Mine Workers (UMW), the largest and most powerful union in the country, was at the center of the protest. Its new president, John L. Lewis, reflected the union's vitality and its commitment to better field conditions. The son of Welsh immigrants, Lewis joined his father in the mines at the age of sixteen. In 1909, he was elected president of his local in Illinois, and from 1911 to 1916 he was a field and legislative representative for the American Federation of Labor, holding various offices in the UMW from 1916 to 1919. He served as president of the UMW for forty years (1920 to 1960), and was cofounder of the Congress of Industrial Organization (CIO) in 1935. An advocate of industrial unionism—as opposed to trade unionism—he nevertheless was a proponent of the capitalist system and an ardent anti-Communist.

Lewis and the UMW were on top of the mountain looking down in 1920. Membership stood at .5 million, but plummeted to 84,000 by 1930. Bitter strikes in 1919 and 1922 closed more than 70 percent of the nation's bituminous coal-producing capacity and 100 percent of anthracite capacity. The ravages that hit the industry strongly affected the union. Operators and miners alike felt the decline of the industry in these difficult years, while the nation as a whole underwent a euphoric economic growth.

Ironically, the buoyancy of the 1920s consumer economy mitigated against a solution to the coal industry's problems. Coal as an energy source was increasingly out of step with the times, especially in the new, consumer-oriented automobile and chemical industries. While the UMW was growing in influence in the 1920s, unionism in general remained anemic until the mid-1930s. Strikes were viewed as impediments to prosperity by many Americans and thus miners received little public sympathy for their cause.

The probusiness climate of the nation in the 1920s worked against a governmental solution to the industry's plight. The three Republican presidents did not wish to tamper with the economic boom in general or the coal industry in particular. Their inaction—and sometimes open hostility to unionism—undermined the interests of coal miners. However, events outside Washington did more to determine the future of the industry than did activities that transpired on Capitol Hill.

The Coal Strikes—1919 and 1922

With the armistice came a series of labor disputes that characterized the instability of the coal industry during the 1920s. The year 1919 was a time of trouble: reconversion to a peacetime economy, inflation, the Red Scare, and massive labor disputes. Bituminous coal miners chose that moment to make their first postwar claim to higher wages and better working conditions. Their action set off a major coal shortage which lasted months after the strike ended.

To manage the shortage, the federal government dusted off the U.S. Fuel Administration (USFA) and reinstituted some wartime fuel controls. Without authorized personnel, the USFA had to delegate its authority to the U.S. Railroad Administration (USRA). But the USRA was being dismantled and authority to deal with distribution devolved to the Interstate Commerce Commission (ICC). Ineptly handled, the management of the shortage resulted in severe misallocations, with utilities and other large consumers acquiring the lion's share of available supplies. Price controls failed, and increases went as high as 75 percent.

Attorney General A. Mitchell Palmer ended the strike by obtaining an injunction against the striking miners. Responding to the miners' great bitterness unleashed by Palmer's actions and the general disarray of the industry, Wilson appointed an investigating commission in March 1920. The commission awarded the miners a 17 percent wage increase, but it ignored mine safety and the question of union representation. In the same year, a threatened strike in the anthracite fields was avoided when Wilson established an Anthracite Commission, which awarded a similar wage increase but also extended UMW recognition to the anthracite fields. These actions momentarily pacified the miners, but they did not resolve the inherent problems in the industry.

The Harding administration dealt with problems in the coal fields in a similar, piecemeal fashion. When a shooting war broke out between miners and operators in the West Virginia coal fields in 1920, President Harding sent in nearly 2,000 federal troops. He did not, however, follow this action with an evaluation of conditions in the industry. In Congress, an attempt to enact an industrial code for the industry attracted few supporters.

Herbert Hoover, then Harding's secretary of commerce, wanted to stabilize the industry by eliminating excess mining capacity and gradually reducing the work force. Hoover's vision of a more orderly and efficient coal industry was limited by his faith in individual action and "cooperative competition" among coal companies. As an advocate of "associatism," according to historian Ellis Hawley, Hoover

> preached the gospel of efficient production and scientific management, the conquest of poverty through economic growth, technological innovation, and elimination of waste, all of which, he seemed to realize, would involve cooperative planning, the systematic use of expert knowledge, and an environment stable enough to attract capital and allow the planners to function. Yet, as an idealist, moral philosopher, and self-made man, he remained wedded to the images of laissez-faire and competitive individualism.[2]

The Harding administration did little to anticipate another coal shortage that could arise from renegotiation of miners' contracts in 1922. After negotiations broke down, a strike erupted. When voluntary measures failed to produce an immediate solution, Harding chose to let the crisis run its course. Hoover and other officials were forced to deal with the strike through emergency measures alone. By May, the nation experienced a serious coal shortage. Finally in August, a settlement was achieved, but shortages persisted.

At Hoover's urging, Congress appointed a Federal Fuel Distributor (FFD) to determine where shortages existed and to work out voluntary agreements on coal prices. Congress also granted additional powers to the ICC. But the FFD had no coercive power and the ICC proved reluctant to exercise its authority over transportation, distribution, and price. Without the crisis atmosphere of the war, and lacking the experience to deal with the myriad problems of the industry, the FFD and the ICC let the states and the coalmen figure a way out of the predicament. By December, the worst of the crisis was over, and the FFD was scrapped the next year.

---

[2]Ellis W. Hawley, "Secretary Hoover and the Bituminous Coal Problem, 1921–1928," *Business History Review*, vol. 42 (Autumn 1968); p. 248.

The only encouraging prospect for longer-range solutions was the establishment of the U.S. Coal Commission—another idea promoted by Hoover. Harding appointed members who, by and large, represented the thinking of Hoover rather than the interests of the operators or miners. A report completed in 1923 was inconclusive. Although critical of some of the worst mining and labor practices, it offered no effective program for change. Calvin Coolidge, who assumed the presidency by the time the report was issued, acknowledged the effort but did not pursue coal mining reform any further.

Hoover, the Depression, and Coal

For the next few years after the 1922 strike, miners, operators, and government officials urged cooperation. But the only major effort to bring some relief to the plight of miners was the signing of the so-called Jacksonville Agreement in 1924. To avoid labor disturbances, especially in an election year, Secretary Hoover urged the operators in the Central Competitive Field to accept a status quo wage contract.

The Jacksonville Agreement stated that the UMW would not seek to increase wages in the nonunion, southern fields in exchange for retaining the relatively high wages in the Central Field. The agreement was based on the hope that mechanized mines in the North would be able to compete with less efficient, nonunion mines in the South. But the gamble did not work, the premises proved faulty, and the agreement crumbled in 1925.

Decline in coal demand brought wage cutting and layoffs. As a result, the UMW began to falter. To make matters worse, an anthracite strike broke out in 1925 and 1926. Lewis decided to strike in Pennsylvania, where bituminous operators had defied the Jacksonville Agreement. The resulting bloody labor dispute only demonstrated the futility of the piecemeal efforts at stabilizing the industry.

The election of Herbert Hoover as president in 1928 brought hope to the coal industry. The onset of depression, however, turned that hope into despair. The coal industry virtually collapsed, which resulted in distress and deprivation to the mining communities. The Harlan County coal field in Kentucky was one of the hardest hit. Serious wage cuts and unemployment ravaged the area. One miner wrote:

> We have been eating wild green . . . . Such as Polk salad. Violet tops, wild onions. forget me not wild lettuce and such weeds as cows eat as a cow wont eat a poison weeds . . . . Our family are in bad shake childrens need milk women need nurishments food shoes and dresses—that we cannot get. and there at least 10,000 hungry people in Harlan County daily. I know because I am one off them.[3]

[3]Cited in Irving Bernstein, *The Lean Years* (Baltimore, 1966; orig. 1960), p. 377.

Then came the strike—and the violence. The hard-fought gains of the miners slipped back into operators' hands. Nationally, the UMW suffered defeat after defeat because of internal strife and the crippling conditions of depression. In 1932, less than 400,000 miners could find work. Hourly wages slipped as low as $.45 an hour in the North and $.20 an hour in the South.

As secretary of commerce, Hoover had learned that bringing stability to the coal industry was exceedingly difficult. As president he faced the impossible task of dealing with coal as one of several economic problems during the depression. But he was limited by his perceptions of those problems and by his commitment to voluntarism and individual initiative, to market forces controlling wages and prices, and to a reliance on private charities to alleviate suffering. Without presidential leadership, the efforts of some members of Congress, state governments, trade associations, regional sales agencies, and the UMW to achieve stabilization met with little success.

Signs of change came with the passage of the Norris-La Guardia Act in March 1932. The act forbade injunctions to sustain antiunion employment contracts or to prevent picketing, strikes, and boycotts. Conditions in the coal fields helped promote this act, which, given the immensity of the problems, was only a small step forward. By 1932, President Hoover himself came to realize that older notions of self-reliance and voluntary activity were not going to take the country out of depression. By that time, however, Hoover's political fortunes had run out.

The 1920s demonstrated how tradition-bound all parties in the coal industry disputes had remained. Operators clung to the vague faith in free enterprise. The split between the North and South fields widened. The Republican presidents encouraged general economic growth. Labor became badly divided and increasingly impotent by 1929. In 1933, hopeful eyes turned to FDR and the New Deal.

A NEW DEAL FOR COAL?

During the "First Hundred Days" of the New Deal, miners, operators, and government officials turned their attention to the National Industrial Recovery Act (1933), which stricken industries hoped would be their salvation. Under the provisions of the act, the President had broad discretionary power to establish and enforce industrial codes of fair competition. The codes were meant to discourage destructive competition, limit production as a way of raising prices, and encourage cooperation within industries. The program was also designed to mitigate against government antitrust suits. To implement the codes, the act set up the National Recovery Administration (NRA), directed by General Hugh S. Johnson.[4]

---

[4]As adopted, the codes actually encouraged business concentration and allowed the largest companies within each industry to dictate practices.

The National Coal Code

The writing of a coal code was a complex task. The badly divided industry had shown little propensity to cooperation. However, leaders in bituminous coal realized that a code was a better solution than less flexible special legislation. But what form should the code take? Southern operators wanted regional or local code agencies. Northern operators and the UMW wanted a unified national code. Operators of "captive mines"—those mines controlled and utilized by major steel companies—felt that they should be exempt from the codes altogether.

Johnson's staff was stamped with more than twenty codes from all sectors of the industry. The most crucial and common provision was wage differentials between northern and southern fields. This was a volatile issue because wages represented approximately two-thirds of the cost of mining. Typical of his handling of codes from other industries, Johnson abruptly announced the completion of a government-drawn code based on those presented to the NRA. After a flurry of criticism, the code was revised, incorporating changes suggested by industry spokesmen.

The coal code attempted to incorporate the interests of several contentious factions. It provided for more than twenty divisional or subdivisional code agencies, which decentralized price-fixing authority and limited centralized enforcement. The agencies were governed by a National Bituminous Coal Industrial Board. Fair trade practices were outlined, and a major set of labor provisions were incorporated, including the eight-hour day, forty-hour week, collective bargaining, a ban on child labor, establishment of grievance committees, but no closed-shop arrangement. Three days after the President signed the code into law, operators and miners completed the Appalachian Agreement, a two-year pact affecting 70 percent of the industry.

The NIRA and Labor

In the short term, the coal miners were major beneficiaries of this experiment in industrial cooperation. The most important piece of legislation was Section 7(a) of the NIRA, which was the basis for the labor provisions of the coal code. Section 7(a) recognized collective bargaining by representatives of the workers' choosing as a legal right. This legitimized the efforts of the previously sagging UMW, and stimulated the union to launch a large-scale campaign in the coal industry.

By 1935, the UMW was 540,000 strong and was the foundation of labor growth in the 1930s. In fact, much of the leadership and financial backing for the CIO—the major rival of the American Federation of Labor (AFL)—came from the UMW. Riding the crest of governmental support for unionism, the CIO set out to organize all workers, from unskilled to skilled, across industrial lines. In 1935, the CIO broke with the AFL, which as a trade union catered only to a small class of skilled workers regardless of industry.

The vigorous union activity spilled over into the political arena. In 1936,

Lewis organized the Non-Partisan League, which pledged to support the re-election of FDR. That same year Lewis abandoned the Republican party; this move became symbolic of the major alignment of labor with the New Deal and the Democratic party.

The NRA code and the prounion stance of the Roosevelt administration provided aid through emergency relief for miners and temporarily raised coal prices. However, they failed to fulfill the intended role of long-range industrial recovery. Little was done to stimulate demand for coal or to confront the problem of overcapacity. The trend toward higher wages meant higher costs for the industry, resulting in increased mechanization or expansion of strip mining. In time, Lewis and the UMW would view mechanization as an effective way to make coal mining less hazardous, but for the present it meant fewer jobs. Higher coal prices also encouraged consumers to shop for other sources of energy. Euphoria over the coal code passed quickly.

The Guffey-Snyder Act

Those groups involved in creating the coal code were aware of its shortcomings from the outset. Prior to the decision to extend the NIRA beyond its expiration date in June 1935, Lewis and supporters in the northern fields had sought a new stabilization bill to bring more centralized controls to the industry. On May 27, however, the Supreme Court declared the NIRA unconstitutional, thus ending the debate over extension. In *Schechter* v. *The United States,* the Court stated that Congress had exceeded its power in granting the Executive Branch and code-drafting committees excessive authority.

As a result, the coal industry, like every other industry and labor group that established codes, had to reevaluate its recovery program. A bill drafted by the UMW, and resembling the old coal code in many ways, became the Guffey-Snyder Act in 1935. Lewis used the threat of a strike and lobbying pressure (with the help of northern operators) to get the bill passed. The act guaranteed collective bargaining, established uniform wage and hour scales, created a national commission with authority to fix prices and influence production, authorized closing marginal mines, and included a production tax to pay for the mines and to rehabilitate displaced miners. Guffey-Snyder also was declared unconstitutional (1936) on the grounds that the labor and price provisions were intimately connected. It was replaced by the Guffey-Vinson Act in 1937 which reenacted the previous act without the wage and hours provisions.

While the various legislative actions attempted to end practices that had crippled the industry in the past, none brought stabilization. Strides were made to protect the interest of the miners, to end the rivalry between northern and southern operations, and to confront falling prices. But the coal industry suffered from problems too great to be resolved by compromise, tinkering, or stop-gap measures. (See Table 8.1 for bituminous production between 1920 and 1950.)

Table 8.1 *Bituminous Coal Production (In short tons)*

		In 1,000 Tons	
	Total	Underground	Strip
1920	568,667	559,807	8,860
1925	520,053	503,182	16,871
1930	467,526	447,684	19,842
1935	372,373	348,726	23,647
1940	460,772	417,604	43,167
1945	577,617	467,630	109,987
1950	516,311	392,844	123,467

Source: Bureau of the Census, U.S. Department of Commerce, *Historical Statistics of the United States* (Washington, D.C., 1975), p. 589.

OIL IN THE 1920S

For reasons that became apparent during World War I, the petroleum industry entered the 1920s on a firmer footing than did the coal industry. Nevertheless, several crucial issues faced the oilmen in the era of prosperity. These included basic economic questions tied to supply and demand as well as business-government relations, the problem of waste versus conservation, and the growing concern over pollution. The life or death of the industry was never in question, but the degree to which the industry operated out of its traditional interests was of major concern.

The Hydra: Rising Demand and Oversupply

The good news for the oil industry in the 1920s was rapidly rising consumption. Demand more than doubled during the 1920s. By 1930, oil represented almost 24 percent of total energy consumption in the United States. The most significant growth was due to increased use of gasoline. In 1920, motor fuel represented only 2.2 percent of total oil product consumption, but it reached more than 42 percent in 1930.

The bad news for the oil industry in the 1920s was massive overproduction. For a few years after World War I, demand for crude ran well above domestic production. Deficiencies were met only through imports, primarily from Mexico. Under the stimulus of war, however, oil producers continued to drill new wells at an amazing rate. In 1919, there were 30,000 new wells; by 1920, there were 34,000 more. Of these, approximately 71 percent were productive. In all, oil was being drilled in 25 states, although the midcontinent field (including parts of Louisiana, Arkansas, Texas, Oklahoma, and Kansas) and the California fields accounted for 80 to 90 percent of the total. As with demand, output doubled during the 1920s. In 1922, production rose to more than 500 million barrels and by 1929, it passed the 1 billion-barrel mark. Internationally, the United States was the largest oil producer; it accounted for two-thirds of the market.

The scale of oil production after the war and the rising demand sparked widespread fears of shortages in existing reserves and speculations about future shortages. Uncertainty over the reliability of importing oil added to the anxiety. The industry was being pulled apart by both its determination to meet the rising demand and its concern over chronic oversupply (which continued almost unabated until 1935). In an attempt to resolve this dilemma, debate focused on questions of price stabilization, production controls, and resource conservation.

Unstable market factors, especially fluctuating prices, created uncertainty in the industry throughout the decade. To counteract the fluctuations in price, supply, and demand, major oil producers turned toward further integration, especially "forward integration" (the construction or acquisition of transportation, refining, and marketing facilities to secure outlets for their crude and its by-products). By 1926, fifteen companies controlled 63 percent of the proven domestic acreage and the largest share of output.

As the majors became more powerful and expanded their activities into various phases of the industry, the number of producers multiplied dramatically. New discoveries in California, Oklahoma, and Texas spawned hundreds of companies, leading to the most intense competition in many years. The majors' attempts at forward integration also meant that strong competition occurred in refining, wholesaling, and retailing. Conflicts between majors and independents, among producers, refiners, and shippers, complicated efforts to resolve production problems.

The role of the government in the oil market of the 1920s was no less clear. Oilmen generally preferred to deal with the problems of shortages, oversupply, exports and imports, and price fluctuations from within the industry, and, sometimes, in the marketplace. Since petroleum was so essential to the life of the nation, the industry's problems had a public dimension that could not be ignored. How problems of production affected the relationship between the industry and government was itself a crucial issue of the decade; concern over shortages and the debate over conservation measures were the manifestations of that issue. In addition, concern over oil pollution began to enter the public dialogue in the 1920s.

Teapot Dome

Teapot Dome is remembered as the most dramatic case of political corruption associated with the scandal-ridden Harding administration. Within the context of energy history, it has additional significance: the scandal's origins were imbedded in the conservation battles of the early twentieth century, and its repercussions affected the debate over reserve shortages and federal oil policy.

The conservation battle revolved around the appointment of Albert Fall as interior secretary. A former Republican senator from New Mexico, Fall had mining, lumber, and railroad interests in the West. His severest critics branded him anticonservationist, but as secretary of the interior he was a relatively able administrator with a traditional western bent toward greater exploitation and utilization of natural resources.

To the leaders of the conservation movement, Fall challenged the notion of wise use of resources. They especially scoffed at Fall's apparent unwillingness to continue withdrawing natural resources from immediate use by private companies. Most significant was Fall's efforts to transfer naval oil reserves from the Navy Department to the Interior Department. With the acquiescence of Secretary of the Navy Edwin Denby, Fall secured the transfer in May 1921.

Fall's critics now focused on the oil reserve-transfer issue, assuming the worst about his intentions. Unfortunately for the secretary, for the Harding administration, and for the Republican party, Fall's own greed played into the hands of his enemies. What became known as the Teapot Dome scandal involved the awarding of federal leases to oilmen in exchange for personal "loans," which Fall used to prop up his sagging financial status. The scandal did not become public until after the untimely death of President Harding, but it quickly became the source of intense partisan debate. What made Teapot Dome especially serious for the Republicans were other scandals associated with Harding's administration.

The oil scandal involved the leasing of two important reserves: Elk Hills, California, and Teapot Dome, Wyoming. In July 1921, Fall awarded a lease on the Elk Hills reservoir to his close friend Edward Doheny, president of Pan-American Petroleum and Transport Company. In April 1922, he granted a lease on Teapot Dome to Harry F. Sinclair of Mammoth Oil Company. Fall stated that the concessions were made so that protective wells could be drilled in order to conserve naval reserves. Under this system, companies could drill for oil but were required to store crude reserves in tanks for navy use at a later time.

Suspicious of Fall and critical of his department, Senator Robert LaFollette (Prog. Rep., Wisc.) and Gifford Pinchot led the effort to investigate the secretary's activities. Senator Thomas Walsh (Dem., Mont.), a member of the Public Lands Committee, was pressured by LaFollette to assume the leadership in the inquiry, which began in October 1923. The beleaguered secretary resigned before the hearings began. A broken man, facing severe financial setbacks, and beset by family hardships, Fall faced yet another personal tragedy.

The investigation clearly demonstrated Fall's guilt. He had received about $400,000 in loans from Doheny and Sinclair. After the protracted investigation and a federal indictment, a jury declared Fall guilty of accepting a bribe from Doheny. He was sentenced to a year in jail and fined $100,000. While there is little doubt about Fall's guilt, he proved to be a scapegoat for a scandal that went beyond his transgressions. During the course of the Walsh investigation, it was learned that several prominent Democrats in the

Wilson cabinet had been on the Doheny payroll at one time or another. However, a thin line was drawn between "paying for influence" and Fall's bribery. More irksome was the fact that Doheny was acquitted of the charge of bribing Fall.

The press and the Democrats had a field day with the scandal. The new President, Calvin Coolidge, was faced with the unenviable task of confronting the various revelations about the Harding administration. In the long run, Teapot Dome was not a major crisis for the Republicans or the nation. However, it raised questions about oil leases, strategic reserves, and—most important—the distinction between private and public control of natural resources.

Coolidge and the FOCB

In the wake of the scandal, Coolidge's immediate job was putting the political controversy to rest. The more difficult task was establishing some clear direction for federal oil policy. He wisely let the Teapot Dome inquiry run its course, and appointed Curtis D. Wilbur as secretary of the navy and Harlan Fiske Stone as attorney general. Both men were honest, effective and handled matters better than had their predecessors. He also established a special commission to recommend improvements in the management of naval reserves.

Beyond the housecleaning activities, the Coolidge administration did little to establish an effective national oil policy. The probusiness climate of the Harding years persisted. The oil industry as a whole resisted any change in its relationship with government. The onset of the trade-association movement within the industry during World War I—which led to the formation of the American Petroleum Institute (API)—convinced many oilmen that self-regulation was the only answer to their problems.

Henry L. Doherty of Cities Service Corporation opposed the majority view within the industry. He believed that production controls and conservation were necessary to protect the industry against wild fluctuations in the oil market. Especially after the oil discoveries in California in 1921, Doherty tried to convince his colleagues that initiative within the industry was preferable to a government-imposed solution to overproduction.

Failing to attract much support among other oilmen, Doherty turned to the federal government. Until then, oil conservation and the elimination of waste had received scant attention on the national level. Because of the prodding of Doherty, Secretary of the Interior Hubert Work and the dire predictions of shortages by J. E. O'Neal (President of Prairie Oil and Gas Company), Coolidge created the Federal Oil Conservation Board (FOCB) in December 1924.

The FOCB was instructed to investigate the industry and formulate methods of conservation to safeguard national security. At first, the board tried to build a consensus on conservation within the industry, but too many interests were represented. Oilmen also resisted production controls. With a fairly stable market and high prices for oil in 1924 and 1925, Doherty's warnings and the FOCB's solutions were ignored.

The FOCB was never independent, since it required approbation from those within the industry. As a result, the final report of the investigation offered few acceptable proposals. In general, the Republican administration was unwilling to move much beyond its support for a favorable tax structure for oil producers (a uniform 27.5 percent depletion allowance) and some easing of antitrust actions. Few were interested in any form of preventive medicine at the time.

Conservation, Waste, and State Regulation

By the late 1920s, the industry was singing a different tune. Oil discoveries in California and in Oklahoma's great Seminole field meant that known reserves of crude outstripped demand for oil products. The net result would be incredibly low prices, a trend that continued into the 1930s with the tapping of the enormous East Texas field and the sharp drop in demand during the depression.

Controlling production gained renewed interest in the late 1920s. Wasteful drilling, storing, and transporting practices reinforced the call for conservation. The "rule of capture" was under attack. Several producers, especially the larger ones, began to realize the danger of indiscriminate drilling. Small producers and "wild-catters," however, were trapped between the plummeting prices of crude and the need to get a quick return on their tenuous investments. The new-found abundance of oil harkened an era of instability for the industry that included great internal turmoil and the possibility of government intervention.

A report issued by API's Committee of Eleven (1925) stated that there was no imminent danger of exhaustion of American oil, and that waste was negligible. This ill-timed report could not have been more wrong. Waste in the oil industry was the result of several factors, the most important of which were poor storage, inadequate pipeline facilities, excessive drilling in productive fields, and ineffective control of flows from wells brought in under extreme gas pressure. Technical developments in oil searching, refining, and pipeline improvements eventually reduced the severest problems for the larger producers, but they were not uniformly applied by smaller producers.

During the late 1920s, the federal government did little to confront waste in any substantive way. The Coolidge administration never really contemplated intervening in the issue. Instead, it urged various forms of self-regulation and left the industry or the states to seek solutions. Doherty's efforts to bring about unit drilling through the establishment of drilling districts did not replace the "rule of capture" mentality of the industry. No compulsory unitization was possible on a voluntary basis, and the federal government was unwilling to back men like Doherty.

State regulation was the only available outlet in the 1920s for oilmen favoring production controls. Oklahoma led the way. As elsewhere, overproduction was a key problem in the Sooner state. By 1927 Oklahoma wells had reached their maximum output. Oilfield waste and the squandering of natural gas was common. By 1912, approximately fifty billion cubic feet of natural gas had been flared, with little or no effort to curb the practice. Boomtowns experienced seepage from pipelines and serious water pollution.

Oklahoma set several precedents in production control and conservation. Industry people were already familiar with practices recommended by the federal government for oil production on restricted Indian lands. In addition, the Bureau of Mines published studies on conservation practices based on experiences in Oklahoma. As early as the 1910s, the Oklahoma legislature passed several conservation measures. And in 1926, the state adopted a voluntary prorationing[5] program as a way to allocate production. Until the depression and the important new strikes in the 1930s, Oklahoma's example proved to be the exception rather than the rule.

The Oil Pollution Problem

The problem of oil pollution was directly related to the problem of waste. But because pollution was not regarded as an impediment to the economic fortunes of the industry, it did not receive much attention from oilmen in the 1920s. Nonetheless, groups most directly affected by the pollution began to protest.

The primary oil pollution problems were linked to water contamination, due primarily to tanker discharges and seepage problems on land. The former attracted the most attention since the polluting of waterways and coastal areas directly affected commercial fishermen and resort owners. Conservationists also decried the discharges because of the impact on fish, waterfowl, and estuaries and bays.

Secretary Hoover was the leading government proponent of oil conservation and antipollution. As an engineer he opposed waste. In his capacity as secretary of commerce, he felt compelled to protect American fisheries, despite his conflicting responsibility to commercial shippers. The resulting government action, however, fell short of Hoover's goals.

Several investigations were conducted between 1922 and 1926; the first general survey of regional pollution was undertaken in the Texas Gulf area. In Hoover's view, all American streams should be categorized by degree of pollution—unpolluted, partially polluted, and polluted beyond hope. He held that the first group should be preserved as is, the second restored to the first category, and the third abandoned to whatever purposes industry wanted. Somewhat elementary, the proposal at least offered a starting point for dealing with the problem.

---

[5]Prorationing is limiting oil output to expected market demand.

Within the oil industry, the call to end polluting practices and to purify waterways was met with grave apprehension. The API was defensive at first, but it realized that industry studies could control the flow of information on pollution. API did not accomplish anything substantial at first; it simply used its data to reduce criticism of the industry and to support further investigations of oil pollution.

In Congress a bill to control oil pollution met stiff resistance. Hoover and his supporters wanted a comprehensive law, which included the regulation of shore plants as well as ships. Both interests fought the proposal, and a much weaker bill was sent to President Coolidge. The Oil Pollution Act of 1924—the first federal pollution control act since 1899—had inadequate enforcement provisions and dealt only with dumping fuel at sea by oil-burning vessels. While it was a disappointment to Hoover and the conservationists, it was the first serious attempt to deal with oil pollution on a national scale.

OIL DURING THE GREAT DEPRESSION

What reason and foresight could not do for the oil industry in the late 1920s, the depression and new gushers in the Southwest accomplished in the 1930s—a move toward production stabilization. By the end of the decade, a framework for dealing with the oversupply was set in place. This alone did not alleviate the problems of the industry or protect the consuming public. But it did move oil policy beyond anarchy toward some broad goals acceptable to several groups involved in this newest oil crisis.

Domestic overproduction and slipping demand shook the industry in the early 1930s. Strikes in the East Texas field in 1930—the largest flush pool discovered at the time—came at the worst possible moment. The depression was affecting almost every sector of the economy and driving down oil consumption. In 1931, daily crude output averaged 2.5 million barrels, while market demand was only 2 million. Between 1929 and 1940, production increased by about 34 percent. Prices, on the other hand, plummeted. During the early 1930s, they dropped 50 percent below the 1929 mark. Crude that sold for $3 a barrel in 1919 plunged to $.10 a barrel in 1931. Overproduction in the fields also meant overexpansion of refining capacity, shortage of storage space, and the use of high-grade oil for inferior purposes. Resources were wasted, oil companies folded, the economy shuddered.

Few oilmen believed that the federal government could solve their problems in the early years of depression—and they had cause to feel that way. The response of the Hoover administration varied little from previous years: calls for industry cooperation and lip service to the defense oil needs of the nation. Divisions within the petroleum industry only exacerbated the problems.

Specific efforts from within the federal government promised little between 1929 and 1933. Interior secretary Ray L. Wilbur tried to renew interest in cooperation among producing states, but to little avail. In March 1929, he issued a proclamation stating that no further permits for oil leases would be issued on public lands. However, these lands yielded just 10 percent of the nation's production, and Wilbur's policy only succeeded in infuriating Westerners, especially small independent producers, without getting to the heart of the production problem. A more useful proposal was a congressionally sponsored tariff of $1 a barrel on foreign crude which was meant to curb imports and boost domestic prices. While Hoover did not like to tamper with foreign trade to alleviate domestic overproduction, he reluctantly signed the bill. These measures did little to reinvigorate the industry, however.

Texas, Oklahoma, and Oversupply

At the same time that national interest was centered on overproduction and falling demand, attention was also focusing on the dramatic developments in the Southwest. Many observers believed that Texas and Oklahoma, and to a lesser extent California, had to lead the way in stabilizing the oil industry. Oklahoma had set the precedent for prorationing prior to the depression. But new strikes and legal battles over regulation made conditions in the Oklahoma fields precarious. Overproduction was serious in 1926, but it was even worse in 1928, when the Oklahoma City field came in.

In 1928, the Oklahoma Corporation Commission, under statute authority, assumed prorationing responsibility for the entire state. Resistance from wild-catters and other independents made enforcement difficult, if not impossible. Court battles over the right of the commission to prorate retarded stabilization. In 1931, with the courts continuing to obstruct the efforts at state regulation, Governor "Alfalfa" Bill Murray (an oilman himself) declared martial law in the state's major fields and sent the National Guard into the affected areas. When the court reversed itself in October, Murray kept the troops in the fields to execute the prorationing orders. The National Guard was called up again in 1932, and by 1933 the governor enacted a complete shutdown of the Oklahoma City field. Finally in the spring of 1934, the Oklahoma legislature passed a law establishing a stronger prorationing system. In a state where the economy was based largely on oil revenues, the disruptions proved devastating.

The diversified economy of Texas was more capable of surviving an oil field controversy than was its neighbor across the Red River. If anything, however, the situation in the Texas fields was worse. The scale of production was greater, and the clash between the several major integrated companies and the hundreds of smaller independents added a layer of complexity unmatched in the United States.

The focus of the controversy was the rich field in East Texas, opened in October 1930. By the end of 1931, the enormous field was punctured with 3,400 to 3,600 wells. In 1932, production peaked at more than 200 million barrels—more than the rest of the state's production. What made regulation so difficult was that the East Texas field was developed almost entirely by small independents, ardent followers of the "rule of capture." Refineries operated by the majors refused to buy East Texas crude, hoping to undermine the independents and grab their leases.

By the summer of 1931, overproduction had gone well beyond any point of reason. The Texas Railroad Commission (TRC), charged with responsibility for oil matters, attempted in April 1931, to establish prorationing under a 1929 law. The TRC met resistance from East Texas operators, who ignored the ruling and put pressure on the legislature to forbid the commission from using market demand as a way of determining production. Similar to the situation in Oklahoma, the commission was also short-circuited by a federal district court order which ruled against the prorationing plan.

As more and more operators in the field criticized overproduction, they squared off against the most relentless producers. The threats turned to violence, and the violence convinced Governor Ross Sterling (the former president of Humble Oil) to declare martial law in the region in August, which resulted in the shutting down of all wells in a four-county area. When the TRC orders were enforced, martial law was abandoned. However, the 4,000 National Guard remained in the field to keep peace.

In the wake of the prorationing order, prices began to rise. By July 1932, oil was selling for $.85 a barrel. When the Supreme Court upheld the right of the Oklahoma prorationing statute (May 1932), the district-court decision affecting East Texas was reversed. The decree had little immediate effect, since the Texas Conservation Act of 1931 prohibited the TRC from restricting production through market demand. In November 1932, the legislature passed the Market Demand Act which allowed the TRC to limit production to available market demand. The worst of the uproar had passed, but only time would tell if the measures taken were simply stop-gap. (See Table 8.2 for production of crude and proved reserves from 1900 to 1945.)

Table 8.2 *Production of Crude Petroleum and Proved Reserves (In thousands of forty-two-gallon barrels)*

	Production	Estimated Proved Reserves
1900	63,621	2,900,000
1905	134,717	3,800,000
1910	209,557	4,500,000
1915	281,104	5,500,000
1920	442,929	7,200,000
1925	763,743	8,500,000
1930	898,011	13,600,000
1935	996,596	12,400,000
1940	1,353,214	19,024,515
1945	1,713,655	20,826,813

Source: Bureau of the Census, U.S. Department of Commerce, *Historical Statistics of the United States* (Washington, D.C., 1975), pp. 593–594.

The Texas Railroad Commission

The ascendancy of the Texas Railroad Commission in the 1930s is a testament to the importance of production controls in stabilizing the oil industry. As one expert noted, the TRC "although it is only a state agency, deals with a commodity that underlies virtually every aspect of modern industrial life."[6] A regulatory body out of the Progressive Era, the TRC acquired its power when it assumed authority over pipelines in Texas during World War I. By the 1920s, the legislature had given TRC additional responsibility: enforcing a new statute prohibiting the waste of natural resources, especially oil. Well-spacing became one of the first ways of implementing the new law.

With the depression and the East Texas gushers, the TRC expanded its influence through prorationing (limiting output for each well to a maximum daily allowance). By 1935, the TRC exercised a variety of other powers. Since Texas possessed almost half of America's oil reserves, it played a major role in setting national prices for oil and controlling available supplies.

The TRC did not operate in a vacuum, however. The TRC maintained close ties to the industry and to the political leaders of the state. Its chief mission was to benefit the economy of Texas and protect the interests of a thriving industry. Integrated companies approved of its actions when prorationing kept wild-catters from exhausting productive wells and driving down oil prices. Independents benefited when the TRC's rulings helped make them more competitive with the majors. The side to be on was the side of the TRC.

The uniqueness of the oil industry can be demonstrated by the fact that rulings emanating from a state commission had significant national and international impact. It was not an industry that defied regulation and control, but one that—because of its vitality and centrality to the economy—was able to avoid stringent federal regulation. Government authorities, while attempting to encourage cooperation with the industry, did little to demand the kinds of controls that fell upon the coal industry.

NATURAL GAS: FUEL AND UTILITY

A close relative of petroleum, natural gas was becoming an important fuel in the 1930s. However, policy makers treated it more like a utility than a conventional fuel. While its history is linked with oil, the development and use of natural gas really requires separate treatment. Like other fossil fuels, the early use of natural gas was local and sporadic. More than coal and petroleum, the great majority of natural gas produced before World War II (about 90

[6]David F. Prindle, *Petroleum Politics and the Texas Railroad Commission* (Austin, Tex., 1981). p. 3.

percent) was squandered or wasted through flaring. In the search for oil, natural gas was viewed initially as a nuisance or an unnecessary by-product of the drilling process. Wanton flaring was reduced only after it was learned that the retention of natural gas in wells was necessary to conserve oil (gas pressure made crude flow), and that natural gas might have a market value of its own.

Growth and Consolidation

Knowledge of natural gas as a fuel goes back thousands of years to the ancient Chinese. In the United States, early settlers noted "burning springs," and miners drilling water and salt wells encountered natural gas. The earliest recorded commercial use dates back to 1821, in Fredonia, New York; the first natural gas company in the United States was aptly the Fredonia Gas Light and Waterworks (1865).

Because transportation was such a problem—the production of airtight, high-pressure pipelines was not perfected until the mid-1920s—natural gas could not move much beyond its point of origin. Only after the shift of oil production across the Mississippi did the use of natural gas begin in the Southwest, Midwest, and West.

In the 1930s, the natural gas industry began to evolve from a regional enterprise to a national one. The first indication of the shift was the completion of a pipeline from West Texas to Chicago. Since long-distance pipeline construction was expensive, several gas distribution or pipeline companies cooperated in the ventures. Vertical integration was often the result, which lead to the purchase of extensive tracts of producing lands and large distribution systems. In turn, holding companies combined gas firms with electric systems, creating new utility monopolies. An FPC report (1934–1935) revealed that more than half of the gas produced and over three-fourths of the interstate natural gas pipelines were controlled by eleven holding companies. The four largest companies controlled 58 percent of the mileage.

The Natural Gas Act of 1938

The quick consolidation of the natural gas industry, along with such abuses as waste, cut-throat competition, and rate discrimination, led to the Natural Gas Act of 1938. As a supplement to state regulation, the law gave the FPC some sway over the natural gas industry. The FPC could regulate interstate transportation and sale of natural gas for resale, and it could determine prices for gas in interstate commerce. Most controversial was the FPC's ability to determine the place and pace of pipeline expansion. The law, however, was not designed to regulate intrastate producers or to determine intrastate prices. While bringing some order to a chaotic business, the Natural Gas Act had severe limits, which made it palatable to the American Gas Association and the producing states.

OIL AND THE NEW DEAL

Despite the severity of the problems that the oil industry faced in the 1930s, the influence of the federal government was circumscribed in several respects. State action, especially in Oklahoma and Texas, undercut the need or desire for federal production controls during peacetime. The states also began to address problems of waste and conservation that affected them directly. Well-spacing, slant drilling, and storage were issues that the states stubbornly guarded as their own concerns.

Never comfortable with federal intervention, the majors and the large independents sought alternatives to government action whenever possible. Unlike some industries, the oil industry did not face a long-term or permanent decline as a result of the depression. Demand was relatively stable, and production could be stabilized, as efforts in Oklahoma and Texas demonstrated. With a powerful lobby and with great growth potential, the oil industry repulsed any serious efforts at stringent control. Beginning in the 1930s, leaders in the industry advocated cooperative programs for dealing with interstate trade and transport—areas of traditional federal regulation. The majors preferred to rely on state controls, to emphasize production quotas rather than minimum prices, and to keep federal regulation at arms length. However, they continued to expect the federal government to promote their interests at home and abroad—and they got much of what they wanted.

Many issues that the states and the oil industry jealously coveted as their own—conservation, workable production controls, interstate transport of "hot" oil[7]—were of national concern. The New Deal was selective in addressing these issues. In general, it adopted the production control proposals of the FOCB but without the major impulse to protect oil resources from depletion or waste. In other words, they borrowed a policy established during a period of relative scarcity to deal with problems in an era of overproduction. This meant price stabilization as a primary goal of New Deal oil policy, but little else.

First and foremost, the Roosevelt administration did not intend to tinker with the structure of the oil industry. Like its predecessors, it was interested in sufficient supplies of oil for national defense and supported a vague notion of resource conservation. It hoped that production could be curbed and prices stabilized under the NIRA, but it did nothing to tamper with the oil depletion allowance or the tariff on foreign oil.

Using World War I agencies as a model, the Roosevelt administration

---

[7]"Hot" oil was oil produced above the mandated prorationing limits.

set up a Petroleum Administration Board (PAB),[8] and through Section 9(c) of NIRA gave the President authority to prohibit interstate shipment of hot oil. According to historian John G. Clark, "The PAB, like the FOCB, was labeled a tool of the majors and of the consuming states."[9] Since the API lead the way in preparing the draft of the oil code, the charge had merit. Despite confrontations between majors and independents over the nature and extent of federal regulation, price-fixing, and other matters, a compromise code with limited federal involvement was established. The government could only recommend production quotas, not impose them. As a sop to Fuel Administrator Harold Ickes, the President was given discretionary power to fix prices for ninety days in an emergency. A fairly innocuous document, the oil code may have aided in reducing production, but its effects on the industry were negligible.

The demise of the NIRA did not generate other legislation, as had been the case with the coal code and Guffey-Snyder. Instead, interest turned to establishing an interstate compact for oil. This approach was similiar in intent to the code but with less direct federal involvement. Primarily through the efforts of API and Oklahoma Governor Ernest W. Marland, an interstate oil compact among the producing states of the Southwest and midcontinent took shape. Feuds persisted, but, in the summer of 1935, six states—New Mexico, Oklahoma, Kansas, Texas, Colorado, and Illinois—ratified the Interstate Compact to Conserve Oil and Gas, and Congress approved it in August.

FDR sided against Ickes over the matter of centralized federal control of oil. And while the compact was not an ironclad program of compulsory control, neither was it a loose voluntary program. The compact provided a mechanism to implement various conservation efforts and complemented state efforts at production control. It reflected the need for production control as envisioned by many oilmen. To compensate for the loss of Section 9(c) of the NIRA, Congress passed the Connally "Hot Oil" Act in 1935, which restored federal authority to police the shipment of hot oil.

Aside from some antitrust activity, the Roosevelt administration moved no closer to federal control of the oil industry than had its Republican predecessors. The industry may have been divided in many ways, but it shared an apprehension for strong governmental intervention. Consumers' interests were left to the good faith of the industry. But in a time of cheap energy, strong consumer protests were not forthcoming.

The domestic oil industry emerged from the depression as a sound enterprise. State regulation and the actions of the New Deal did little to force a change in the industry's structure. Oilmen could be smug for the moment, as they rode the crest of the nation's second energy transition. Oil was king. And oil drove major integrated companies overseas in search of more oil and more markets.

---

[8] Oil was the only commodity not administered directly by NIRA.

[9] John G. Clark, "Federal Management of Fuel Crises Between the World Wars," in George H. Daniels and Mark H. Rose (eds.), *Energy and Transport* (Beverly Hills, Calif., 1982), p. 142.

FURTHER READING

Harold W. Aurand. *From the Molly Maguires to the United Mine Workers.* Philadelphia, 1971.

Douglas C. Drake. "Herbert Hoover, Ecologist," *Mid-America,* vol. 55 (July 1973), pp. 207–228.

George N. Green. "The Oil and Gas Industry in Texas," in Ben Procter and Archie P. McDonald. *The Texas Heritage.* Arlington Heights, Ill., 1980.

Ellis W. Hawley. *The New Deal and the Problem of Monopoly.* Princeton, N.J., 1971; orig., 1966.

——————."Secretary Hoover and the Bituminous Coal Problem, 1921–1928," *Business History Review,* vol. 42 (Autumn 1968), pp. 247–270.

Linda J. Lear. "Harold L. Ickes and the Oil Crisis of the First Hundred Days," *Mid-America,* vol. 63 (January 1981), pp. 3–17.

John G. McLean and Robert W. Haigh. *The Growth of Integrated Oil Companies.* Boston, 1954.

Burl Noggle. *Teapot Dome.* New York, 1962.

Norman Nordhauser. "Origins of Federal Oil Regulation in the 1920s," *Business History Review,* vol. 47 (Spring 1973), pp. 53–71.

David F. Prindle. *Petroleum Politics and the Texas Railroad Commission.* Austin, Tex., 1981.

CHAPTER 9

Energy Abroad: The United States and International Oil

Compared with other expansionist powers, the United States was late in seeking energy sources abroad. Although major oil companies had an interest in developing international markets in the late nineteenth century, American penetration into the world's oil fields can be traced to events surrounding World War I.

In 1914, American oil companies only controlled producing properties in Mexico and Rumania. Foreign production amounted to just 15 percent of the total crude output outside the United States. For most majors—especially Jersey Standard and its affiliates—marketing considerations motivated their activities abroad before World War I. The postwar economic growth of the United States provided capital for more foreign investment and greater opportunity for American companies to compete internationally. The fear of domestic crude shortages also stimulated interest in exploiting foreign oil sources.

Not until the late 1920s, however, did American firms begin to make significant in-roads into the oil areas of Asia and the Middle East, and even into productive regions in Latin America. The financial risk posed limits to all but the largest companies. Moreover, American firms were constrained by powerful competitors, especially British and Dutch companies, who had active support of their governments. Attempts to block American companies from entering Asian and Middle Eastern ventures grew out of a legitimate fear that a "Standard Oil Monopoly" would spread abroad. In addition, there was an intense desire to control oil supplies in order to enhance national power.

The strategic importance of oil was not lost on American political leaders. Oil was inextricably linked to national security and industrialization. As the United States emerged as a global power in the postwar years, government interest in world oil supplies and oil markets also grew. Republican and Democratic administrations alike favored American economic penetration abroad, and they supported the efforts of American oil companies to compete against companies from other nations.

The majors, especially, were never quite certain as to the extent of government support. At home, independents felt threatened by the international ventures of the majors and feared competition from foreign oil. While the federal government supported the growth and prosperity of the domestic oil industry, it also promoted the interests of the majors as long as those interests did not interfere with other U.S. commitments abroad. As a consequence, U.S. oil policy undulated with the currents of domestic and international events. American oil companies abroad were at their strongest when they advanced the interests of the nation and at their most vulnerable when they were caught in diplomatic crises.

JERSEY STANDARD GOES ABROAD

The prewar history of American oil companies abroad belongs to Jersey Standard and is primarily a story of exporting enterprise. In the mid-1860s, 28 to 59 percent of all American-refined oil was exported. In 1866, the total reached 69 percent and never dropped below 64 percent through the mid-1880s. Most exported oil was sold overseas through independent merchants. In time, several of the component companies within the Standard Trust were involved in foreign business. Standard of Ohio invested in a refinery in Galicia in 1879; New York Standard developed the Oriental trade in kerosene; Standard affiliate Waters-Pierce built a marketing network in Mexico in the mid-1880s.

Production of oil at the gigantic Russian fields of Baku in the 1880s initiated the European side of the world petroleum industry and gave Standard its first international competition. For a brief period during the 1890s, Baku oil production surpassed that produced in the United States, and it was the cause of the so-called oil war in the 1880s between Russian and American oil. Standard was not timid in the encounter; it first cut prices and then established foreign subsidiaries to monitor the trade. This led to the formation of the Anglo-American Oil Company, Ltd. in 1888, which marketed American oil and put British business under Standard's direction. The new affiliate supervised the trade east of Suez more effectively than did the American companies.

Anglo-American transformed Standard's interests abroad. From marketing it branched out into producing properties. By 1907, Jersey Standard was a giant multinational business with fifty-five foreign enterprises, and, by 1911, it had sixty-seven affiliates involved in foreign trade.

While strong in Europe, Canada, and Latin America, Standard had yet to make headway in Asia, Africa, or Oceania. With the 1911 dissolution, these latter areas went to other Standard oil units. Practically all the companies continued to expand abroad, especially Jersey Standard and New York Standard. Jersey Standard, fearing antitrust action if it expanded in the United States, put its efforts into building markets and refining and producing abroad.

MULTINATIONALS IN LATIN AMERICA

Latin America, especially Mexico and Venezuela, offered American companies their most immediate opportunities for exploiting foreign sources of oil. Before American oil companies gained concessions in Mexico, significant portions of the economy had come under the sway of the United States. American mining interests in Mexico, for example, had a long history well before oil was produced. American capital, especially, provided the means to develop the economic potential of the southern neighbor, but at a price that Mexicans were not always willing to pay.

Before 1900, oil ventures in Mexico were modest and did not threaten large-scale exploitation of the local economy. In 1900, however, foreign interest in Mexico turned from marketing and refining to production. Edward L. Doheny incorporated the Mexican Petroleum Company and began drilling in 1901. By 1910, a true bonanza was underway. Although Aguila Company, a British firm, became the largest producer in Mexico, more than half of the 34,000 barrels a day in the early 1910s were produced by American companies. At that time, Mexico ranked third behind the United States and Russia in oil production.

Unfortunately for foreign oil companies, the bonanza coincided with the eruption of revolution in Mexico. Beginning in 1911, the revolution brought to an end the thirty-five year rule of Porfirio Diaz. The Mexican dictator viewed foreign investment and exploitation of resources as a means to economic progress for his country, and he saw it as a means to gain personal wealth.

Intellectual and spiritualist, Francisco I. Madero, led the social revolution, which resulted in the overthrow of the dictator. Rumors circulated that Standard had backed Madero because Diaz's policies favored the British. If this is true Standard may have calculated poorly, for once the revolution was set in motion the outcome was unpredictable. The evolving socialist cast to the revolution clearly ran counter to the capitalist doctrines espoused by foreign companies.

Soon the revolutionary leaders came to view reform of oil policies as the centerpiece for a new relationship with the world powers. But wishing was not going to make it so. In the case of the United States, the vast resources of the oil companies and Washington's strong support for economic expansion made any drastic shift in policy unlikely. The credibility of the revolutionary leaders was also undermined by the rise and fall of one new Mexican government after another.

The importance of Mexican oil in a world market kept oil companies from becoming timid in the face of the revolution. After Madero put a tax on oil production, for example, multinationals refused to cut back production. When General Victoriano Huerta overthrew Madero in 1913, foreign investments dwindled, but oilmen continued their activities. Resentment of American oil companies was not powerful enough at the time to offset the economic interest in continued oil production.

In 1914, revolutionary zeal for national control of Mexican oil was neutralized by wartime demands. The search for oil in the Western Hemisphere accelerated, and Mexican production more than tripled by 1919, making Mexico the second largest producer in the world. By war's end, almost every major American oil company had investments in Mexico.

As the war subsided so did the oil boom in Mexico. Increased taxes imposed by successive revolutionary governments and talk of expropriation discouraged new investments. The situation was aggravated by labor problems, salt-water seepage in wells, and the continual debate over ownership of subsurface rights. With opportunities cropping up elsewhere, especially in Venezuela, the determination of oil companies to wait out the revolution subsided. Between 1921 and 1929, Mexican production declined from 193 million barrels to 45 million. By 1926, Mexican production was more than 50 percent less than what it had been during the peak years of the war.

Through the early years of the revolution, the U.S. State Department supported the rights of businessmen in Mexico, but it was not an activist agent for the oil companies. Complex diplomatic issues often went beyond the narrower interests of oil. For example, President Wilson authorized American forces to bombard Vera Cruz and occupy the city in April 1914, to redress grievances against the Huerta government. Businessmen were appalled by the display, not wanting their interests sacrificed for the sake of upholding American honor.

A change in policy toward Mexico in the 1920s also affected business interests there. The Mexican Constitution of 1917 called for more radical political and social reforms, including the curbing of foreign ownership of lands, mines, and oil fields. A 1918 decree made oil a national resource, with title to oil lands converted into concessions. The Alvaro Obrègon government imposed higher taxes on foreign industries in the early 1920s, and the Mexican Congress enacted a law in 1925 to accommodate eventual nationalization of the oil industry.

The State Department did little to break the logjam over the higher taxes and only protested weakly about the proposed nationalization. Its new approach in the 1920s was more conciliatory, largely because the old-style interventionism was accomplishing very little. One example of this changing attitude was the so-called Clark Memorandum (1928), a major step in advancing the Good Neighbor Policy. It redefined the Monroe Doctrine as "a case of the U.S. v. Europe, and not of the U.S. v. Latin America." In light of the shifting tone of American policy, the interests of the oil companies were not set aside, only placed in a new context.

Outside Mexico, the pattern of oil company penetration and governmental support varied from situation to situation. Nothing better demonstrates the diversity of experience than the contrast between activities in Venezuela and Colombia. From the early 1920s onward, there was a steady transfer of American oil interests from Mexico to Venezuela. This was due in part to the increasingly hostile climate in Mexico but also because of the promise of the Venezuelan fields and the accommodating political climate.

Royal Dutch-Shell drilled the first commercial well in 1914. By 1928, Venezuela ranked second in world production.

American interest in Venezuela surfaced before the abandoning of Mexico in the 1920s. In response to the postwar oil shortage scare, more aggressive British activity, and the request of oil companies for diplomatic aid, the Wilson administration helped U.S. companies secure concessions as early as 1919. Standard of Indiana and Gulf played the crucial role in the penetration by American firms in the early 1920s. (It was not until the mid-1930s that Jersey Standard came to dominate Venezuela, largely at the expense of Gulf.) By 1928, more than thirty-five firms had concessions, and Americans controlled more than fifty percent of production.

The success of American oil companies in Venezuela was accomplished primarily at the expense of Royal Dutch-Shell and British influence in Latin America. The British could not expand concessions in the wake of rising American economic power throughout the world. Moreover, unlike in the Middle East and Asia, neither British companies nor their government had the leverage to compete with Jersey Standard or match the influence of the U.S. government in Latin America.

The case in Colombia presented quite a different picture. Colombia would never become an oil-producing country on the scale of Venezuela, but interest in oil was widespread throughout Latin America. U.S. prospects, however, were reduced because of anti-American feelings in Colombia. The anti-American attitude was the result of Theodore Roosevelt's role in severing Panama from Colombia in 1903 in order to gain a canal route through Central America. Despite local protests, American prospectors received a concession in 1916 and triggered another oil boom. In 1920, Jersey Standard undertook large-scale operations. It urged the State Department to improve relations with Colombia through a new treaty that would pay for injuries caused during the revolt. Unlike the situations in Venezuela and Mexico, the oil company played a central role in obtaining concessions and working toward an accommodation with the host government.

The 1920s were a heyday for American oil interests in the Western Hemisphere and Canada. In South America, U.S. companies made important headway in marketing, where every country except Peru imported oil. Impressive networks were developed in Brazil and Argentina, with Jersey Standard as the leading marketer and followed far behind by Shell. Refining developed more slowly; few companies refined imported crude in host nations until the late 1920s.

Production proved very successful in Venezuela, but it was the only country where petroleum legislation was entirely favorable to the oil companies. In Colombia, Ecuador, Bolivia, Argentina, and elsewhere, they continued to seek more leverage and less constraints from unfavorable legislation and taxation. The companies also fought hostile terrain and sweltering climates in their search for oil.

However, oil companies were bold in seeking their fortunes. The interests and aspirations of Latin American nations were subservient to American economic fortunes and physical security. Oil companies risked little in asserting their claim to the black gold of the region with the Monroe Doctrine as their guide.

OIL IN THE MIDDLE EAST

It was logical for American oil companies to expand into Latin America, given its proximity to the United States and the early successes in Mexico. But American oil companies were not the pioneers in the rich fields of the Middle East. With few markets in the area and little diplomatic interest, that area fell to the European powers to first exploit what would become the greatest oil bonanza of modern times.

The opening of the Middle Eastern fields began very modestly in Persia (known as Iran after 1935). An Australian gold miner and mineral explorer, William K. D'Arcy, struck oil in 1908. The next year, with financial support from the Burmah Oil Company, he formed the Anglo-Persian Oil Company (APOC). The risky venture survived because, six days before World War I began, the House of Commons obtained royal consent to bring APOC under British control. The major impetus was the fact that the British navy had converted from using coal to using petroleum. When APOC offered to secure Middle Eastern oil in exchange for financial support from the British government, a great opportunity presented itself. The APOC negotiations eventually led to the establishment of British Petroleum (BP), a leader in international oil.

At about the same time that D'Arcy struck oil in Persia, similar activity was taking place in Mesopotamia (called Iraq after 1921). A Turkish concession led to the creation of the Turkish Petroleum Company (TPC) in 1912, which was composed of APOC, Royal Dutch-Shell, German interests, and Armenian Calouste S. Gulbenkian (who played a central role in the TPC negotiations).

Had it not been for World War I, the Middle Eastern fields might have taken many more years to be developed. Ready availability of oil elsewhere provided for the immediate needs of industrialized powers. But the war dramatized the strategic importance of oil beyond its immediate markets. The development of Middle Eastern oil, therefore, was future-oriented, emphasizing production rather than marketing outlets. Moreover, the strategic importance of oil supplies made government involvement crucial. In this context, American companies were at a disadvantage, lacking the kind of governmental involvement practiced in Europe.

Soon after the Versailles peace settlement, the British government sought to exclude all foreign oil companies from areas mandated to them, especially Palestine and Mesopotamia. With the British army occupying a large portion of the old Ottoman Empire, English business acquired an obvious advantage in the region. At an Allied conference in San Remo, Italy (1920), the British worked out an arrangement with the French to aid their respective oil companies in acquiring concessions in the Middle East and to bar other nationals. The French were receptive, since they had their own mandates in Lebanon and Syria and had acquired the German interest in TPC as part of the wartime settlement. They needed a strong economic ally in the area to promote their fledgling oil industry. The San Remo agreement virtually divided the Middle East oil rights between the two nations, with the British acquiring about 50 percent of the world's proven resources. The United States obviously felt threatened by this power play.

OIL AND THE OPEN DOOR POLICY

San Remo set off a chain of events that eventually led to the participation of American companies in the Middle East. Momentum for American participation came primarily from Jersey Standard. In the wake of the 1911 dissolution—which left it with direct control over only 8 percent of production for its refining capacity—Jersey Standard needed crude. Walter C. Teagle, its dynamic president, led American oilmen in requesting State Department support to obtain concessions in the British-held areas.

In part, the oilmen blamed the U.S. government for not taking the lead earlier, but they failed to realize that the world situation had changed substantially since the war. By 1920, however, there was a uniformity of spirit and determination among American oilmen and their government. Rejecting the San Remo agreement, support grew for an "open door" principle to be applied to commercial matters. Secretary of State John Hay had circulated the first open door notes in 1899 and 1900, in response to a potential partitioning of China. On the surface, the notes expressed concern for maintaining the political and territorial integrity of China, but more practically they implied support for American economic penetration. It was in this latter sense that the revived open door policy was applied to Middle East oil.

Beginning in 1920, the State Department began a strenuous effort to gain American entry into Mesopotamia. Government officials reminded the British that the United States had played a major role in keeping Allies supplied with oil during the war (three-fifths of foreign demand) but was being cast aside after the emergency passed. Beyond the rhetoric, the State Department sought to develop international agreements to settle the controversy. Congress also became involved; it passed the Mineral Leasing Act in 1920, which stated that no leases of public lands could be extended to nationals of countries that did not extend similar privileges to Americans. However, a proposal for the formation of a government-owned company to search for oil was not enacted.

Jersey Standard realized that penetration into the Middle East fields required two things. First, several American oil companies had to participate to convince the State Department that Standard was not simply looking out for its own interests—although it was looking out for its own interests. Second, direct negotiations with the TPC members were imperative.

Standard's strategy worked on the State Department. Under increasing pressure from Washington, and with the TPC concession on somewhat shaky footing, resistance to American participation ebbed. Tactically, bringing American firms into the consortium as a minority partner did not threaten the European partners' control. For the British, especially, such a gesture bought some needed good will with the United States at a time when a developing naval rivalry threatened to sap the economies of both nations.

In the summer of 1922, TPC accepted American entry. Originally, Jersey Standard had assembled seven companies including itself into the consortium: Standard of New York (Socony), Texas, Gulf, Sinclair, Atlantic Refining, and Pan American Petroleum and Transport (sold to Standard Indiana in 1925). When the final agreement was reached in 1928, the American syndicates, without Texas and Sinclair, received 23.75 percent of the newly organized (1929) Iran Petroleum Company (IPC), and they became partners with APOC, Shell, CFP, and Gulbenkian. Three years later, all but Jersey and Socony had dropped out of the American group. Hardly a victory for the open door principle, membership in IPC gave American oil companies their first foothold in the Middle East.

THE RED LINE AND AS IS AGREEMENTS

American entry did little to make the international oil industry more competitive. Two important agreements in 1928 set the pattern for Middle East oil development, until after World War II, and effectively limited competition in production and marketing of crude. Contributing to this situation was the rising surpluses of world oil that stimulated an interest in limiting output and allocating markets. American companies in IPC quickly lost their interest in the open door and worked in concert with British, Dutch, and French interests to reinforce this noncompetitive system.

IPC was particularly interested in establishing guidelines that would both preclude competition from nonmember oil companies and reduce competition among the members. In July 1928, the Group Agreement (or "Red Line" Agreement) was accepted as a basic policy. Members would not seek concessions or begin operations independently within an area circumscribed on a map of the Middle East by a red line. This area encompassed Turkey, Iraq, Saudi Arabia, and adjoining sheikdoms (it did not include Iran, Kuwait, Israel or Trans-Jordan). With the exception of Saudi Arabia, the remaining area was already under the control of IPC members. This was a self-denying agreement meant to maintain long-term control of oil by companies who dominated world markets and production.

The Red Line Agreement restricted production without effectively addressing marketing. A series of price wars in the 1920s encouraged the major companies to seek a solution as quickly as possible. Royal Dutch-Shell and Socony began a major price war which started over Russian oil but spread throughout the world. Sir Henri Deterding of Royal Dutch-Shell tried to end the crisis. As part of his plan, in August 1928, he rented Achnacarry Castle in Scotland, ostensibly for a grouse-shooting outing with Walter Teagle of Jersey Standard and Sir John Cadman of APOC. The three men represented the major clout in international oil.

By September, the three oilmen had secretly formulated a set of principles to stabilize the world's major marketing areas. Under the arrangement, each company retained its current share of the world market—"as is"—which would effectively block new competitors from those established markets. (The United States was originally excluded from the agreement for fear of antitrust suits.)

A pricing arrangement was also agreed upon, often referred to as "Gulf Plus" pricing. This meant that all oil, regardless of where it was produced or the cost of its production, would be priced as if it were produced in American oil fields along the Gulf of Mexico. The cost of transporting the oil from the gulf to the point of sale would be added to the price. This plan protected the price of American oil—usually the highest in the world—and also offered great profits to companies selling cheap oil to nearby markets. Cartel arrangements were later agreed upon, which allowed swapping of petroleum contracts to take advantage of profits on the new arrangement.

The "As Is" Agreement was not fully revealed to the public until 1952. By 1932, however, it had been approved by all American companies operating abroad. Through the 1930s, the international oil community had an outline for maintaining prices overseas. And while the agreement was never fully implemented, it added to the noncompetitive nature of the world oil industry. Oilmen had worked out, on paper at least, some of their most difficult problems by 1930. But as Calouste Gulbenkian stated: "Oilmen are like cats. One never knows when listening to them whether they are fighting or making love."[1]

OIL IN THE FAR EAST

American penetration into Asian oil fields proved, if anything, more difficult than did penetration into the Middle East. In the nineteenth century, Jersey Standard had a near monopoly in marketing in the area. But stiff competition from European companies eventually eroded Standard's control, and it turned attention to the acquisition of producing territories.

The greatest impediment to American production in Asia was Royal Dutch-Shell. In 1890, a small Indonesian company was chartered to exploit oil in the Dutch East Indies, which became Royal Dutch. In 1900, the rise of an aggressive and brilliant Dutchman, Henri Deterding, as manager of the company proved to be the turning point in its fortunes. Soon Deterding

[1]Cited in Mira Wilkins, *The Maturing of Multinational Enterprises . . . 1914 to 1970* (Cambridge, Mass., 1974), p. 87.

brought together the three largest foreign competitors of Standard—Royal Dutch, Shell Transport and Trading Company, and the French Rothschilds. Together in 1903, they formed a new marketing organization, Asiatic Petroleum. Needing more marketing outlets for his own company, Deterding made an alliance with Shell in 1907. Shell agreed to the arrangement, because it needed more production for its marketing operations. A marriage of convenience, Royal Dutch-Shell soon expanded into Europe and became one of Standard's chief international rivals.

Royal Dutch-Shell did not have sufficient power to push Standard out of the Far East, but it did all it could to frustrate further American activity. Between Deterding's company and the Dutch government, Standard was blocked from acquiring concessions in the Dutch East Indies. Similarly, Burmah Oil blocked Standard in Burma and India. Just before the outbreak of World War I, however, Standard got a toehold in the Dutch East Indies, through its own Dutch subsidiary. Standard, however, did not discover commercial quantities of oil in South Sumatra until 1922, and the Dutch government did not yield to Standard and State Department pressure for additional concessions until 1928.

Throughout the 1910s and 1920s, Standard found itself in intense price wars with Royal Dutch-Shell and Burmah (which was linked to APOC in India). In most cases the United States government provided little assistance. One exception occurred in 1922, when the Department of the Interior declared the Netherlands a nonreciprocating country, which strained relations between the two nations but helped to change the concession policy of the Dutch. Other companies attempted to develop interests in Asia and the Pacific, most notably Socal in the Philippines and the Dutch East Indies and Sinclair in Portuguese Angola and the Gold Coast of Africa. Socony, a rising oil power in the area, operated as a distribution outlet for Jersey Standard in the 1920s.

MIDDLE EAST OIL IN THE 1930s

Conditions in the United States and abroad changed sufficiently in the 1930s that a whole new round of development in the international oil industry occurred. The extensive production and marketing activity of the international oil industry in the 1920s combined with the bonanza strikes in Texas and Oklahoma to create a serious oil glut. Fears of depletion had long subsided in the United States. Domestic production continued to rise, but exports declined because of worldwide economic problems and other than American suppliers meeting demand.

The changing conditions contributed to intensified competition for the limited foreign markets—and a shift in the response of government. The Hoover administration encouraged voluntary restrictions on oil imports, followed by a tax on imported crude in 1932. Between 1929 and 1939, official support for American companies operating in the Middle East subsided, due primarily to excess supplies at home and from Latin America. The Roosevelt administration, preoccupied with the depression, devoted little time to developing a coherent policy for foreign oil.

The story of American participation in international oil in the 1930s is largely the story of oilmen themselves. While oil companies operating abroad received lukewarm governmental support, they were also free from much official supervision in conducting their affairs.

Socal in Bahrain: Crossing the Red Line

Socal was the first company outside the IPC to extend American interests in Middle East oil. After an unsuccessful search for foreign oil in the 1920s, Socal, in 1930, finally acquired prospecting rights on the Persian Gulf island of Bahrain—generally regarded on the fringes of the red line. Socal operated through a new subsidiary, the Bahrain Petroleum Company, Ltd. (Bapco).

The British were unhappy with this foot in the door. Bahrain was situated in a strategic location essential to the security of India. But the British had not responded to offers to develop Bahrain's potential as an oil-producing area themselves. Gulf Oil, however, accepted an option in 1927, but because Gulf was a member of IPC at the time it posed no immediate threat to British interests. Gulf offered the option to IPC, as was required by the Red Line Agreement, but it was rejected. Despite British obstructionism, Gulf transferred its option to nonmember Socal in 1928. A compromise with the British was struck, and Socal acquired the concession through a subsidiary incorporated in Canada with British citizens in top management positions.

With the confusing negotiations behind them, Socal discovered oil in 1932. Since Socal was not a party to IPC agreements, its activities also threatened entry into Saudi Arabia—another territory within the red line but undeveloped by the IPC.

Saudi Arabia and the Origins of ARAMCO

From an American point of view, Saudi Arabia had little meaning until World War II underscored its strategic importance. However, this desert nation sat atop oil reserves estimated to contain nearly half of all oil in the noncommunist world.

Aside from its physical obstacles to oil exploration, Saudi Arabia was at the center of the Muslim world: it was custodian to the sacred cities of Mecca and Medina. An impoverished nation, it had come under the rule of the House of Saud, where kinship and central authority dominated the philosophy of government. The latest king, Abdul Azziz Ibn Saud, was an exceptional leader, but one with few material resources. Revenue came primarily from the annual pilgrimage to Mecca. Hearing about the strike in Bahrain, the king hoped to seek revenue through oil concessions. But he was suspicious of non-Arabs exploiting the resources of his country. He was even dubious about the prospects of finding oil at all. In fact, in 1930, he had turned down Socal's request for a concession.

King Saud changed his mind in 1933. The Bahrain strike was one reason; it gave him some hope and confidence in Socal. He had tried to remain friendly with the British, but he was particularly suspicious of a concession that might encourage their influence in his country. On the other hand, the king did not have a strong preference for Americans. But he had developed good relations with Protestant medical missionaries before World War I, and he was aware of the vast resources that the United States possessed. Still, he was wise enough to play the British off against the Americans when the need arose.

Saud turned to Socal because it offered something he wanted—gold. Gold meant real wealth, something tangible, and he agreed to a concession provided he received a healthy advance against future royalties. This insured the king of income whether or not Socal struck oil. The concession consisted of the eastern half of Saudi Arabia. The agreement further provided that the king would not tax the company. In return, Socal would make every effort to employ Saudi nationals and agreed not to interfere in the internal affairs of the nation. Although the IPC had bought up several concessions to keep competitors out of the region, the Red Line Agreement could not prevent non-members from seeking their own concessions.

To pursue the concession, Socal established the California Arabian Standard Oil Company (CASOC). CASOC's task in discovering oil was formidable: desert conditions were brutal. It took time to convert illiterate nomads into oil workers. And the company had to operate under the constraints of religious fundamentalism. The most dutiful among the followers of the Koran remained suspicious of Western ways and Western technology. Furthermore, CASOC operated with little aid from the American government. A diplomatic post was not established in Saudi Arabia until the eve of World War II.

The striking of oil in commercial quantities in March 1938, was a major feat. But its immediate impact was to aggravate the problem that Socal, Bapco and CASOC faced—inadequate markets. When Bahrain became productive, Socal encountered difficulty in finding markets in areas where IPC had a stranglehold. Lacking a foreign marketing organization and failing to attract buyers, the company first turned to building its own refinery. CASOC then approached Texas Company, which had a worldwide marketing organization but inadequate crude. The resulting agreement gave Texas 50 percent of Bapco and consolidated its marketing facilities east of Suez into a new subsidiary, California Texas Oil Company, Ltd. (which became Caltex in July 1936). In a separate agreement, Texas received 50 percent interest in CASOC in exchange for cash payments. It was a marriage made in oil heaven, and the beginning of the most important American oil company in the Middle East, later called the Arabian-American Oil Company (ARAMCO).

LATIN AMERICAN OIL IN THE 1930s

An optimistic future seemed to lay ahead for American oil companies in the Middle East. The greatest impediment was the potential breakdown in amicable relations with rival multinationals. In the Latin America of the 1930s, however, the host countries became increasingly important. The assertiveness of governments in Bolivia and Mexico permanently changed the relationship between oil firms and the countries in which they operated. More important, questions of who controlled underground mineral rights and who controlled the economic destiny in the developing nations were being raised, and these issues had worldwide repercussions.

The relationship between most oil companies and their host governments in Latin America had been uncomplicated. Oil companies received concessions for which they paid some form of royalty. Since it was most expedient, these arrangements were made with one or a few individuals, who were in controlling positions, in the host country. Governmental regulations were few and taxes remained low, giving oil companies great latitude in their operations. In cases where the strikes proved successful, the firms amassed great wealth. In some cases, the oil companies provided employment, new towns, and a higher standard of living within certain sectors of the country. But these benefits were not commensurate with the profits accrued. As a matter of course, the contact between oil companies and the native populations was accomplished by great indifference to local mores and customs. American roughnecks and drillers were often crude, tough, and insensitive, while management personnel were aloof and condescending toward the locals. Racial hostility was sometimes at the heart of these relations.

In the 1930s, growing nationalist fervor in Latin America unleashed the deep resentment against all foreign intruders. Oil companies faced a strong wave of criticism, unmatched in any previous era. In Chile, Brazil, and Uruguay, which had yet to become producing oil countries, rumblings against foreign exploitation became heated. In the producing countries of Argentina, Colombia, and Venezuela, tensions between the oil companies and the governments mounted.

Bolivia and Jersey Standard

The first crucial stand by a host government occurred in Bolivia. Jersey Standard struck oil there in the 1920s. After acquiring new sources in Mexico and Venezuela, it began negotiations in 1936 to sell out to the Bolivian government. However, in March 1937, a military junta seized the company's properties and turned them over to a newly formed government company. Standard protested strenuously, seeking the aid of the State Department and exhausting what legal remedies it could through the Bolivian courts. The State Department failed to take an active role until 1940, and a settlement was not reached until 1942. Had Jersey Standard wanted to continue operations in Bolivia, this incident would have taken on greater significance. Nonetheless, it was a signal—though largely ignored—to companies operating in Latin America.

The Mexican Expropriation

The Mexican Expropriation of 1938 is generally recognized as the turning point in the ability of developing nations to control their mineral resources and to devise models for economic self-determination. It was also an important test for the United States' Good Neighbor Policy. The policy, intended to win goodwill and continued economic and political suasion in Latin America, disavowed the long-standing practice of intervention as a legitimate means of protecting American interests.

The insensitivity of the oil companies to the interests of Mexico, and an overreaction to pressures by the Mexican labor unions, turned a controversy into a confrontation.[2] In 1935, some ten thousand workers, belonging to nineteen separate unions, formed a single national union—Sindicato de Trabajadores Petroleros de la Republica Mexicana (STPRM). Affiliating with the Confederacion de Trabajadores Mexicanos (CTM), it established a strong and growing labor confederation. In a general assembly held in 1936, the unions drafted their first collective-bargaining contract. Their primary demands were higher wages and increased benefits.

The Mexican courts declared a worker strike, from May to June 1937, to be legal, and a Mexican commission declared that the oil companies could afford to raise wages and benefits. The companies argued that they were already paying the highest wages in Mexico, and that the union demands amounted to "confiscation by slow strangulation." Workers responded that the companies' rebuttal stated the case in relative terms only. The companies operated their businesses with harsh discipline, provided appallingly poor living conditions, and demanded excessively hard work. These issues, plus resentments stirred by years of revolution, meant that the workers would not relent.

In December, the Federal Labor Board declared in favor of the union. In March 1938, the Mexican Supreme Court rejected the companies' appeal and gave them six days to enter into a new contract. A temporary suspension was granted, but it only exacerbated the controversy. Faced with the impasse, President Lazaro Cardenàs declared that the refusal of the oil companies to act left him no choice but to invoke a 1936 law empowering him to expropriate foreign property. On March 18, Cardenàs confiscated the property of seventeen American and European companies.

The Mexican government began preparations to run the oil industry itself. Petromex Petroleos Mexicanos (Pemex) took over operations, primarily employing unskilled workers who had to learn all facets of the industry over-

---

[2]The largest oil interest in Mexico was Royal Dutch-Shell, followed by Jersey Standard, Consolidated (Sinclair), Cities Service, and Gulf.

night. Little confidence was placed in the venture from within or without Mexico. Nonetheless, the emotional response within the country was thunderous. Expropriation Day became a national holiday, and the revolution appeared to have produced a visible sign of success. A March 22 gathering of the CTM at the National Palace attracted 200,000 people, who cheered President Cardenàs.

The oil companies worked for a reversal of the expropriation decision. They staged boycotts to deprive Mexico of tankers for shipping oil and additives. They participated in secondary boycotts meant to cut off needed machinery to Pemex. They railed against the Mexicans in their company publications. And then they turned to the federal government for aid.

American officials were shocked at the expropriation, but they faced a dilemma. The U.S. government had supported the principle of expropriation, in the abstract at least, but they also wanted the restoration of oil companies' property and continued American participation in extracting oil. The expropriation meant that all U.S. economic interests in Latin America might eventually be in jeopardy.

The goals of the Good Neighbor Policy complicated the government's role. Would the expropriation be the first major test? How would the goals of the Good Neighbor Policy clash with the interests of the oil companies? The immediate reaction of Secretary of State Cordell Hull was anger and disgust. He told the Mexican ambassador that confiscating foreign property was the sign of a nation slipping into decadence and backwardness. He tried to convince FDR that the issue should be met through a defense of the principle of property rights. But Hull was constrained by a president not particularly sympathetic to the big oil companies. Hull was also at cross-purposes with the Ambassador to Mexico Josephus Daniels, who was exceedingly sympathetic to the Mexican Revolution and the position of the Cardenàs government in the oil controversy.

What was available to the State Department—other than accepting expropriation—was economic suasion and the withholding of aid. Efforts to accomplish these ends proved unsuccessful, however. The Treasury Department suspended the agreement for purchases of Mexican silver, but it soon resumed open market purchases since the mines were owned primarily by Americans. In 1938 and 1939, the United States blocked Mexican oil sales to the United States Navy, encouraged other Latin American and European nations to boycott Mexico, and tried to throw more oil business toward Venezuela through higher quotas. None of these efforts led to a reversal of policy in Mexico.

The Mexican government and the circumstances of the late 1930s forced the State Department to choose the "high road" and accept expropriation. Facing American economic boycotts and threats, Mexico turned to Germany and Japan as oil markets. FDR stepped in at this point, easing tension with Mexico by sending Vice President Henry Wallace to the inauguration of the new President of Mexico, Avila Camacho (a moderate). But more important, the United States promised Mexico a continuing market for its other minerals if it would agree to embargo such goods from the Axis powers. This gave Hull room to work for a settlement.

In 1940, Sinclair Oil settled with Mexico on its own, but the battle raged over what was fair compensation. Oilmen believed that the "potential" value of their property should be figured into the equation. Mexico did not see it that way. A final agreement was reached in 1943, amounting to about $29 million. This was way below the oil companies' bloated figures but more than Mexico had initially offered. There was no challenge to the Mexican claim of expropriation in the agreement, although Hull and the oil companies held out hope for re-entry at some future date.

For Mexico, the expropriation was not a single victory over foreign economic exploiters; rather, it was a culmination of the revolution. It signaled a way for weaker nations to deal with strong ones, and it was one of the very few victories against the "Colossus of the North." Less dependent on foreign investment and expertise in the 1940s, Mexico now had to face the difficult road of turning a moral victory into a practical one.

For American oil companies, the expropriation was a humiliation and a foreboding of things to come. But it was also a valuable lesson in dealing with host countries, a lesson that some multinationals took to heart in the Middle East and throughout the rest of Latin America. Many companies, however, ignored the lesson.

For the United States government, the event demonstrated that economic interests and strategic interests are not always compatible. The Good Neighbor Policy survived—not as a major shift in U.S. goals—but as a subtler form of our old Latin American policy.

The rise of American multinational oil companies coincided with the emergence of the United States as a global economic power. The old "world of empires" at the turn of the century had faded, but a new era of economic expansionism found American firms in the thick of the scramble. As World War II would demonstrate, America's new economic interests in Latin America, the Middle East, and Asia would be transformed into broader strategic interests. Not only had the United States become the leading producer of oil, but it was establishing a reputation as a leading explorer, marketer, and transporter of crude and refined petroleum products.

National and international energy issues were linked since World War I. The benefits of this new arrangement were manifest in the success of Jersey Standard, Socal, and the other multinationals. But as the Mexican expropriation demonstrated, energy expansionism confused the lines between national policy and economic interests, and it raised serious questions about the exploitation of underdeveloped countries. Domestically, the conflict between majors and independents, between oil exports and domestic supplies, was aggravated by the penetration of American multinationals abroad. Few could deny, however, the important role of the United States in the growth and transformation of the international oil industry.

FURTHER READING

Philip J. Baram. *The Department of State in the Middle East, 1919–1945.*
    Philadelphia, 1978.
Lloyd Gardner. *Economic Aspects of New Deal Diplomacy.* Madison, Wis., 1964.
George W. Grayson. *The Politics of Mexican Oil.* Pittsburgh, 1980.
Clayton R. Koppes. "The Good Neighbor Policy and the Nationalization of Mexican
    Oil: A Reinterpretation," *Journal of American History,* vol. 69 (June 1982),
    pp. 62–81.
Robert B. Krueger. *The United States and International Oil.* New York, 1975.
Lorenzo Meyer. *Mexico and the United States in the Oil Controversy, 1917–1942.*
    Austin, Tex., 1972.
Edith T. Penrose. *The Large International Firm in Developing Countries.*
    Cambridge, Mass., 1968.
Mira Wilkins. *The Emergence of Multinational Enterprise: American Business
    Abroad from the Colonial Era to 1914.* Cambridge, Mass., 1970, and
    American Business Abroad from 1914 to 1970. Cambridge, Mass., 1974.
Joan Hoff Wilson. *American Business and Foreign Policy, 1920–1933.* Boston, 1971.
Bryce Wood. *The Making of the Good Neighbor Policy.* New York, 1967; orig. 1961.

CHAPTER 10

World War II and Energy

World War II was an energy-intensive conflict, dependent on the flow of oil and ushering in the atomic age. If anything, World War II had a greater impact on American energy history than did World War I. The United States, relatively speaking, escaped the monumental human carnage that befell Russia, Poland, Great Britain, Germany, China, and Japan. But the duration and scale of this grueling war, which began in Asia in 1937 and ended there in 1945, sorely tested the material resources of the nation. Production of land vehicles, airplanes, ships, heavy equipment of all types, and specialized armaments was conducted on an unprecedented scale, using vast quantities of coal and other energy sources. Demand for oil, gasoline, aircraft fuel, and lubricants strained production, refining, and transportation facilities. Shortages and the unique requirements of global warfare led to innovations such as synthetic fuels, synthetic rubber, and the development of atomic weapons.

While drawing on the experiences of the first world war, the Roosevelt administration moved beyond them to meet the exacting requirements of the new war. With a commitment to a two-ocean navy, a program of peacetime conscription, and a growing sentiment (at least by late 1940 or early 1941) to provide Great Britain with "all aid short of war," defense preparations began more than two years before Pearl Harbor (December 7, 1941).

As before, World War II demanded a central role for the federal government in war production. If Americans had not come to accept the central role of government in the economic life of the nation by the 1940s, they were not shocked by it. More than Woodrow Wilson, Franklin Roosevelt demonstrated an unwillingness to share executive authority with Congress or his staff. He effectively maintained power by distributing responsibility among several underlings, forcing them to compete among themselves for influence. Yet the President did little to discourage greater business concentration, intimate relations between big business and the military, and stronger links among the federal government, the universities, and the private sector.

While the Wilson administration's war production program focused on domestic problems, the Roosevelt administration cast a wider net. The extended role of American multinationals in Latin America, Asia, and the Middle East meant that petroleum was not simply a means to an end but an end in itself. For the United States, protection of international sources of oil and

maintenance of good relations with host governments was as crucial as producing adequate fuels and lubricants for the war effort.

The importance of the Middle East as a source of oil was firmly established during the 1940s. Hemispheric solidarity also became a central concern
of the United States. The global perspective that the United States acquired
in the cold war years is traceable, in part at least, to the growing importance
of international sources of energy as perceived in World War II.

PREPARING FOR WAR

As early as December 1940, Roosevelt challenged the nation to become an
"arsenal of democracy." To help the British repulse the German *Wehrmacht*
without directly involving a reluctant America in the conflict, he directed a
war of mass production. In 1938, the United States began to strengthen its
military in the name of hemispheric defense. The President authorized a War
Resources Board in 1939, whose purpose was to insure that the nation's defense needs were being met. This modest action led to charges that he was
leading the nation into war. Ultimately Roosevelt stripped the board of its
power, not because of the criticism, but because he was unwilling to relinquish control of the defense program. In 1940, he established a cabinet-level
Council of National Defense and a National Defense Advisory Commission,
drawn from the private sector.

As the war in Europe intensified, Roosevelt recast his preparedness program, creating the Office of Emergency Management. One of its principle
agencies, the Office of Production Management, took the lead in the war
production program in January 1941, but its status was modified in September with the creation of the Supply, Priorities, and Allocation Board. The
shuffling of authority did little to prepare the nation adequately for war. But
at least by the Pearl Harbor attack, the United States had a departure point
for war production.

In early 1942, the War Production Board (WPB) was established, and it
quickly became the most important government agency in the coordination of
war production. FDR appointed Donald M. Nelson to head WPB. Trained as
a chemical engineer and serving as a vice president in merchandising for
Sears Roebuck, Nelson garnered wide respect within and outside government. Under Nelson's control, the WPB came closer to centralizing the war
production program than had its predecessor agencies, but the President retained ultimate authority. Conflict among wartime agencies, however, often
meant that efficiency was sacrificed for control, resulting in shortages, delays,
and labor problems.

On the positive side, industrial and agricultural production attained un-
believable levels. In fact, they reached the point where output—especially in
weaponry—created an overabundance by late 1943. During the war the nation spent $186 billion for munitions production alone. Overall, industrial
production increased 96 percent; agricultural production, 50 percent. While

war needs were largely responsible, there was also a major increase in consumer goods, made possible by rising employment, healthier payrolls, and a public determination to buy the things denied them during the depression.

These staggering achievements were not accomplished without difficulties. Insufficient raw materials and their allocations were the most nagging problems. Until the WPB acquired the authority to allocate crucial war materials in mid-1943, there were recurring shortages, squabbles between businesses, and in-fighting among governmental agencies over pet projects. Major shortages occurred in aluminum, steel, gasoline and fuel oil, rubber, and certain foods. All the items were eventually acquired and allocated, often through rationing programs.

Government and business leaders also faced problems of converting civilian manufacturing to wartime production, building new facilities, and developing efficient priorities systems. The federal government supplied five-sixths of the funds required to construct new plants. In fact, by the end of the war, the government owned more than 90 percent of the facilities that produced aircraft, ships, synthetic rubber, and magnesium; 70 percent of all aluminum-producing facilities; and 50 percent of the plants producing machine tools.

Financing alone was not enough to promote an effective conversion program. The Roosevelt administration shied away from a war program based on government operation of essential industries. Its prodding of industry was often too mild, leading to foot-dragging by companies reluctant to give up lucrative business ventures for patriotic duty. Nonetheless, the caution that the WPB exhibited reduced the chance of disrupting the economy and generally allowed conversion to keep pace with available raw materials.

Labor posed a crucial problem for the war effort. In September 1940, a peacetime draft was instituted, resulting in 12.3 million Americans in the armed forces by July 1945. This meant that new sources of labor for war industries had to be tapped. The largest number was drawn from the ranks of the unemployed—about 9 million—but also from among school-age youth, married women, those previously in agriculture, retired citizens, and minorities (especially blacks). In all, the labor force increased from 54 to 64 million between 1940 and 1945.

While payrolls increased drastically and wages began to rise, labor problems took several forms. Training of new people took time. The movement of workers to defense areas created housing shortages, crowding, health problems, and high absenteeism, caused by working long hours. Federal officials attempted to ease labor discontent by placing labor representatives in all defense agencies and appointing labor leaders to some key positions in the war production program. A War Manpower Commission and a National War Labor Board were established. Most of the labor leaders pledged a "no-strike" policy during the war in return for adequate wages, decent working conditions, and fair security. But numerous strikes, especially "outlaw strikes" by those not taking the pledge, occurred.

Friction over wages continued throughout the war. Government officials fell back on what became known as the "little steel" formula, which stated that wages could rise equal to the rise in the cost of living. Although it never became an iron-clad policy and was broken by some unions, it provided a broad framework for dealing with the wage issue. Tension between the government and workers persisted, with some administrators calling on the President to use the draft as a way of keeping dissident workers in line. However, FDR preferred that business and labor resolve their own problems.

COAL AND THE WAR EFFORT

Coal was not the indispensable source in World War II that it was in World War I. Many of its functions were usurped by petroleum, its by-products, and natural gas. Coal production reached an all-time high in 1944 (about 620 million net tons), but it was no longer the dominant fuel in the aggregate. Coal was becoming a more specialized fuel with only four major markets— railroads, home heating, coke producing, and electric power generation.

Adequate supplies and effective delivery of coal, especially in the production of steel, was nonetheless an important concern. But the industry continued to be plagued by its old ghosts—overproduction and low prices. The Bituminous Coal Act of 1937 and other regulations helped the industry to show a profit in 1940—the first time in more than ten years. On the eve of war, however, the government was still propping up a sick industry with an uncertain future.

Almost all government contact with the coal industry prior to and during the war came through the Interior Department. In November 1941, Secretary Harold Ickes was named Solid Fuels Coordinator for National Defense. Eventually an Office of the Solid Fuels Administration for War replaced the coordinator. WPB was also drawn into the picture; it had responsibility for coal-mining equipment and supplies. This led to the typical interagency squabbling, characteristic of the whole war production program. Unfortunately for the coal industry, cooperation between the Interior Department and emergency agencies deteriorated badly by September 1942. Finally, in 1943, difficulties were reduced by the establishment of the Mineral Resources Coordinating Division.

What was required of the industry during the war was expansion—exactly the opposite of what it had been trying to do prior to the conflict. The call for higher production focused attention on manpower. The draft had taken many skilled miners out of the coal fields, but soon government agencies sought to have the army release soldiers to work the mines. This confusing cycle led operators to turn increasingly to mechanized mining. Despite the problems, coal production increased, and it helped relieve the steel shortages.

For the United Mine Workers and its president, John L. Lewis, the war offered an opportunity to advance the cause of miners. With 400,000 miners participating, Lewis suspended work four times in 1943. These strikes led to critical shortages along the East Coast and made Lewis extremely un-popular. In the wake of the strikes, FDR seized the mines but eventually granted substantial wage increases to the UMW in order to get experienced miners back on the job.

OIL: THE ESSENTIAL RESOURCE

Petroleum may not have been the be-all and end-all of the war effort, but it came very close. Military demands for oil had grown astonishingly since World War I, and the uses of petroleum in industry had multiplied more rapidly than anyone could have imagined. By 1939, virtually all naval vessels and approximately 85 percent of the world's merchant ships were burning fuel oil. During the peak of operations on the western front, the U.S. Army Air Force alone consumed fourteen times the total amount of gasoline shipped to Europe between 1914 and 1918. A typical army division required fuel to operate mechanized equipment having 187,000 combined horsepower. In World War I, the typical division utilized equipment with about 4,000 combined horsepower.

Petroleum was high stakes in the war. Part of the wartime strategy was protecting existing oil supplies, gaining additional sources, and restricting or curtailing the enemy's supplies. On paper the Allies appeared to have an overwhelming advantage in petroleum supplies. The United States produced 60 percent of the world output in 1939, while the Axis powers depended primarily on imported oil. These statistics are deceptive, however. Germany initiated a crash program to produce synthetic oil derived from coal. It also captured the substantial oil fields in Galicia and Rumania, plus the stockpiles of oil in France. While the Japanese oil reserves prior to Pearl Harbor were not massive, they provided a cushion until the Japanese overran the Dutch East Indies, Indochina, and Burma.

While the Allies had access to great reserves, they faced serious problems in maintaining their long supply lines across the Atlantic. Because of the dangers of venturing into the Mediterranean, the Allies had to ship oil supplies from the Middle East via South Africa. By as early as May 1942, about 55 tankers servicing the Atlantic seaboard were sunk by Axis submarines.

While plans were worked out to protect oil tankers, American officials set as their goal the maximum production of oil in U.S. fields. They were ultimately successful, supplying 80 percent of the seven billion barrels of crude oil used by the Allies between December 1941, and August 1945. This represented one-fifth of all oil produced in the United States since 1859 and more than half of all supply tonnage shipped overseas during the war.

Accomplishing this feat required industry cooperation as well as a return of governmental policy to maximum production. Federal authorities sought to increase production much like the Wilson administration had done—through subsidies, favorable tax provisions, easing of antitrust activity, effective allocation programs, and a general climate of government-business cooperation. An orderly transition to full production was impossible, however, because of rapidly accelerating war demands. Within a few hours of war, shortages were noticeable. German submarines threatened tankers in the Atlantic; shipments from California and the gulf states to the Northeast were disrupted; and overland transportation was insufficient to take up the slack.

The Petroleum Administration for War

The initial response of government to increased production was slow and haphazard. Congress was reluctant to expand federal controls—especially in the face of congressional pressure from the producing states. In the end, the President took the necessary steps to mobilize the oil industry. Characteristically, FDR was vague about which agency would have primary responsibility. In May 1941, he authorized the Office of Petroleum Coordinator for National Defense (OPCND) with Secretary Ickes in charge. In April 1942, the agency changed its name to the Office of Petroleum Coordinator for War (OPCW), and in December, to the Petroleum Administration for War (PAW).

The initial responsibility of the OPCND was not clear, but it entailed gathering information about military and civilian oil needs and making recommendations for the distribution and allocation of oil supplies. As envisioned by Ickes, the office was to centralize governmental oil activities, to organize itself on lines parallel to the oil industry, and to include an industry committee to advise the staff. Eventually, a central office was established with five district offices and several suboffices. The staff was composed primarily of oil industry people. The Petroleum Industry Council for National Defense, later the Petroleum Industry War Council, was also established.

The OPCND was treated with apprehension within the oil industry. Oilmen were particularly dubious of Ickes, who they believed was an enemy of the industry and a critic of its free market philosophy. They were chary that Ickes had favored nationalizing the industry. The secretary's abrasive personality did not help to dispel their concern. However, Ickes gave little indication that he planned to do more than accomplish maximum production. To alleviate anxieties, he chose Socal Vice President Ralph K. Davies as deputy coordinator, and relied on several industry leaders in running the OPCND and later PAW.

While Ickes set the tone for the government's wartime oil policy, his office did not have absolute sway over development of that policy. In what became a serious intergovernmental battle, Ickes protested against the State Department policy of issuing export licenses for shipment of oil to Japan. Ickes also found that pricing policy was beyond his control. Given these limits, his approach throughout the war was to intervene on the industry's behalf to acquire scarce materials, to soften governmental antitrust policy, and to increase incentives for greater production. Being a pragmatist, he realized that advocacy of the oil industry was the only way to gain influence over oil policy.

The establishment of the Petroleum Administration for War was more than a renaming of the OPCND. It gave Ickes the additional clout he had wanted to perform his duties. In 1942, Ickes made it known that his position as petroleum coordinator hampered his effectiveness. He was particularly frustrated with the lack of centralized government responsibility for oil policy; forty different agencies had jurisdiction over some phase of it. Although FDR was unwilling to grant Ickes the status of "oil czar," he did allow the fiery bureaucrat to submit a tentative proposal. While forced to make several compromises, the creation of PAW in December 1942, gave Ickes more power to issue rules governing the production, transportation, and distribution of petroleum and its by-products. Control over allocation of scarce materials remained with WPB and the regulation of prices with the Office of Price Administration (OPA). In particular, battles with OPA consumed an enormous amount of PAW's time.

The PAW's job was awesome and the problems were never-ending. It is surprising that so much was accomplished amid such intense and complex issues. To make sure that oil production satisfied essential domestic needs, Ickes tried to curb oil exports prior to American involvement in the war. On June 11, 1941, he "ordered" Secretary of State Cordell Hull and Administrator of Export Controls Russell Maxwell to stop exports to Japan. Ickes had no authority to do this, and he only succeeded in infuriating Hull and drawing a reprimand from the President. FDR reminded Ickes that exports to Japan was a foreign policy issue, not an allocations issue. As the war progressed, however, total exports declined until the United States entered the war.

PAW also sought to increase supplies of oil by promoting conservation, such as well-spacing, better secondary recovery, and unitization. In 1943, it issued an order to compel producers to drill no more than one well for every forty acres. Without any formal enforcement powers, it used coercion, such as denying priorities for drilling and refining equipment to uncooperative producers. These policies succeeded only in raising hostility from independents, who felt preyed upon by PAW actions.

Tankers, Trains, and Pipelines—The Problem of Transporting Oil

Bringing enough petroleum from the Southwest oil fields to the Atlantic Seaboard posed the most serious problem. During the early 1940s, it took almost 1.3 million barrels of oil daily to supply eastern needs. What made the supply problem most difficult was the almost total dependence on tankers. Only 5 percent of the oil to the East Coast traveled through pipelines, by rail, or by barge. British requests for tankers in 1941 and stepped-up German submarine attacks in 1942 cut off most tanker deliveries to the East Coast.

Alternative transportation or conservation were two means of counteracting the tanker loss. Ickes urged the reduction of all nonessential uses of oil. He also asked companies to eliminate wasteful tanker runs and to utilize more rail transport. In July 1941, oil companies along the East Coast began a campaign to convince motorists to curtail unnecessary driving. Service stations were asked to cut back their hours. But enforcement of these conservation programs was impossible for the government agencies. Ickes, for the time being, was reluctant to propose rationing.

Voluntary compliance seemed the only immediate alternative. In August, several oil companies began cutting deliveries to wholesalers and retailers. Very reluctantly some oil companies turned to railroad transportation, despite the tremendously higher cost (almost ten times as expensive). The decision resulted in a thirty-fold increase in oil shipments by rail. Fortunately, the British returned about half of the borrowed tankers in October and promised to return the others soon. This allowed Ickes to remove all the restrictions on gasoline sales in the East.

The experiences of 1940 and 1941 led Ickes to examine a longer-range solution to the transportation problem. He decided upon an aggressive campaign for government pipeline construction. To keep the development of pipelines in private hands, eleven major oil companies announced a plan for a National Defense Pipelines and Emergency Pipelines Corporation in 1941 to finance a privately owned system. Midcontinent independents obstructed the project. Local obstacles, especially the denial in granting rights-of-way, also stymied it. FDR's authorizing the study of the problem resulted in a bill that granted rights-of-way to interstate pipeline companies. But WPB refused to allocate steel to pipeline projects, charging that PAW did not utilize available transportation effectively.

Renewed efforts were made after the United States entered the war. In March 1942, Ickes sponsored a meeting in Tulsa, bringing together leading pipeline operators from around the nation. The participants adopted the Tulsa Plan, a ten-point program to establish an extensive national pipeline network using public and private funds. The plan resulted in two massive projects directed by the federal government—the "Big Inch" and the "Little Big Inch." After oil shortages almost reached crisis levels in 1942, the WPB allocated necessary building materials to the Big Inch project. Within 350 days, 1,254 miles of pipeline were constructed, constituting the main line of the Big Inch (the total line ran 1,476 miles). Completed in summer 1943, Big Inch ran from the Southwest to Phoenix Junction, Pennsylvania; the total cost was $78.5 million.

While Big Inch met the need for supplying crude to the East Coast, a second major line, the Little Big Inch, would carry refined petroleum products. This "product pipeline"—completed in December 1943—extended 1,475 miles (a total of 1,714 miles) from Beaumont, Texas, to Linden, New Jersey. It cost $67 million to build. Between 1943 and 1945, both lines delivered almost 380 million barrels from the Texas fields to the East Coast. Projects, primarily dependent on private investment (about $127 million), built another 31 smaller lines. The dramatic increases in pipelines especially served the interests of the majors at the expense of midcontinent and gulf coast independents.

Refining and Aviation Fuel

Refining proved to be much less of a problem than anticipated. However, Ickes and some of his associates were concerned about the availability of aviation fuel. Refineries were often too far removed from sources of production, although Little Big Inch went a long way in solving that problem. Still, it took PAW until 1943 to obtain top priority for acquiring equipment to construct special refineries to produce 100-octane aviation fuel. Sufficient quantities eventually were produced, allaying Ickes' worst fears of a critical shortage.

DWINDLING SUPPLIES AND WARTIME SCARCITIES

The Rubber Shortage and Buna-S

Of all the shortages, the rubber shortage was the most serious and was resolved in the most curious way. By early 1942, the Japanese had seized the Dutch East Indies and Malaya, the source of 90 percent of America's crude rubber. Stockpiled amounts were far from sufficient, and other natural sources in the Southwest and Mexico took too long to grow. These problems were magnified by the staggering wartime demand: armored tanks required 1 ton of rubber each; a B-17 Flying Fortress, .5 tons; and a battleship, a whopping 75 tons.

Synthetic rubber was the answer. The basic technology had been developed in czarist Russia. In Nazi Germany, a whole array of synthetics were being produced out of low-grade coal found in Silesia. American development of synthetic rubber, using a petroleum base, had been seriously delayed because of an agreement between Jersey Standard and an infamous German partner, I. G. Farben. Together they controlled the patent on Buna S, the most common form of synthetic rubber, and also on another synthetic, butyl.

Since an agreement between the two in the late 1920s restricted independent development of synthetic rubber, American companies were in the cold about producing an alternative to natural rubber using petroleum. What made things worse is that, as the war began, the Germans were increasingly unwilling to share secrets about synthetic rubber. In addition, Farben apparently had been conducting industrial espionage in the United States. Because of its close association with Farben, Jersey Standard was faced with charges of criminal conduct and anti-American activity. The government brought civil action against the company in 1942, but Jersey Standard agreed to release all rubber patents—royalty-free—for the duration of the war.

Jersey Standard's synthetic rubber technology was not the only alternative to the rubber shortage. Butadiene, a major component in synthetic rubber, could be derived from alcohol. As a result of its farm price-support program, the federal government had enormous stores of grain for making alcohol. Whiskey distillers had plants that could be converted to the production of grain alcohol with little trouble. Despite the efforts of agricultural groups, other forces were determined that synthetic rubber was to be based on petroleum or natural gas derivatives, not on alcohol.

WPB's Chemicals Branch argued that alcohol was in short supply and would not be able to produce sufficient quantities of synthetic rubber. The real reason for petroleum-based production, however, was quite different. For obvious reasons, Jersey Standard championed their synthetic rubber alternative, as did other members of the oil industry. Furthermore, the Reconstruction Finance Corporation (RFC), which was to provide funding for the project, and the Rubber Reserve Company, a subsidiary of RFC, also opted for petroleum-based production. As economist Robert Solo argued: "They were bankers, and like bankers, they put their trust in the big customers, with substantial assets on hand."[1] Lacking in technical competence, the RFC and the Rubber Reserve failed to acknowledge other promising alternatives. Ickes too came out in favor of petroleum-based production, which only strengthened the case.

With the Germans battering away at Russia in 1942 and no production of synthetic rubber, Congress tried to gain control over the rubber crisis. Senator Guy Gillette (Dem., Ohio) accused Jersey Standard of blocking the use of grain-based alcohol for synthetic rubber production; he then conducted hearings on the matter. Under pressure from the investigation, the Chemicals Branch of WPB announced that instead of a critical shortage, there was a huge surplus of alcohol. As a result, the Rubber Reserve Company reallocated 220,000 of the proposed 700,000 tons of planned synthetic rubber to alcohol production. Beyond this, Congress passed the Rubber Supply Act of 1942, which set up a nonexecutive-controlled agency to promote production of synthetic rubber from alcohol produced from grain and forest products. The President vetoed the bill but did not defend the rubber program.

As rubber supplies dwindled, FDR appealed to Americans to donate "whatever you have that is made of rubber" to a national scrap drive. Within four weeks, 450,000 tons of scrap rubber were collected. However impressive, much of the supply could not be reprocessed. Gas rationing seemed to be a necessary evil, but the President was reluctant to anger powerful opponents of rationing (petroleum companies, automobile interests, state officials fearful of losing gas tax revenues), especially with the election of 1942 just around the corner.

Instead of moving to rationing, FDR appointed an investigating committee led by Bernard Baruch. If the committee recommended rationing, at least FDR would look as if he had tried all other alternatives first. The Baruch committee strongly criticized the planning and organization of the synthetic rubber program, but it believed that it was too late in the war to change courses. Instead, in September 1942, it made three recommendations: (1) it

[1]Robert A. Solo, "The Saga of Synthetic Rubber," *The Bulletin of Atomic Scientists* (April 1980), p. 32.

urged expansion of synthetic rubber output, using petroleum to obtain butadiene; (2) it recommended the appointment of a rubber director to oversee the government's activities in the area; and (3) it supported gas rationing to save tires. After the election, FDR initiated gas rationing for the whole nation, and in January 1943, he imposed a ban on all pleasure driving. This was, at best, a plan made out of desperation. The real victory came with the massive production of synthetic rubber.

Many accounts credit the Baruch committee with stimulating the reorganization of the synthetic rubber program, which led to massive production by 1944. The government spent $700 million to construct 51 plants primarily in Texas, Louisiana, southern California, West Virginia, and Ohio. By 1944, synthetic rubber production soared to 800,000 tons a year—equal to the harvest of 180 million rubber trees. This production represented 87 percent of the rubber used in the United States at the time.

What this story does not tell is the importance of alcohol-based synthetic rubber and a lucky turn of events in the war. With Germany still on the offensive in Russia in early 1943, the Baruch committee called for an output of 450,000 tons of Buna-S; only 181,000 tons were produced. Fortunately, the Russian counteroffensive began in 1943, and the cross-channel invasion by the combined British and American forces was postponed for a year. The projected demand for rubber eased substantially, and the rubber program was given more time to develop. Of the 180,000 tons of synthetic rubber produced in 1943, 130,000 tons came from alcohol-based production and only 20,000 from petroleum derivatives. In 1944, about 362,000 of the 558,000 tons of Buna-S was made from alcohol.[2] If there was a success story in the wartime race to produce synthetic rubber it was not the petroleum-based synthetic rubber program.

Gas Rationing

The need to conserve rubber played a large role in the decision to ration gasoline, and the repercussions of that decision fell directly on the driving public. Gas rationing was short-lived, an inconvenience rather than a permanent readjustment in the transportation habits of American people. However, it continues to be a reminder of the vulnerability of a mechanized society cut off from its major energy supply.

Organizing and monitoring a national gasoline-rationing program bordered on the impossible. Rationing was carried out by a sticker system, which entitled drivers to coupons for gas purchases. A car owner with an "A" sticker received the smallest allocation—three or four gallons a week. Those with "B" stickers had essential driving, such as commuting to a war production plant, and received supplemental allowances. The "C" card was reserved for

[2]Petroleum-based synthetic rubber was produced in large quantities late in the war. Until then, the technical difficulties in setting up a new program and the demand for high-octane aviation fuel (which required the same cut of petroleum as did butadiene) kept its production modest.

doctors and others with specialized driving needs; they too received extra allowances. "T" stickers were for truck drivers who received unlimited gasoline, and "E" stickers were issued for emergency vehicles and granted the similar privilege.

The system was subject to extensive abuse. Most people tried to convince the local OPA board (OPA was in charge of the program) to give them a better sticker because of the essential nature of their contribution to the war effort. As a consequence, probably one-half of all American drivers received B and C stickers.

More serious were illegal attempts to tamper with the system. Truck drivers sometimes sold their excess coupons to service station owners. Counterfeiters found new inspiration copying rationing stamps. OPA offices were raided and coupons were stolen. In a Cleveland office, coupons worth 5 million gallons were stolen; in Washington, 20 million. Black market activities often fell under the sway of organized crime, but they also involved local merchants, service station owners, and other small businessmen who turned up coupons for loyal customers. It was estimated that illegally purchased gasoline amounted to 1 million gallons a week or even as high as 2.5 million gallons a day. (OPA estimates placed gasoline purchased with counterfeit coupons at 5 percent.) Despite the cheating and illegal activity, rationing, during its duration, cut the average automobile use by one-third.

The gas-rationing plan had a significant effect on the patterns of life for many Americans, at least in the short run. The reduction in traffic in major cities was notable, and the drop in the auto death rate laudable. However, some sectors of society felt the impact more directly in their pocketbooks. As several state officials feared, revenues from gas taxes fell sharply. People engaged in the auto tourist trade suffered. PAW and OPA encouraged the use of public transportation, which brought about a temporary boon in passenger train traffic. Resort areas in Florida serviced by rail, for example, did a brisk business.

Gasoline rationing and fuel oil rationing for home heating made Americans aware that the nation was living in a war mode. In large measure, Americans recognized these restrictions as emergency measures only; they had little lasting impact on the conservation practices of the nation. A point about energy frugality had been made, but it was a small point.

INTERNATIONAL OIL, AMERICAN SECURITY, AND THE WAR

In the form of international oil, energy was a major component of American security. The political, military, and economic interests of the United States and the strategic importance of Latin America, Asia, and the Middle East were never more clearly linked than during World War II. In the short run at least, the war imposed an intimate relationship between foreign policy goals of the nation and the activities of American multinational oil companies. From time to time—as in the case of Jersey Standard's connection with I.G. Farben—the question of loyalty to U.S. war aims cropped up. The momentum of New Deal antitrust actions carried into the war and momentarily challenged the oil companies. Yet these pressures did little to undermine a working relationship that benefited both parties. The American multinationals needed governmental support and protection; the United States needed oil, stable relations with friendly producing nations, and access to future supplies and markets.

Hemisphere Solidarity and Oil

American oil policy in the Western Hemisphere was strongly influenced by the desire for hemispheric solidarity in confronting the Axis. The Good Neighbor Policy had laid the groundwork for cooperation between the United States and Latin America, but the Mexican expropriation, a change of leadership in Venezuela, and other problems linked to American business activities had to be resolved to bring economic interests in line with security needs.

As war approached, relations with Mexico were strained. Mexico's oil sales to Germany—one-third of their oil exports at the time of the Munich crisis in September 1938—rankled the State Department; but it also made it imperative to settle the dispute over expropriation. As a settlement was being worked out in 1942, the ties between the two nations strengthened. Rejecting a neutral stance as it had taken in World War I, the Mexican leadership sensed that the encroachment of war and Nazism into the Western Hemisphere would have disastrous effects on them. A most dramatic gesture was the arrival of Mexican oil tankers to American ports. In fact, German submarine attacks on Mexican tankers provoked Mexico into declaring war in May 1942. As Allies, Mexico and the United States extended their cooperation further. While the congenial relationship between the neighbors was sure to end with the last shot of the war, much had changed since the expropriation controversy that took place four years earlier.

Relations with Venezuela did not proceed as smoothly. The ascendancy of General Isaias Medina as president in May 1941, signaled a significant change in the relationship between the oil companies and the government of Venezuela. Under the previous regime, oil companies lived in an almost utopian world. The host government allowed them extensive freedom of action and even participated in the effort to keep oil workers from unionizing. Medina rejected that approach and announced that he would seek much higher profits from the oil companies. The State Department feared expropriation and urged the oil companies to act cautiously. A rise in output in 1941 was followed by a sharp decline the next year, leading to more denunciations from Medina. As a precautionary measure, the State Department advised the companies to replace their officials with those having no previous ties to the old regime. Expropriation was avoided, but Medina pressed for a new concession agreement.

Under the new arrangement, output increased rapidly. By 1944, Venezuela was once again second only to the United States in production. A crisis had been avoided by making oil company interests subservient to national wartime interest. Furthermore, the lesson of Mexican expropriation was not lost on the State Department while it was formulating its Venezuelan policy.

A less satisfactory relationship developed with Canada. In 1942, the War Department approved the so-called Canol (Canadian Oil) Project, which would allow U.S. airfields in Alaska to be supplied with oil and would also keep open the Alaskan Highway by tapping the Norman Wells field in the Arctic area of northern Canada. Despite the reservations of the Canadians and Jersey Standard's Canadian affiliate, Imperial Oil, the War Department forged ahead with its plan, neglecting to consult with PAW officials. The combined road and pipeline project was completed in 1944, at a cost of $134 million, only to be abandoned by the War Department the next year. Because of limited interest from the Canadian government and Imperial Oil, the pipeline was dismantled and sold for scrap after the war. An impulsive, ill-conceived plan was hastily developed on the flimsy justification of national security. Luckily, this project was more the exception than the rule in the development of wartime hemispheric oil policy.

Stanvac in Asia

During the war, the United States had the least success exploiting oil in Asia than in any other part of the world. As the Japanese swept through the China Sea and the Pacific, they not only gained control of the oil reserves in the area but also forced Western companies to sabotage their own facilities in order to avoid capture.

In the 1930s, Standard-Vacuum Oil Company (Stanvac) held a position unique in the Asian oil business. It had marketing outlets in China and Japan and controlled supplies in the Dutch East Indies. Stanvac was of such crucial importance in the Asian oil market that, in cooperation with Royal Dutch-Shell and the American government, it could effectively control the supply of oil to Japan.

As a relatively independent subsidiary of Jersey Standard and Socony-Vacuum (consolidated into Stanvac in 1933), and as the only American company operating a distribution business in China and Japan prior to World War II, Stanvac played a vital diplomatic role as well as an economic one in Asia. Beginning in 1938, Stanvac, fearing a Japanese attack on the Dutch East Indies, quickly aligned itself with American policy in Southeast Asia, and played a major part in implementation of that policy in 1940 and 1941. However, with the coming of war and the Japanese advances, no company with links to the United States could effectively undermine Japanese control of oil production in Asia. Stanvac thus lost its preeminent role in the Far East.

Saudi Arabia, Oil, and the War

Writing in the *Nation* in 1944, I. F. Stone warned:

> The proposed Arabian oil deal brings us to the first great crossroads of post-war international policy. In one direction lies a new world order; in the other, a return to imperialism, with all it entails. To go into a colonial country and buy oil concessions by favors to desert sheiks, to embark on a long-range program for the exploitation of natural resources which belong to other people, is imperialism, however we choose to disguise it.

Stone was expressing fears not of economic penetration by private companies but by the American government itself; that is, its actions resembled British, Dutch, and French participation in the oil business. Conditions during World War II, brought American policy makers face to face with that choice in Saudi Arabia. A whole new relationship between the United States and the Middle East was being shaped during the war, a relationship smeared with oil.

The contribution of Middle Eastern oil to the American war effort was negligible. By as late as 1943, the British controlled 80 percent of Middle Eastern oil production, while the United States controlled a paltry 14 percent. Despite the paucity of production accessible to the United States, American policy makers believed that King Saud's goodwill was the key to increased American influence in the Middle East and the road to greater oil production. The war alerted government officials to the possible inadequacies of future American oil reserves and the potential abundance of Saudi reserves (although they never imagined the real extent of the Saudi reserves this early). They were also aware of the strategic importance of the Middle East in protecting growing American interests abroad.

King Saud's financial problems proved to be the catalyst that led to an aggressive American oil policy in the Middle East. World War II interrupted transportation and supplies, which seriously reduced oil production and further exploitation of the oil fields. Pilgrimages to Mecca were also curtailed, sharply reducing the king's revenues. Saud immediately turned to his concessionaire, but CASOC had advanced Saud nearly $7 million against future royalties and was unwilling to pay more. While Saud was pro-Allies, his own financial shortcomings and the instability of Saudi Arabian economy led him to negotiate with Japanese and British concession-seekers.

Fearing a vastly reduced concession in Saudi Arabia, executives from CASOC told their gloomy story to American government officials. The President and the State Department realized that a great deal was at stake. Not only was CASOC's concession in jeopardy, but British oil interests might use the situation as a pretext to undermine the American monopoly in Saudi Arabia.

While CASOC leaders had little trouble convincing the State Department of the dangerous situation, they were uncertain how to meet the king's financial demands. Since FDR favored some action, doors began to open. Under existing law, the U.S. government could not extend Lend-Lease aid directly to the Saudis because they were not a belligerent. FDR then suggested that the British advance a portion of their $400 million Lend-Lease aid, and, between 1941 and 1943, British advanced them more than $30 million. This gesture, however, enhanced Britain's relationship with King Saud and opened the door to possible future concessions. CASOC officials saw the danger in this plan and continued to lobby for direct aid.

Despite their apprehensions about the British, CASOC managers were overjoyed. They were relieved of a great financial burden, derived prestige from the reflected glow of the American aid package, and protected their concession from an immediate British incursion. But they also helped to create momentum for further governmental involvement in the economic affairs of the Saudis, as well as possible competition for oil concessions.

Once the United States government became involved in extending aid to Saudi Arabia and upgrading its diplomatic mission, the idea of direct participation in the oil concession did not seem far-fetched. After all, the idea of government participation in formerly private economic affairs was not alien to the New Dealers. The idea eventually received support from several formidable individuals within the administration, namely Secretary Ickes, Secretary of War Henry L. Stimson, Secretary of the Navy Frank Knox, Undersecretary of the Navy William L. Bullitt, and FDR himself.

Believing that the government could compete with British interests in the Middle East more effectively than did the oil companies, Ickes supported the creation of the Petroleum Reserves Corporation (PRC). CASOC opposed the PRC obtaining the whole concession from Saudi Arabia, but it was in a difficult position because it depended heavily on government financial and diplomatic assistance.

The State Department, especially Secretary Hull, opposed the PRC, believing that the project was unnecessary and not acceptable to King Saud. It urged that Ickes and his supporters reconsider and accept an offer more in line with the traditional policy toward oil companies. One viable offer, it believed, was CASOC's plan to allow the government to buy large quantities of oil at a substantial discount.

Despite the opposition, Ickes forged ahead with the blessings of the President. In June 1943, the PRC was officially established under the aegis of the Reconstruction Finance Corporation. Like the abortive United States Oil Corporation of the 1920s, PRC failed to secure a concession. CASOC came close to completing an agreement to sell one-third interest in the existing concession in return for government financing of its Ras Tanura refinery. According to one recent study, Ickes broke off the negotiations because of pressure from Jersey Standard and Socony-Vacuum, who actively obstructed governmental participation in the oil business.

Undaunted, Ickes sought a different route for the PRC—the building of a 1,000-mile pipeline from the Persian Gulf to the eastern Mediterranean. CASOC reluctantly agreed to the project and, uncharacteristically, so did the

State Department. Ickes welcomed the support, hoping to secure immediate success for the PRC. The State Department, however, looked at the project from its long-range impact on relations with Saudi Arabia, not the narrower interests of Ickes. But bitter opposition from the oil industry, the British, and key members of Congress killed the project and felled the PRC. CASOC, having changed its name to the Arabian American Oil Company (ARAMCO) in 1944, eventually built its own pipeline.

The failure of direct governmental participation in international oil suggested that strained relations with the British be improved. Such a move was supported by the State Department and the major oil companies. The State Department originally suggested the creation of a bilateral commission to manage Middle Eastern oil production. This would insure markets for Saudi oil but also preserve good relations with Britain. In 1944, an Anglo-American Petroleum Agreement was negotiated, which outlined the orderly development of reserves and discussing international oil trade.

While the majors preferred this approach as compared to the PRC, the domestic independents regarded it as threatening. The agreement was revised in September 1945, but it was never ratified. Suspicious of the goals of the American and British governments and concerned about the ascendancy of ARAMCO, Jersey Standard and Socony-Vacuum cooperated with the independent companies to kill the agreement.

The failed negotiations led to a reversion to the more traditional practice of private development with government backing. By the end of the war, American multinationals were more influential than ever before. Yet the policy interests of the United States had been made clearer by the various wartime ventures. The extension of Lend-Lease aid to the Saudis was the first step in placing the Middle East at center stage in American foreign policy. The roles of the United States and Great Britain in the area were reversing. Most important for U.S. energy history, the foundations of an almost unfathomable industry were erected. A new oil giant emerged—ARAMCO—and the Red Line Agreement faded and died. As one historian noted about Saudi Arabia and the Middle East: "War made the region prominent; oil made it vital."[3]

THE SYNTHETIC LIQUID FUELS PROGRAM

Scholars make a great point of the federal government's aggressive interest in international oil during World War II, but they rarely mention the synthetic fuels program meant to augment future energy reserves.

The vast American coal deposits provided the most convincing argument for seeking reserves through the production of synthetic fuels. The idea of converting coal into liquid fuels had its origins in the eighteenth century. Not until the late 1920s, however, did German scientists and engineers de-

---

[3]Michael B. Stoff, *Oil, War, and American Security* (New Haven, Conn., 1980), p. 209.

velop three processes for synthesizing oil and gas from coal. By the outbreak of World War II, several large plants were in full operation, providing one-third of the total fuel capacity for Nazi Germany's war machine.

The Bureau of Mines (BOM) had conducted research with shale oil in the 1920s and with synthetic fuels since 1935. In January 1943, Michael Straus, director of the War Resources Board, wrote his superior Harold Ickes that he was tired of "piddling around" with the small appropriations for the synthetic fuel research and wanted to build a plant immediately. Ickes was intrigued with the idea—and suspicious enough of the motives of oil companies in developing only those projects that brought immediate profit—that he gave Straus the authorization. In 1944, the Synthetic Liquid Fuels Act was passed over the objection of some congressmen who feared government involvement in energy development.

Few people realized the monumental task of beginning a new energy industry from scratch. Central to its success was acquiring pertinent engineering data and necessary patents. Through prodding from the oil industry, the BOM (which was in charge of the project) looked to the capture of German documents to make greater headway in establishing a viable fuel production program. A few technical teams had already begun to investigate German military and industrial secrets, but, in 1945, the BOM sent a team to Germany, as part of the Technical Oil Mission, with the expressed purpose of uncovering what they could about German synthetic fuel production. In all, more than 3,000 teams investigated thousands of factories, businesses, and scientific centers, looking for valuable material and crucial information. They interviewed scores of German scientists, uncovered tons of materials, and explored key installations.

Despite the wealth of information, the synthetic fuel program languished after the war. National security interests and energy self-sufficiency were adequate reasons to continue the project. But energy available through the exploitation of foreign oil and the reluctance of the majors to tolerate a new competitive industry, worked against the synthetic fuel program. Its time had not come—at least not in a nation where "energy crisis" was not part of the vocabulary in 1945.

Energy abundance, indeed material abundance in general, is a key to understanding the successful prosecution of the war and the society that emerged in the wake of that war. As in World War I, adequate energy sources had been vital to the war effort in the 1940s, and the United States had not been found wanting. Similarly, energy industries and the federal government cooperated to maximize production. Despite its precedent-setting involvement in the economic life of the nation, the New Deal administration did not tamper with the capitalistic underpinnings. It also adjusted its foreign policy to blend economic and strategic interests in Latin America and the Middle East.

But just as energy was vital to the war effort, the impact of the war was vital to the economic growth and global power of the United States for years to come. The war previewed those energy sources that would be crucial to postwar America, petroleum, natural gas, and electrical power, and another with ominous potential—atomic energy. Using wars as historic dividing points is often superficial, but for U.S. energy history, World War II has special significance.

FURTHER READING

Irvine H. Anderson. *ARAMCO, the United States, and Saudi Arabia*. Princeton, N.J., 1981.

——————. *The Standard-Vacuum Oil Company and United States Asian Policy, 1933–1941*. Princeton, N.J., 1975.

Herbert Feis. *Petroleum and American Foreign Policy*. Palo Alto, Calif., 1944.

John W. Frey and H. Chandler Ide. *A History of the Petroleum Administration for War, 1941–1945*. Washington, D.C., 1946.

Arnold P. Krammer. "Technology Transfer as War Booty: The U.S. Technical Oil Mission to Europe, 1945," *Technology and Culture*, vol. 22 (January 1981), pp. 68–103.

Aaron David Miller. *Search for Security: Saudi Arabian Oil and American Foreign Policy, 1939–1949*. Chapel Hill, N.C., 1980.

Richard Polenberg. *War and Society*. Philadelphia, 1972.

Michael B. Stoff. *Oil, War, and American Security*. New Haven, Conn., 1980.

William M. Tuttle, Jr. "The Birth of an Industry: The Synthetic Rubber 'Mess' in World War II," *Technology and Culture*, vol. 22 (January 1981), pp. 35–67.

Part Three

Energy-Intensive Society, 1945–1970

CHAPTER 11

Electricity and the Economies of Scale

While many countries were devastated by World War II, the United States emerged as the premier world power envied for its material wealth. Internationally the United States had no rivals; at home, the pieces of a crumbling economy had been put back together. While the country faced predictable shortages, inflation, and the convulsions of demobilization for a short time after the war, the potential growth of the economy was anyone's guess. The wartime "production miracle" left behind a sense of economic omnipotence and a restored faith in the capitalist system. The past was past. The future was everything again.

Forces at work before the war—the automobile and the airplane, mass communications and mass production—had an even greater economic and social impact after the war. The rise of the electronics industry and the advent of television added powerful new dimensions to the technological revolution of the modern era. From a nation of cities emerged an urban nation: industrial cities were replaced by metropolises; suburbs fanned out in ever-increasing numbers; local issues were transformed into regional and national issues. Critical social problems—racism, bigotry, unemployment, poverty—had not disappeared. But with the upbeat mood of middle-class America in the late 1940s, these problems seemed less crucial, more likely to be resolved through general prosperity. The expectations of the postwar years were often unfulfilled, but the country had found its moment in history.

ELECTRICITY IN AN ENERGY-INTENSIVE SOCIETY

In this setting, energy continued to play a vital role in shaping the American economy and reflecting the moods of its people. Faith in unbridled material progress was linked to visions of a high-technology society, where every family drove a new car, had a modern ranch-style home, and accumulated every appliance that could be plugged into a wall socket. In spirit at least, the consumerism of the late 1940s and beyond was much like that of the 1920s. Similarly, this acquisitiveness was built on the assumption of available, abundant, and cheap sources of energy.

The rapid rise in production and consumption of electrical power went hand in hand with economic growth in the postwar years. The increase in electrical power generation—about 8.5 percent a year—kept pace with impressive economic growth (6 percent of the world's population was producing half of the world's goods), and outstripped the birthrate and the rise in the GNP. Utility companies put their faith—and their money—into large, centralized systems. Economies of scale dictated that the unquenchable demand for energy made larger generating units profitable and, thus, desirable.

However, the combination of vast growth in the utilities industry and dwindling political support for public power projects, reduced the public versus private power debate by the late 1950s. Public power units already in service generally remained in service, even under Republican rule. But there was little increase in public power beyond the prewar levels. The one major exception was TVA, which continued to expand its markets to justify its generation of electricity.

While the public power issue faded, other questions took its place. The role of electrical power as a force for innovation was one. A revolution in mass communications, entertainment, and electronics was stimulated by new electrical technology and the availability of cheap electrical power as a dependable energy source. Moreover, because of the scale of electrical power development, the utilities' demands for massive supplies of coal, oil, and nuclear fuels raised serious questions about the utilization and exploitation of natural resources. The increased use of polluting fuels and the efforts to exploit the remaining hydroelectric sites (largely in undeveloped parts of the country) made "environmental costs" a significant issue by the late 1960s. The blessings and curse of energy abundance—technical innovation and environmental costs—evolved side by side in the maturing of electrical power in postwar America.

THE POSTWAR UTILITY INDUSTRY: A PROFILE

In 1970, the electric utility industry was the largest industry, in terms of capital assets, in the United States. It generated as much power as the Soviet Union, United Kingdom, Japan, West Germany, and Canada combined, or more than half of all electricity in the world. The electric utility industry was also the single largest issuer of securities in the United States.

The trend toward centralization began well before World War II, but the electric utility industry became even more monolithic in almost every phase of business after the war: ownership, planning, coordination, decision making, and economic influence. In terms of actual number of power systems (3,300 to 3,500 in 1970), the industry was fragmented. About 2,400 units were involved solely in the transmission and distribution of power. Of those generating power, 800 were municipal or federally financed cooperatives producing about 10 percent of the nation's electricity; between 250 and 300 privately owned utilities and two major federal systems produced the rest, or about 90 percent.

With the exception of the Tennessee Valley Authority, the privately owned utilities were the primary source of accelerated growth in unit, station size, and voltage increase in the United States. Along with growth in individual units, there was a continual increase in the interconnection of systems. "Power pools," sometimes informal in nature, allowed for power exchange, centralized dispatching, cooperative planning, and the development of new systems. The number of power pools with unaffiliated corporate members increased from four in 1960 (12 percent of national capacity) to seventeen in 1970 (50 percent of national capacity).

The new power pools moved toward an integration of systems, sometimes with federal support and encouragement. This trend was viewed as an efficient means of delivering energy to consumers, but it was also a means to encourage concentration and monopolistic practices within the industry. An unanticipated side effect was the increased potential for massive blackouts, such as the one that struck the East Coast and Canada in 1965.

An important change in the postwar electric power industry was the switch in primary energy sources. Hydroelectric capacity increased after World War II by 5.2 percent annually, but total generation grew by 8.5 percent. Thus hydroelectric's share of total generation was declining. The postwar high for hydroelectric generation was 35.1 percent in 1946; in 1970, it had dropped to 16.2 percent of the total. On a regional basis, hydroelectric power was only dominant in the Pacific Coast states, where it represented a little over 55 percent in 1970.

While railroad coal use declined significantly, and coal lost ground to other energy sources, it remained an important source for the electric power industry after World War II. Between 1954 and 1970, coal generated about half of the electric power for the nation as a whole, and consumed more than half of the coal produced. Coal-fired plants in the East, burning primarily bituminous coal, utilized almost 38 percent of the steam coal; the south Atlantic used another 21 percent.

Yet even steam coal was gradually replaced by other fuels by the mid-1960s. Natural gas fields in the south central states and southern California provided a major alternative. Easier to handle, cleaner, and requiring simpler furnaces for burning, natural gas became particularly important in the south central region, where about 81 percent of the proven reserves exist. By 1969, natural gas supplied more than 23 percent of the power used to produce electricity in the United States. Residual oil (fuel oil) also made in-roads into the coal markets, especially on the East Coast. For example, in the 1960s, residual oil increased in use on an average of 17 percent a year. In the 1950s and 1960s, many experts believed that nuclear power would dominate electrical power production in the near future. But in 1970 nuclear-generated electricity represented less than 2 percent (see Table 11.1).

Table 11.1   *Consumption of Fuels by Electric Utilities*

	Total Coal Equivalent	Coal	Oil	Gas
	1,000 Short tons	1,000 Short tons	1,000 42-gal bbl	Mil. cu. ft.
1945	92,642	74,725	20,228	326,212
1950	138,421	91,871	75,420	628,919
1955	206,929	143,759	75,274	1,153,280
1960	266,064	176,634	85,340	1,724,762
1965	369,331	244,788	115,203	2,321,101
1970	583,456	320,818	335,504	3,931,996

Source: Bureau of the Census, U.S. Department of Commerce, *Historical Statistics of the United States* (Washington, D.C., 1975), p. 826.

FEDERAL POWER POLICY

The debate over public power did not completely subside with the end of the New Deal; but it changed in tone, if not substance. The Truman administration kept it alive through new TVA-like projects. Gone was FDR's "birchrod in the cupboard" mentality and the justification of public power as a means of invigorating the national economy. Republican opposition to extending public power remained vocal. Under President Dwight Eisenhower, the opportunity for severely limiting the public power idea, if not rolling back existing projects, surfaced.

The basic structure of the federally owned and financed electric utility system remained much the same as it had been in the 1930s, however. TVA was the only federally owned corporation for regional development. The Bonneville Power Administration marketed power from the Grand Coulee, Bonneville, and other dams in the West. Between 1944 and 1950, two additional power administrations, which disposed of output from federal dams, were also established: the Southwestern Power Administration (1944) and the Southeastern Power Administration (1950).[1] In addition, the Rural Electrification Administration still operated as a mechanism for financing electrical development. In recent years, rural electric cooperatives still provide electric power to about 98 percent of all American farms, serving more than 25 million people.

While the structure of the federal electric utility system remained intact, controversy persisted over its mission. Within the Truman administration, no single policy emerged other than a broad commitment to sustaining the system and possibly extending it. The lack of a uniform policy can be

[1] In 1967, the Alaska Power Administration was added and, in 1977, the Western Area Power Administration.

traced to several factors. First, Harry Truman had not inherited a coherent policy. Second, intra-agency and interagency rivalries for establishing energy policy pitted vested interest against vested interest. Third, World War II had made demands on the electric utility system to meet the crisis but had shed little light on a coherent peacetime policy.

The Department of the Interior and Electrical Power

The absence of a clear strategy, or firm executive direction, allowed the Department of the Interior to take a central role in attempting to guide national power policy. In 1941, Secretary Harold Ickes established a Division of Power to cooperate with the Bureau of Reclamation—the agency in the Interior Department that built and operated electrical plants—in reviewing plans for new projects and contracts for the sale of power. But Ickes's efforts at centralization were not eagerly accepted within his contentious department nor by rival government agencies. His attempt to pry REA from the Department of Agriculture in 1945–1946 was a good example of the tensions he had created.

Despite the failure of Ickes's plans, the Department of Interior helped set the tone for the administration's support of public power. In January 1946, he issued a "Memorandum on Power Policy" that codified the most important congressional legislation on the subject. Out of the synthesis came "primary objectives" that reasserted the concept of public power: that federal dams should play a vital role in producing electrical energy; that power should be sold at low cost primarily to public agencies and cooperatives for the benefit of domestic and rural consumers; and that power disposal should not encourage monopolization.

In essence the memorandum outlined areas of debate over public power, which acquired a national forum in the presidential election of 1948. Truman's general campaign tactic was to pillory the Republican-dominated 80th Congress—a force that he believed obstructed postwar recovery and sabotaged the extension of the New Deal into the postwar years. Appealing to the New Deal constituency, Truman used the power issue in his aggressive attack. He charged that the Republicans tried to cut off the Democrats' attempts to bring cheap power to the masses. He further charged that the Republican strategy of limiting power projects in the West was an attempt to make that section "an economic colony of Wall Street." His solution was more public power projects: valley authorities along the Missouri, the Colorado, the Columbia, and in the central valley of California.

Truman's offensive on this and other issues returned him to office in 1949, to the great surprise of some political pundits. Public power advocates within the Interior Department were overjoyed with the President's stand. Planning was soon underway for extending more transmission lines and developing coal-fired plants to supplement hydroelectric projects. Republicans countered through congressional action, especially by withholding funds for the stringing of new lines, which crippled expansion of the projects. In the election, Truman had won the first round over public power, but would he win the match?

The Waning of Public Power—CVA and the Korean War

An important test of the extension of public power was the squabble over a Columbia Valley Authority (CVA). A CVA bill was introduced in 1945, but Republican opposition, the war's end, and the death of FDR weakened interest in the project (especially among Westerners). When Ickes resigned from the Interior Department in 1946—due to his growing unpopularity in the Truman administration and his unwillingness to accept a less influential role—impetus for public power projects was stunted.

Interagency jealousies and "turf-guarding" made it impossible to sustain an interest in new projects within the department. As a result, the White House wrote a new bill for a CVA in 1949. But the timing was poor. The postwar depression was over and no legitimate comparison as depressed areas awaiting regional development could be made between the Columbia River Valley and the Appalachian region (where TVA ruled). The valley authority idea, in other words, could not be sold as an effective means of economic recovery. Moreover, the bill never left its committee because Republicans had identified public programs of this type with socialistic approaches to government. As the Cold War heated up in the late 1940s, "socialism" became the ultimate "four-letter word." Anything that smacked of governmental involvement, interference, or encroachment in the private sector was thus branded by right-wing politicians.

Truman continued to support public power nonetheless. The failure of CVA and the energy shortages in the winter of 1948 and 1949 made the President more determined to push for new projects. He established the Water Resources Policy Commission (headed by Morris L. Cooke), whose task was to evaluate multipurpose river projects. The final report of the Cooke Commission called for a continuation of the mixed power system, but it came down in favor of the principle of public power. Beyond this, the report offered few guidelines for developing a cohesive power policy.

The Korean War (1950–1953) blunted the call for additional public power projects. The Interior Department using the war to enhance its influence, tried to be designated as the chief coordinating unit for electrical power under the Defense Production Act of 1950. Like World War I and World War II, distribution of authority was spread among several agencies that were directed to meet the emergency—not to establish long-range policy objectives.

Ike and the Partnership Approach

The growing unpopularity of President Truman during an increasingly unpopular war gave Republicans real hope for victory in 1952—and with it death to public power. In their candidate, Dwight David Eisenhower, the Republicans had a leader who promised to end the Korean conflict, to roll back the New Deal, and to place "business in the saddle" once again. The former Supreme Allied Commander, NATO leader, and president of Columbia University was the kind of executive who the Republicans believed would reduce government spending, help to dismantle the "bloated" federal bureaucracy, and terminate federal power projects.

Adlai Stevenson, the former governor of Illinois and Democratic standard-bearer, was a perfect foil for Eisenhower on the public power issue. To the same degree that Stevenson was an ardent supporter of public power (especially the brand espoused by the Interior Department), Eisenhower rejected the program and the principle. On the surface, Eisenhower's criticism was a standard right-wing charge of the day—government action equalled socialism. In campaign speeches in the West, he identified "creeping socialism" with the TVA, other federal power projects, and the New Deal in general.

Eisenhower's public identification with the slogan belied his more moderate approach to public power once he entered office. The Eisenhower years were not characterized by effective roll-backs in public power programs but by an emphasis on "partnership." The cry of "creeping socialism" appealed to Ike's more conservative supporters, but not among the great middle class—Democrat and Republican alike—who had given him victory in 1952. The new president wanted the major responsibility for developing electrical power to rest with state and local authorities and private industry. If their efforts fell short, he believed the federal government then had to give assistance as a "partner." Eisenhower had not rejected federal involvement in power projects outright; he merely changed the priority of participation.

The partnership approach was not easy to promote as long as it remained an abstraction. From a political perspective, the administration needed a project before the 1956 election. It rested its hopes on the Upper Colorado River Storage Basin Project, authorized by Congress in 1956. The project had the advantage of being region-wide, complex, and requiring the involvement of several levels of government as well as private industry. But one project did not establish a whole new direction in policy. Undercutting the "partnership" approach was the administration's largely negative method of establishing policy—cutting appropriations, stopping or slowing new projects. In many cases, western Republicans with special interests in these projects were appalled at their leadership's actions.

TVA and Dixon-Yates

The administration's unsuccessful assault on TVA—not its lack of an adequate demonstration project or budget-cutting—seriously hurt its credibility on public power policy. TVA was undergoing a major transition in the 1940s and early 1950s as a result of continued growth and a clear shift in mission. In many ways, it was a much different institution than Eisenhower had remembered it to be, but to Republicans it was still a Frankenstein monster of the New Deal years.

During World War II, TVA's growth was dramatic, installed capacity increased from 1 million kilowatts in 1940 to 2.5 million in 1946. Much of the new capacity went into the production of aluminum for aircraft, which required considerable amounts of electricity. The war also provided the impetus for building twelve new dams. When the war ended, many believed that TVA's major problem would be overcapacity. However, new industries moved into the area, especially Atomic Energy Commission facilities, where uranium was being reduced, and the TVA continued to encourage consumers to utilize more electricity.

TVA's efforts at further expansion led to a crucial decision—major construction of coal-fired steam plants to supplement the existing hydroelectric plants. With most of the good hydroelectric sites already developed, the turn to thermal generation was the most expedient means of increasing capacity. Congress authorized the first large steam facility in 1948, to be constructed in Johnsonville, Tennessee. Soon six major projects were underway. Dependence on steam generation also led to a change in the transmission system: lines would carry much higher voltages over longer distances and thus would require significant new rights-of-way. In 1939, TVA produced virtually all its power in hydroplants; by 1956, 70 percent was produced in coal-burning steam plants.

Republicans had fought the Johnsonville project, but they were unable to overcome the well-entrenched support for TVA. Eisenhower's election offered the first real chance to confront the authority. But the administration was not going to make a head-on attack on such a successful operation. Instead, the Republican leadership would try to stop its growth by cutting federal funds for expansion. If additional power were necessary in the existing service area, private utilities would have to take up the slack. TVA would have to supply its customers of preference—municipalities, cooperatives, rural electric authorities—without asking for federal funds to finance increased capacity.

The administration's plan was sidetracked by the Dixon-Yates controversy, which arose over contracting with a private utility to supply additional power in the Tennessee Valley. In 1952, TVA asked the Bureau of the Budget to approve funds for a steam plant to service Memphis. The project was vigorously opposed by local utility companies, especially Middle South Utilities and the Southern Company. The Truman administration approved the capacity increase, but Congress waited until it received the Republican budget from President Eisenhower. As expected, the allocation was left out of the budget.

As an alternative, the administration supported a proposal by Edgar Dixon, president of Middle South, and Eugene Yates, president of Southern Company, for building a steam plant jointly constructed and operated by their companies. To complete this plan with the least amount of political flack, the Dixon-Yates plant would contract with the AEC to supply power to the TVA service area near Memphis. The power that Dixon-Yates supplied to Memphis would then be considered as a replacement of power which TVA would continue to supply to the AEC facility in Paducah, 150 miles away. This complex arrangement was meant to satisfy advocates of public power by including TVA in the transaction. The AEC resisted the plan because it would pay more for power without any compensation.

What was intended as a back door to undermining TVA turned into a fiasco. Senator Estes Kefauver (Dem., Tenn.)—interested in his constituency's welfare and concerned with his own presidential ambitions—secured appointment, in 1955, as chairman of a subcommittee to investigate the Dixon-Yates deal. The committee was stacked three to one in favor of public power, and it immediately charged that the administration had hidden the fact that the government adviser, who helped to devise the power plan, worked for the financial institution backing the deal. The Democrats were quick to expose a Republican "giveaway" program to private utilities.

Luckily for the administration, Memphis decided to build its own steam plant, and the President—while denying Kefauver's charges—cancelled the Dixon-Yates contract. Kefauver continued to press the issue, which got him the nomination as the Democratic vice-presidential candidate in 1956. Despite some additional sniping, TVA was left unassailed.

In 1959, Congress passed the Revenue Bond Act, which required new TVA power programs to be financed from the sale of bonds not from the federal treasury. Rather than constraining its growth, the act freed TVA from the yearly fights over appropriations and gave it "breathing space" for further development.[2]

Despite the flurry of charges and skirmishes, the debate over a national power policy was limited to relatively few issues. Neither Truman nor Eisenhower had a clear electricity policy. In large measure, policy decisions were being made in the states or within operating company areas—with no coordination of any kind. The relationship between patterns of consumption and future energy needs were virtually ignored at the national level, except in terms of economic growth and prosperity. As long as the notion of energy abundance dominated the thinking of the day, politics superseded planning.

Power Policy in the 1960s

The brief years of the Kennedy administration saw a return to liberal Democratic lip service to public power. As a New Englander, John Kennedy was no great advocate of public power. But as a Democrat in the tradition of Roosevelt and Truman, he appreciated the central role of the federal government in establishing energy policy. The belief that future energy supplies would be plentiful and prices stable also colored the views of the Kennedy administration. Questions of energy availability and the role of the govern-

[2]Thomas K. McCraw, "Triumph and Irony—The TVA," *Proceedings of the IEEE*, vol. 64 (September 1976), pp. 1372–1380.

ment in energy policy were overshadowed by the Cold War, civil rights, and economic growth.

In line with the relatively optimistic energy outlook of the day, priority was given to the study of interconnection of systems, especially those linking the Pacific Northwest and Southwest. When the FPC initiated the National Power Survey in January 1962, it looked toward a systematic national power network evolving out of the disparate systems. Efforts at funding major additions to the federal power system fared less well in the early 1960s.

Under Lyndon Johnson, controversy arose over interconnections and transmission of power. In part, this was stimulated by the 1965 blackout, which plunged much of Canada and the eastern United States into darkness for as long as thirteen hours. At 5:16 p.m. on November 9, 1965, a single relay switch malfunctioned at the Sir Adam Beck plant in Ontario, Canada. Overload in the lines occurred, reversing the flow of 1,500 million watts back into the United States with electricity surging toward every outlet. All open lines collapsed and a region spanning from Toronto to New York to Buffalo to Boston went black. Within twelve minutes 30 million people over 80,000 square miles were affected.

The extent of the problem was greatest in areas with concentrated populations, such as New York City, where people were trapped in subways and elevators and water and gas supplies were cut. Luckily the blackout did not occur in the dead of winter. Previous winter blackouts were smaller in scale but brought on much worse suffering. In fact, New York City took on an almost carnival-like atmosphere. Aside from the object lesson about the vulnerability of vast interconnections, the only long-term impact of the blackout was the brisk hospital business in July and August, when scores of "blackout babies" were born.

In response to the blackout, the President appointed a Task Force on Electric Power. It recommended moving toward regional planning and regional integration of systems rather than toward a national system. But most significant for the future energy debate was the emergence of a commercial nuclear power industry during the Johnson years.

Richard Nixon's presidency is memorable for many reasons, but with respect to energy, these years were significant as prelude to the "energy crisis" of the 1970s. Like its predecessors, the Nixon administration was conditioned by a long history of energy abundance. Staunchly probusiness, it supported the growth of energy industries without giving much serious attention to evaluating the state of those industries. In the case of electrical power generation, some observers were talking about an industry crisis in 1968. Primary fuel supplies, which were predicted as stable, became increasingly expensive and in short supply by the end of the decade. Technical improvements in the systems had not advanced rapidly enough to offset increased fuel prices.[3] Marketing, load management, and other managerial problems

---

[3]Richard F. Hirsh, "Conserving Kilowatts: The Electric Power Industry in Transition," *Materials and Society*, vol. 7 (1983), pp. 295–305.

also undermined the effectiveness of the industry. Indeed, by as early as 1964, the industry's hope of rapid and continued expansion was being replaced by expectations of more modest growth. An array of brownouts and blackouts, short supplies of natural gas, and environmental controversies were harbingers of things to come. Despite the ominous signs, the period 1969 to 1973 produced no change in national power policy—such as it was.

ELECTRICAL POWER AND THE ENVIRONMENT

In the 1960s, the major controversy surrounding electrical power generation in the United States began to shift from the public versus private debate to questions of the environmental impact of power production. The rise of the modern environmental movement (discussed more fully in Chapter XVI) at the end of the decade provided the backdrop. The broadscale societal critique of America in the wake of the civil rights movement, the Vietnam War, student revolts, and the emergence of a counterculture set the stage for a new environmental awareness and concern for quality-of-life issues. In the realm of electrical power, the large-scale utilization of coal and the development of nuclear power became the focal point of debate.

Coal and Pollution

Since coal-fired steam plants were abundant in the 1960s, the environmental controversy immediately focused on coal as a pollutant. Unlike nineteenth-century Americans who judged the debilitating effects of smoke pollution by its sensory effects only, modern Americans had the benefit of more sophisticated scientific measures that pointed to a range of problems. Air pollution was one problem, but the mining and use of coal also contributes to water pollution, and strip mining produced land despoliation.

Air pollution from the burning of coal is one of the most destructive of environmental blights. Sulfur oxides in particular are highly toxic; they directly attack plant life by stunting growth, reducing seed output, and weakening resistance to disease.[4] In the United States, most low-sulfur coal is located in the West, but the bulk of coal production is in the East, where coal is rich in sulfur. Even in locations where low-sulfur bituminous or lignite is utilized for producing steam, sulfur oxides are a problem. An environmental impact statement prepared for two power plant sites at Colstrip, Montana, predicted that crop and grass damage could be as high as 20 percent within a 500 mile radius.

Particulates in coal smoke are also very toxic. Soot in the particulate discharge contains benzopyrene, which is a recognized carcinogen in cigarette

---

[4]Sulfur oxides are a main component in acid rain, which also attacks plant life, kills aquatic life, and leaches soil nutrients.

smoke. Nitrogen oxides, a component in smog, and carbon dioxide, linked to a possible "greenhouse" effect,[5] are the by-products of fossil-fuel burning. Other air pollutants include waste heat and the problem of "fogging," which occurs around cooling towers under certain climatic conditions. While power plants are not responsible for all the air pollution from the burning of coal, they are responsible for a great amount of it. On a national basis in 1970, electric power plants discharged 50 percent of all sulfur oxides (41.8 billion pounds), 25 percent of nitrogen oxides (9.24 billion pounds), and 25 percent of all particulates.

Water pollution is a serious but sometimes overlooked result of the utilization of coal by power plants. Drainage from coal mines polluted about 6,700 miles of streams by the mid-1970s (more than 90 percent of which are in the Appalachians). Fourteen heavy metals are found in American coal—and they are all toxic. Coal also contains radioactive isotopes, which have a potentially severe impact on sources of drinking water. It is not uncommon to find a mixture of sulfuric acid, iron, and aluminum salts in coal drainage. While in a slightly different category, thermal pollution is an important form of water pollution. Since massive quantities of water are needed in the steam-heating process, great amounts of hot water are returned to their sources with severe effects on aquatic life.

Strip Mining

Strip mining, or surface mining, rivaled air pollution as the most publicized aspect of the controversy over burning coal. Strip mining causes soil erosion, loss of top soil, water pollution, and acid mine drainage, as well as creating large amounts of solid waste and lowering ground-water tables. In strip-mined areas, community disruption led to almost 18 percent loss of population. By 1961, hundreds of miles of streams and thousands of acres of land were disturbed or ruined by strip mining. A 1969 report by the Appalachian regional commissioner stated that approximately 5,700 miles of streams had been polluted in the Appalachians, and the water quality of 10,500 miles of streams was affected. By that time, some 470,000 acres of land had been stripped and not reclaimed ("orphan lands"), 81 percent in the Appalachians alone.

The rationale for turning to strip mining was economic. In order to compete with cheap imported oil and natural gas, mining companies had to find a less expensive means of acquiring coal. Strip mining was more in line with the economies of scale in other industries. Improved mining technology was a key factor in making strip mining feasible on a large scale. Giant shovels, as tall as some skyscrapers, could strip thirty to forty feet of overburden in one gulp. The use of explosives and augers allowed miners to get at the coal easily. Through surface techniques, as much as ninety percent of the coal in

---

[5]Excessive carbon dioxide in the atmosphere can raise the earth's temperature and disrupt climatic equilibrium.

a seam could be removed as compared with fifty percent through deep mining.

In the long run, the economies of scale turned a labor-intensive operation into a cheaper, capital-intensive one. Two dozen men could operate a strip mine that produced millions of tons of coal. Mining companies, therefore, escaped the labor problems that haunted the industry with an increase in productivity. The leadership of the United Mine Workers favored strip mining, although it meant a reduction in jobs: employed miners would receive better pay and would be working under safer conditions.

According to coal historian Robert F. Munn, "The strip mining of coal is new as a problem but old as a practice."[6] The steam shovel was invented in 1839 but was not used for stripping until 1881. The demands for coal in World War I stimulated strip mining in West Virginia and gave rise to more extensive use of the technique in other areas after the war. But as late as 1950, deep mines still accounted for more than two-thirds of coal produced in the United States.

Through its early years, strip mining was an eastern phenomenon. In the late 1960s, however, it was viewed as an important technique for mining low-sulfur coal in the West. Coal companies and other firms with an interest in coal production, including competitors in the oil industry, began buying up leases in the Dakotas, Montana, and Wyoming. The reduction in operating costs helped to offset the high transportation rates that had limited the exploitation of western coal in the past. In some cases, electric power plants were sited near points of extraction and transmission lines were extended for hundreds of miles to distant power markets. But the transition to western coal was only beginning in the 1960s. While about 50 new strip mines appeared in the West, 2,000 remained in the Appalachians.

Coal and Environmental Reform

The controversy over coal pollution carried with it a series of difficulties for electric utilities and coal producers. As early as 1958, conservationists, journalists, and sportsmen began to attack electric utilities for creating air pollution and coal producers for employing strip mining. Deflecting the criticisms as best they could, they hoped to avoid open public debate and stiffer environmental legislation. During the 1960s, coal producers and their trade associations, electric utilities, the UMW, and companies with strong mining interests (including oil companies and railroads) united in their opposition to stringent environmental laws or sanctions. According to historian Richard H. K. Vietor, a "coal coalition"—a cohesive political coalition of coal-related industries—emerged as early as 1960. All but three of the biggest producers of coal were subsidiaries of large, noncoal corporations by the mid-1970s.[7]

[6]Robert F. Munn, "The First Fifty Years of Strip Mining in West Virginia, 1916—1965," *West Virginia History* (October 1973), p. 66.

[7]Richard H. K. Vietor, *Environmental Politics and the Coal Coalition* (College Station, Tex., 1980).

Whether a "coal coalition" actually existed is subject to debate, but it is clear that a clash between environmentalists and coal and utility interests was likely to arise.

Air pollution became a national problem in the United States, in part at least, because of the criticism of coal use (and also because of a rising concern over smog). Through the encouragement of health officials and academics, the Department of Health, Education and Welfare (HEW) sponsored the first National Conference on Air Pollution in 1958. The conference was not a classic confrontation between environmentalists and business leaders. Health officials, although unclear about the effects of air pollution on humans, were sufficiently concerned to propose that industry and government work together on its reduction. The conference attracted few people from the coal industry and just as few conservationists. (At that time, conservationists had yet to turn attention from efficient use of resources to questions of the quality of the environment.) In the 1958 conference, as well as the second conference in 1962, participants were enmeshed in debate over who possessed regulatory authority to deal with air pollution—the states or the federal government. By the third Conference on Air Pollution (1966), both coal and environmental interests were well-represented. The coal industry realized that it had to shape federal and state air pollution laws in order to protect its interests. In 1965, the industry's press conducted a lively dialogue on air pollution.

In the mid-1960s, a relatively innocuous law—the Clean Air Act of 1955—underwent several revisions that were potentially injurious to the coal and electric utility industries. The 1955 law affirmed that air pollution was a local problem, and the role of the federal government should be restricted to support and assistance in technical research. The 1967 Clean Air Act changed the emphasis somewhat, conjuring up the spirit of "cooperation" between industry and government. In the broadest sense, the effect of these revisions was that industry was brought into the policy-formation phase of air pollution legislation, resulting in a Clean Air Act that was "coal's law." Only with the Clean Air Act of 1970 would significant strides be made toward a national policy of air quality not tied so inextricably to the coal interests.

A national campaign against the most blatant forms of strip mining did not get very far in the 1960s. The issue did not reach the proportions of a *cause célèbre* until the late 1970s. Pennsylvania was the first state in which strip mining became a serious political issue. In 1961, the legislature passed the Pennsylvania Surface Mine Reclamation Act. In states that followed Pennsylvania's lead the results were the same: sufficient legislation but little enforcement. The scope of the environmental movement was not sufficiently broad in the late 1960s to confront the strip-mining issue.

CONSUMERISM AND ELECTRICITY

While the preoccupation of many consumers of electricity in the 1970s would be blackouts and brownouts, skyrocketing rate increases, and appeals for energy conservation, the postwar generation still wondered at the marvels wrought by the age of electricity and succumbed with childlike glee to all manner of products thrust on the market.

In many ways, the postwar era was truly an age of electrical marvel and wonder. Mass communications and entertainment were revolutionized by television. The electronics industry was born. Air conditioning systems virtually changed the environment, especially in the sultry climes of the South.[8]

TV: Tube of Plenty or Cultural Wasteland?

The "magic mirror," the "dream machine," the "idiot box" reflect the conflicting images of the most influential form of mass media ever devised. More than any people on earth, Americans took to TV as an essential fixture in their homes—a companion, an adviser, a diversion, an escape.

Transmitting pictures electronically had its origins in the late nineteenth century. But not until 1936 did the British Broadcasting Corporation initiate the first open circuit television system. In the United States, RCA began regular television service with experimental station WQXBS in 1939. By May 1940, there were twenty-three television stations on the air. World War II forced a halt in the production of receivers, but, by 1948, video was making a strong bid for public attention. In that year, over forty stations were operating, serving more than twenty major cities in the United States. TV receivers were sold as quickly as they could be produced.

With the precedent established by radio, commercial television was the only serious option in the United States. Large networks, ABC, NBC, CBS, soon dominated, often siphoning funds from their radio companies to pay the bills. By 1958, TV sets almost equalled the number of American homes. Radio and motion pictures lost ground to the rapidly rising medium.

Technical and organizational improvements were often the most tangible achievements of the industry. By 1968, about twenty million receivers were color sets. Community Access Television (cable TV) has been changing the very structure of the industry in recent years. While diversity and quality of programming lagged behind technology, the introduction of "educational," or public, broadcasting offered an alternative. Television as the transmitter of ideas, images, and emotions quickly found itself at the center of national debate over several key social, psychological, and even philosophical issues. The debate goes on: Is TV a radical force that shapes culture and patterns of behavior, or is it merely an "electric fireplace" that acts as background for other activities?

The Computer

The development of the electronic computer stands on a par with television as a major innovation in modern times. Until recently, computers have not

---

[8]The term "air conditioning" was coined in 1907. During the 1930s, production of equipment began on a commercial scale, and, by 1950, the industry was firmly established. Since 1960, the air conditioning business has been phenomenal. In the words of industry spokesmen, air conditioning passed through an era of "customer acceptance" into an era of "customer demand."

been a consumer item in the same sense that televisions have been. Yet their impact on the world of science, business, communications, and even entertainment has been staggering.

The development of the computer industry can be traced to Charles Babbage and his "Analytical Engine" during the mid-nineteenth century, although digital computers began with the abacus. About a century after Babbage worked on his Analytical Engine, Howard Aiken, a graduate student at Harvard, conceived of a mechanical automatic calculating machine similar to Babbage's. With the financial backing and technical support of International Business Machines (IBM), Aiken developed his Mark I, which he completed in 1944. Several others contributed to the development of the modern computer, and a new industry began to develop in the 1940s. Demand became especially acute as a result of World War II. With the development of UNIVAC I (Universal Automatic Computer)—whose most significant feature was stored programming—commercial development of electronic computers was underway in 1950–1951.

IBM, thrust into the computer business with the production of UNIVAC, delivered its first computer, the 701, in 1953. In that year, Remington Rand controlled the whole market. By 1955, IBM had a 56.1 percent share; in 1957, a 78.5 percent share. Along with the consolidations, the industry passed through several technical phases from the 1950s to the 1970s. In the second generation (beginning in 1959), technological advances were diffused, the transistor was adapted to computer use, and an array of "software" was introduced. A third generation of computers based on integrated circuits was started around 1965, and the development of minicomputers was made possible through advances in semiconductor components. In the 1970s, the computer industry passed into a fourth generation that was noted for large-scale integration, an explosion in the variety of computers, and computer-related products. The modern middle-class home is filled with reminders of this generation—handheld calculators, digital clocks, video games, and home computers.

Computers no longer simply keep account records, issue monthly bills, store personal information; they also run appliances, monitor temperatures in buildings, help operate automobiles, guide weapons systems, compose music, and have turned the telephone into a sophisticated communications center. Like television, computers are put to wondrous uses, but they are also subject to abuse. Intentional misuse, such as embezzling, falsifying records, and stealing information, are most comprehensible. The computer, Hal, in Arthur C. Clarke's *2001: A Space Odyssey* is a reminder of the potential for the invasion of privacy and unauthorized access to information that exists in the modern world of electronics.

In recent years, Americans have become less awestruck by the wonders of electronics and electricity itself. In the immediate postwar years, however, the so-called electronic revolution was discussed by scholars and commentators as being a central force in the evolution of American society. In the 1960s, media scholar Marshall McLuhan, designer R. Buckminster Fuller, policy adviser and social scientist Zbigniew Brzezinski, and others regarded electrical technology as a force for positive change—to enhance the sense of community, to break down centralized authority, to restore social harmony, and to bring about ecological balance.[9]

To others, the implications of the "electronic revolution" have been and will continue to be quite different. The electric utility industry, the television industry, and the computer industry have all moved toward consolidation and centralization, as have many other businesses. Computer centers in the Pentagon and interconnected electrical systems are major centralizing forces. Rather than providing a clean source of power, the generation of electricity through the use of coal, oil, and nuclear power creates serious pollution problems. Social impacts of electronic technology are not necessarily harmonious, benign, or pleasant.

As the United States matured and became more complex over time, its energy systems have followed a similar course. Providing heat, light, and power is out of the hands of the modern American. Few people chop down trees and burn the resulting logs, or jump on a horse and ride into the sunset. Electrical power, despite the ease with which it is accepted in present-day culture, is part of an energy system much too large for an individual to comprehend or control easily. Its generation is on a massive scale. Its transmission spans thousands of miles. Its applications are many and varied. That electricity has become an integral part of modern America is a cliché. That it has defied policy making is confounding. That it can be applied to useful ends, squandered carelessly, and sometimes misused speaks to its significance.

FURTHER READING

Erik Barnouw. *Tube of Plenty*. New York, 1977.

Neil Fabricant and Robert M. Hallman. *Toward a Rational Power Policy*. New York, 1971.

Craufurd D. Goodwin (ed.). *Energy Policy in Perspective*. Washington, D.C., 1981.

Erwin C. Hargrove and Paul K. Conkin. *TVA*. Urbana, Ill., 1983.

Charles J. Johnson. *Coal Demand in the Electric Utility Industry, 1946–1990*. New York, 1979.

George Katona. *The Mass Consumption Society*. New York, 1964.

Elmo Richardson. *Dams, Parks and Politics: Resource Development in the Truman-Eisenhower Era*. Lexington, Ky., 1973.

William Rodgers. *Brown-out: The Power Crisis in America*. New York, 1972.

A. M. Rosenthal and Arthur Gelb. *The Night the Lights Went Out*. New York, 1965.

---

[9]James W. Carey and John J. Quirk, "The Mythos of the Electronic Revolution," parts I and II, *American Scholar*, vol. 39 (Spring and Summer 1970).

Bruce A. Smith. *Technological Innovation in Electric Power Generation, 1950–1970*.
    East Lansing, Mich., 1977.
Nancy Stern. *From ENIAC to UNIVAC*. Bedford, Mass., 1981.
Richard H. K. Vietor. *Environmental Politics and the Coal Coalition*. College
    Station, Tex., 1980.
Aaron Wildavsky. *Dixon-Yates*. New Haven, Conn., 1962.

CHAPTER 12

Entering the Atomic Age: Nuclear Power in Peace and War

One can hardly avoid speaking in superlatives about nuclear power. It has come to be identified with hideous weapons capable of total human annihilation; with confrontation between superpowers; and with a revolutionary source of energy that possesses great potential but also generates equally great fears.

The "Atomic Age" began at 5:30 P.M., Monday, July 16, 1945. At that moment, Project Trinity—the detonation of the first atomic device at Alamogordo, New Mexico—met with success. From that day forward, the military use of atomic energy set the agenda for the development of nuclear power and its applications: technical innovations, the rise of "atomic diplomacy," control of fissionable materials, regulation of the nuclear industry, questions of health and safety, and an array of public reactions and responses.

Spawned by war, nuclear power is a special form of energy. Because of its military applications, the U.S. government regarded the development of atomic energy as crucial to national defense and national security; it, therefore, became the exclusive producer of fissionable material. The federal government, having a monopoly on nuclear energy, determined all its uses. As a result, commercialization did not occur in the energy market, was not subject to immediate scrutiny from the business community or the public, and was subordinated, at least in the early decades, to weapons development. Through the 1960s, nuclear power's *potential* as a commercial source, rather than its widescale application, was at the center of debate. A legacy of World War II research and development, commercial use of atomic energy was a future interest not a present obsession.

THE DISCOVERY OF ATOMIC ENERGY

The origins of the concept of atomic energy go back to the Greeks, but it was not until 1896 that Henri Becquerel discovered radioactivity. In 1902–1903, Ernest Rutherford and Frederick Soddy learned that atoms of certain elements—uranium, thorium, radium, and others—were spontaneously being transformed, or transmuted, into other atoms. They were ejecting small particles—alphas (neutrons) and betas (helium ions)—at great velocities and thus giving off heat. Despite this substantial discovery many questions remained: What was the exact structure of the atom? Where did the energy in the atom come from? Could energy be released from the atom on demand?

Work on these questions proceeded for the next several years. Rutherford and his colleagues developed a model of the atom in 1911 and demonstrated a nuclear reaction in 1919. In 1932, two of Rutherford's students, John Cockcroft and E.T.S. Walton, constructed a machine in which they could bombard a lithium atom with protons, producing two helium nuclei.

Rutherford, despite his contributions to atomic science, downplayed the possibility of extracting usable energy from the nucleus; "moonshine" he called it. Additional contributions nonetheless moved scientists closer to that goal. As early as 1930, Ernest Lawrence at the University of California developed a particle accelerator, a cyclotron, that could propel protons, electrons, and heavier particles at their targets.

The work of Otto Hahn and Fritz Strassman in Germany directly led to the harnessing of nuclear power. In 1938, they discovered a new phenomenon, nuclear fission or the release of energy through the "splitting" of heavy atomic elements. Since the release of energy through fissioning was enormous, a controlled chain reaction could provide a continuous source of energy for productive use.

THE ATOM IN WORLD WAR II

The Einstein Letter

The significance of the Hahn-Strassman discovery was not lost on some of America's new refugee scientists from Europe, especially Leo Szilard, an Hungarian emigré. The feasibility of creating a self-sustaining chain reaction through the fissioning process was established by 1939. What made these experiments crucial in the eyes of Szilard was the realization that German scientists might also achieve a chain reaction, giving Adolph Hitler access to a potent new weapon capable of making Nazi Germany a superpower.

Failing to get the American military interested in the weapons potential of the atom, Szilard and fellow Hungarian physicist Eugene Wigner enlisted the aid of another refugee scientist, Albert Einstein, to approach the President. A letter, under Einstein's signature, was presented to FDR in October 1939. In part, the famous document read:

> Some recent work by E. Fermi and L. Szilard . . . leads me to expect that the element uranium may be turned into a new and important source of energy in the immediate future. . . . This new phenomenon (nuclear chain reaction) would also lead to the construction of bombs, and it is conceivable though much less certain that extremely powerful bombs of a new type may thus be constructed.

The letter also intimated that experiments with uranium similar to those being conducted in the United States were being made in Berlin. In response, FDR told intermediary Alexander Sachs: "Alex, what you are after is to see that the Nazis don't blow us up." He then turned to Major General Edwin M. "Pa" Watson, his secretary, and said: "Pa, look into this. It requires action."[1]

Science as a National Resource

What the Americans did not know was that Germany was far from developing an atomic bomb. Since German scientists could not give any assurances that a bomb could be developed quickly, Hitler gave the project low priority. Furthermore, several leaders in the Nazi regime ridiculed nuclear physics as "Jewish physics."

While nuclear power had scant support in the United States, the impression that Germany was forging ahead with their atomic research kept interest alive. Part of the reason for the slow and modest response was the lack of a mechanism for studying such projects. In 1939, FDR had no personal science adviser and no standing science advisory committee. Science as a national resource had yet to achieve high status. The President, however, did establish an ad hoc Uranium Committee, but it accomplished little. For security reasons the committee excluded emigré scientists from participating in its decisions, thus eliminating input from those with the most intense interest in and knowledge about atomic science.[2]

Greater interest in nuclear power began with the creation of the National Defense Research Committee (NDRC) in 1940, followed the next year by the creation of the Office of Scientific Research and Development (OSRD). Vannevar Bush—engineer, mathematician, president of Carnegie Institution, and chairman of the National Advisory Committee for Aeronautics—was appointed head of the OSRD. The OSRD absorbed the Uranium Committee and the NDRC, which was under the direction of chemist James B. Conant, president of Harvard University. Bush and Conant were crucial to the development of fission energy for weapons use.

A major turning point in nuclear weapons development came with the MAUD Committee report. (MAUD was the code name for a British atomic energy research project.) The report, which reached the United States in spring 1941, stated that if pure Uranium 235 (U-235) was available in sufficient quantities, any neutron produced could cause fission. Since the neutron bombardment would be fast, the chain reaction would cause a massive explosion. The report went on to say that plutonium, produced through transmut-

---

[1] Cited in Corbin Allardice and Edward R. Trampnell, *The Atomic Energy Commission* (New York, 1974), p. 7.

[2] Some scholars have observed that because the emigré physicists were excluded from work on the most secret wartime projects (for instance, radar), they were free to pursue what they knew best: fission and nuclear physics.

ing a U-238 isotope, might also be used for bombs.[3] Finally, the MAUD report added that bombs could be made small enough to be carried on existing aircraft, and—most important—they could be produced within two years.

The feasibility of developing a superweapon stimulated renewed interest in nuclear research. Moreover, American leaders conjectured, if British scientists were making such progress, what about Germany? By fall 1941, the United States was involved in naval skirmishes with Germany in the Atlantic, on the brink of war with Japan in the Pacific, and extending massive aid to Great Britain. Convinced that the country would soon enter the war, the President instructed Bush to proceed rapidly with research and planning. However, no steps toward construction of a bomb were to be taken without further instructions. FDR also suggested to Winston Churchill that the United States and Great Britain enter into an atomic energy partnership to develop a bomb.

The Manhattan Project

In *A World Destroyed: The Atomic Bomb and the Grand Alliance* (1975), Martin J. Sherwin observed: "Linking fundamental research to military applications, the [Manhattan] project transformed scientists into weapons-makers and, at its end, introduced a world in quest of peace to history's deadliest weapon of war." The nuclear weapons development program came under the control of the Manhattan Engineering District (MED), a special organization under the U.S. Army Corps of Engineers. At its peak, the Manhattan Project employed 150,000 people and spent more than $2 billion to develop the atomic bomb.

The uniqueness of the enterprise was demonstrated by the personnel and their relationship to one another. General Leslie R. Groves was selected to spearhead the project. The former deputy chief of construction was an engineer long on management skills but short of patience with university scientists. His drive and determination were crucial to the project, but he was obsessed with security. Workers were subject to intensive investigations, censorship of correspondence, and even surveillance. What the scientists especially disliked was Groves' policy of "compartmentalization" of the work, which was carried out to such an extreme that only a few people knew what they were working on. "Compartmentalization" preserved secrecy, but it often led to morale problems and severely limited the free exchange of ideas that scientists so highly prized.

Despite his apprehensions about the scientific staff, Groves had to be pleased with the stellar quality of the group. Bush and Conant had advisory roles. Project leaders included Arthur H. Compton for plutonium work, Ernest O. Lawrence for electromagnetic separations, and J. Robert Oppenheimer for weapons work. Among the myriad scientific notables were Enrico

---

[3]Since U-235 is a rare isotope in naturally occurring uranium, the production of plutonium (PU 239) would provide an important source of fissionable material.

Fermi, Edward Teller, and Hans Bethe. With such a team the theoretical problems of nuclear physics would be worked out—but could theory be turned into a tangible by-product?

On December 2, 1942, a telephone message flashed from Chicago: "The Italian navigator has landed. The natives are friendly." The message was a signal that Enrico Fermi and his team of scientists had produced the world's first controlled nuclear chain reaction. Under the stands of Alonzo Stagg Field at the University of Chicago, Fermi had accomplished a feat that shifted the orientation of the Manhattan Project from research to practical application.

Even before Fermi's successful experiment, huge industrial facilities were constructed and made ready for use. At Hanford, Washington, the army built a massive plutonium production complex; at Oak Ridge, Tennessee, the field headquarters, isotope separation plants were constructed; at Los Alamos, New Mexico, the weapons research and development complex was built. Other sites for key research and operations were located throughout the country.

Hiroshima and Nagasaki

The success of Project Trinity was cause for celebration among the Manhattan Project team. Yet even before the trinity test, several of the scientists began to express second thoughts about what they "hath wrought." One of the physicists, Werner Heisenberg, later argued: "In the summer of 1939 twelve people might still have been able, by coming to mutual agreement, to prevent the construction of atom-bombs."[4]

The mood in 1939 was not amenable to such a possibility. But in late 1944, when it became known that the Germans were far from constructing atomic weapons, the initial incentive for developing the bomb was gone. For many scientists, there were other incentives: less trustworthy powers might develop the bomb if the United States did not, such as Russia; and atomic power might be harnessed for peaceful purposes after the war.

Most scientists contemplated their apprehensions privately. But some attempted to influence policy in 1944 and 1945. The eminent Danish scientist Niels Bohr was concerned about the postwar implications of atomic weapons. O. C. Brewster, an engineer for Kellex at Oak Ridge, wrote a long letter to Washington expressing his fear that civilization could be destroyed. Even Einstein and Szilard openly expressed their concerns. Szilard did not use the moral issue to make his case; he feared that use of the bomb would be harmful to America's long-range interests.

The protest infuriated Groves and led Compton to appoint committees to discuss the issues surrounding the soon-to-be completed bomb. The most significant was the Committee on Social and Political Implications, headed by James Franck. The Franck group recommended that nuclear weapons needed

---

[4]Cited in Arthur Steiner, "Scientists, Statesmen, and Politicians: The Competing Influence on American Atomic Energy Policy, 1945–46," *Minerva*, vol. 12 (October 1974), p. 469.

to be considered as "a problem of long-range national policy rather than of military expediency," that is, their use would ruin the chance for an international agreement on nuclear power and could precipitate an arms race. Furthermore, if the use of the bomb became a real option, then Japan—the remaining target since the surrender of Germany took place before the weapon was ready—should be warned in advance. An alternative proposal called for a demonstration staged for Japanese officials.

The Franck report and other advice had little affect on policy. Harry S Truman, who became president upon the death of FDR, on April 12, 1945, wavered little in his determination to use the bomb if and when it was completed. Truman appointed an Interim Committee to advise him on the use of the new weapon. The committee recommended that the bomb should be used against Japan as soon as possible and without prior warning. Doubts remained, however, and Truman approached Arthur Compton in private. "Arthur," he said, "you are a Christian man, a scientist, and an educator. In your personal view, all political and military views aside, what should I do?" He gave Compton a week to think about the question, after which time the scientist advised him to drop the bomb.

There is little doubt that Truman would have chosen this course irrespective of Compton's reply. In the context of seven long years of devastation—including the fire-bombing of Dresden and Tokyo—employing the atomic bomb did not seem as horrible as it would appear in hindsight. Many leaders viewed it simply as a larger version of existing weapons; the dangers of radiation were lost on most contemporaries. Truman was also operating within a government committed to completing a bomb before the Germans produced one and to the "unconditional surrender" of its enemies.

Dropping the bomb, however, was not a foregone conclusion. Some of Truman's military advisers favored a land invasion of Japan as least costly in lives and material. Others were convinced that the atomic bomb would end the war quickly and save American lives. The President sided with the latter group. In addition, he had the consent of the British government to use the bomb against Japan. And finally, the diplomatic implications of the act—controlling the postwar course of world affairs—was not lost on Truman. More than FDR, he was suspicious of Russian intentions in Europe and Asia once the war ended.

On August 6, 1945, the B-29 *Enola Gay* dropped the first atomic bomb ("Little Boy") from 31,600 feet onto the city of Hiroshima. The effects were that 80,000 people perished, almost 14,000 were missing, another 38,000 were injured. Of the city's 90,000 buildings, 62,000 were totally destroyed and another 6,000 were damaged beyond repair; 4 square miles of the city were razed. Three days later, a second bomb ("Fat Man") was dropped on Nagasaki, killing at least 35,000. On August 14, Truman announced that the Japanese had accepted the Allied surrender terms.

Euphoria over the end of World War II was mixed with the stunning nature of the act which ended it. Reconstruction of the attacks on Hiroshima and Nagasaki, and reanalysis of the circumstances surrounding the decision to drop the bomb, could not obscure the fact that warfare and international relations would never be the same.

THE ATOM AND THE COLD WAR

Maintaining the Nuclear Advantage

In the postwar years, maintaining control over nuclear power was an American goal with two dimensions. On the domestic side, the fundamental question was *how* rather than *if* the federal government would manage nuclear power. In the international context, the basic issue was how the United States could maintain its atomic monopoly without undermining good relations with its friends or unduly aggravating its apparent enemies.

The military significance of nuclear power afforded little debate over the necessity of government control. Thus, the initial postwar debate centered on where regulatory powers should lie. In its early stages, control of nuclear power transcended the old debates over public versus private power. Those who believed that government should not be in the energy or weapons business provided few answers on how the government could avoid it. The situation was not completely analogous to the Ancient Mariner and his albatross, but, for some, the comparison was not far from the mark. According to one observer: "After the war the American taxpayer discovered that he was the owner of a $2.2 billion business hardly heard of before."[5]

Before the war ended, military planners had already developed postwar plans for a peacetime agency to manage nuclear power. With the aid of the War Department and the support of the President, Representative Andrew Jackson May (Dem., Ky.) and Senator Edwin C. Johnson (Dem., Co.), the respective heads of the military affairs committees, presented a bill in 1945 that would create a board to oversee the atomic energy program. The purpose of the bill was to give the military a central role in the future development of nuclear power.

The May-Johnson bill was ill-conceived, and, according to one critic, confused the need for security with the need for haste. When news of the bill reached the scientists at the Chicago and Los Alamos laboratories, there was a storm of protest. The younger scientists, with fresh memories of General Groves, objected to the central role of the military.[6] They quickly called for public hearings and lobbied hard to defeat the bill. Their efforts, the continuing debate in the Senate, and the withdrawal of Truman's support killed the May-Johnson bill.

An alternative bill came from the Senate Special Committee on Atomic Energy. The freshman senator from Connecticut, Brien McMahon, chaired

[5]S. David Aviel, *The Politics of Nuclear Energy* (Washington, D.C., 1982), p. 15.

[6]The more senior scientists—Bush, Conant, Compton, and Lawrence—served on the advisory panel of the War Department.

this committee which had been formed during the debate over the May-Johnson bill. The McMahon bill offered a form of regulation similar to that in the May-Johnson bill, but it was markedly different in two ways. First, it deemphasized the military role in regulation. Second, the bill stressed the potential for civilian applications of nuclear power. On August 1, 1946, President Truman signed into law the Atomic Energy Act, giving the government a monopoly over nuclear power.

The question of international control of nuclear power was preconditioned by U.S. wartime experiences and shaped by the onset of the Cold War. Everyone recognized that the atomic bomb would give the United States a military advantage after the war, but both FDR and Truman realized that the bomb also had value as a diplomatic tool.

According to Professor Martin Sherwin, the potential diplomatic value of the bomb began to shape FDR's overall atomic energy policy as early as 1943. The President, especially at Churchill's urging, saw an Anglo-American monopoly of nuclear power as an essential counterweight to the postwar ambitions of other countries, particularly the Soviet Union. Truman was much more suspicious of the Soviets than FDR, and much more adamant that the possession of the bomb could make Josef Stalin more cooperative. His suspicions apparently extended to the British, since he proved less willing to nurture an Anglo-American monopoly than was Roosevelt.

Thus, a true desire for internationalization of the bomb did not exist at the war's end. Truman and several key advisers believed that the Russians would make significant concessions in exchange for neutralization of the bomb. Truman's "atomic diplomacy" was also built on the false assumption that the Soviets were many years away from developing their own nuclear device.

Where the USSR stood on the issue of the American nuclear monopoly remained murky through the late 1940s. At Potsdam, the last wartime conference between the Allies, Truman revealed to Stalin that the United States possessed a tremendous new weapon that it intended to use on Japan. The Soviet leader responded with indifference. Certainly he must have been concerned. But he was unwilling to reveal his feelings on the matter, possibly because Soviet scientists were working on their own bomb, or because Stalin already had been apprised of the existence of an American bomb.

The President nonetheless realized that some semblance of international control was needed. In November 1945, Truman, British Prime Minister Clement Attlee, and Mackenzie King of Canada issued a declaration calling for international control over atomic energy, that is, a willingness to share information for peacetime uses. They also recommended that the newly created United Nations establish a commission on nuclear power, and, in January, 1946, the General Assembly created the United Nations Atomic Energy Commission (UNAEC).

At the first meeting of the UNAEC, the United States presented a proposal for international control. After some alterations, the plan took the name of its presenter, Bernard M. Baruch. The Baruch plan called for international ownership and inspection of all atomic facilities and offered a transition period that would allow for the curtailment of American manufacture of atomic weapons and destruction of its stockpiles. At that point, atomic weapons would be outlawed. The Soviets balked: the United States would maintain its nuclear monopoly during the transition period, and the plan would generate unprecedented powers of inspection. The Soviets presented a counterproposal that simply called for the outlawing of nuclear weapons.

From the vantage point of Szilard and Bohr, there was little earnest interest in internationalizing atomic power from either the American or the Russian side. The situation became critical when the White House announced on September 29, 1949: "We have evidence that within recent weeks an atomic explosion occurred in the U.S.S.R." The Russian bomb, detonated in Siberia, was built at least two years before American intelligence sources had predicted. America's monopoly was over, the Cold War deepened, and the opportunity for international control slipped away.

The AEC and the JCAE

As an international policy, maintaining control over atomic power rested largely with the President. Domestically, it depended in large measure on the institutions established through the Atomic Energy Act of 1946: the Atomic Energy Commission (AEC) and the Joint Committee on Atomic Energy (JCAE). The AEC was unlike any government agency ever established. The five-man commission was meant to insure against the caprice and limited expertise of a single administrator. Below this body was an elaborate administrative system headed by a general manager who coordinated many program directors and field managers. In addition, the AEC included several advisory bodies, most notably the General Advisory Committee (GAC), which provided guidance in scientific and technical matters, and a Military Liaison Committee.

What was most unique about the AEC was its dual functions. It held a virtual monopoly over atomic energy development, including exclusive control and ownership of fissionable materials. At the same time, it was responsible for establishing regulations and standards for those licensed to use fissionable material. All atomic energy devices were licensed through AEC; all property and facilities associated with atomic energy were owned by AEC; responsibility for promoting research and disseminating basic scientific and technical information about nuclear power was granted to AEC. Never had a technology's control been so centrally coordinated, especially a technology that had yet to demonstrate its range of applications.

Little wonder that AEC's initial appointees were awaited with great interest. After a two-month search, Truman chose four Republicans and one Independent to serve on the commission. David E. Lilienthal was selected as chairman. Lilienthal's appointment, in particular, set off a political storm. The former chairman of the TVA and coauthor of the Oppenheimer-Lilienthal plan (then the Baruch plan), Lilienthal had outstanding credentials as an administrator. But powerful men attract powerful enemies, and he was subjected to a scathing and relentless attack by Senator Kenneth McKellar (Dem., Tenn.) during the confirmation hearings. Lilienthal had apparently short-circuited McKellar's efforts to exercise his patronage power within TVA several years before. The crusty, old senator claimed that Lilienthal had been part of a Communist cell within TVA. Prolonging the confirmation hearings only raised bad feelings, and it delayed the organization of the JCAE and disrupted the work of AEC project workers.

The Atomic Energy Act did not leave regulatory powers solely in the hands of AEC, however. Congress made sure that it was not excluded from assuming a pivotal role in national defense and national security policy vis-á-vis nuclear power, and it was always alert to protect its interests within the system of checks and balances. Senator Johnson and others had worked diligently on the McMahon Act to insure a strong role for the legislative branch. However, no existing committee appeared to be able to handle such a task. In the sense that AEC was an executive creation, the Joint Committee on Atomic Energy was a legislative innovation.

The eighteen-member committee had substantial jurisdiction in the area of regulation, and it had power as a regular standing committee in Congress. It made the AEC not only accountable to the executive branch but also to the legislative branch. The JCAE's primary functions were maintaining legislative power on all atomic energy bills; acting as a watchdog over matters of secrecy and security; maintaining policy and review functions on nuclear programs; and providing and gathering information on nuclear power.

Through its acquisition of data on nuclear power, the JCAE became an indispensable source of information with great influence and power. By the late 1950s, the JCAE was not simply reviewing policy, it was making it. Before 1974, only one bill proposed by the JCAE was questioned on the floor of Congress.

The Reactor Development Program

Establishing a control mechanism for dealing with nuclear power and the continuation of the weapons program preoccupied the AEC and the JCAE in the immediate postwar years. However, interest in the peaceful uses of nuclear energy began to attract some attention by the late 1940s. During the war, interest in generating power through the use of atomic energy ran high. In fact, in meetings with FDR, Churchill pressed for the rights to commercial use of atomic energy. The French were also interested, but did not have the close working relationship with the United States that Britain enjoyed.

The AEC moved in the direction of nonmilitary programs quite slowly. Before the passage of the 1946 act, some members of Congress queried whether military and nonmilitary nuclear programs should be separated. Truman rejected the idea, believing that the entire area of atomic energy development belonged within the proposed AEC.

Within the commission, interest in potential commercial uses for atomic energy evolved through the various reactor development programs. Yet building reactors to produce electricity was a minor consideration throughout the 1940s. The wartime reactors at Hanford were used to produce plutonium, and while valuable experience about reactor design and use were gained, they were not prototypes for the energy-producing reactors of subsequent years.

The AEC, nonetheless, was charged with encouraging peaceful applications of nuclear power. Consequently, Lilienthal set up an Industrial Advisory Group in 1947, which requested that the AEC declassify and publish more technical information as well as establish a reactor development program. In late 1948, the AEC created its first Reactor Development Program (RDP). Although modest, the program and the establishment of the Division of Reactor Development in 1949 made a beginning in the direction of peaceful uses of atomic energy.

The wartime reactor projects were the foundation for subsequent development. During the first phase of the RDP, the commission established the National Reactor Testing Station in Idaho to study various reactor concepts. One of four initial projects was made operational at the Idaho site. Two other early projects experimented with breeder reactors.[7] The final project was a land-based prototype for a submarine reactor. Three additional projects were added between 1950 and 1952, but at this juncture only a limited number of industrial firms—GE, Westinghouse, Phillips Petroleum, North American Aviation, and Union Carbide—were involved.

The achievements of the initial reactor program were modest and the costs high. In order to attract more interest from the private sector, the AEC began to ease its control of technical data. In 1949, the AEC granted more liberal access to selected industrial representatives, and, in 1951, it initiated an Industrial Participation Program, which granted security clearances to industry personnel and offered funding for promising reactor designs.

By the 1950s, nonmilitary use of nuclear power had made little headway, despite the reactor programs and growing interest within the JCAE. Industrial demand for electricity from nuclear power was negligible in the short run because of the availability of cheap fossil fuels. Planning for the long run required great expenditures without immediate rewards, and the AEC's financial support for reactor research was insufficiently attractive to many private firms. Most important, civilian projects were subordinated to weapons development in the postwar years. In 1948, more than 80 percent of the commission's budget went into military projects.

Of Nuclear Subs and the "Super"

The Cold War undermined peaceful uses of atomic power, as resources were devoted to the construction of bigger and better bombs and the stockpiling of those bombs. Nuclear weapons were at the heart of the growing tensions

---

[7]A breeder reactor produces more fissionable material than it consumes.

between the United States and the Soviet Union after World War II. Even
the issue of peaceful uses of the atom found its way into the "war of words"
in the 1940s and 1950s.

The United States' loss of its atomic monopoly in 1949 was a turning
point in the Cold War. Although it had a four-year lead over the Soviets in
nuclear technology and possessed a large stockpile of atomic weapons, the
United States viewed the Russian detonation of an atomic device as a serious
and *immediate* threat to its security (despite the fact that the Russians did not
have the capability to deliver atomic bombs to American targets in 1949).

During the late 1940s and 1950s, the development of nuclear weapons
continued at a fast pace. Through the almost single-handed effort of Admiral
Hyman Rickover, the AEC focused major attention on ship propulsion. Rickover believed that the technology of the light-water reactors was sufficiently
developed in the early 1950s that construction of nuclear submarines could
begin. A submarine with such an independent source of power could stay
underwater almost indefinitely, and it was sure to revolutionize undersea
warfare. Rickover got his wish, and, in 1954, the *Nautilus*, with its Westinghouse pressurized-water reactor, was completed. In 1955, *Seawolf*, boasting
a GE sodium-cooled power plant, was christened.

The single most impressive leap in nuclear destructive power was the
perfection of the hydrogen bomb, or the fusion bomb.[8] The "super," as it was
called, was 1,000 times more powerful than the fission bomb and represented
an incalculable leap in nuclear destructiveness. Immediately after the war,
few scientists and political leaders gave much thought to developing such a
bomb. But because the Cold War so decisively eroded the United States' sense
of security—and thus the adequacy of the A-bomb as a deterrent—supporters
of the H-bomb (Edward Teller, Lewis Strauss, Brien McMahon, and others)
were able to present their case to Truman.

Despite the opposition of the GAC, especially chairman Oppenheimer,
Truman gave the go-ahead on January 31, 1950. Within four years, AEC's
investment in plant facilities increased by more than $2 billion, operating
costs more than doubled, and manpower grew by a factor of three. In October 1952, thirty-three months after Truman's order, the first fusion bomb was
exploded at Eniwetok Atoll in the Pacific. The blast was equal to ten million
tons of TNT and utterly obliterated one island.

The "New Look," the Red Scare, and Atoms-for-Peace

By the time Dwight Eisenhower became president, the central role of nuclear weapons in America's foreign and military policy was already established. Eisenhower's "new look" for the armed forces was designed to scale
down European rearmament, emphasizing the deployment of nuclear weapons to replace manpower—"substituting machines for men." This policy was

---

[8]Instead of splitting heavy elements to create an energy release, the H-bomb produced energy
through the fusion of light forms of hydrogen to create helium.

emphatically embraced by Secretary of State John Foster Dulles, who spoke about an American policy of "massive retaliation" against Soviet aggression. While Eisenhower tended to treat confrontation with Russia more cautiously than did his melodramatic secretary of state, there is little doubt about the centrality of nuclear arms in the American foreign policy of the 1950s. When the Soviets detonated a fusion device of their own in August 1953, the nuclear arms race became even more ominous.

On the domestic scene, an ugly side effect of the Cold War and the nuclear arms race was the "Communist-in-government" controversy during the late 1940s and early 1950s, often referred to as "McCarthyism."[9] Proponents of McCarthyism charged that the Soviet acquisition of the bomb was due to espionage, subversion, and treasonous acts by unpatriotic Americans. The "witch hunts" conducted by McCarthy and others turned up little real evidence of massive subversion. There were, to be sure, a few "atomic spies" (Klaus Fuchs, for example, who was high up in the British nuclear establishment). The alleged crimes of others were not so clear, such as Alger Hiss and the Rosenbergs. However, it was the unrelenting use of the "big lie" and wild accusations that brought down many innocent people and threatened all Americans' civil liberties.

The AEC, and those associated with it, were not immune from the hunt for subversives. In 1949, the JCAE decided to investigate the AEC because of rumors that "Communists" were receiving AEC fellowships. The inability to account for several grams of uranium heightened congressional suspicion and led to charges against Lilienthal for mismanagement of the commission. In all, forty-five hearings were dragged out over several months. A report issued in October cleared the AEC, including the disappearance of the uranium (found in a vault at the Argonne National Laboratory). But the hearings took their toll on the daily operations of the commission and led to Lilienthal's resignation.

Five years later, about the time the McCarthyite craze was dissipating, the AEC upheld the decision of a review board denying J. Robert Oppenheimer, then chairman of the GAC, security clearance. Oppenheimer's earlier associations with left-wing groups, his continued friendship with colleagues associated with the left, his unfortunate misrepresentation of a 1943 conversation concerning the leakage of information to the Soviets, and his lack of enthusiasm for the development of the H-bomb was strong ammunition for his enemies. The award of the prestigious Fermi prize to Oppenheimer in 1963 did little to make up for the loss of his security clearance, which, in practice, denied him the ability to carry out research.

In the context of nuclear escalation, increasing world tensions, and the limited development of commercial atomic power, Eisenhower's "Atoms-for-Peace" speech is significant. On December 8, 1953, the President appeared before the UN General Assembly and proposed that the nations capable of

[9]Named for the junior senator from Wisconsin, Joseph McCarthy, who built his political career on the new Red Scare.

producing fissionable material contribute to a pool from which other nations could draw for nonmilitary purposes. This meant sharing civilian nuclear information. The speech also called for an International Atomic Energy Agency (IAEA).

Some observers viewed the plan as a way to create a large enough demand for fissionable material to limit what otherwise might be used to build weapons. Taking the argument a step further, others argued that Eisenhower, while pointing out the horrors of nuclear war, was trying to offer hope through expansion of the civilian uses of atomic energy. The appeal, through indirect means, sought some form of arms control and possibly disarmament. On a more pragmatic level, Atoms-for-Peace would allow the United States to maintain its commanding lead over the Russians, neutralize potential adversaries, and also provide a great propaganda outlet.

By taking the lead in developing peaceful uses for the atom, the United States could retain its overall leadership in nuclear power. This was particularly important because the British were moving rapidly toward large-scale power generation through atomic energy. The United States, therefore, supported ventures like EURATOM—a Western European nuclear cooperative designed to establish an integrated program for development of an atomic energy industry. EURATOM was significant because it offered energy-poor Europe an important new power source. Like the Marshall Plan, it would give the United States another way to promote stability in Western Europe, thus strengthening American interests in the Atlantic region.

While Atoms-for-Peace passed the Senate, it stood little chance of success in the 1950s. Suspicions and tensions stimulated by the Cold War were too great. The reception of the plan at home was lukewarm. Democrats criticized it for not going far enough. Liberals did not sufficiently trust AEC leadership to back the plan wholeheartedly. Right-wing Republicans saw it as a "give-away" program through which Eastern European countries could acquire enriched uranium.

While Atoms-for-Peace was good propaganda, the United States followed through with only mild support for the IAEA. When cheap oil became available from the Middle East, the idea of nonmilitary nuclear power development on a world scale petered out.

COMMERCIALIZATION OF NUCLEAR POWER

Atomic Energy Act of 1954

Given the events of the 1950s, it is amazing that commercialization of nuclear power occurred at all. But with the passage of the Atomic Energy Act of 1954, nonmilitary applications received a substantial boost. The energy market had little to do with this important event, since there was no pressing need for a new source of power in the United States. There was, however, a strong interest in enhancing American prestige. Several government leaders believed that it was important that the United States lead the way in the development of nuclear power, especially beyond weapons-making. Since nuclear power was a government-dominated and government-sponsored energy source, the mechanism for carrying out that goal—the AEC and the JCAE—was already in place.

Atoms-for-Peace set the tone for the commercialization of nuclear power. The election of a business-oriented Republican president in 1952 also gave a boost to commercial development. Direct support for commercialization, however, came from Congress and the AEC. In late 1952, the JCAE issued a report outlining the history and problems involved in developing atomic power for peaceful uses; however, the lame duck period was inappropriate for bold new legislation. In August 1953, the AEC began work to amend the 1946 law. After lengthy hearings, the Atomic Energy Act of 1954 (or the Cole-Hickenlooper Act) was passed.

The 1954 act combined the spirit of Atoms-for-Peace with a call to develop civilian nuclear power in the private sector. It authorized greater international cooperation for the AEC, by providing for more latitude in the dissemination of scientific data. It also sought to increase participation by private enterprise in the development and construction of reactors. Private firms would be allowed to own reactor facilities, with the government retaining ownership of the nuclear fuel.

The AEC was not retreating from nuclear power development altogether. It retained most of its regulatory powers, including issuing permits for entering the industry and constructing facilities; purchasing the industry's nuclear products or licensing such sales; and setting security and safety standards. The 1954 act also opened the door to JCAE decision making in the commercial reactor program.

The Power Reactor Demonstration Program

The 1954 act removed legal impediments to commercial development, but development itself was not automatic. Questions of technical feasibility and cost had to be considered. To move beyond simple speculation, the AEC announced its Power Reactor Demonstration Program in January 1955. The AEC would provide funding for research and development, and utility companies would build and operate the plants. Since the emphasis of the program was on large units, small utilities could not afford to participate. Of the four projects proposed, only one was successful. It was based on a pressurized water reactor (PWR), which had been through extensive development and testing in the navy's submarine propulsion program. However, little new research and development occurred during this first round.[10]

---

[10]The first full-scale electric power demonstration plant was authorized for Shippingport, Pennsylvania, in 1953. Completed in 1957, it incorporated a PWR.

Dissatisfied with the pace of round one, Senator Albert Gore (Dem., Tenn.) and Representative Chet Holifield (Dem., Calif.) of the JCAE introduced a bill to accelerate the reactor construction program. It called for the AEC to construct six nuclear power facilities of different designs (total cost, $400 million) and financed completely by the government. These facilities were in addition to projects already in operation.

The Gore-Holifield bill set off a political controversy. This was an opportunity for Democratic legislators to challenge the Eisenhower administration's plan for private development of nuclear power, and, in essence, to aggravate the public versus private debate that was raging over electrical utilities.[11] The bill passed the Senate but was defeated in the House when Republicans closed ranks, bringing with them Democrats from the coal states (who felt threatened by competition from nuclear power).

JCAE members had flexed their muscles despite the defeat. In response, the AEC moved more quickly toward commercialization. By the end of the Gore-Holifield debate, a second round of demonstrations, announced in September 1955, was directed at smaller utilities. Soon, a third round was announced (in January 1957). Round three encouraged both large and small companies to construct reactors of newer designs, especially moderated heavy water reactors and homogenous reactors.[12]

Technical problems similar to those in the previous rounds recurred. Trying to solve technical problems in a demonstration project was self-defeating. Thus, the AEC turned to a "modified" third round, announced in 1962, concentrating on proven designs to demonstrate that light-water reactors were reliable for commercial development.

Sputnik and Nuclear Power

The JCAE placed its hopes on the Kennedy administration to provide more aggressive leadership in developing nuclear power. President Kennedy's Cold War rhetoric—asserting that the United States would not back away from the challenges of world leadership—buoyed the spirits of the JCAE. Its hopes, however, were not fulfilled. Budget requests for 1962 and 1963 gave low priority to atomic power. After the successful launching of the Russian satellite, Sputnik, in 1957, it became apparent that the United States may have been ahead in the development of nuclear weapons but had slipped behind in rocketry. Sputnik also made it clear that the Russians now had the capability to direct an intercontinental ballistic missile (ICBM) at the United States from many miles away.

---

[11]See the section on Dixon-Yates in Chapter XI. For more on the public versus private debate, see Bonnie Baack Pendergrass, *Public Power, Politics, and Technology in the Eisenhower and Kennedy Years: The Hanford Dual-Purpose Reactor Controversy, 1956–1962* (New York, 1979).

[12]An homogenous reactor used fluid fuels with the fissionable material in solution or in suspension.

The belief that the country was no longer invulnerable to enemy attack, and the more general sense that American science was in a state of atrophy, convinced the Kennedy administration that research funds should concentrate on missile development and the space program. Kennedy also commissioned an Interdepartmental Energy Study Group to evaluate the nation's energy sources. As a consequence of these actions, nuclear power development—a symbol of American prestige—lost its glimmer.

In 1962, the AEC issued a report claiming that nuclear power was now commercially viable. But it created no waves of enthusiasm. The report was a hope, more than an assertion, that commercial nuclear power had arrived. In 1961, two-thirds of the reactor program's emphasis was on weapons and other military applications.

The AEC, therefore, had yet to make nuclear power development appear attractive to the private sector. The modified third round was an attempt to do that, as was the Private Ownership of Special Nuclear Fuels Act (1963), which allowed private companies to own nuclear fuels used to generate electricity and for other nonmilitary purposes. It was hoped that the new law would allow companies to predict their fuel costs more accurately, free the uranium industry from dependence on the government, and reduce the cost of financing private utilities with public monies.

Another approach to aid in commercialization was the development of "turnkey plants." Jersey Central Power and Light Company set a precedent by agreeing to purchase a 515,000-kilowatt nuclear plant from General Electric at a fixed price ($66 million). GE would build the facility and simply turn it over to Jersey Central when it was ready. While the costs were high for the contractors, both GE and Westinghouse used the technique to develop a market for nuclear power plants until about 1967. Cost overruns and flawed projections of energy demand eventually forced the companies to withdraw from the turnkey market, or to increase their bid prices.

Until the late 1960s, the question of economic feasibility dominated the debate over the nuclear option. Despite serious errors in estimating capital costs, demand for nuclear power facilities was on the rise. High coal prices and growing sensitivity to pollution problems associated with coal made nuclear power more attractive to utility companies. The great northeast blackout in 1965 also stimulated interest in nuclear power generation. As its response, the Federal Power Commission called for more interconnections and pooling of regional utility companies, which justified investment in larger units, including nuclear plants. In some general way, private utilities still feared government competition—"atomic TVAs" so to speak—thus adding another incentive to construct their own nuclear facilities.

By the end of 1967, American utility companies had ordered seventy-five nuclear plants; about half of all power plant capacity ordered was nuclear. By the end of 1969, ninety-seven nuclear plants were in operation, under construction, or had been contracted. For the moment, the future for the fledgling industry looked bright.

HEALTH AND SAFETY: THE FIRST ENVIRONMENTAL CHALLENGE

Beginning in the late 1960s, opponents of nuclear power seized on its health and safety risks, creating a major environmental controversy. Nuclear safety had been a secondary issue in the early development of nuclear power. The furious race to produce the bomb in World War II, the quest for strategic superiority engendered by the Cold War, and the search for prestige through commercialization of atomic energy received top priority. While proponents of nuclear power were aware of the dangers of radioactivity, they had confidence that the technology was safe or could be made safer. Moreover, the AEC's dual role as promoter and regulator of nuclear power had been heavily weighted to the former.

Questions of health and safety were raised as early as the 1950s, although they did not completely upstage or restrain the development of nuclear power. One of these issues—fallout from atmospheric testing—attracted a great deal of public attention; the other—reactor safety and siting of reactors—received less publicity but was no less significant.

The Fallout Scare

The testing of an H-bomb in the Marshall Islands on March 1, 1954, one of six large detonations conducted between March and April, led to an international crisis. A Japanese tuna boat, *Lucky Dragon*, in the vicinity of the blast was showered with fallout. All twenty-three seamen were exposed to radiation. On September 24, fisherman Aikichi Kuboyama died—the first casualty of an H-bomb. The fact that Kuboyama was Japanese made the event extremely symbolic.

Soon after the *Lucky Dragon* returned to port, Japan was in the throes of panic. A tuna scare swept the islands, and memories of Hiroshima and Nagasaki revived anti-American feelings. The Japanese government demanded a formal inquiry. In the United States, public debate over nuclear testing was widespread. Soon the furor was worldwide. According to historian Robert A. Divine: "The genie had escaped from the bottle—all the Eisenhower administration could do now was try to reassure a frightened world that the danger could be contained."[13]

The panic, however, was not easily contained, especially when Japanese doctors found traces of Strontium-90 in the bones of the *Lucky Dragon* victims.[14] With Kuboyama's death and the news of a Soviet nuclear test, fear of fallout reached serious proportions. Little by little the perils of fallout were made public, with the hope that the truth would quash the wildest rumors. An AEC report (February 1955) argued that while testing created risks to

---

[13]Robert A. Divine, *Blowing on the Wind: The Nuclear Test Ban Debate, 1954–1960* (New York, 1978), p. 22.

[14]Strontium-90 is a product of nuclear reaction not found in nature. It lodges in the bone, where it gives off radiation that can cause cancer.

health and genetic development, these risks were minor compared to the advantages in terms of national security. The AEC then promised to take adequate precautions in the future. This was a weak rationalization, but the administration tried to live with it and weather the criticisms.

A move to underground testing through a nuclear test-ban treaty with Russia did not materialize until 1963. In the meantime, informal efforts at curtailing atmospheric testing and government claims that the radiation problem was minor appeared to allay the worst fears. In the minds of many Americans, the fallout scare reconfirmed that nuclear power equaled the bomb. In a poll conducted by the utilities industry in 1972, 60 percent of the adults surveyed associated "nuclear" with violence or anxiety. Of the adults surveyed, 83 percent associated "atomic" with violence or anxiety, as did 90 percent of the youth.

Reactor Safety and the Price-Anderson Act

As nuclear power moved toward commercialization in the 1950s, a concern for safety was one of several issues that needed to be addressed. On the surface, the AEC was aware of the potential dangers of a nuclear accident. However, the AEC's role as promoter of nuclear power put it in the position of encouraging nuclear development first and then seeking safety standards. Reactors were evaluated on a case-by-case basis, with safety problems confronted as they arose. Convinced that the chance for a major accident was remote, AEC seemed to regard safety as an engineering problem.

A mechanism for dealing with safety issues was established within the commission as early as 1947—the Reactor Safety Committee—chaired by Edward Teller. The committee's primary responsibility was to evaluate and audit technical health and safety factors of reactor hazards. Teller later commented that the committee was not very popular and had been referred to as the "Committee for Reactor Prevention." In 1950, a second advisory group, the Industrial Committee on Reactor Location Problems, was established to deal with nontechnical considerations of siting plants. To avoid duplication and to refocus the safety program, the two groups were merged into the Advisory Committee on Reactor Safeguards (ACRS) in 1953. With the passage of the 1954 act, however, the ACRS lost its important role in the licensing process, partly because the members of ACRS were part-time consultants. Shortly before the passage of the act, a full-time reactor hazards review group—the Hazards Evaluation Staff—was established.

The 1954 act included at least twenty-five references to health and safety and greatly increased the scope of the licensing program. Exactly how health and safety were to be protected, however, was not spelled out clearly. Into the 1960s, AEC regulations were vague on this point. There were no specific safety standards, applied universally, for all reactor projects and no independent safety research program. Emphasis on promotion made safety a specific, rather than a general, problem to be dealt with as the need arose.

Controversy over safety was first dramatized in the case of the Fermi plant, built at Lagoona Beach, Michigan. In January 1956, the Power Reactor Development Company (PRDC), a consortium of twenty-five equipment manufacturers and utility companies, applied for a license to construct a fast breeder. AEC interest was high because this would fulfill its goal of having the industry move beyond the light-water reactor.

Within AEC, several questions were raised about the proposed site (which was thirty miles from Detroit and Toledo). A partial fuel meltdown in an experimental breeder reactor in November 1955, further complicated the evaluation process.[15] Meetings between the PRDC and the fast breeder sub-committee raised several safety questions. In June 1958, the ACRS issued a report that contained serious reservations about the state of breeder reactor research and the proposed Fermi plant.

The issue became political when JCAE Chairman Senator Clinton P. Anderson (Dem., N.M.) learned of the existence of the Safeguards Committee report. The AEC refused to give him the document, arguing that it was an internal memorandum not a formal report. This set off a major jurisdictional battle. While the debate raged, the AEC issued a "conditional" construction permit, subject to later review, stating that the safety problems would have to be solved prior to the operation of the plant. The idea of a "conditional" permit, although not supported unanimously within the commission, became an accepted means for dealing with reactor safety problems.

Senator Anderson had another point of view. Incensed at AEC's secrecy, he threatened to seek separation of AEC's regulatory functions from its promotional functions. Short of accomplishing that, Anderson secured passage of the Price-Anderson Act in 1957. The act established the ACRS as a statutory body to review every license application and to issue a public report in each case. In addition, it required public hearings for all application proceedings, contested or not. Anderson won a partial victory by forcing the AEC to conduct some of its business in the open.

The best-known portion of the Price-Anderson Act—the indemnification measures—actually increased AEC's influence as a promoter of nuclear power. Many private companies were hesitant to invest heavily in nuclear power plants because of a concern over the potential liability should a major accident occur. A 1957 AEC report (WASH-740) concluded that the likelihood of an accident resulting in a major release of radioactive material outside the reactor ranged from 1 in 100,000 to 1 in 1 billion per reactor year. In the worst case, however, such an accident might result in 34,000 fatalities, 43,000 injuries, $7 billion in property damage, and contamination of 150,000 square miles.

The AEC regarded these estimates as evidence of the safety of nuclear reactors. To private companies, the report only added to their uneasiness. As early as 1955, the AEC encouraged the insurance industry to explore its own

[15]Nuclear fuel is unpredictable when it melts. Even when the fission stops, the heat produced may cause the core to melt through the reactor vessel into the earth ("China syndrome"), or molten fuel can react with the coolant or the air causing a chemical explosion.

ability to provide liability policies, leading to the formation of three insurance syndicates willing to extend such coverage. Utility companies were still hesitant until the passage of Price-Anderson. It limited the liability of an individual company ($560 million) and provided governmental subsidies to cover liability above insurance coverage. Price-Anderson, therefore, not only confronted the safety issue but stimulated commercial development as well. In the 1970s, the indemnification measures would be singled out by opponents of nuclear power as a public admission of the dangers of nuclear power.

Despite the questions raised about reactor safety, there was little in the way of public protest during the 1950s. Other issues, such as health hazards to uranium miners, were likewise ignored or overlooked. The activity that most closely resembled an organized protest was the efforts of the AFL-CIO to force a public hearing on the construction permit for the Fermi plant (and eventually on other siting and licensing issues). In 1957, the AEC held a public hearing on the PRDC permit—the first public hearing on licensing of nuclear plants. But the commission reconfirmed the permit in 1958, and, despite further legal action from the union, the Supreme Court upheld it in a landmark decision in 1961.

Nuclear Accidents, Siting, and Remote Location

During the early 1960s, nuclear power safety took on greater importance as a public issue. Some nuclear accidents had already taken place outside of the United States. In 1957, Windscale Pile Number One in England experienced a nuclear fire, resulting in a release of radioactive contaminants into the air over England and into Western Europe. According to an exiled Russian scientist, radioactive waste buried in the Ural Mountains exploded in 1958, causing hundreds of deaths. In the United States, an experimental reactor exploded at the National Reactor Testing Station in Idaho Falls. The AEC claimed that the resulting three fatalities were due to an electrical power-surge blast; union officials claimed they died from radiation. In any event, these accidents took the safety question out of the realm of the abstract and into the real world.

An immediate effect of the Idaho accident in 1961 was guidelines for siting nuclear reactors away from large urban populations. In 1962, AEC set down a procedure for relating plant size to distance from dense populations, formalizing the concept of "remote location." This policy led the AEC to deny Consolidated Edison of New York a permit to build a reactor in Queens. Similar decisions were reached concerning the building of reactors in Los Angeles and Burlington, New Jersey. By the late 1960s, however, the remote location concept had not evolved into a clear set of standards, and, in some cases, the AEC was relaxing its demands to accommodate utilities.

Local opposition to siting of nuclear power plants was most prevalent in California. The Northern California Association to Preserve Bodega Head and Harbor challenged the industry's seismic evidence supporting the building of a plant at Bodega Bay. In 1964, Pacific Gas and Electric, the company planning to construct the plant, agreed to work jointly with the Sierra Club to find an alternative site. Additional protests arose in 1967 over the building of plants along fault lines in southern California.

The glut of licensing requests after 1966 strained AEC's review system and limited its efforts at ordering safety modifications in existing plants. A partial meltdown at the Fermi plant in 1967 was a clear warning about the need for careful licensing and monitoring practices. In this instance, the safety controls worked, no large-scale release of radioactivity occurred, and no one was injured. But the plant had been plagued with problems from the start. While it was issued a new operating permit and operated on a limited basis through 1972, it was ultimately shut down and dismantled. By the time antinuclear protests heated up in the 1970s, the meltdown at the Fermi plant became the centerpiece of suspicion.

The building of the Monticello reactor in Minnesota also publicized the nuclear safety issue. The Northern States Power Company (NSP) requested permission to construct the reactor in 1966. What made the project unique was the extent to which well-organized citizen involvement played a role in the construction and operating license stages. The controversy revolved around a battle between the AEC and a state pollution control agency over regulating plant emissions. In May 1967, the Minnesota Pollution Control Agency (MPCA) was formed and attempted to gain jurisdiction over radioactive emissions from the plant. AEC claimed sole responsibility—a position with which the Supreme Court concurred in 1971. But public protest went beyond the jurisdictional battle; it raised the question of citizens' rights in licensing and siting of plants. In response to the protests, a Symposium on Nuclear Power and the Public was held at the University of Minnesota.

The tone of antinuclear protest in the 1970s was established in Minnesota and at similar meetings in New York, Vermont, and California. By 1969, others were questioning the environmental dangers of radioactivity. For its part, the AEC had no ready answers. Its Safety Research Program proved inadequate and was terminated in 1965. After that time, questions of nuclear safety within AEC focused primarily on reactor safety, and the general position of the commission was that reactors had enough engineering safeguards to make them safe. The range of safety issues was too narrowly conceived by the AEC at this point, and, as critics of nuclear power argued, safety measures had to be considered from the mining of uranium to the disposing of radioactive wastes.

By the 1970s, expectations and anxieties over nuclear power had built up to a high pitch. The technical feasibility of large, electricity-generating nuclear plants was established. Nuclear power reached its peak in 1967; contracts in that year alone were equivalent in megawatts to all prior years. Construction permits were granted for twenty-three reactors. But just as quickly as the new industry was born, it faced marked and immediate decline. In 1968 and 1969, the economic feasibility of nuclear power was seriously questioned. An anticipated shortage in fossil fuels did not occur; cost overruns in the plants under construction exceeded the most liberal estimates; higher interest rates and a tight-money economy slowed the flow of production; and increased public concern over safety and siting threatened to stall or block further projects. By September 1968, only fourteen plants, generating about 2,800 megawatts of power, were operable.

For the AEC, the years ahead would also be difficult. The development program had been costly and had been carried largely by government funds. The AEC spent more than $2 billion in bringing nuclear reactors to commercial implementation. With the decline in the nuclear power market in the late 1960s, some questioned the wisdom of the heavy governmental commitment. But other criticisms of the commission posed more serious problems. While the AEC considered light-water reactor technology to be sufficiently developed for wide usage, accidents, further research on the effects of radiation, and siting problems tested AEC's credibility.

The potentially most serious challenge to the development of commercial nuclear power was the rising environmental movement. Local protests made way for demands for stricter regulation, efforts at discrediting safety reports, pressure for environmental impact studies, and even obstruction of plant construction. Nuclear proponents argued that public misinformation or ignorance of the technology accounted for a great deal of the skepticism. But public information programs launched by the AEC or the industry had a ring of propaganda to them.

There was no escaping the fears of nuclear holocaust. During the Cuban Missile Crisis in October 1962, school children were given instructions on how to protect themselves from an atomic flash. Many Americans were frightened into digging fallout shelters in their yards. Efforts at a nuclear test-ban treaty (1963), and commencement of the Strategic Arms Limitations Talks (SALT) in Helsinki in late 1969, offered some hope. But the link between peaceful and military uses of nuclear power—irrational or no—persisted. Nuclear power was the most significant new energy source of the postwar years precisely because it was the most awesome.

FURTHER READING

Corbin Allardice and Edward R. Trapnell. *The Atomic Energy Commission.* New York, 1974.

Wendy Allen. *Nuclear Reactors for Generating Electricity.* Santa Monica, Calif., 1977.

S. David Aviel. *The Politics of Nuclear Power.* Washington, D.C., 1982.

Lawrence Badash. *Radioactivity in America.* Baltimore, 1979.

Frank G. Dawson. *Nuclear Power.* Seattle, 1976.

Steven L. Del Sesto. *Science, Politics, and Controversy.* Boulder, Colo., 1979.

Harold P. Green and Alan Rosenthal. *Government of the Atom.* New York, 1963.

Morton Grodzins and Eugene Rabinowitch. *The Atomic Age.* New York, 1963.
Richard G. Hewlett and Francis Duncan. *Atomic Shield, 1947–1952.* University
     Park, Pa., 1969.
—————— and Oscar E. Anderson, Jr. *The New World, 1939–1946.* University
     Park, Pa., 1962.
George T. Mazuzan and J. Samuel Walker. *Atomic Safety: Licensing and Regulating
     Peaceful Atomic Energy, 1946–1962* (in press).

CHAPTER 13

OPEC and the Changing World Order

Oil was a major international issue after World War II. As the strategic and economic importance of oil in world affairs unfolded, American policy makers were exposed to the interplay among domestic and foreign oil production, transportation, marketing, and consumption. However, it took the energy crisis of the 1970s to make them understand that developing nations in the Middle East, Africa, and Latin America had acquired greater control over their own oil resources during the past two decades. If a revolution occurred in the world of oil in the postwar years, it occurred in terms of that shift in control.

As a period of transition for international oil, the postwar years complicated the task of those who made energy policy. Consumption and trade patterns were in flux. The center of oil production shifted dramatically from the Western Hemisphere to the Middle East. The Cold War introduced an array of tensions. And at home, the insistence of domestic oil producers for protection from imports, and the demands of environmentalists for protection from air pollution and the oil companies further blurred perceptions of the rapidly shifting energy picture. Energy may well have been the issue of the 1970s, but it only became such because crucial changes had taken place during the previous twenty-five years.

OIL IN THE POSTWAR WORLD ECONOMY

The place of petroleum in the world economy changed markedly after 1945. The war hastened the transition from coal to oil in Europe and Japan by destroying, temporarily at least, much of the coal production and transport capacity. The war also accelerated the growth of petrochemicals, especially crucial items such as synthetic rubber, fertilizers, plastics, and synthetic fibers. Between 1949 and 1971, world energy consumption more than tripled. While coal met nearly 67 percent of the energy needs in 1949 and oil less than 25 percent, by 1971 coal use dropped to about 33 percent and oil use rose to 43 percent (natural gas was 21 percent). Gasoline and residual fuels for industry accounted for the bulk of oil demand in non-Communist nations.

Not only were there new oil markets in the postwar years, but also new marketers. In 1950, the "Seven Sisters" controlled world oil supplies.[1] They had interlocking joint ventures in major concession areas and controlled most transportation, marketing, and refining. In the late 1940s, the primary flow of petroleum was from South America to the United States and Europe, and from the Middle East to Europe and Asia.

By 1961, however, the control of oil was being challenged by "independents" venturing into the Middle East and North African oil regions; by host governments working out new arrangements with the oil companies and, in some cases, nationalizing their own oil industries; and by competing cartels, especially OPEC. That year, there also was a great expansion in the volume of oil produced, and the flow of petroleum was more complex: from the Middle East to the United States, Canada, and to Southeast Asia and Japan; from North Africa to Western Europe; from Indonesia to Australia and Japan; and from the USSR to several markets. The Middle East—not the Americas—was the center of world production.

Another important development was the rise in the trade in crude compared with petroleum products. By 1950, over half of the total international petroleum trade was in crude, and, by the 1970s, that figure increased to more than 80 percent. This was primarily the result of the postwar tendency to situate refineries in consuming markets. In Europe, especially, the reasoning was simple—with shortages in dollars, problems in foreign exchange, and trade restrictions, it was cheaper to import crude and utilize local refineries. For American companies operating in the Middle East, it was cheaper to ship crude to Europe and refine locally in the large European markets. This practice further enhanced the importance of Middle Eastern and North African oil reserves.

Cold War politics and diplomacy complicated the oil situation. For example, rebuilding Western Europe was a major goal of United States foreign policy in the late 1940s. European recovery, among other things, meant the restoration of markets for American goods. A sound and stable Western Europe was also a bulwark against Russian expansion. In a commencement address at Harvard University, Secretary of State George C. Marshall presented the Truman administration's proposal for European recovery. Dubbed the Marshall Plan (1948), it provided aid under provision that economic rehabilitation be carried out jointly among the participating nations.

Europeans used Marshall Plan funds to purchase large quantities of imported oil. Pressure from the United States and the participating nations led the oil companies to offer oil at lower prices than initially quoted. Between 1950 and 1953, the average price of oil to Europe dropped 25 percent. This helped to spur recovery, but it also increased European dependence on im-

---

[1]The following seven companies controlled virtually all the reserves in less-developed regions of the world and a large share in developed countries: British Petroleum, Royal Dutch-Shell, Mobil (Socony-Vacuum), Exxon (Standard of New Jersey), Socal, Texaco (Texas), and Gulf.

ported Middle East oil. Similarly in Occupied Japan, imported oil was used to stimulate industrialization. By 1950, the Japanese government allowed multinational oil companies to obtain equity with Japanese refining. Japan, like Western Europe, increased its dependence on foreign oil.

VENEZUELA AND THE 50-50 PLAN

While the stature of the Middle Eastern oil industry grew in the late 1940s, Latin American oil, with the exception of Venezuelan oil, became less important as an exported item. American companies produced oil primarily in Venezuela, but also in Argentina, Colombia, and Peru. Government companies in Brazil and Chile had limited output, and Mexico and Bolivia operated their expropriated industries at a relatively low level of production.

In Mexico, once the most important producer in Latin America, Pemex almost reached productive capacity in 1945 with very small exports. In fact, exports were almost completely eliminated after the industry was nationalized (1938). The expropriated companies sought to exclude Mexican oil from world markets, and Pemex was unable to maintain sufficiently high production. Compounding these problems in the late 1950s and 1960s were government policies forbidding exports, largely as a way of converting crude into refined products to be used internally. As a result, Mexico lost a great amount of foreign exchange earnings.

A precedent set in Venezuela in 1948 changed the relationship between host countries and oil companies in Latin America and throughout the world. Despite the faltering of the Latin American oil industries, Venezuela remained a world leader and continued to increase production until the late 1950s. The continued significance of Venezuelan oil allowed the government to extract new concessions from Creole Oil and other companies operating in the country.

Memories of the Mexican expropriation also made the oil companies cautious in dealing with Venezuelan leaders. After the overthrow of General Isaias Medina's government, the new *Accion Democratica* government raised taxes on oil production. In an unprecedented move, foreign oil companies signed contracts with labor unions in Venezuela (the *Accion Democratica* government supported labor's grievances) in 1946. Two years later, a new labor contract included a revision in the income tax law, which required the oil firms to split profits 50-50 with the government.

The industry suffered little in this series of events, as production rose dramatically and foreign taxes were credited against the companies' American income taxes. However, the precedent formalized the view that oil had "intrinsic" value—not value tied only to demand—and it enhanced the power of the host government in controlling its precious resource. This concept, promoted by Venezuela, was not lost on the producing countries of the Middle East and North Africa.

SAUDI ARABIA AND THE "GOLDEN GIMMICK"

The impact of the Venezuelan precedent was felt most significantly in the Middle East in general and in Saudi Arabia in particular during the 1950s. Because of the growing strategic and economic importance of the Middle East to the United States, any change in the relationship between the Saudis and the oil companies had an impact on national policy. The steady flow of Saudi oil was important to many interests: to the military, increased production meant conservation of strategic reserves in the Western Hemisphere; to the State Department, economic stability for Saudi Arabia was an important safeguard against the spread of Soviet influence in the Middle East; to "crude-poor" independent oil firms, potential concessions; to Socal and Texaco, financial success; and to King Saud, vital revenue for the modernization of his country and the enhancement of his personal wealth.

The decision of Socal and Texaco to admit Exxon (Standard of New Jersey) and Mobil (Socony-Vacuum) into ARAMCO in 1947 set in motion a series of events that led to crucial changes in American-Middle Eastern relations. Exxon, especially, found itself in dire need of additional supplies of crude. Its production was being absorbed by markets in North America, and it felt threatened by CASOC's control of vast and cheap reserves in Saudi Arabia. To keep Socal and Texaco out of its European and Japanese markets, Exxon, along wtih Mobil, sought a way into ARAMCO in 1946.

Exxon initially faced resistance from Socal and Texaco. But it was also bound by the Red Line Agreement barring members of the IPC from seeking concessions in Saudi Arabia. Several things were working in Exxon's and Mobil's behalf, which led to their admission into ARAMCO. The U.S. government favored more penetration of American firms into Saudi Arabia to insure rapid economic development—and thus increase American influence there. The Saudi government saw an opportunity to open more concessions and accrue additional revenue. Socal and Texaco needed more capital and were looking for a way of sharing the risk of their venture. Finally, Exxon and Mobil convinced the IPC partners that the Red Line Agreement was no longer valid under new interpretations of American antitrust law (although lawsuits kept this issue alive until a settlement was reached with IPC members in 1948).

The precedent set by the inclusion of Exxon and Mobil into the concession areas of Saudi Arabia was followed by the inclusion of other oil companies, who the Saudis were willing to greet with open arms. ARAMCO's position was threatened in particular by the efforts of J. Paul Getty. To obtain a concession, Getty offered to pay $.55 a barrel royalty as compared with the $.21 royalty that ARAMCO paid. (Like other oil firms, ARAMCO paid a fixed royalty.)

The Saudis could accept the offer, but because of their relationship with ARAMCO, a new arrangement to raise revenue was first in order. Possible alternatives were to request an increase in production or to change the royalty arrangement in some way. While ARAMCO could not ignore the Saudi demands for higher revenue, the alternatives seemed equally unpalatable. ARAMCO did not want to raise prices to its European customers, which would undercut postwar recovery, nor did it want to increase production markedly, for fear of driving down prices and creating a serious glut. It also wanted to avoid raising royalty payments which would cut into profits. As a result, it turned to the U.S. government for help.

A happy solution was found—happy for ARAMCO, Saudi Arabia, and the U.S. government at least. That solution was a foreign tax credit, or the "golden gimmick" as it was later called. Used in dealing with Venezuelan oil, and common among other industries abroad, the foreign tax credit allowed taxes imposed by a foreign government to be credited against U.S. taxes. Instead of changing the royalty schedule, the Saudis simply levied an income tax on ARAMCO. In November 1950, it imposed a 20 percent tax with an increase to 50 percent later on. The payment to Saudi Arabia increased from $56 million in 1950 to $110 million in 1951, while ARAMCO's tax payment to the United States decreased from $50 million to $6 million.

The State Department, the Treasury Department, and the Internal Revenue Service did not oppose the action. It was regarded as the least painful way—for the company and the government, if not the American taxpayer—to deal with a difficult economic and diplomatic problem. For the State Department, the golden gimmick helped to bolster the Saudi government without either relying on direct foreign aid or reducing ARAMCO's profits. ARAMCO lost nothing, and indeed gained stature in Saudi Arabia by retaining its sources of production. The Saudis were also satisfied because they now shared profits 50-50 with the company. The golden gimmick was soon imitated in Iran and Kuwait, and eventually was used by the British in their dealings in the Middle and Near East.

Tapline and Zionism

Part of the agreement that Socal and Texaco reached with Exxon and Mobil in the late 1940s dealt with participation in the building of a trans-Arabian pipeline (Tapline) to deliver Saudi oil to the Mediterranean. The project was completed by 1950 at a cost of about $200 million and through the efforts of more than 16,000 workers. The herculean task was matched by the political storm that it created.

The Trans-Arabian Pipeline Company was formed in 1945, and the project was approved by ARAMCO the following year. Aside from the technical problems in a project of this type, rights-of-way or wayleaves had to be obtained from the different states and territories along the proposed route. The initial plant was to establish the terminus in Palestine, but mounting Arab-Jewish tensions led the company to choose an alternative route through Lebanon and Syria. The dealings proved most difficult, but ultimately a 1,040-mile pipeline was completed between Saudi Arabia and the coast of Lebanon.

The Tapline issue was indicative of how the growing Arab-Israeli conflict affected oil exploitation in the Middle East and complicated the development of American foreign policy in the region. In 1947, Great Britain relinquished its mandate over Palestine; the following year, the United Nations voted to partition it. While American policy on a Jewish homeland vacillated over the years, the United States initially endorsed the UN proposal.

Since the Arabs greeted the plan with intense opposition, the United States withdrew its endorsement and called for a temporary UN trusteeship as an alternative. Convinced that they would have to work in their own behalf, the Jews proclaimed the formation of the state of Israel in the wake of the British withdrawal from Palestine in May 1948. This action led to a full-scale war between the new Israelis and the Arab League (Egypt, Syria, Lebanon, Transjordan, Iraq, Saudi Arabia, and Yemen). In the meantime, U.S. policy reversed itself again when Truman decided, after receiving conflicting advice, to recognize the state of Israel. Through the efforts of the UN, an armistice was reached in 1949, but the state of Israel remained and so did this new Middle East dilemma.

Opposition to Zionism and the creation of the state of Israel came especially from the Departments of State and Defense. Citing American oil interests in the Middle East and the threat of Soviet activity in Iran and Turkey, diplomats and military leaders argued vigorously against a pro-Zionist foreign policy.

The State Department, in particular, argued that such a shift in policy could weaken King Saud's role in the Arab world and make him increasingly vulnerable to Iraqi and Syrian extremists. To what degree the State Department's anti-Zionism was also anti-Semitism must be left to conjecture. Nevertheless, the department's strong adherence to a policy tied to American oil interests, and the President's support for the creation and maintenance of Israel, mixed political, economic, and strategic goals in such a way as to insure that future U.S. policy in the region would be less predictable and more contradictory.

THE IRAN CRISIS

The rising tide of nationalism in the Middle East challenged the role of American oil companies there, but without the immediate results experienced in Mexico. Through the 1950s, the American contingent among the Seven Sisters did not relinquish their control of oil. The Iran crisis bears that out most dramatically.

Three years before the 50-50 arrangement was reached in Saudi Arabia, the Iranian *Majlis* (Parliament) demanded the renegotiation of its concession with British Petroleum (BP). Resistance from BP, the precedent of the 50-50 arrangement, and other issues led to a growing interest in the nationalization of the Iranian oil industry. In 1951, Premier Razmara, an opponent of nationalization, was assassinated. He was replaced by Dr. Mohammed Mossadegh, who had led the opposition to BP and strongly favored nationalization. Im-

mediately after Mossadegh's rise to power, a bill passed the *Majlis* nationalizing the assets of BP. "For the happiness and prosperity of the Iranian nation," the bill read, "and in the interest of world peace, it is hereby resolved
that the petroleum industry shall be nationalized throughout the territory
without exception, that is to say: all the operations of exploration, extraction,
and exploitation shall be conducted by the government."[2]

The exhilaration of this victory over economic imperialism soon dissi-
pated. The British were determined to take legal action against any company
purchasing or distributing oil from Iran. The major international oil companies soon boycotted Iranian oil, leaving the country no distribution channels
to sell a product essential to its economic survival. To compensate for the loss
of Iranian oil, production in Saudi Arabia, Kuwait, and Iraq was stepped up.
The proclamation of nationalization failed, in and of itself, to release Iran from
the foreign domination its new leaders despised.

As a result of the British pressure, the new Iranian government faced
two years of economic distress. In May 1953, Mossadegh wrote to the newly
elected U.S. President Dwight Eisenhower complaining about BP's efforts to
destroy Iran's economy. When Eisenhower finally answered, he sided with
the British claims, insisting that Iran had to live up to its obligations.

While Truman was still president, however, the United States had gone
beyond simply echoing British claims against Iran; it had devised a consortium of major U.S. companies and BP to stimulate production. To clear the
way, Truman called off an FTC antitrust investigation of Exxon, Socal, Texaco, Mobil, and Gulf in January 1953. The Departments of State, Defense,
and Interior were most instrumental in persuading Truman to take this course
of action. The decision coincided with BP's willingness to take a 40 percent
share in the consortium, which would also include Compagnie Française de
Pétrole (CFP), five American majors, and a small group of independents.

The consortium was assured because of the fall of the Mossadegh government in August 1953, in which the Americans played a central role. After
the British Foreign Minister Anthony Eden failed to sanction a coup using
anti-Mossadegh elements in Iran, the project fell to the U.S. Central Intelligence Agency (CIA). Although leary of acting without British support, the
CIA decided to promote a coup, but only after Winston Churchill, sitting in
temporary command of the Foreign Office in Eden's absence, gave the British sanction. Supporters of the Shah (currently in exile), aided by paid agents,
forced Mossadegh out of office. General Fazlollah Zahedi replaced Mossadegh, the Shah returned to claim the Peacock Throne, and the consortium
agreement was signed in 1954.

For the U.S. government, the American multinationals, BP, and the
current government of Iran, the new arrangement was a substantial victory.
American oil policy and foreign policy were effectively linked. Soviet influence in Iran was blocked. Independent oil companies lost competitive ground

---

[2]Cited in Fuad Rouhani, *A History of OPEC* (New York, 1971), p. 48.

to the U.S. majors. The British found a route of reentry into Iran. And the Iranian government enjoyed a return of oil revenues. Under the new consortium arrangement, production in Iran was owned by the National Iranian Oil Company (NIOC), which sold oil to traders established by the consortium. The consortium could purchase oil at a discount, but it could not own the concessions. In time, this new way of establishing proprietary rights over oil would become the norm. For the moment, the majors continued to dominate Middle East oil.

The Die Is Cast

Relationships changed between the Seven Sisters and host governments in other parts of the Middle East and in North Africa. These changes signaled a shift from the tight controls that the majors had enjoyed for several decades. In 1952, the 50-50 system replaced the previous arrangement with the IPC in Iraq, and, by the early 1960s, IPC's concession area was substantially reduced. The Iraqi government took over 99.5 percent of the concession area by 1961. In Libya, independent companies were favored in awarding concessions after oil was discoverd in the 1950s. The Libyan government awarded seventeen companies some eighty-four concessions. Both the implementation of the 50-50 plan throughout the Middle East and the thwarted nationalization effort in Iran were harbingers of a new oil future.

OPEC AND THE WORLD OF OIL

The profit-sharing plans initiated in the postwar years ushered in a new era in the relationship between the Seven Sisters and the host governments, especially in the Middle East. While the major oil companies continued to set prices and determine distribution of much of the oil produced in the world, the rising oil-producing nations were determined to direct their own economic affairs. Whether the oil companies realized it or not, the days of unilateral decision making by the Seven Sisters was passing. The creation of the Organization of Petroleum Exporting Countries (OPEC) in 1960 was the most visible sign of changing times.

The decision of the oil companies to reduce the posted price[3] for oil in 1959 and 1960 was the catalyst to the formation of OPEC. For the producing nations, a decision to reduce the posted price meant a decrease in revenue. The reductions announced by Exxon in 1959 and 1960 amounted to a drop of about 15 percent, or a loss of about $270 million for the five major Middle East producers. The argument that the oil glut was driving down prices—a

---

[3]The posted price was one of several prices for crude oil. It was an "internal accounting price" used to calculate royalties and taxes paid to the host governments. For several years, it remained close to the actual market price of oil, but as the oil glut grew, the differential between the posted price and the market price widened.

glut that Exxon blamed on cheap Russian oil, but that also could be blamed on increased production by independent and state companies and the institution of an import quota in the United States—was not sufficient for the producing nations. Posted price, they argued, did not affect the price that the majors received for crude; it only affected royalty payments and taxes. Furthermore, the producing nations resented that the oil companies announced the reductions without consulting them.

The Arab nations were quick to state their opposition to the price cuts. In April 1959, soon after Exxon's initial announcement, an Arab Petroleum Congress met in Cairo. Formally, the congress discussed matters affecting only the interest of the Arab countries. Informally, views about the creation of an organization for producing nations were expressed. Taking part in the informal discussions were representatives from Iran and Venezuela, who were invited observers. Dr. Juan Perez Alfonzo, the Venezuelan minister of mines and hydrocarbons, proposed that an "Oil Consultation Commission," composed of various producer governments, meet annually to discuss common interests and problems. Perez Alfonzo's motives were somewhat self-serving. When the posted price was reduced in 1959, Venezuelan leaders feared that Middle East oil would gain greater competitive advantage and would threaten Venezuelan revenues. A system of regulating production and holding up prices could serve the dual purpose of protecting Venezuela's limited reserves from rapid depletion at cheap prices and also weaken the grip of the multinational oil companies. Perez Alfonzo got strong support for his plan, especially from Sheik Abdullah Al-Tariki of Saudi Arabia, who pushed the proposal, and the commission was formed.

It was not until the second price reduction in August 1960, that interest in cooperative action turned into a substantive plan. Differences among the members led to the termination of the commission. The new price reduction, however, united the various parties behind a common foe. In response to the price cut, a meeting of the major producing nations was convened in Baghdad in September, and OPEC was formed. Founding members included Venezuela, Saudi Arabia, Kuwait, Iran, and Iraq. Jointly they represented 67 percent of the world's oil reserves, 38 percent of its production, and 90 percent of oil in international trade. They demanded that the oil companies restore former price levels and agree to consult with OPEC before reducing prices in the future.

Measured against its impact in the 1970s, the accomplishments of OPEC in the decade of the 1960s were modest. It moved cautiously, unsure of the extent of its combined strength, wary of a crisis on the scale of Iran's several years before, and internally divided over nationalist goals.[4]

OPEC, however, served an important role as a clearinghouse for infor-

[4]Its membership increased markedly during the 1960s, however. Qatar entered in 1961; Libya and Indonesia were admitted in 1962; Abu Dhabi (the United Arab Emirates) in 1967; and Algeria in 1969. OPEC admitted whom it wanted, systematically excluding developed nations, such as the USSR.

mation and as a forum for sharing views. In a negative sense, it affected prices by preventing further reductions in the posted price. It increased revenues primarily through the growth in production volume, but at the expense of internal harmony—that is, intense competition for sales among members. The organization was not yet in a position to allocate production and control prices. For that reason, the oil companies were not seriously worried about OPEC during the 1960s. The Seven Sisters continued to deal with each country separately and tried to set one against the other at every opportunity. Snubbing OPEC was a luxury that the Seven Sisters enjoyed only for the moment.

THE SUEZ CRISIS, THE SIX-DAY WAR, AND OAPEC

The relationship among Middle East oil-producing nations had a political as well as an economic dimension. Anti-Zionist tensions mounting in the Arab world strengthened the political bonds. The establishment of the state of Israel and the Tapline issue set the stage, but the Suez Crisis in 1956 exacerbated the problem. On July 27, 1956, Egyptian President Gamal Abdel Nasser nationalized the Suez Canal. This decision came in the wake of deteriorating relations between the United States and Egypt; in Israel, there was fear of imminent war.

In late 1955 and early 1956, Israel began to increase its military preparedness in the face of Soviet arms shipments to Egypt. The Israelis were also worried by the U.S. offer to lend Egypt $56 million for construction of the Aswan Dam, which was intended to increase arable land and supply electrical power. (The British and the World Bank also agreed to contribute loans.) In July 1956, however, Secretary of State John Foster Dulles bluntly informed Nasser that the United States would renig on its promise.[5] In retaliation, Nasser nationalized the canal (and eventually made it unusable), announcing that the tolls would be used to defray the expenses of building the dam. Furthermore, the Egyptian president refused to guarantee the safety of Israeli ships.

But it was the French and British who reacted most violently to the nationalization of the canal. Their citizens were major stockholders in the company that owned it, and they were dependent on Middle East oil to a much greater extent than was the United States. Three months of negotiations failed to produce a solution. A plan, coordinated in advance, called for Israel to invade the Gaza strip and the Sinai peninsula, followed by the intervention of England and France. By November 6, British and French forces controlled the Suez Canal. This provocative action placed the United States

---

[5]Dulles and other officials of the Eisenhower administration were suspicious of Egypt's ties with the USSR, angered at Egypt's recognition of the People's Republic of China, and disappointed in Nasser's inability to improve his nation's sagging economic conditions.

in the precarious position of standing with the Soviet Union in opposition to its NATO allies. Under pressure from the United States and the USSR, the British, French, and Israelis accepted a cease-fire, and United Nations forces were sent in as a buffer between Egypt and Israel. The immediate crisis was over, but the animus between Israel and the rest of the Arab world was stronger than ever.

A little more than ten years later, another Egyptian-Israeli conflict threatened the stability of the Middle East and encouraged closer ties among oil-producing Arab nations. In June 1967, Israel attacked Egypt as a preventive measure against a feared Egyptian assault—the so-called six-day war. Nasser claimed that Israel was getting support for its aggressive actions from the United States and Great Britain. In response, the Arab states agreed to stage an oil boycott. Iran and Venezuela had no interest in the political problems of the Arabs, and thus refused to participate. The boycott, however, was over quickly because Arab producers were hurt more than their opponents. Venezuela and Iran took advantage of the boycott by increasing imports to Europe. The United States, for its part, emerged relatively untouched. OPEC survived the war but was shaken badly.

In August, Arab finance and oil ministers met in Baghdad to discuss events in the aftermath of the six-day war. They agreed that a unique organization of Arab states would allow them to use their oil for political interests. In Beirut, in January 1968, the Organization of Arab Petroleum Exporting Countries (OAPEC) was formed. The founding members included Saudi Arabia, Kuwait, and Libya—none of whom participated in the war. At the time, all three countries were under conservative regimes. For that reason, Iraq and Algeria refused to join.

The purpose of the organization was to extend political power through economic means, with the hope of uniting the Arab world, by using oil as a common link. Since OPEC had non-Arab members with divergent national interests, it was not considered a proper vehicle for the nonfinancial objectives of the OAPEC founders. While OAPEC posed a potential threat to Israel, division between conservative and radical states kept it from fulfilling its goals in the 1960s. In addition, the new Arab organization was weakened by its apparent undermining of OPEC. As circumstances changed during the 1970s, OAPEC gained more credibility. At the very least, its formation demonstrated the growing significance of oil as a political and diplomatic tool in the Middle East and as a weapon in the unresolved tensions between Israel and its Arab neighbors.

CAPITULATION IN LIBYA

What OPEC had been unable to do collectively—break the twenty-year-old profit-sharing arrangement and drive up the posted price—the relatively weak North African state of Libya accomplished independently. By its actions during the late 1960s, Libya altered the international oil system irrevocably.

The Libyan victory came on the heels of Colonel Muammar Qhaddafi's successful overthrow of King Idris in 1969. The ultranationalist regime quickly turned its attention to increasing oil revenues. While OPEC looked toward collective action to force changes in the international oil system, Libya and other North African producers juggled concessions. They played one oil company off against the other, hoping to drive up royalties and taxes.

Libya granted many of its concessions not to the Seven Sisters but to independents, such as Continental, Marathon, and Occidental. These companies were particularly vulnerable to the host government's pressure because they were almost completely dependent on North African crude. The rise of Qhaddafi coincided with events favorable to Libya's goal of seeking a larger market share. First, the Suez Canal remained unnavigable after the six-day war, making oil shipments difficult. Second, Tapline was severed in early 1970, disrupting further oil supplies from the Persian Gulf. Third, tankers were in short supply. Finally, spare capacity of oil declined as demand dropped in the 1960s. All these events gave the Libyans an opportunity to fill the gap, especially in Europe.

Qhaddafi and the Libyans recognized the significance of these new circumstances and began playing off one company against the other. Discussions were conducted with the giant Exxon and the dwarf Occidental.[6] At a key juncture, the Libyans broke off negotiations with Exxon and concentrated on the much more vulnerable Occidental. This was an excellent tactic, since practically all of Oxy's revenue outside the United States came from Libyan oil. To put additional pressure on the oil companies, Libya imposed production cutbacks. Without the aid or support from Exxon, Oxy had little choice but to accept Libya's demand to raise the posted price and income taxes. This action forced the independents to yield. Fearing trouble with other producers in Africa and the Middle East, the majors also felt compelled to accept the new arrangement. By the end of the year, most producers were receiving a 55 percent tax rate and enjoyed a higher posted price.

Libya's victory was an important object lesson for the oil companies and for OPEC. It was only the beginning of attempts by the producing countries to gain further control of their oil supplies and the pricing mechanism. Internal disputes within OPEC continued, and the commanding role of the Seven Sisters was not so easily quashed. Yet the international oil system had been disrupted. The zenith of American power in the world of oil had been reached. And new, unpredictable economic and political forces were gaining strength in the rush to control the precious black gold. The 1970s would bring a climax and a new starting point to the contest over the control of oil (see Table 13.1).

---

[6]Occidental was only a small oil company in comparison to Exxon. Due to its Libyan output, it had become a respectable oil supplier, but very dependent on the host government.

Table 13.1   *Major Oil-Producing Nations (production in million metric tons of coal equivalent)*

	1950	1960	1970	1977
USSR	56	217	519	807
U.S.	421	564	792	686
Saudi Arabia	39	95	280	680
Iran	47	77	282	415
Venezuela	114	220	288	179
Iraq	10	70	112	163
Nigeria	—	1	80	155
Libya	—	—	235	149
United Arab Emirates	—	—	55	146
Kuwait	25	125	224	144

Source: Adapted from *RF Illustrated*, vol. 4 (April 1980), p. 3.

FURTHER READING

Loring Allen. *OPEC Oil*. Cambridge, Mass., 1979.

Kenneth R. Bain. *The March to Zion: United States Policy and the Founding of Israel*. College Station, Tex., 1980.

John Blair. *The Control of Oil*. New York, 1976.

Edward W. Chester. *United States Oil Policy and Diplomacy*. Westport, Conn., 1983.

Robert Engler. *The Politics of Oil*. Chicago, 1961.

Neil Jacoby. *Multinational Oil*. New York, 1974.

Burton I. Kaufman. *The Oil Cartel Case*. Westport, Conn., 1978.

Stephen G. Rabe. *The Road to OPEC: United States Relations with Venezuela, 1919–1976*. Austin, Tex., 1982.

Anthony Sampson. *The Seven Sisters*. New York, 1975.

Benjamin Shwadran. *The Middle East, Oil and the Great Powers*. New York, 1973.

Carl Solberg. *Oil Power*. New York, 1976.

Louis Turner. *Oil Companies in the International Systems*. London, 1978.

Frank R. Wyant. *The United States, OPEC, and Multinational Oil*. Lexington, Mass., 1977.

CHAPTER 14

The United States as Oil Importer

The transition of the United States in 1947 from net exporter to net importer of oil signaled an important change in the relationship between the domestic and international oil industries. Diminishing domestic production of oil and rising consumption complicated the process of making energy policy. These circumstances sparked the domestic oil industry to insist upon government protection from imported oil. The energy picture was blurred further by environmentalists demanding governmental protection from air pollution and the oil companies. From Truman through Nixon, the federal government was caught in a crossfire in its attempts to set energy policy; crisis management was as close as it came.

POSTWAR DEMAND AND THE GROWTH OF THE OIL INDUSTRY

Between 1945 and 1947, a serious oil shortage retarded postwar recovery, and a fuel crisis in the winter of 1947–1948 crippled the Northeast. After 1947, however, the domestic oil industry experienced a period of great expansion. Between 1945 and 1959, production increased more than 50 percent, from 1.7 billion barrels to 2.6 billion barrels. Exports accounted for a diminishing share of the total demand, dropping from 7.8 percent in 1945 to 2.4 percent in 1959.

Several factors accounted for the postwar production boom. Consumption, which increased by about 80 percent between 1945 and 1959, grew as a result of the use of railroad diesels, the mechanization of farms, the use of oil and natural gas for home heating, and, especially, the increased gasoline sales. About 55 percent of refiners' revenues came from gasoline. Rising prices for crude—from $1.70 a barrel for East Texas crude in 1945 to $3.25 in 1958—stimulated further exploration and production.

The size and structure of companies after the war demonstrated that petroleum was a growth industry. Like its counterpart, electric utilities, the oil industry was gigantic. Its capital expenditures made up one-sixth of the

Gross Private Domestic Investment in the United States. Of the twenty-four manufacturing corporations with over $1 billion in assets in 1957, ten were oil companies. Three of those companies, Exxon, Gulf, and Mobil, had assets of $4 billion which exceeded those of the major automobile companies. While the total number of companies engaged in the various phases of oil production was large (12,000), only about half were producers and only thirty-three companies (in 1957) accounted for two-thirds of domestic production. The twenty major companies produced more than 47 percent of the oil in 1958.

Given the vitality of the oil industry, most business and government leaders regarded the continued good fortune of the domestic companies as synonymous with the economic health of the nation. International events and certain problems at home threatened that unbridled enthusiasm, and thus made the development of a national oil policy almost impossible.

TRUMAN AND ENERGY POLITICS

World events strongly influenced the Truman administration's energy policies. Close contacts between the State Department and American multinationals sometimes meant that oil policy worked at cross-purposes with other interests, especially the solid preservation of the domestic oil industry. Encouragement of international oil companies to expand imports, for example, was met with criticism from domestic producers, who claimed that imports in excess of economic need would retard the development of North American resources.

The establishment of a cogent energy policy was made more difficult by competing forces within the administration. A chronic problem, not unique to the Truman administration, was the friction between the State and Interior departments. The State Department promoted the interests of the multinationals as far as maintaining (or increasing) American economic and strategic interests abroad. The Interior Department was jealous of the other's influence over international energy matters, believing that it should have primary authority over domestic energy policy. Some officials, including Harold Ickes, envisioned the transformation of the Interior Department into a Department of Energy, Resources, and the Environment, thus consolidating energy policy formation under one roof. Truman balked at such an idea, suspicious of Ickes and uncomfortable with the prospect of so drastically centralizing energy policy. Other departments, especially Agriculture, resented Interior's power play and sided with the President.

Yet the administration's reorganization of the Interior Department after the war decentralized peacetime energy planning somewhat, although it did not undermine the department's general influence. Responsibility for petroleum was removed from the Bureau of Mines and placed in the independent Oil and Gas Division (OGD), established in May 1946. OGD's duties included helping to coordinate governmental oil and gas policies, analyzing data on supply and demand, acting as a communications link with the oil industry and the state governments, and administering the Connally Hot Oil Act. OGD proved to be strongly industry-oriented.

The National Petroleum Council (NPC) was also established. It was an industry advisory body made up of the presidents of most major oil companies as well as representatives from trade associations, industry producers, and refiners. Beyond OGD and NPC, influence over energy policy was dispersed among several other governmental agencies in the State and Commerce departments, the various armed services, the National Security Resources Board (at least through the Korean War), and even the Bureau of Mines.

The Paley Commission

The Korean War (1950–1953) put energy policy back on a wartime footing temporarily, but it also dashed hopes of reconciling the various attempts to develop peacetime energy plans. However, the war did increase concern over the depletion of renewable resources, which led to the creation of the Paley Commission. In 1950, Truman established the President's Materials Policy Commission to be chaired by William S. Paley, chairman of the board of Columbia Broadcasting System. The commission was charged with examining the relationship between crucial raw materials and national defense.

Energy was but one of several issues addressed by the Paley Commission, but it was an important one. The commission's report *Resources for Freedom* (1952), predicted a doubling of energy requirements by 1975. Optimistic in tone, the report concluded that the goal could be achieved through new recovery and utilization technologies and by more rapid development of the resources of poorer nations. *Resources for Freedom* placed faith in the private sector rather than in the government to meet the future energy needs; it emphasized supply-side solutions rather than conservation programs. But it also recommended the development of a "comprehensive energy policy" by the federal government—not a new concept but one that needed to be reiterated. Despite its message, the report was relegated to an obscure spot on most agencies' shelves.

Domestic Producers and Multinationals: Oil Policy as Bigamy

By the early 1950s, the most crucial oil issue involved imports. Except during the Korean War, domestic oil supply exceeded demand by a substantial margin. To compensate for the rising imports, the Texas Railroad Commission and other bodies began to reduce allowable domestic production. This decision could not, in and of itself, control the market in the face of unrestricted imported oil. Small producers called for quotas, while others, including state conservation agencies, wanted flexible controls that would prevent imports from undermining domestic oil markets. The larger independents, the majors, and the Truman administration advocated curbing imports through voluntary action, without formal controls.

Once again the Truman administration found itself caught between its foreign and domestic interests. On the one hand, it did not want to see domestic producers lose markets to cheap foreign oil, and a national security argument was being formulated to secure that objective. On the other hand, the administration was chary to restrict the imports from American multinationals or to strain relations with Latin America and Canada by curtailing imports. Fortunately for the Truman administration, the Korean War and the booming domestic economy stimulated exploration and increased domestic production capacity as well as imports. The quota question was momentarily deferred.

The dualism of the administration's oil policy was apparent in its approach to other energy-related issues. While the State Department encouraged the activities of American majors abroad, the FTC warned the President about the possible dangers of worldwide cartels. These cartels, it argued, could hurt U.S. foreign policy by raising the prices of materials for programs like the Marshall Plan. In 1950, the FTC began an investigation into antitrust violations among overseas petroleum companies. The study was completed by the fall of 1951, but, despite congressional pressure, it remained secret during the course of the Korean War. In 1952, Truman requested legal proceedings against those companies, but he quickly broke off the criminal suit to clear the way for the Iran consortium. Short-term goals prevailed; cartels were acceptable if they advanced national interests.

The Tidelands Oil Controversy

Conflicting oil interests aside, the federal government had been a constant supporter of both the domestic and foreign American oil industries. But federal intervention into what was perceived as local energy issues met with strong resistance. The so-called tidelands oil controversy embroiled the Truman administration in an affair that tended to blur rather than clarify the energy goals of the federal government.

The tidelands oil controversy actually began in 1937, when Interior Secretary Harold Ickes questioned state ownership of submerged lands. Concerned that companies would too quickly exploit the last remaining oil lands in the country, he wanted Congress to declare that coastal waters were in the federal domain. The issue languished, but it arose again during World War II. The Navy Department wanted to set aside offshore reserves, and Ickes urged FDR to seek clear title to the coastal waters through the courts.

Officials in the coastal states were surprised by the action. They had assumed the right to utilize coastal waters at least to the three-mile limit. The controversy really did not focus on "tidelands" but on the submerged land beyond the tidal areas along the continental shelf. Questions of fishing rights, harbor development, or reclamation were not at stake. Oil was the issue.

In 1945, President Truman issued an executive order proclaiming that the continental shelf was under federal control. Through the efforts of state officials and oilmen in 1946, a quitclaim bill on federal rights to offshore land to the three-mile limit swiftly passed the House. Just as swiftly, Truman vetoed the bill, arguing that the Supreme Court—not Congress—should decide the matter.

In a 1947 decision pertaining to California, the court affirmed the federal claim. The decision was repeated in cases involving Texas and Louisiana in 1950. The court conceded that Congress had the power to nullify those decisions by granting the rights to the states. This concession led to another bill and another veto. For good measure, Truman issued an executive order four days before the end of his tenure, setting aside offshore oil lands as a navy reserve. If the states and the oil companies were to have satisfaction, it would have to be through the Republican administration.

An additional side effect of the tidelands controversy was the resignation of Harold Ickes as Secretary of the Interior in 1946. Truman and Ickes had never gotten along, but when Truman nominated oilman Edwin W. Pauley as undersecretary of the navy, Ickes broke with the administration. Having an oilman in charge of naval reserves stirred up memories of Teapot Dome, and Ickes openly fought the nomination. (Furthermore, Ickes was offended that Pauley had been involved in unethical campaign practices.) The President was furious, but before a major confrontation could occur Ickes stepped down. Truman ultimately withdrew the nomination of Pauley, but the storm it created only added to the emotional tenor of the tidelands dispute.

The Government as Energy Producer: The Synthetic Fuel Program

While the tidelands oil controversy spoke to the question of federal versus state authority, the synthetic fuel program smacked of public versus private energy development. As discussed earlier, the Synthetic Liquid Fuels Act was passed (1944) with an eye toward bolstering strategic reserves of liquid fuel. To that end, between 1944 and 1955, Congress appropriated $88 million for the project. The development of an adequate, independent liquid fuel supply seemed justifiable during the Cold War when the "national security" claim became a powerful force in the evolution of federal energy policy.

As might be expected, the oil industry showed little interest in the synthetic fuel program after the war. While the industry may have welcomed the knowledge gained from basic research in the synfuel area, it loathed the prospect of the government conducting industrial experiments to produce a competitive fuel.

The Interior Department led the way in the synfuel program. Little by little, progress was made. The Bureau of Mines spearheaded programs in coal hydrogenation, gas synthesis, and oil-shale mining and retorting conducted at sites in Rifle, Colorado; Laramie, Wyoming; and Louisiana, Missouri. The postwar oil shortage and the rising tensions with Soviet Russia gave impetus to the program. But as oil production began to rise again, and as a coalition of conservative Republicans and oil-state Democrats formed to fight synfuel development, chances for legislative support of the program dimmed. Compelled to develop American markets for their Middle East oil, the majors cancelled their own synfuel projects.

The battle lines were drawn over the commercial feasibility of synthetic liquid fuels. The Bureau of Mines fought to keep their program. Critics emphatically stated that synfuel could not be competitive in the present market, and thus questioned the government's role in developing them. Given the transition to excess capacity in the domestic oil industry, and the rising tide of oil imports, the assertion of commercial feasibility stood on weak ground in the early 1950s.

The election of Dwight Eisenhower sealed the fate of the program. When the new administration terminated synfuel development in 1954, it closed one avenue for those advocating an independent liquid fuel supply on national security grounds. The decision also committed the administration—whether it realized it or not—to increasing dependence on imported oil.

EISENHOWER AND OIL

Despite the ideological differences between the Truman and Eisenhower administrations, a major shift in energy policy was not forthcoming in the 1950s. The Republican administration consciously attempted to break with many of the policies of its predecessor but was often constrained by myriad vested interests. As in the cases of electrical and nuclear power, the Eisenhower administration wanted to reduce federal involvement in oil matters. However, by promoting the national security claim in protecting the domestic oil industry from imports, it could not fulfill its goal.

Imports and Import Quotas

The control of imports in the name of national security was but the broadest rationale for such a step. The President was especially concerned that Congress would act if the executive branch failed to take steps to insure the vitality of the domestic industry. With the Korean War coming to an end, the import problem became acute. The battle lines were drawn over revision of the Reciprocal Trade Agreements. The coal industry was interested in seeing quotas for oil, especially because residual oils were winning over former coal consumers. The multinationals and the Eisenhower administration, for different reasons, opposed quotas. The majors needed the American markets; the administration did not want to jeopardize relations in the Western Hemisphere and the Middle East.

A continuation of Truman's voluntary program appealed to Eisenhower. However, by the end of 1955, the ratio of crude imports to domestic production had reached 10.3 percent and was continuing to rise. In response to the growing dilemma, the President appointed a cabinet-level committee to study the problem. It recommended that imported crude and residual oils not exceed the proportion of domestic production (with 1954 as a base year). The President accepted the recommendation but made the program voluntary. Lacking compulsory power, it failed. By the summer of 1956, foreign oil (at $1.95 a barrel as compared to $2.75 for domestic oil) was eroding the domestic oil market. Demands to restrict foreign oil were more numerous than ever.

The Suez crisis galvanized the call for quotas and reinforced the national security claim. With its regular supplies cut off, Europe had to rely on shipments from the United States. Domestic producers argued that the instability of the Middle East and its unreliability in supplying oil made dependence on imports unwise. Majors countered that the crisis proved the importance of foreign oil and the problems inherent in antagonizing Arab governments. A special report from the cabinet-level committee edged Eisenhower toward a quota system. The major issues continued to be national security and protection of the domestic industry. Fewer and fewer advisers maintained that large imports, in and of themselves, would save domestic reserves.

The changing political climate convinced Eisenhower to institute a formal import quota. The program was voluntary and, without adequate enforcement, a scramble for shares in the import market ensued. The next logical step—one that the President was reluctant to take—was mandatory quotas. Advisors counseled him that if he did not do something quickly, Congress was sure to act. At least, they rationalized, a mandatory program directed by the executive branch could be more easily manipulated than one imposed by Congress. On March 10, 1959, the President instituted mandatory quotas. Neither crude nor refined products could enter the country without a license issued by the Interior Department. Furthermore, imports were not to exceed a predetermined ratio based on projected domestic demand.[1]

The Mandatory Oil Import Program (MOIP) was hardly a panacea for the nation's energy problems. Import quotas stabilized the U.S. oil market, protecting the price of domestic oil from foreign competition. But this created an artificial energy environment in which oil prices failed to respond to the prevailing market and consumers footed the bill for propped-up domestic oil. Some experts argued that the MOIP also kept the United States from gradually adjusting to the economic changes wrought by the energy crisis in the 1970s. The MOIP was an attempt to resolve economic, political, and diplomatic problems simultaneously in the short run, but it could not halt the long-term economic shifts that were underway at home and abroad.

On a practical level, MOIP was a nightmare to administer. It allowed domestic and foreign oil to coexist within the American economy. Moreover, it was flexible enough to permit the expansion of imports as demand grew— and this flexibility was at the heart of the problem. Maximum import allowables were set for crude and refined products, but these allowables had to take into consideration the interests of long-time importers as well as new entries into the business. MOIP had to determine how imports would be distributed

---

[1]In 1959, imports represented less than 10 percent of demand. Ultimately the ratio was set at 12.2 percent which remained in force until 1970.

to American refiners, but, for political reasons, it also had to give preference to Canadian, Mexican, and Venezuelan oil over the production of Middle East oil. The formulas for these tasks were complicated, especially because every vested interest in and out of the country demanded exemption from the program. Inequities were frequent but predictable for a program attempting to be all things to all people.

Who benefited and who lost from the program? Domestic producers certainly won; so did the international firms to some degree. Since MOIP supported domestic prices at $1.25 a barrel above the world market, these companies found their own domestic operations more profitable. Favorable treatment under the program also extended to such varied groups as small refiners and northeastern utilities. The coal industry, while not devastated by MOIP, found little to cheer about. Most certainly, the group that carried the greatest burden from the program was the consuming public, who bore the burden of higher priced domestic oil. Since MOIP had no single goal, and involved more than economic issues, it must be viewed as a symptom of policy making at the time, that is, an effort to find immediate solutions to complex problems.

The Tidelands Oil Controversy—Act II

MOIP is an example of how the Eisenhower administration shunted its non-interventionist inclinations to meet a pressing problem. In the case of the tidelands controversy, its effort to mute the federal role in energy development was more successful. After sixteen congressional hearings had failed to resolve the tidelands issue, it became a lively topic in the 1952 presidential election. In their platform, the Republicans promised the "restoration to the States of their rights to all lands and resources beneath navigable inland and offshore waters within their historic boundaries." The Democratic candidate, Adlai Stevenson, defended Truman's policy on the tidelands and, in so doing, alienated leaders in oil states, especially Texas.

Living up to his campaign promises, Eisenhower signed the Submerged Lands Act in 1953. It granted California, Florida, Texas, and Louisiana rights to the submerged areas within the three-mile limit. The law also allowed the states to claim additional lands within their "historical boundaries." Sustained by court decisions, Texas and Louisiana were able to extend their jurisdiction three leagues, or about 10.5 miles.

While reversing the Truman policy, the Eisenhower administration did not adhere to an unbridled states' rights stance. In 1953, it supported passage of the Outer Continental Shelf Act which gave the federal government exclusive jurisdiction over the ocean bottom beyond the newly established limits. The State Department also negotiated treaties to avoid international conflict over the issue of freedom of the seas. In years to come, federal sales of offshore leases would revive the tidelands controversy. For the moment, the Eisenhower administration quelled the debate.

NATURAL GAS: A POSTWAR FUEL

Natural Gas in the Truman Years

After World War II, natural gas became an important fuel in its own right. The industry experienced tremendous expansion in production and consumption in the 1950s. In part, increased demand was due to the versatility of natural gas. What had once been a fuel primarily utilized by the petroleum industry became an important source of home heating. Between 1945 and 1955, the number of households burning natural gas increased from about 11 million to more than 21 million; residential consumption increased from 607 billion to more than 2,000 billion cubic feet per year.

Natural gas was clean burning and relatively inexpensive. It also generated by-products other than heat: solvents, films, plastics, adhesives, synthetic rubber, fiberglass, insecticides, gasoline additives, paints, lacquers, and drugs. Natural gas was particularly important in the production of synthetic fibers, especially nylon, orlon, and dacron.

Changes in the postwar economy fostered the rise in consumption. Concentration of Americans in cities and suburbs was crucial to the economies of scale and the geographic demand for natural gas. The needs and desires of a rapidly growing, more affluent population manifested itself in the great postwar housing boom. Many middle-class homes were equipped with gas heating and air conditioning. Improved pipeline systems made delivery of natural gas easier. And the continued marketing of various gas appliances promoted increased usage.

While the industry expanded greatly through the late 1950s, areas of production and consumption were more differentiated. With the decline of reserves in the Appalachian region, four southwestern states—Texas, Louisiana, Oklahoma, and New Mexico—dominated production. These four states produced more than 80 percent of the country's natural gas. Consumption, however, was concentrated in California and seven midwestern and Mid-Atlantic states, which had about 60 percent of the residential gas users.

The uniqueness of the energy source, and its production and consumption patterns, posed some serious regulatory problems. Since the bulk of natural gas was produced in the Southwest but consumed in other areas, regional rivalries complicated the regulatory picture. Moreover, the limited degree of regulation imposed on the petroleum industry frustrated gasmen who felt that their industry was overregulated. During the Truman years, natural gas legislation became a political battleground, pitting politicians in producing states against politicians in consuming states and a Democratic administration committed to antimonopoly against free-market Republicans.

As natural gas production expanded in the 1940s, renewed interest in regulating the industry also grew. In 1944, the FPC initiated an investigation that gasmen believed would lead to greater federal price control. In response, congressional leaders from producing states sought deregulation or at least the weakening of FPC jurisdiction over the industry. Senator Robert Kerr

(Dem., Okla.), a wealthy oil and gas producer and founder of Kerr-McGee Corporation, led the fight with the introduction of the Harris-Kerr bill in 1949. President Truman, who opposed any weakening of FPC authority over natural gas, vetoed the bill in 1950. This decision only provoked proindustry forces rather than quieting them.

Eisenhower and the Phillips Decision

During the Korean War, industry supporters were incensed by the decision to place natural gas under the control of the PAD. The gas interests believed that the Democratic administration would use the war as an excuse to extend industry regulation. Their only hope was a reversal of policy under the newly elected Republican president and his supporters in Congress.

Before executive or congressional power could be mustered, the Supreme Court handed down a crucial decision in the case of *Phillips Petroleum Company* v. *Wisconsin* in 1954. The case revolved around the question of whether Phillips was a "natural gas company" and thus subject to FPC price regulation. The Court decided that Phillips was a "natural gas company" and its sales in interstate commerce were subject to FPC rates. The Court also found in the 1938 Natural Gas Act the intent to give the FPC jurisdiction over "all sales in interstate commerce." Most important, FPC was ordered to regulate price at the well-head.

This was not a particularly welcomed decision for the FPC and certainly not for gas producers. The FPC found itself burdened with regulating sales of thousands of independent producers, and it did not move quickly to implement the ruling. Eisenhower, his supporters in Congress, and his appointees to the FPC were uncomfortable having to enforce regulations that conflicted with their own views of limited government. Not surprisingly, legislative efforts were made to blunt the Supreme Court's ruling. In 1956, both houses— with the support of the FPC—passed the Harris-Fulbright bill which would deregulate the field price of natural gas.

In a supreme irony, Eisenhower vetoed the bill for reasons that were more political than economic. Before Harris-Fulbright passed the Senate, Senator Francis Case (Rep., S.D.) announced that a lobbyist had given him $2,500 in return for his support of the bill. Until that point, Case favored deregulation, but upon returning the money, he decided to vote against the bill. Senate leaders were outraged and believed their work had been sabotaged. An obligatory investigation tried to dispel the idea of a bribe, but President Eisenhower felt compelled to veto the bill for fear of a political backlash. The "arrogant" gas lobby had clumsily tried to run the vote in their direction, even though the momentum was moving that way.

Further attempts to deregulate field prices were stalled throughout Eisenhower's second term. The gas industry had missed a rare opportunity. The veto of Harris-Fulbright did little to relieve the FPC of its bureaucratic burdens, let alone settle the extent to which the federal government would regulate prices.

Natural Gas in the 1960s

Instead of attempting to eliminate the FPC's power to control field prices, the Kennedy administration intended to uphold the *Phillips* decision; it also planned to simplify the regulatory process. The FPC shifted from setting rates for individual producers to setting rates on an area-wide basis.

During the 1960s, a two-tier price structure was evolving. The federal government regulated prices for interstate sale but not for intrastate. Intrastate prices were subject to supply and demand, instead of being tied to the cost of production (the measure used by the FPC in setting prices). Until the mid-1960s, the difference between the two price structures was not great, with interstate prices rising gradually through the period. By 1970, however, the disparity in price was wide, and producers attempted to sell their gas where they could get the highest price, that is, the intrastate market. (This market was also expanding because of increased industrial and residential demand in the Sunbelt.)

In addition to the interstate-intrastate problem, demand was outstripping production in the 1960s. Consumption more than doubled, while the number of gas wells brought in declined by more than 25 percent. Reserves declined and the amount of reserves committed to interstate pipelines dropped significantly.[2] Gas shortages began to appear in the interstate market, and the long-standing division between producing and consuming regions was changing dramatically.

Into the 1970s, a new round of debate over regulation and deregulation began.[3] With the lion's share of new production (90 percent in 1971) and a growing portion of total production (40 percent in 1971) of natural gas going to the intrastate market, the FPC was losing its jurisdiction. For the industry, rising demand in the interstate market was not being rewarded with higher prices. A time of reckoning was at hand that would only complicate the jarring effect of the coming "energy crisis." (For consumption figures, see Table 14.1.)

OIL IN THE KENNEDY-JOHNSON YEARS

Like their predecessors, JFK and LBJ tended to look to the future through the eyes of the present. Both the Kennedy and Johnson administrations tried to cope with the immediate problem of excess capacity of oil, while overlooking the possibility of a future period of scarcity.

---

[2]Pollution from other fossil fuels made natural gas a logical alternative. In 1964, the Board of Supervisors of Los Angeles County banned the burning of high-sulfur fuels, resulting in the exclusive use of natural gas as an industrial fuel. While environmental factors were becoming important in selecting nonpolluting fuels, in this case, they helped encourage the depletion of natural gas reserves.

[3]A key issue, which persisted throughout the 1970s, was the accuracy of industry reserve estimates. FPC was wary of industry estimates, believing that reserves were underestimated in order to force FPC to raise prices.

Table 14.1   *Consumption of Natural Gas (in billion cubic feet)*

	Total	Residential	Commercial	Industrial
1945	3,900	607	230	3,063
1950	6,026	1,198	388	4,440
1955	9,070	2,124	629	6,317
1960	12,509	3,103	1,020	8,386
1965	16,033	3,903	1,443	10,687
1970	22,046	4,837	2,057	11,825

Source: Bureau of the Census, U.S. Department of Commerce, *Historical Statistics of the United States* (Washington, D.C., 1975), p. 831.

With the economy operating sluggishly in the early 1960s, the Kennedy administration was more concerned with demand deficiencies than with excessive exploitation of domestic oil or the long-term effects of oversupply. One economist referred to the Kennedy energy policy as a "strategy of studied inaction."[4] This is an accurate portrayal of an administration that conducted several energy studies but made little real effort to establish a national energy policy.

Focus remained on the MOIP, and especially the process of allocation (or calculating allowable imports). Pressure to change the quota system came from producers, who regarded the program as badly managed, and from consumer groups, who believed the average American citizen was carrying the burden of such controls. With little incentive to alter the basic goals of MOIP, the Kennedy administration provided continuity with the immediate past.

The Johnson administration faced a more complex set of energy problems, particularly because American economic conditions were beginning to shift. Through 1966, however, the consensus within several federal agencies was that future energy needs could be met adequately at prices near current levels. Attempts at a comprehensive energy plan were more perfunctory than effective.

Various factions within the executive branch, Congress, and the oil industry exploited MOIP. The Council of Economic Advisers sought to liberalize quotas as a way of combatting inflation. The Department of Commerce wanted exemptions for the petrochemical industry to improve the balance of payments. A wide array of groups sought exclusions from the program. The international oil companies, while accepting the quotas as in their best interest, pressured for various exclusions and exemptions. All in all, the MOIP was deteriorating and losing sight of its original purpose.

After 1966, the Johnson administration demonstrated even less inclination to develop a comprehensive energy plan. Murmurings about inflation,

[4]William J. Barber, "Studied Inaction in the Kennedy Years," in Craufurd D. Goodwin (ed.), *Energy Policy in Perspective* (Washington, D.C., 1981), pp. 287–335.

national defense, and protectionism were on the rise. But these issues were smothered by the administration's increasing preoccupation with the Vietnam War and the needs of the Great Society programs. The 1967 Arab-Israeli war and the subsequent Arab oil embargo should have been regarded as significant danger signals, but they were not. The ability of American producers and refiners to lessen the blow of the temporary oil cutoff from the Middle East further reduced any sense of impending scarcity or rising prices.

One bit of irony took place during the last days of the Johnson administration: the oil depletion allowance was reduced from the long-standing 27.5 percent to 22 percent. The fact that Johnson was president when this happened—a political leader who stridently defended the oil industry during his congressional career—is intriguing. The 27.5 percent depletion allowance had stood since 1926. Despite opposition from the Roosevelt, Truman, and Kennedy administrations, it not only survived but was enhanced.

The change in the depletion allowance occurred with the passage of the Tax Reform Act of 1969. By that time, many oil stalwarts were gone from Congress, and high taxes and tax reform became important political issues. As the public awareness of the depletion allowance rose, it became a symbol of tax inequity. However, by reducing the percentage of depletion, the oil companies were not forced to bear a heavy tax bite. Prices were raised to compensate for the reduction, and the companies continued to deduct many intangible costs of exploration, drilling, and development. The Treasury Department estimated that between the depletion allowance and the foreign tax credit, producers saved as much as nineteen times their original investment in a well. Furthermore, the depletion allowance—like the foreign tax credit—benefited larger producers more than it did small producers or wild-catters.

OIL AND THE ENVIRONMENT

By the 1960s, oil was no longer identified only with material progress, mobility, industrial growth, and national security; it was also linked to health risks, environmental despoliation, and overconsumption. Few people, if any, wanted to abandon oil as a source of energy, but a growing number began to recognize its dangers when misused.

Waste, Conservation, and Industrial Pollution

The problem of waste at the wellhead was long viewed as an economic problem with environmental overtones. Conservation practices helped to produce oil in a systematic and rational fashion—protecting prices and limiting wild fluctuations in supply. It also provided a side benefit, which was the reduction of oil field pollution. These practices, however, were usually motivated by economic interests, especially for the large companies that controlled major sources of supply and benefited from industrial stability.

In the years prior to 1909, oil conservation laws tried to cope with the most egregious practices, concentrating on casing requirements and plugging of wells. With the major discoveries in the Southwest and the rise in demand for gasoline, legislation shifted to production controls, such as prorationing and unitization. After World War II, with a system of production controls in place, attention returned to preventing oil field pollution.

Population growth, urbanization, and industrialization in the producing states had a profound effect on this change in attitude. Most important, the increased demand for water—for urban consumption, for various industrial uses, and for agricultural irrigation—encouraged the passage of laws to prevent the contamination of fresh water supplies. In the late 1940s, several states adopted more sophisticated petroleum conservation laws to protect groundwater and reduce external damage caused by oil field discharges.

These laws took several forms but incorporated more precise language on environmental matters. In some cases, jurisdiction over the control of salt water, waste disposal, or water pollution was extended to existing regulatory commissions. Other laws called for replugging of oil wells and regulating the disposal of wastes from wells. A law passed in Michigan in 1951 authorized the supervisor of wells to plug wells on private property if the owners neglected to do so. A 1953 Kansas law outlined procedures for regulating the disposal of wastes and directed the State Board of Health to maintain records of maximum pressures for wells. Most producing states extended their conservation laws in some fashion by the early 1960s, although neither total compliance with the laws or consistent enforcement necessarily followed.

Limited success was achieved in controlling petroleum-related pollution in the Gulf Coast refining region. Hydrocarbons and other chemical pollutants blanketed the skies over the Beaumont-Port Arthur area and along the Houston Ship Channel. Water pollution in estuaries, tidelands, and especially in the channel added to the environmental deterioration. Much of this pollution was industrial in origin, traceable especially to the refineries.

The oil industry preferred to deal with pollution questions internally. However, those most directly affected by the contamination began to speak out. In the early 1950s, a citizen's group from the area of the Houston Ship Channel met with officials from local industries to lodge their protests. Their actions led to the establishment of an air and water pollution control section in the Harris County Health Department in 1953. Additional successes were thwarted by the state court, which handed down several decisions making it more difficult to prosecute those companies responsible for the pollution. Texas also created a Water Pollution Control Board that shifted initiation for political action from the local area to a rural-dominated legislature with little interest in antipollution measures.

As conditions worsened in the region, a call for action revived. The argument that further pollution threatened economic growth was particularly persuasive. A 1967 report by federal investigators stated that the Houston Ship Channel had the worst water pollution problem in the state. Federal pressure encouraged the Texas legislature to pass a clean air act in 1965 and a water quality act in 1967. Again, enforcement of the laws proved to be the most serious impediment to reducing pollution. By the late 1960s, federal laws required states to meet national pollution standards, and local authorities put pressure on the Texas Air Quality Board to bring suit against the most flagrant violators. Pollution problems were addressed if not eliminated.

Santa Barbara and Offshore Oil

Nothing riveted attention on the environmental dangers of oil production like the Santa Barbara oil spill in 1969. Aside from the scale of the leak, the incident brought into question the rush to exploit offshore oil, corporate responsibility for environmental disasters, and the need for environmental protection.

By the time of the spill, in January 1969, 925 wells had been constructed along the coastal tidelands from Santa Barbara to Los Angeles. In 1955, the California legislature passed the Cunningham-Shell Tidelands Act which dealt with leases and royalties. It barred drilling in specified "sanctuaries" within the three-mile limit to preserve the seascape. Beyond the three-mile limit, the federal government controlled the leases, granting its first one in 1963. Fearing that poorly regulated wells in the "federal zone" could pollute the state's beaches, California demanded jurisdiction beyond the three-mile limit. The state was denied its request. Interestingly, the world-famous spill originated on a federal lease.

Industrial concern over oil leaks was negligible before the Santa Barbara incident. However, world attention turned to the problem in March 1967, when the supertanker *Torrey Canyon* ran aground sixteen miles off the coast of England, spilling most of its 120,000 tons of crude into the sea. In May, President Johnson initiated a study of oil pollution problems, but no major change came in federal offshore policy. In fact, a few oil slicks appeared along the Santa Barbara shoreline in 1968, but Secretary of the Interior Stewart Udall gave assurances that no major problem existed.

On January 28, 1969, Union Oil's Well A-21 blew. The hole was capped in just thirteen minutes, but almost as quickly natural gas and oil began to bubble in the sea as thousands of gallons of crude oozed from a fissure in the ocean floor. By February 1, the oil had extended to 5 miles of beach. Eventually, the leak released 235,000 gallons of crude, creating a slick of 800 miles.

This was not simply a local crisis. A blowout on a federal lease posed several uncomfortable problems for newly inaugurated President Richard M. Nixon. The official directly accountable was Secretary of the Interior Walter J. Hickel.[5] While not taking strong immediate measures to curtail offshore drilling, Hickel did order a review of drilling and casing procedures and asked

---

[5]The former governor of Alaska had faced strong opposition from conservationists during his confirmation hearings, because of his close ties to the oil industry and his less-than-sterling environmental credentials. Hickel later proved to have stronger conservationist convictions than first thought.

for voluntary compliance with suspension of operations until the review was complete.

During February and into March, the crisis continued with no clear resolution and no immediate end to the pollution of the beaches. Efforts to use chemical dispersants on the oil were started and stopped several times by the Federal Water Pollution Control Administration (FWPCA). Union Oil tried several other methods but to no avail. Beaches, boats, and wildlife were engulfed in the sticky muck.

Washington responded with investigations and studies. Hickel established two committees in the Department of the Interior to examine the problem and to tighten drilling regulations. Nixon appointed a Presidential Panel on Oil Spills to deal with immediate and future problems. In Congress, Senator Edward S. Muskie's (Dem., Maine) Public Works Subcommittee on Air and Water Pollution and Congressman John Blatnik's (Dem., Minn.) House Public Works Subcommittee on Rivers and Harbors held hearings. In California, Governor Ronald Reagan ordered state reviews of offshore oil regulations.

The investigatory process offered little immediate relief to Santa Barbara. Lawsuits against Union Oil from commercial fishermen and owners of beachfront property soon followed, as well as state lawsuits against the federal government. Citizen groups, especially GOO—Get Oil Out—protested against the remaining oil operations. Efforts to permit Union Oil to resume offshore production simply led to renewed blowouts and leaks. By March 6, the oil was washing up on San Diego beaches, and it was not until the end of the month that the worst leaks were plugged.

The aftermath of the Santa Barbara crisis was significant. Union Oil assumed liability for the blowout, but the financial settlements were well below the total damage costs. Congress revised the Outer Continental Shelf Lands Act by tightening regulations on leases and making offshore operators liable for cleaning spills. The worst fears about the damage to the California coast were not realized, however. While more than 3,500 birds died, damage to wildlife and the beaches was not permanent. But the spill was a dramatic event that helped stimulate the growth of the modern environmental movement and moved the federal government toward the passage of the National Environmental Policy Act (NEPA) in 1969.

The Automobile and Air Pollution

As dramatic as the Santa Barbara oil spill proved to be, emissions from the internal combustion engine have been the most significant environmental by-product of oil production in recent times. In the early twentieth century, street cleaners sang the praises of the motor car—no more horse manure! But the environmental panacea of one generation proved to be the bane of another. In the postwar years, the symbiotic relationship between the petroleum industry and automobile manufacturers matured to the point where gasoline-powered vehicles were the essential form of transportation for the whole nation. The technical limits of the internal combustion engine and the scale of automobile use produced a devastating form of pollution—photochemical smog (PCS).

The automobile was not simply the transportation of preference; it was a way of life. It reshaped urban America, transforming industrial cities into metropolises. Along with the housing explosion that followed World War II, the increased dependence on the automobile accelerated the decline of central cities and the rise of new suburbs. The new suburbs, especially, were deeply imprinted by the automobile. Suburban sprawl followed highway development, and suburbs were scaled and designed for automobiles, not pedestrians—drive-in banks, drive-in movies, drive-through restaurants, and shopping centers.

The age of the "automobile suburb" was also the era of the superhighway and the development of the interstate system. The Interstate Highway Act of 1956 was the culmination of years of effort to move the United States toward a national system of high-speed highways linking the major cities across the continent. The passage of the 1956 act not only reinforced the goals of earlier laws, but it committed the nation to a toll-free system and a greater dependence on automobile travel than ever before. Congress provided allocations for a 41,000-mile express highway system, with 90 to 95 percent of the cost absorbed by the federal government. To finance the system, the Highway Trust Fund was established, drawing revenue from taxes especially those from fuels, truck use, and tire sales. The fund provided a seemingly inexhaustible financial source not subject to congressional or executive budgeting. It also undermined any federally sponsored mass transit programs. The entire interstate network was to be completed by 1971, although it remained unfinished into the 1980s.

The commitment to highway construction in the postwar years was matched by rising demand for automobiles. In 1946, the industry produced 1.8 million new cars, which fell far short of existing orders. The 3.2 million produced in 1947 were still inadequate. But by early 1949, expanded production and a dip in demand caused by recession created a balance. After such setbacks as the Korean War, the automobile industry experienced a real boom. By 1968, more than 83 million cars were registered in the United States and continued to increase by 5 percent annually for another decade. In the same year, automobiles traveled between 800 billion to 1 trillion miles.

While small, imported cars made in-roads into the American market beginning in 1957, American automobile manufacturers concentrated on bigger cars with larger engines. The Big Three, GM, Ford, and Chrysler, were not convinced that a large enough market existed for small cars. As long as gasoline was abundant and cheap, they would produce more powerful automobiles. High-compression engines offered more horsepower and greater acceleration for highway travel. Automatic transmissions—an option on 91 percent of the cars sold by 1970—made driving easier. These were luxuries of a high-octane age, luxuries to which the Big Three committed their futures.

The side effects of more cars, bigger engines, and automatic transmissions were loss of fuel economy and increased air pollution. Before the 1960s, these were not major concerns for automobile manufacturers, oil companies, or the public. But some pollution crises in the postwar years were harbingers of things to come. In 1948, there was a major air pollution crisis in the steel-mill town of Donora, Pennsylvania. A temperature inversion kept a dense smoke cloud of sulfur dioxide and particulate matter close to the ground for six days. On the fifth day, October 30, seventeen people died, followed by two more deaths the next day. In all, almost 43 percent of the townspeople became ill with more than 10 percent (1,440) "severely affected." The tragedy at Donora made Americans aware of the health hazards of air pollution. Those dangers were reconfirmed by the "killer smog" that hit London in 1952 (4,000 deaths) and the serious smog attack in New York City in 1953 (200 deaths). Congress enacted the National Air Pollution Control Act in 1955 to generate research on the subject; but the potential threat of automobile emissions took several years to evaluate and even longer to address.

A relatively new source of air pollution, automobile emissions posed different problems than did more conventional sources such as coal smoke. In the 1940s, citizens in Los Angeles began to notice a haze that made their eyes tear. It was often white or sometimes yellow-brown. They referred to this irritation as "smog." The word was taken from a combination of "smoke" and "fog," the term originally used to describe the thick clouds that engulfed London in 1952. The major toxic component of London smog was sulfur dioxide (like at Donora), which attacks the cells lining the air passages in the lungs and reduces the resistance to other pollutants in the air. Los Angeles smog was quite different, and it took some time to understand its unique properties.

Beginning in 1947, Los Angeles reduced sulfur dioxide emissions by banning the use of coal and fuel oils for industrial purposes—but the smog problem increased. Studies began to indicate that the complex and various pollutants existing in automobile emissions came from four sources: engine exhaust, crankcase blowby (through the engine ventilation system), the carburetor, and the fuel tank.

Los Angeles smog proved to be primarily "photochemical smog," that is, a form of pollution caused by the action of sunlight on various chemical compounds suspended in the air. Nitrogen oxide is the major component in PCS—a yellow-brown gas that reduces atmospheric visibility and is toxic to humans in large doses. Auto emissions also include carbon monoxide, hydrocarbons, oxidants [ozone and peroxyacyl nitrates (PAN)], lead, and waste heat. Individually or together, these components pose a health hazard to humans and they damage vegetation; they eat away at rubber, textiles, dyes, and other materials; and they modify weather conditions.

Los Angeles, the "smog capital of America," became the living laboratory for studying the causes and effects of massive doses of automobile emissions. In 1959, eye irritation was reported in Los Angeles County on 187 days; in 1962, 212 days. Motor vehicles were responsible for 80 percent of the hydrocarbons in the air; more than 90 percent of the carbon monoxide; and about half of the nitrogen oxide. A typical car produced in 1963 (without pollution control devices) discharged 520 pounds of hydrocarbons, 1,700 pounds of carbon monoxide, and 90 pounds of nitrogen oxide in one year.

Multiplied by thousands of cars, the smog problem in Los Angeles was critical. California became the logical testing ground for several emissions control devices and some pioneering legislation. As early as 1953, Los Angeles County Supervisor Kenneth Hahn inquired of Detroit auto makers as to whether research was being conducted to eliminate emissions. The response was vague. With the threat of mandatory federal regulations, the auto industry began to install crankcase blowby devices (which returned unburned gases to the combustion chambers) on their cars. These devices became mandatory in California by 1962–1963. The auto companies installed them on all 1963 models.

This was a significant advance because crankcase blowby produced 25 percent of the engine's hydrocarbon emissions. But this was only a start. By 1965, no effort was made to control exhaust emissions—responsible for 55 percent of the hydrocarbons, 100 percent of the carbon monoxide, 100 percent of the nitrogen oxides, 100 percent of the lead, and most of the waste heat.

By 1966, California required exhaust control devices on all new cars, significantly reducing hydrocarbons as well as carbon monoxide. But the 12 percent drop in hydrocarbon emissions experienced in Los Angeles between 1965 and 1968 was accompanied by a 28 percent rise in nitrogen oxides. By 1968, nitrogen dioxide, which is highly poisonous, exceeded the "adverse" level on 132 days.

The serious increases in nitrogen oxides was due to the inability of available antiemissions devices to act on them, as well as to the increase in automobiles and rising gasoline consumption. A new technical fix was sought from the automobile industry, and, in response, catalytic exhaust devices were developed to convert NO and NO_2 into harmless by-products. However, leaded gasoline played havoc with the catalysts. One solution to this problem was to use lead-free or unleaded gasoline. (Another was the unauthorized removal of the devices by motorists.)

Outside of California, the states moved slowly to combat automobile emissions. By 1966, motor vehicles contributed more than 60 percent of pollutants in the atmosphere. Temperature inversions in at least twenty-seven states and the District of Columbia produced serious smog problems by 1970. The more widespread use of trucks and airplanes exacerbated the nation's air pollution problems.

It became apparent during the 1960s that smog was not a local problem but a national problem requiring the attention of the federal government. While California still led the way in emission control legislation, at least, federal laws moved toward a recognition of the problem. For the first time, the 1963 Clean Air Act gave the federal government limited enforcement power over interstate pollution. An amendment to the 1965 act recognized the need to control motor vehicle pollution nationally, and it empowered HEW to establish and enforce standards to control air pollution from new motor vehicles. The 1967 Air Quality Act was the first piece of federal legislation designed to control lead emissions. Federal funds became available to defray part of the cost of inspection programs. Hydrocarbon emissions came under federal jurisdiction in 1968. An amendment to the 1970 Clean Air Act authorized the Environmental Protection Agency to set emission standards for new automobiles and other motor vehicles.

Legislation and technical fixes were a start in the battle for clean air. No magic solutions were achieved overnight. The automobile and oil industries continued to resist tougher standards. The public paid homage to clean air but resented carrying the burden of responsibility through higher costs and reduced automobile performance. Cities groped with ways to keep air quality from diminishing further. But as long as Americans cherished the automobile, emissions problems would remain. The intimacy between the individual and an energy source was nowhere more apparent than in the relationship between Americans and their cars.

The United States as a net importer of oil in the postwar years meant a great deal more than a shift in an economic equation. By 1970, Americans had quotas on imported oil, no clear policy on the deregulation of the oil and gas industries, an environmental *cause célèbre* in the Santa Barbara Oil Spill, a growing air pollution problem, and the disruption of the international oil market. To a contemporary audience, the brewing energy crisis—or crises— took a back seat to the Vietnam War, the race riots in the cities, and the demands of everyday life. But it was a brewing crisis nonetheless.

FURTHER READING

Ernest R. Bartley. *The Tidelands Oil Controversy.* Austin, Tex., 1953.

Douglas R. Bohi and Milton Russell. *Limiting Oil Imports.* Baltimore, 1978.

Barry Commoner. *The Closing Circle: Nature, Man and Technology.* New York, 1971.

E. Anthony Copp. *Regulating Competition in Oil.* College Station, Tex., 1976.

Donald N. Dewees. *Economics and Public Policy: The Automobile Pollution Case.* Cambridge, Mass., 1974.

Robert Easton. *Black Tide: The Santa Barbara Oil Spill and Its Consequences.* New York, 1972.

Edward W. Lawless. *Technology and Social Shock.* New Brunswick, N.J., 1977.

Bruce I. Oppenheimer. *Oil and the Congressional Process.* Lexington, Mass., 1974.

Mark H. Rose. *Interstate: Express Highway Politics, 1941–1956.* Lawrence, Kan., 1979.

M. Elizabeth Sanders. *The Regulation of Natural Gas.* Philadelphia, 1981.

Richard H. K. Vietor. "The Synthetic Liquid Fuels Program: Energy Politics in the Truman Era," *Business History Review,* vol. 54 (Spring 1980), pp. 1–34.

PART FOUR

The Scarcity Decade—1970s

CHAPTER 15

Energy Crisis: "The Moral Equivalent of War"

The 1970s represent the coming of the third energy transition in the United States. Unlike the two previous transitions, the latest one has less to do with the shift from one major energy source to another and more to do with change in attitudes shaped by the energy crisis and the environmental movement.

The link between national and international energy issues was never clearer than in the 1970s. The Arab oil embargo in 1973 and the Iran crisis in 1979 raised serious questions about American vulnerability, especially in the acquisition and control of energy resources. The energy crisis found the United States without a clear strategy for addressing or combatting the problems. American dependence on petroleum was made painfully obvious. Faith in unrelenting material progress was shaken. And optimism in continuing affluence was undermined, at least temporarily, by apprehension and even fear of the future. The days of cheap, abundant energy were slipping away, and with them a sense that America the Abundant was slipping away too.

OPEC COMES OF AGE

In 1970, Libya's victory over its concessionaires was a prelude to OPEC's rise to power. By 1973, the producing countries of the Persian Gulf and North Africa virtually completed the process of controlling their own oil supplies and strongly influencing oil prices.

At a meeting in Caracas in December 1970, OPEC moved to negotiate with the multinationals on a regional basis. They also decided upon a 55 percent minimum income tax rate. In response, the oil companies agreed that collective action was the only way to counteract OPEC's growing power. As a first step, companies involved in Libyan production established a "safety net agreement" for participants. In addition, the London Policy Group was created to develop a program of collective action. However, when the Shah of Iran made it clear that any effort at global negotiations would be interpreted as a sign of the companies' "bad faith," the collective approach collapsed.

OPEC achieved a clear victory over the multinationals at Tehran in February 1971. The Tehran Agreement resulted in a $.30 a barrel increase in taxes to be followed by a $.50 increase by 1975. In dollars, this meant rise in revenue of more than $13 billion. The oil companies had gone into the Tehran meeting hoping to link an agreement with the gulf producers to one with Libya. The Shah and Colonel Qhadaffi, especially, balked at the idea and convinced the companies to abandon their scheme. It was becoming clear that the Seven Sisters and the major independents would accept stable supplies and consistent financial arrangements rather than insisting on negotiating leverage.

In March, a similar agreement was signed in Tripoli. Libya received an increase of about $.65 a barrel. By acquiring better terms than the gulf producers, Libya once again introduced great instability into the settlements. The decision of the United States to float the dollar in August exacerbated the problem of establishing a workable revenue settlement and price agreements. Since the price of oil had traditionally been expressed in dollars, a devaluation meant the virtual erosion of the gains OPEC achieved at Tehran and Tripoli. When the dollar fell sharply in December, OPEC convinced the oil companies to boost the posted price, to offset the reduced value of the dollar.

Into 1972, the relationship between producing nations and the companies changed dramatically. In January, officials of OPEC and the multinationals met in Geneva to consider currency parity and direct governmental participation in the companies themselves. The currency issue was resolved by linking the posted price to a group of currencies; gold became the reference point for parity. On the question of participation, the companies had few options but to accept the principle. A general agreement was struck with five gulf producers in October. Under its provisions, the governments would receive 25 percent equity in the companies, which was increased to 51 percent by 1983. By December, Saudi Arabia, Qatar, and Abu Dhabi implemented the plan, while Kuwait held out for a better arrangement. (Negotiations in Saudi Arabia were prolonged because the Saudis were more interested in a profitable buyback arrangement with ARAMCO than in direct control.)

Independent of the Geneva negotiations, some OPEC members chose expropriation. Maverick Libya nationalized 51 percent of BP prior to the conference. In August 1973, it nationalized 51 percent of Occidental and then unilaterally announced 51 percent participation in the remaining concessionaires. Iraq nationalized all of IPC.

THE YOM KIPPUR WAR AND THE EMBARGO

The outbreak of the Arab-Israeli war, known as the "Yom Kippur war," in 1973 provided a catalyst for OPEC's emergence as the world leader in crude oil pricing and production.[1] No longer would the Seven Sisters possess unrivaled power; no longer would the producing nations consult with the international companies before announcing a price increase. The OPEC cartel was not omnipotent, but, on the other hand, the international companies did not wither away. The days of cheap energy were being replaced by an era of rising prices; an oil industry dominated by private companies made way for increased governmental domination. The Yom Kippur war did not spark these trends, but coming on the heels of global price inflation, rising nationalism in the Third World, and the shift in oil exploitation from the Western Hemisphere to the Middle East and North Africa, it was the proverbial straw that broke the camel's back.[2]

After President Nasser died in late 1970 the new Egyptian leader, Anwar Sadat, promised a renewed war with Israel to recover lands lost during the six-day war of 1967. On October 6, 1973—Yom Kippur—Egypt and Syria launched a coordinated attack on Israel. Egyptian troops poured onto the eastern bank of the Suez Canal, while Syrian forces claimed a foothold in the Golan Heights. The initial advantage went to the oil-financed and Soviet-armed Arabs, but by mid-October an Israeli counterattack reversed the fortunes of the war. Like the Soviets, the Americans gave up any pretense of neutrality, airlifting weapons, tanks, and planes into Israel.

In April, President Sadat had said that oil would be a weapon in any future Arab-Israeli conflict. He was correct. As early as the summer of 1973, King Faisal of Saudi Arabia warned the leading executives of ARAMCO that the United States faced serious consequences if it continued to aid Israel. The Nixon administration failed to heed the warning. In August, Faisal assured Sadat that Saudi Arabia would restrict oil exports and cut production if American policy did not change. While reluctant to become involved in a conflict that would disrupt their economic interests, the Saudis' anti-Zionist views and their unwillingness to be isolated from a united Arab front made their threats and promises very real. Petro-dollars could turn a third-rate military power like Egypt into a serious threat to Israel.

While oil did not simply finance an attack on Israel, it did provide an opportunity to enhance OPEC control, and, for the Arab members at least, it offered a chance to influence diplomatic relations with the West. The onset of war coincided with the beginning of a new round of price discussions in Vienna, which was inspired by the momentum of price increases that began as far back as 1970, not by the war.

---

[1]Nigeria joined OPEC in 1971; Ecuador and Gabon in 1973.

[2]Ironically but significantly, the proliferation of new international oil enterprises by the early 1970s demonstrated the vitality of oil exploration and production in the Middle East and North Africa, but at the same time it undermined the Seven Sisters' power. By 1972, at least 50 new integrated companies were in operation. More than 350 firms—other than the Seven Sisters—had obtained exploration rights in more than 120 areas. Increased competition, including the entrance of the Soviet Union into the oil business, made the major international oil companies more vulnerable to OPEC's influence.

The immediate concern of the international oil companies was the Saudis' demand for the posted price to be increased from about $3.00 a barrel to $6.00. Company officials left the meeting to confer with government leaders. Rather than resume negotiations with the companies, OPEC members met in Kuwait on October 16 and unilaterally increased the price to $5.12. This was an economic move based on the notion that oil meant only profit to the companies, but to OPEC it was the vital depletable resource that determined future development of the member nations.

While the price increase was not the result of the war, the Arab-Israeli conflict produced the embargo. During the Vienna negotiations, Israel suffered military reversals and requested immediate replacement of material from the United States. The Saudis had blocked strong sanctions against the United States in the early days of the war, but they felt compelled to threaten an oil embargo if further aid was extended to Israel. Executives of ARAMCO tried to dissuade President Nixon from taking such action. But on October 19, he authorized a $2.2 billion weapons airlift. Believing they were left with no alternative, the Saudis supported an Arab (OAPEC) boycott of oil against the United States and other supporters of Israel—the Netherlands, Portugal, South Africa, and Rhodesia. King Faisal ordered ARAMCO to reduce production and to bar all oil shipments to the United States. A total production cutback of about 25 percent was envisioned. ARAMCO, convinced that the U.S. government could do little to protect it, obeyed the order.

The news of the embargo was disturbing to Americans. Since the 1967 embargo had such little impact, however, there was disagreement over the potential damage of the current decree. While the emotional impact was great, the embargo was never airtight in any practical sense. Iraq did not sustain its boycott for long, and Libya continued to supply oil to the West. Even some Saudi oil made its way across the Atlantic. Economic interests were often more powerful than was politics. Furthermore, non-Arab sources of oil were tapped from Colombia, Italy, Chile, Bolivia, Peru, and elsewhere. The Seven Sisters helped to mitigate the effects of the embargo by increasing production from their non-Arab wells and allocating available supplies as equitably as possible. This action was hardly humanitarian; the international companies could ill afford to be closely linked with OAPEC's political reprisal.

The embargo produced tangible results for OPEC. Imports of oil in the United States dropped from six million barrels a day in September to five million in subsequent months. Japan and European nations dependent on Middle East crude yielded to Arab demands, putting distance between themselves and a pro-Israeli stance. A snowballing effect had begun with the prewar price increases, OPEC's ability to make unilateral decisions on the posted price, wartime oil shortages, and the political interests of the Arab nations, not to mention the preoccupation with wartime diplomacy in consuming nations. By December, price per barrel rose 130 percent to $11.65. Spot market prices were as high as $22 a barrel. In 1974, the price of Arabian oil delivered to the United States was $12.25 per barrel, as compared to $3.65 a year earlier.

THE EMBARGO'S AFTERMATH AND IRAN

After a six-month duration the embargo ended, on March 18, 1974. In its wake, a new order had developed in international oil. To the industrialized nations, the rapidly rising prices and the embargo were, at the very least, an overreaction on the part of OPEC, and, at most, exploitation by a dangerous cartel. From OPEC's vantage point, the price revolution was a justifiable response to the inflationary economic policies of the industrialized nations in the short term and to the efforts of the international companies to control supplies and exploit the Third World in the long run. For members of OPEC, the embargo was a political protest against U.S. aid to Israel. Into 1974, there was an uneasy respite for both producers and consumers. The future, however, was more uncertain than ever.

Between 1974 and 1978, the world oil market remained relatively orderly. Demand for OPEC oil temporarily dipped because of slow economic growth throughout the world, increased production from the North Sea and Alaska, and de facto conservation practices. In fact, OPEC's production in 1978 was only slightly higher than in 1974—prices did not keep pace with inflation. Some members continued their takeovers of oil production at home; others increased taxes, but without a commensurate rise in the posted price of oil.

A "one price" system was evolving, which meant the end of the posted price and reduced margins of profit for the multinationals. Saudi Arabia, Abu Dhabi, and Qatar dropped an alleged "bombshell" in November 1974, when it cut the posted price by $.40, raised the income tax rate to 85 percent, and increased the royalty share to 20 percent. During 1974 and 1975, most members of OPEC also showed a willingness to cut production to maintain the current price levels. To further enhance their standing, several members moved "downstream" into transportation, refining, and marketing.

The stability of the world oil market was broken in the late 1970s by events outside of the control of either OPEC or the multinationals. On New Year's Eve 1977, President Jimmy Carter referred to Iran as "an island of stability" in the troubled Middle East. By the next year, America's preeminent ally, the Shah, was forced into exile and was replaced by Ayatollah Khomeini, the leader of the Islamic Revolution.

Oil exports fell by five million barrels a day after the Shah's flight, turning a small surplus in world production into a shortage (made up only in part by the Saudis and others). With the new government, exports increased again, but production was never allowed to return to the old levels. Vestiges of "Western exploitation" were banished—meaning an end to the consortium. The spirit of the Islamic Revolution suggested a quick turnabout in American-

Iranian relations, manifest in greater political and strategic instability in the Middle East and uncertainty in the world oil market.

The dramatic events in this emotion-charged, vacillating nation broke the temporary stability of the oil market. With the Soviet invasion of Afghanistan in December 1979—and concern about further Russian advances along the Persian Gulf—uncertainty turned to pessimism. Oil prices reflected the lack of equilibrium. The spot market became increasingly important, with oil selling for $45 a barrel by December.

THE ENERGY CRISIS AT HOME

Prelude to Embargo: Nixon and Oil Quotas

"Energy crisis" was on everyone's lips after 1973. But even the jarring impact of higher energy prices and limited supplies was short-lived. It would take the Iranian crisis and a whole new round of rising prices and scarce supplies to reinforce the notion that the era of cheap energy was coming to an end. By 1979, Americans wanted to believe that technology, Yankee ingenuity, diplomatic élan, or some other force would see the United States through the energy crisis, but grave apprehension lingered.

During the early 1970s, consumption and production trends in oil and natural gas were strong indicators of the predicament the United States could face if its energy supplies were cut. Excluding Alaska, oil production steadily declined. In 1972 and 1973, an average of 360,000 barrels less a year were produced. In 1968, for the first time in U.S. history, more natural gas was sold than was discovered. Practically all the increases in energy consumption after 1970 came from oil imports. In 1970, foreign oil accounted for approximately 22 percent of consumption; by 1973, 36 percent.

A key to the potential disruption of the economy and society due to oil shortages was rising consumption. Energy consumption had doubled since 1950, while population rose by only 1.3 times. In 1970, the average American consumed more than three times the energy of his forefathers in 1900. Energy hungry technologies, consumerism, and the rise of the automobile account for much of this increase.[3]

The United States was never more dependent on oil and natural gas than in the 1970s. In 1973, on the eve of the embargo, oil furnished almost half of the total energy needs of the nation. By 1977, petroleum and natural gas furnished 75 percent. The claim that the root cause of America's energy woes in the 1970s was consumption rather than production has some merit.

---

[3]It should be noted that energy consumption has not been evenly distributed in American households. Those people in the upper 10 percent income bracket consume as much natural gas, twice the gasoline, and one-fifth more electricity than do the lowest 20 percent.

The level of consumption that Americans came to expect was due in large measure to the availability of abundant and cheap supplies. In confronting the possibility of scarcity and rising prices, government leaders faced not only complex economic questions but political problems linked to national security, international relations, the interests of the nation's businesses, and the accustomed lifestyle of its citizenry. High energy consumption had long been an integral part of American life. Government leaders, therefore, found it difficult to heed the danger signals of the pre-embargo years.

When Richard Nixon took office in January 1969, signs of a looming crisis were ample. The winter of 1969–1970 was the coldest in thirty years. A predicted scarcity of natural gas became a reality. Brownouts struck most cities. Clashes between environmentalists and energy producers were increasing. OPEC was showing signs of rising from obscurity in the world oil market. And Libya's role as "trendsetter" was being established.

The warnings increased executive and congressional dialogue over developing a national energy policy. (Yet this was a long-standing goal as far back as World War I.) Like several of his predecessors, Nixon set out to evaluate fuel policies as a means of orientation. His administration addressed the energy problems from several vantage points, but often in the same particularist fashion of the past. Close ties with big business meant that the Nixon administration had no drastic plans for dealing with the oil industry. But despite his apparent conservative credentials, the President was no ideologue. Interest in deregulation of natural gas and the easing of other regulatory policies contrasted with a concern over inflation. The promotion of alternative energy sources, especially coal and nuclear power, met with resistance from environmentalist groups. As the Nixon administration soon discovered, clarity of purpose was difficult to achieve in the field of energy.

At first, the new administration gave few hints of changing the well-established course of the past. The Cabinet Task Force on Oil Import Control concluded that the quota system had to be abandoned, but Nixon decided to maintain MOIP and increase the quotas gradually over the succeeding five years. Although he created an Oil Policy Committee to evaluate MOIP, Nixon sided with the FPC and the Interior and Commerce departments over the quota issue rather than give ground to Congress to set energy policy.[4]

Events in 1970 and 1971 would force the President to pay more attention to energy matters. The inflationary effects of the quota system soon began to trouble the administration, as did fuel shortages along the East Coast (an area extremely dependent on oil imports). After liberalizing the quotas several times, Nixon abandoned them in April 1973. By that time, the program had already distorted the allocation of resources and made it difficult for the nation to adjust to domestic depletion of oil and the rising price of foreign crude.

---

[4]The task force recommended a tariff system to replace MOIP. This would have meant increasing congressional prerogatives over oil imports.

In June 1971, Nixon delivered his first energy message. In terms of breadth, it was probably the most comprehensive message of its type ever sent to Congress. The emphasis was long term rather than short term. It called for expanded programs in nuclear power, coal conversion, outer-shelf development, and oil-shale reserve leasing. The message alluded to developing "clean" energy by requesting that Congress tax leaded gasoline. Finally, it called for a Department of Natural Resources. Without an emergency, the message went largely unheeded.

By 1973, the Nixon administration was enmeshed in the Watergate scandal, while energy policy was ensnared in the debate over combatting inflation. Between these two imposing problems, coherent policy became all the more difficult to achieve. The embargo was the icing on the cake. In August 1971, Nixon imposed a mandatory wage-price freeze as Phase I of his Economic Stabilization Program. Phase I (and Phase II which followed soon after) actually worsened the fuel shortage.

In April 1973, Nixon issued his second energy message, which was a strong plea to step up production through natural gas decontrol, leasing of the outer continental shelf, pushing ahead with the Alaska pipeline, and easing environmental standards. In addition, the administration announced a new oil import program. Quotas were replaced by a "license fee" that would open the market to more imports but maintain a price differential in favor of domestic refined products. The administration wanted simultaneously to increase supplies—through imports and domestic incentives—and keep inflation down.

Linking anti-inflation measures to reversing the trend toward an energy shortage posed several problems. A determination to aid domestic independents led to a voluntary allocation plan and then to a mandatory allocation program for heating oil and propane gas. Adding the allocation program to price controls tended to reduce the oil companies' incentive to increase supplies, deepened the winter heating oil shortage, and actually led to a sharp price hike. Thrashing around for alternative plans, the Cost of Living Council issued Phase IV controls in August 1973. This program attempted to stimulate exploration and curb inflation by establishing two price categories for domestic crude—one for old oil, one for new oil. It only created more turmoil.

The oil industry was being torn apart by Phase IV. The regulations had varying effects on oil businesses, depending on their access to crude supplies, their marketing, and their investment strategies. Domestic producers wanted the world market price for their oil. Independent refiners, especially, wanted controls to protect themselves from the majors, who might reserve the cheaper crude for their own refineries.

The Embargo

When the Arab oil embargo was announced in October, the Nixon administration was unable to meet the crisis effectively. The competition between anti-inflation measures and energy scarcity made policy formation almost impossible. Problems in Middle Eastern relations, support for Israel, and competition with the USSR left the United States without a clear world view. Moreover, the cancer of Watergate preoccupied the President and his staff, weakened the administration's leadership capacity, and increasingly demoralized the country.

The quadrupling of oil prices and the lack of adequate preparation for a transition to a period of relative scarcity, left the United States facing a critical juncture. On November 27, Nixon signed the Emergency Petroleum Allocation Act, which jettisoned voluntary oil and gas allocation measures and embraced governmental regulation as a way out of the crisis. The act established a new allocation plan, provided authority for gas rationing, and maintained price controls. In addition, it established Project Independence, a rather diffuse idea to free the United States from foreign oil by 1980.[5] The thrust of the act was modest, and its orientation was essentially crisis management.

In December, a new administrative structure, the Federal Energy Office (FEO), was also established. A part of the Executive Office of the President, FEO replaced the Special Energy Committee and the National Energy Office. It was given responsibility over fuel allocation, rationing, prices, and Project Independence. This reorganization was as close as the administration had come to establishing its proposed Department of Natural Resources.

The flurry of activity in Washington was not sufficient to assuage the anxieties of Americans. Throughout the decade, shifting combinations of states and other interest groups pushing for or contesting specific programs further complicated the situation. As several commentators pointed out, the impact of the embargo was perhaps as much psychological and emotional as practical. By November, some gas stations were shutting down because of shortages. In metropolitan areas, especially in car-dominated California, lines of automobiles stretched around the block waiting to fill up. Gas-guzzling cars were becoming pariahs, and Detroit was bracing itself for hard times. Carpooling and the sad state of mass transit were subjects of animated discussion.

Who was to blame? In the eyes of most Americans, it was the oil companies, followed by the federal government and the Arabs. The oil companies' public image struck its nadir in 1973–1974. The popular belief was that the oil companies contrived the energy crisis to increase profits. Announcements of oil company profits for 1973 did little to alter that view. The leading thirty companies averaged a 71 percent increase from the previous year, with more than 80 percent for Exxon and over 90 percent for Gulf. The announcement of some companies that rising revenues indicated that profits in previous years were unreasonably low, or Mobil's statement that it was fair to expect consumers to pay for the new development of oil supplies, were not well received.

---

[5] Under Project Independence, the President called for Americans to conserve more energy, while the government stimulated the production of coal and lignite. In the following two years, Congress responded by establishing a nationwide 55-mile-per-hour speed limit, by granting tax breaks for home insulation, and by requiring carmakers to produce higher mileage cars.

Public relations efforts only drew more cynicism. Wrapping themselves in the free enterprise banner, the companies pouted about the overburden of regulations and the financial risks of securing oil supplies. They trumpeted dreams of providing a better world for their customers. It was not enough for many Americans that a Texaco dealer was "giving you everything he's got." The announcement of a congressional investigation of oil companies seemed to confirm what many people already believed (although its 1974 report generally exonerated the companies of wrongdoing).

Arab oil nations fared only a little better with the public. OAPEC's embargo was often confused with OPEC's price increases. Iranians and Libyans magically became Arabs, while the decrying of Middle Eastern countries was often couched in bigoted overtones. Primal forces seemed to be tampering with the age-old connection between consumers and their pocketbooks (or in many cases their gas-guzzling automobiles).

The energy crisis was real enough. It may not have been a crisis of dwindling supplies, but it was a crisis of control and the result of wasteful consumption and a short-sighted energy policy. The Seven Sisters were losing their grip on production and were desperately trying to retain downstream influence. But they also garnered huge profits as oil prices skyrocketed. Applauded for their successes in years past, they were a new source of derision. Rumors of oil companies holding back supplies during the embargo—or moving tankers at a snail's pace across the Atlantic—may have been conjecture, but they were regarded as plausible and even likely by many Americans.

The embargo was short-lived and not as calamitous as feared, but it did more than tweak the nose of the industrialized nations. As a public recognition of the changing status of the world oil industry and the value of oil in the world economy, the 1973–1974 crisis was significant. That many Americans chose to believe that the shortages were manipulated and the crisis artificial tended to make it all the more difficult to move toward a coherent energy policy. A warning had been delivered but it was not fully appreciated.

Ford and the Postembargo Assessment

The end of the embargo in May 1974, coincided with heightened tensions over Watergate, leaving the Nixon administration incapable of moving toward a cogent energy policy. There were, however, some structural adjustments in the nation's energy bureaucracy in 1974. In June, the Federal Energy Administration (FEA) was created in order to continue FEO functions, as well as to centralize further executive control over energy policy. To that end, relevant offices within the Interior Department and the energy division of the Cost of Living Council were absorbed by FEA. Its major responsibility was to complete the Project Independence report (which was accomplished in November), and to administer an entitlements program for allocating "old" crude oil to refineries.

When Gerald R. Ford assumed the presidency in August 1974, he faced the major task of responding to the energy crisis. Without an electoral mandate and saddled with the onus of a Republican president leaving office in disgrace, the moderate-to-conservative Ford decided to follow through with many of the broader goals set by Nixon officials. The Ford administration faced several crucial questions that had heavy political overtones—decontrol of oil and gas, oil supply security, debate over alternative energy sources, various environmental issues, the public role in energy development, and business-consumer relations.

The question of oil price decontrol was the central issue in late 1974. (The debate over natural gas regulation also continued to rage.) For Congress, the immediate concern was whether oil price controls should be extended beyond the February 1975 deadline. Without controls, domestic oil was likely to increase by more than $7.00 a barrel. The Ford administration showed its predecessors' general commitment to decontrol but faced similar economic constraints and conflicting vested interests. Within the oil industry, most majors and independent producers favored decontrol to increase profits, while many independent refiners and marketers favored some controls to maintain their subsidies under the government's entitlements program.

With the industry and Congress divided over the question, the President struggled for a compromise solution. But Ford's proposal—immediate decontrol accompanied by a windfall profits tax—could not get through Congress. Instead, Congress wrote its own bill, the Energy Policy and Conservation Act of 1975 (EPCA), which continued price controls and mandatory allocation of domestic oil for a little more than three years. On natural gas decontrol, Congress likewise balked.

EPCA addressed oil supply security, an issue of great importance to the administration. Under the act, a strategic petroleum reserve was authorized along with various standby authorities. It also called for U.S. participation in the International Energy Program. In February 1974, Secretary of State Henry Kissinger convened the Consumer Energy Conference, designed to bring together an alliance of oil-consuming nations to bargain collectively with OPEC. While recognizing energy security as an international issue, efforts at international cooperation did not effectively meld the economic and political interests of the participating nations or effectively undermine OPEC's influence.

The Ford administration also gained little ground in changing or even clarifying what the federal role should be in developing new energy sources. Because of its control of vast public lands, its stake in atomic energy and hydroelectric power, and its regulatory functions, the federal government was not going to move out of the energy business any time within the foreseeable future. The Ford administration continued to call for the development of alternative fuels and allocated funds to coal research, solar research, and conservation programs, but it did not change the broad research priorities already in place.

Controversies arose over a uranium enrichment program, utility bailouts, and even an Energy Resources Finance Corporation. However, the only significant structural adjustment in the Ford years was the establishment of the Energy Research and Development Administration (ERDA), the Nuclear Regulatory Commission (NRC), and the Energy Resources Council. ERDA and NRC divided the responsibilities of AEC, which was abolished. ERDA became the major government vehicle for research and development for all forms of energy, while NRC assumed AEC's regulatory functions over nuclear power. The Energy Resources Council was designed to coordinate the formulation and implementation of national energy policy, but the government's energy functions remained somewhat diffuse within the bureaucracy.

As historian Robert A. Divine noted, "The inability to come to grips with the energy crisis was Ford's gravest failure as President."[6] The flurry of activity belied the development of clear lines of policy. With the 1976 election nearing, Ford accepted expediency by accepting a compromise with Congress. Abandoning the concept of decontrol, he was willing to extend price controls in exchange for the Democratic Congress's promise to drop a plan for a heavy tax on gasoline. The result eased the rise in price of gasoline and home heating oil, but it also frustrated the oil and gas industry and ignored long-range solutions. The failure to take a tough stand on energy, however, must be shared by Congress. Like the Nixon administration before it and the Carter administration after it, the Ford administration was strapped with an uncooperative Congress that did little to provide a comprehensive energy strategy.

Rampant inflation in the 1970s also complicated policy making. Inflation was a worldwide phenomenon, accelerated by heavy demand for commodities—especially oil. In the United States, interest rates soared and real income fell steadily; between November 1973, and March 1975, buying power dropped by almost 9 percent. Inflation increased at an annual rate of over 7 percent, with accompanying industrial recession and high unemployment. Trying to find a focus for economic policy, the Ford administration had a difficult time factoring in energy policy. As a result, it left to the Carter administration the difficult task of confronting a new era of high energy costs and possible changes in American lifestyle.

Carter's "Moral Equivalent of War"

While the Ford administration sought to confront the energy crisis with the tools of its predecessors, the administration of Jimmy Carter sought to move the nation in a new direction. Carter, the former governor of Georgia, was the first post-Watergate and postembargo president. While never successfully grasping administrative or political control of the nation's highest office, he moved the nation closer to a holistic view of the energy problem. With the energy crisis somewhat in the distance, he had an opportunity to set in motion a new national energy policy. However, the Carter administration was more successful in changing the tone of the debate over energy than in changing the substance of the policy.

[6]Robert A. Divine, *Since 1945* (New York, 1979), pp. 222–223.

The energy crisis did not become the lively political issue people expected in the 1976 presidential campaign. Many observers agreed, however, that Carter's promise to deregulate natural gas carried sway in Texas and Oklahoma. With gas shortages in the winter of 1976–1977, the increasing dependence on foreign oil (46 percent in 1977; See Figure 15.1), the continual decline in domestic production, the breakdown of the entitlements program, and perpetually high fuel costs, the energy issue did not remain dormant for long.

James Schlesinger—an economist who served as chairman of the AEC, director of the CIA, and Secretary of Defense under Richard Nixon—quickly became the force behind the Carter energy plan. One of the few non-Georgians to have access to the President, Schlesinger gained Carter's admiration and trust before the election. Through the Office of Energy Policy and Planning, he began to devise a master plan for energy.

On April 18, 1977, Carter announced his National Energy Plan (NEP). In what is now a well-worn phrase, the President described the energy situation as "the moral equivalent of war"—strong language even in the wake of the 1973–1974 crisis. At the heart of NEP was the notion that the United States was facing its third energy transition. The goal of the plan was to ease into the transition, to give the country sufficient time to implement major changes. This was neither crisis management nor long-range planning; it was interim planning.

NEP set several goals for 1985: reduction in annual energy growth to less than 2 percent; reduction in gas consumption by 10 percent; reduction of imports to one-eighth of total energy consumption; increased utilization of coal by two-thirds; and the establishment of strategic petroleum reserves. It also envisioned major improvement in energy efficiency for existing buildings and acceleration in the use of solar energy. In all, the plan included about 100 proposals ranging from taxes and incentives for conservation to new information systems, from development of a wide range of alternative energy sources to new transportation studies.

At the heart of the NEP, was the Crude Oil Equalization Tax (COET). In general, the administration hoped to reduce dependence on imported crude, retain domestic price controls with a new pricing system, and bring supply and demand of natural gas into balance. The COET was meant to raise oil prices sufficiently over three years to reduce demand, while diverting the increased revenues to the government for use in various programs.

Although the NEP offered several attractive features, it was sure to draw fire from the full range of political and economic interest groups. The administration's strategy was to use the dramatic momentum of a call to action to push the omnibus bill quickly through Congress. The legislators resented this, and rightly so. While the administration had a legitimate right to be concerned about bald obstructionist tactics, the plan was too complex to be dealt with in any cavalier fashion.

Yet under old-fashioned political maneuverings, Speaker Thomas "Tip" O'Neill (Dem., Mass.) pushed the plan through the House in August, vir-

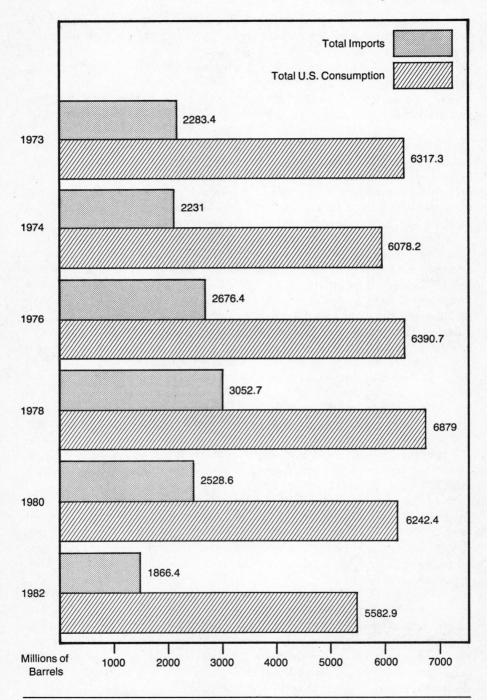

Figure 15.1   U.S. Petroleum Imports
Source: Adapted from *Houston Post* (October 9, 1983), p. E1.

tually without change. The Senate did not bend so easily. After long deliberation, diversion by other pressing issues, and intense lobbying activity, the National Energy Act was finally passed in 1978.

The plan as enacted contained many of the original provisions, including conservation incentives and taxes, prohibition against the use of oil and gas in new electrical generating plants and industrial plants, voluntary standards of electrical rate designs, and a revised natural gas act. The COET was killed in committee, and a tax on industrial users of oil and gas also failed to be included. As a result, the act had no provisions for oil pricing—its major shortcoming. In fact, OPEC was never mentioned, and, thus, EPCA remained in effect until new alternatives were presented to Congress.

As might be expected with such a significant piece of legislation, criticism abounded. Some questioned the inconsistencies in the act. Others doubted that the targets could be achieved within the time limit. Almost every specific provision was questioned—environmental protection, production incentives, development of alternative energy sources, and the extent of federal regulatory authority. Most vested interests believed that the act favored everyone but themselves.

One of the most controversial features was the Natural Gas Policy Act. The first major revision of natural gas law in several decades, it represented the culmination of a long and bitter debate. The year 1968 had been a real turning point for natural gas. Not only was it the first time that more gas was sold than discovered, but the supply situation for interstate pipelines changed for the worse (while President Nixon openly supported policies more favorable to producers).

Federal regulation of interstate pipelines resulted in less interstate gas and more intrastate gas as producers shifted to the unregulated market. By 1970, 77 percent of gas sold under new contracts stayed in producer states. A major result of expansion of the intrastate market was the increased use of natural gas for steam generation by electric utilities and industrial plants—especially in Texas, Oklahoma, and Louisiana. The shift also helped to produce gas in the traditional eastern markets.

A virtual natural gas war broke out between producing states in the Southwest, which demanded deregulation, and consuming states in the Northeast, which sought more favorable regulation. The energy crisis aggravated the producer-consumer conflict, increased criticism of the FPC, and generally left the industry in turmoil.

Despite his promises for deregulation, Carter shifted from an apparent alignment with the producing states to a closer relationship with traditional Democratic support for the northern metropolitan core and the eastern coal interests. The 1978 act moved toward eventual deregulation of "new" natural gas, while extending controls into the intrastate market. The old distinction between the intrastate and interstate markets was eliminated with the government having a stronger, if more temporary, role in natural gas regulation.

Supporters of the act argued that the extension of regulations ended the supply advantage of the producing states; that producers would gain deregulation in time; that the coal interests were given some protection from natural gas competition; and that government regulators gained more effective leverage in setting standards. Opponents claimed that government estimates of supplies and reserves, upon which regulations were based, had major discrepancies. Furthermore, the new act resulted in higher prices for consumers and producers. Anti-industry critics of the act noted that true market forces did not control supply and demand of natural gas, thus, eventual deregulation would only mean higher prices not more supply.

In addition to the National Energy Act, the Carter administration raised the energy issue to cabinet-level importance. In March 1977, the President submitted legislation to create a Department of Energy (DOE); he signed the bill in August. DOE replaced the FEA, ERDA, FPC, and the Energy Resources Council.

The idea for a cabinet-level department was the logical conclusion of what the Nixon and Ford administrations had been working toward, with roots ever farther back. But translating the idea into reality created substantial problems. DOE never got off to a good start because energy officials simultaneously tried to formulate the NEP and construct the department. Secretary James Schlesinger, whose appointment was no surprise, was faced with a "department in disarray," as *Time* noted. "Though DOE was set up to bring order, drive and direction to the uncoordinated activities of the 50 federal agencies involved in energy matters," a June 19, 1978 story claimed, "Secretary Schlesinger's superagency has been sinking into a bureaucratic stupor." The "dual track" of legislation and administration was too much, too soon. Where previous administrations had dragged their feet on energy questions, the Carter administration failed to tie its shoes before marching off.

No sooner had the new legislation and the new department come into existence than the administration faced its own energy emergency. The Iranian crisis in late 1978 produced renewed disruptions in the world energy market and new shock waves in the United States. In addition, double-digit inflation reappeared in Spring 1978. Consumer prices had doubled since 1967, trade deficits were enormous, and the dollar continued to decline in value in international monetary markets. Like the Ford administration, the Carter government battled interlacing economic and energy woes.

The impact of the 1979 crisis was more tangible and easily as dramatic as the embargo five or six years earlier. Weekend and even weekday closing of gas stations hit the big cities. For a time, 90 percent of New York City's stations shut down early or closed. California, again, was hit the hardest, with lines at stations stretching for blocks. In May, it took drivers up to five hours to fill their tanks. By the summer, shortages struck other populous states. Taking the lead from California, seven states—Connecticut, Florida, Maryland, New Jersey, New York, Texas, Virginia, and the District of Columbia— initiated an odd-even gas rationing system that July.[7] While the system was

---

[7] Cars with license plates ending in odd numbers could fill up on odd-numbered days, and vice-versa.

abused, it was a sign of the crisis coming home. Picking up the theme, the Calvary Presbyterian Church in Glendale, California, announced its more magnanimous gesture: "Odd or Even, all are welcome."

For most people the shortage was no laughing matter. By April 1979, gasoline was nudging toward $1 a gallon—unheard of in the United States at the time. While there were 5 to 20 percent fewer allocations for the gas stations, some problems in finding gasoline grew out of panic psychology. Fights broke out in lines, service station attendants were bribed, gasoline was stolen.

As in 1973–1974, many people believed the shortages were contrived. A Gallup poll taken in the spring of 1979 showed that only 44 percent of the public thought the energy situation was very serious (about the same as those polled in 1977); 77 percent believed the shortage was caused by the oil companies. In addition, heating oil was in limited supply and prices increased from $.55 a gallon in the winter of 1978 to $.90 in December 1979.

President Carter called for less driving and more attention to thermostat settings in the home and at work. But he also tried to assuage the worst fears of Americans. Using the crisis to recoup losses for his original energy proposals, especially COET, the President outlined a plan for phased decontrol that would be accompanied by a windfall profits tax. The tax would be used to subsidize mass transit, develop synfuels, and give energy assistance funds to the poor. As leverage with a public suspicious of the oil companies, Carter noted: "Just as surely as the sun will rise the oil companies can be expected to fight to keep the profits they have not earned. Unless you speak out, they will have more influence on Congress than you do."[8]

The timing for new legislation insured success. However, Carter had to shoulder the onus of higher prices due to decontrol, and the new Windfall Profits Tax Act of 1980 was predictably unpopular with many in the business world. But, despite what the polls might have shown about public suspicion over a real energy crisis, government leaders and businessmen had little to be optimistic about in 1980.[9] When would the rollercoaster ride end?

FURTHER READING

Roger M. Anders. *The Federal Energy Administration*. Washington, D.C., 1980.
Alice L. Buck. *A History of the Energy Research and Development Administration*. Washington, D.C., 1982.
Robert Engler. *The Brotherhood of Oil*. New York, 1977.
John C. Fisher. *Energy Crises in Perspective*. New York, 1974.

[8]*Time* (April 16, 1979), p. 67.

[9]For a persuasive overview of postwar U.S. oil policy, see Richard H. K. Vietor, "Market Disequilibrium and Business-Government Relations in Oil Policy, 1947–1980," *Materials and Society*, vol. 7 (1983), pp. 379–394.

Jack M. Holl. *The United States Department of Energy*. Washington, D.C., 1982.
Abdul Amir Q. Kubbah. *OPEC: Past and Present*. Vienna, 1974.
Louis Morano. "Multinationals and Nation-States: The Case of Aramco," *Orbis*,
    vol. 23 (Summer 1979), pp. 447–468.
Ian Seymour. *OPEC: Instrument of Change*. London, 1980.
Joseph S. Szyliowicz and Bard E. O'Neill (eds.). *The Energy Crisis and U.S. Foreign
    Policy*. New York, 1975.

CHAPTER 16

Energy and Environment: The Debate Over Growth

Scarcity replaced abundance as a major focus during the 1970s. In fact, the third energy transition was the first to be linked to the notion of scarcity. What made the energy crisis more confounding was its confluence with the burgeoning environmental movement. Concern over energy scarcity clashed with concern over ecological, or environmental, scarcity. A sense of the finite quantities of energy sources (or access to them) came face to face with a sense of the finite nature of a habitable physical environment. It is not surprising that so much of the environmental protest of the 1970s was a response to energy issues: nuclear power, the Alaska pipeline, oil spills, air pollution.

Out of the turmoil of the 1970s came a reexamination of the nation's energy needs and environmental concerns. Was American life to be dominated by middle-class acquisitiveness or bohemian aesthetics? The real choices, of course, were not to be found in extremes. While few solutions emerged during the 1970s, a perception of energy and environment in more holistic terms began to evolve.

The embargo and the Iranian crisis raised serious questions about the supply and price of oil, but the onset of the energy crisis rested on more than these issues. Since the 1960s, the environmental implications of energy took on major proportions, and the environmental values of Americans had broadened. As Samuel P. Hays argued: "The term 'environment' in contrast with the earlier term 'conservation' reflects more precisely the innovations in values."[1] Local protests made way for "movement" organization. An emphasis on quality of life issues—a greater appreciation of natural environments, more attention to health matters, and a better understanding of pollution—complemented or replaced narrower concerns over the squandering of resources.

Quality of life issues had roots in the American past, especially the antipollution protests of the industrial cities. More than in the past, a concern about the *effects* of environmental degradation was matched with an interest in *causation*. Environmentalists warned about "ecodisasters," but they also questioned the economic, political, and social structures that produced these

---

[1]Samuel P. Hays, "From Conservation to Environment," *Environmental Review*, vol. 6 (Fall 1982), p. 17.

problems. Such inquiry came at a time when fuel scarcity, faltering productivity, inflation, and other anxieties were intensified by the energy crisis. As a counterweight to environmentalist protests, others, notably, business leaders, government officials, and economists, warned about energy shortfalls, threats to national security, and the deterioration of the standard of living.

While American society was not polarized during the 1970s, the convergence of the energy crisis and the environmental movement posed uncomfortable choices. New technologies and untapped energy sources offered means to counteract OPEC's control of oil—but they also posed environmental threats. A change in energy consumption habits, capital outlays for pollution control devices, and an emphasis on "soft" energy paths might help preserve the environment, but it might also threaten economic growth. Encased in these seemingly tangible issues were fundamental questions of values, lifestyle, and the future aspirations of the nation.

THE RISE OF THE MODERN ENVIRONMENTAL MOVEMENT

The publication of Rachel Carson's *Silent Spring* (1962) is often cited as the beginning of the modern environmental movement. Carson's attack on pesticides was significant, but a single event did not cause such a diverse movement. The modern environmental movement arose during the 1960s, to be sure, but its roots and antecedents were imbedded in the European and American pasts—in conservation, preservationism, naturalism, antipollution, and public health campaigns.

The movement's more recent origins are found in natural environment issues such as outdoor recreation, wildlands, and open space; in concerns over environmental pollution; and in the maturing of ecological science. It is also linked to the "sixties" generation. Cynics have argued that political and economic elites sponsored or supported environmental activities as a way of distracting protesters from antiwar, antipoverty, or civil rights activities. However, the political and social turmoil of the 1960s presented an opportunity for raising questions about environmental protection, and it provided willing supporters, especially among idealistic teens and young adults.

The environmental movement, however, was rooted in more than youthful idealism. While drawing its major support from middle- and upper-middle classes, politically it functioned as a coalition of groups that cut across class lines and varying interests.[2] Older preservationist groups—the Sierra Club (1892) and the National Audubon Society(1905)—experienced a revival of interest in the 1970s. More recent groups with corporate backing—Re-

[2]Richard N. L. Andrews, "Class Politics or Democratic Reform," *Natural Resources Journal*, vol. 20 (April 1980), pp. 221–241. For a contrasting view, see William Tucker, *Progress and Privilege* (New York, 1982).

sources for the Future (early 1950s) and Lawrence Rockefeller's Conservation Foundation (mid-1960s)—promoted efficient utilization of resources. Legal remedies received attention from the Environmental Defense Fund (1967) and the Natural Resources Defense Council (1970).

Aggressive, often militant, protest and citizen action was carried out by groups such as Friends of the Earth (splintered from the Sierra Club), Zero Population Growth, the National Wildlife Federation, and Ecology Action. And individuals—biologists Rachel Carson and Barry Commoner—popularized and promoted the study of ecology. Beyond the borders of the United States, "Green parties" and "ecoactivists" inaugurated their own versions of environmental protest.

Environmentalists generally shared an appreciation of the fragility of ecological balances, a notion of the intrinsic value of nature, a personal concern for health and fitness, and a commitment to self-reliance. They by no means espoused uniform political views or reform tactics. Some accepted governmental intervention as a way to allocate resources or preserve wildlands and natural habitats. Others were suspicious of any large institution as the protector of the environment. Some believed that the existing political and social structure was capable of balancing environmental protection and economic productivity. Still others blamed capitalism for promoting uncontrolled economic growth, materialism, the squandering of resources, and even the coopting of the environmental movement for its own ends.

EARTH DAY, NEPA, AND ENVIRONMENTALISM

What made the environmental movement so remarkable was the speed with which it gained national attention—if not universal acclaim. Nothing epitomized that appeal better than Earth Day. In *Earth Day—The Beginning*, the staff of Environmental Action declared: "On April 22, [1970] a generation dedicated itself to reclaiming the planet. A new kind of movement was born—a bizarre alliance that spans the ideological spectrum from campus militants to middle Americans. Its aim: to reverse our rush toward extinction." Across the country, on 2,000 college campuses, in 10,000 high schools, and in parks and various open areas, as many as 20 million people celebrated purportedly "the largest, cleanest, most peaceful demonstration in America's history." In form, Earth Day was so much like a sixties-style peace demonstration that the Daughters of the American Revolution insisted that it must be subversive. As a symbol of the new enthusiasm for environmental matters, and as a public recognition of a trend already well underway, Earth Day nonetheless served its purpose.

The Nixon administration gave its blessings to Earth Day. In his first State of the Union message, the President declared: "Clean air, clean water, open spaces—these should be the birthright of every American." On January 1, 1970, four months before Earth Day, Nixon signed the National Environmental Policy Act of 1969 (NEPA). Many people trumpeted their approval of the President's gesture; others reserved judgment or remained cynical. NEPA, emerging in the wake of the Santa Barbara oil spill, was primarily the work of several congressional Democrats, especially Senators Edmund Muskie (Maine), Henry Jackson (Wash.), and Gaylord Nelson (Wisc.), and Representative John Dingell (Mich.).

While opposing the bill until it cleared the congressional conferees, the Nixon administration ultimately embraced NEPA as its own. Going on record against "clean air, clean water, and open spaces" served no purpose. But lip service alone would not quell the momentum of the new environmental movement.

While far from "the Magna Carta of environmental protection" that some people proclaimed, NEPA called for a new national responsibility for the environment. NEPA was not simply a restatement of resource management; it also promoted efforts to preserve and enhance the environment. The provision mandating action required federal agencies to prepare environmental impact statements (EISs) in advance of all major recommendations, reports, or actions on legislation germaine to the environment (and these were to be made public).

NEPA also provided substantial opportunity for citizen participation, especially through access to information in agency files. It established the Council on Environmental Quality (CEQ) to review government activities pertaining to the environment, to develop impact statement guidelines, and to advise the President on environmental matters. While NEPA could be manipulated, it increased accountability for environmental actions.

The CEQ was essentially a presidential instrument, however, and government environmental programs remained widely dispersed. In early 1970, a presidential council recommended the establishment of a Department of Natural Resources and the Environment to codify several departments and agencies. In-fighting immediately broke out among the affected departments—Interior, Agriculture, Commerce—with a new intensity. Nixon was not prepared for the council's recommendation and had to address this sensitive issue carefully. A compromise avoided a major confrontation between the Interior and Commerce departments, while simultaneously paying homage to government reorganization and the politics of the environment. In June 1970, it was announced that pollution control programs and the evaluation of impact statements would be the responsibility of a new body—the Environmental Protection Agency (EPA)—while another group of programs would be placed within the Commerce Department. Everything else would remain the same. Secretary of Commerce Maurice Stans, who had close ties to the President, seemed to have gained the most, while Secretary of the Interior Walter Hickel, who had fallen out of grace with the White House, lost key programs and eventually his job.

By the end of 1970, environmentalism had gained national attention. However, for the remainder of the decade the interplay between energy policy and environmental protection would be a key to the future of both.

OIL AND THE ENVIRONMENT

The energy crisis exposed the conflict between increasing domestic oil and gas production and environmental protection. Questions of resource exploitation and conservation arose in response to concern over long-term scarcity. Exploring for oil in undeveloped regions, land or sea, set off debates over economic productivity versus preservation.

Blowouts and Oil Spills

The search for new sources of petroleum inevitably led to increased interest in offshore wells. Ocean drilling and greater tanker traffic also guaranteed more blowouts and spills. In February 1970, the *New York Times* reported three Exxon oil spills in one month: 15,000 gallons off the coast of Florida, 3 million gallons in Nova Scotia Bay, and 50,000 gallons a day for several weeks in the Gulf of Mexico. During 1975 alone, there were 12,000 reported spills resulting in 21 million gallons of oil dumped into U.S. waters. And these were only a fraction of the spills throughout the world during the same period.

In 1977, the Coast Guard initiated more stringent regulations for tankers, but illegal flushing continued. An exploratory well some fifty-seven miles off the Yucatan Peninsula experienced a massive blowout on June 3, 1979. While the Ixtoc well in the Bay of Campeche was a Pemex venture, it threatened the Texas coast as much as the Mexican coast. The explosion and fire destroyed the rig and created a slick sixty to seventy miles long and growing, which struck beaches all along the gulf. The ultimate discharge not only exceeded the Santa Barbara spill but also the Ekofisk blowout in the Norwegian North Sea (1977)—the largest on record at the time.

The Ixtoc blowout renewed the controversy over oil exploration along the continental shelf. In the wake of the energy crisis, the Nixon administration and its successors had continued to authorize leasing of federally controlled sites through the Department of the Interior. Coastal states, especially California, were wary of leaving the fate of their coastlines to the Interior Department and the oil companies. Even after the passage of NEPA, many environmentalists believed that impact statements for the leases were more ceremonial than substantive.

The Alaska Pipeline

The major battle over oil production during the 1970s was fought on the land not on the sea. It was a conflict over the Alaska pipeline. Oil exploration was not taken seriously until World War II. But intense interest did not arise until the world oil glut receded during the late 1960s. After an unsuccessful attempt near the Sagvanirktok River, Atlantic Richfield (ARCO) struck a massive field at Prudhoe Bay in 1968 (estimated at 4.8 billion barrels). A rush was on.

In September 1969, oil leases—bringing $900 million to the federal treasury—were awarded. Oil companies were eager to begin development, and there was growing support for the construction of a pipeline to run 800 miles from Prudhoe Bay south to the port of Valdez. (This would mean the delivery of oil to the West Coast rather than to the Midwest through a pipeline crossing Canada.)

Environmentalists fought hard against the pipeline, largely for the sake of wilderness preservation in one of the few remaining frontiers of the United States. The 1973 oil embargo undermined their case, and, in that year, Congress passed the Trans-Alaska Pipeline Authorization Act. Thousands of people poured into Alaska seeking jobs with the Alyeska Pipeline Service Company.

The biggest blow to the environmentalists was a provision declaring that a previous environmental impact statement—criticized as innocuous—satisfied the requirements of NEPA. Without the EIS weapon for further court challenges, environmental groups dropped their challenge in January 1974. The first oil began to flow three years later. The most pessimistic opponents of the pipeline bemoaned the weakening of NEPA. The more optimistic rationalized that the oil companies were forced to modify their original plans to include environmental safeguards.

The Clean Air Amendments

Environmental protest against the petroleum industry and its allies extended to end-use. A general concern for clean air, with a specific interest in automobile emissions, produced the controversies. The meteoric rise in environmental concern, the dissatisfaction with existing federal laws, and the lackluster accomplishments of the states provided the momentum for the 1970 Clean Air Amendments. Dealing with both auto emissions and stationary sources of pollution, the new legislation was the most stringent air pollution law ever passed in the United States. With respect to auto emissions, the law required a 90 percent reduction in hydrocarbons and carbon monoxide by 1975 and a 90 percent reduction in nitrogen oxides by 1976.

In one sense, the Clean Air Amendments had grown out of rising expectations. The 1967 Air Quality Act was a step in the right direction, but it was insufficient to produce a national ambient standard or to protect adequately public health. Supporters of more stringent measures believed that the Nixon administration had been lax in enforcing existing laws and thus should be given less discretion in the protection of the environment.

Implementation of the Clean Air Amendments was made difficult by a reluctant automobile industry and the energy crisis. The 1970 act gave the auto industry a temporary way out of meeting the tougher standards. Under the provisions of the act, the EPA administrator could grant a one-year delay if the auto companies made "good faith" efforts to meet the new standards. Some critics questioned whether the manufacturers had, in fact, made such a gesture, since they relied on the research and development work of independent companies for emission-control technology rather than utilizing their own resources.

EPA Administrator William Ruckelshaus denied the delay on the grounds that the companies were capable of meeting the 1975 deadline. Four auto companies then sued EPA for refusing to extend the deadline, and, in 1973, the Court of Appeals ruled in favor of the plaintiffs. The onset of the energy crisis prompted Congress to extend the deadline further, and apprehension about the safety of the catalytic converters again pushed back the deadline.[3] In 1977, a three-year suspension was granted.

The Clean Air Amendments were a legislative means of applying new standards to the battle for clean air. While auto-related pollution declined steadily after 1973, the serious problem of nitrogen dioxide emissions remained largely unchecked. Programs for changing driving habits were voluntary, and only lip service was paid to improving mass transit in most major cities.

The energy crisis produced a mixed record with respect to auto emissions. The American automobile industry, especially Chrysler, was woefully unprepared to meet the challenge of fuel economy demanded by the rise in gasoline prices. Americans turned to small Japanese and European cars, while Detroit plunged into a deep depression. Alternatives to the internal combustion engine were not quick in developing either. One exception was the greater availability of the more economical and less-polluting diesel engine.

Faced with the crisis in the automobile industry, the federal government sought to ease air pollution and safety standards. In this way, the energy crisis blunted enthusiasm for more stringent air pollution laws. However, the mandated 55-mile-an-hour national speed limit and the decline in gasoline usage (by more than 5 percent) contributed to some reductions in air pollution.

COAL, STRIP MINING, AND ELECTRICAL POWER

The energy crisis stimulated interest in America's most abundant energy resource—coal. The environmental implications of coal mining and coal burning, however, detracted from its rise as a panacea to the nation's energy woes. For reasons of economy and efficiency, surface mining (or strip mining) of coal had become the preferred method in several areas of the country—and also invited the greatest criticism from environmentalists. In 1970, the Geological Survey estimated that 2,450 square miles of land had been strip mined in the United States. By 1971, strip-mined land amounted to almost 75,000 acres a year. Throughout the decade more than half of the annual coal tonnage came from surface mines.

[3]The catalytic converter is an add-on device for reducing carbon monoxide and hydrocarbons.

Efforts to regulate strip-mining practices underwent a substantial meta-morphosis during the 1970s. What was considered a local problem grew to national prominence. As early as 1971, legislators had introduced more than twenty-four bills relating to strip mining. Opposing the coal and utility interests were more than thirty national and regional organizations, including traditional conservation groups, Indian and agricultural groups, church groups, and ad hoc organizations like COALition Against Strip Mining. Debate focused on federal leasing practices, the shift of coal production westward, strip-mining prohibition in key areas, reclamation, pollution control, and regulatory responsibility.

The activities of the Tennessee Valley Authority (TVA) received particular attention. By 1970, TVA was the single largest electric utility in the nation. Electric utility companies accounted for more than half of the coal consumed in the United States, and TVA was the largest purchaser. About 66 percent of its energy source came from fossil fuels. Paradise steam plant was TVA's first "mine mouth" plant, burning 21,000 tons of coal each day from beds in the immediate area. Resistant to strong strip-mining control, TVA used its preeminence as a coal consumer to purchase coal at bargain rates. In 1974, it secretly considered a proposal to strip mine reserves that it owned in the Daniel Boone National Forest but was thwarted by a newspaper exposé of the plan. TVA reclamation director James Curry stated: "Strip mining is part of the American way."[4]

The Federal Strip Mining Control Act of 1977 was the culmination of efforts to curtail the greatest abuses. Ironically, it was passed at a time when the Carter administration was encouraging greater coal production to offset losses in petroleum supplies. The act was not passed without substantial controversy. President Gerald Ford vetoed strip-mining control bills twice before the 1977 act was passed. Pressure from the coal interests and utilities, as well as a fear of high coal prices, kept Congress from overriding the vetoes.

Carter's election and the elevation of environmentalist Morris Udall to chairman of the House Interior Committee led to reintroduction of a strip-mining bill. The 1977 act, as passed, provided for federal control of strip-mine reclamation (unless the states were willing to enforce strict laws themselves), established a new Office of Surface Mining, and required most operators to restore mined land to its approximate original state.

The new law was not as strict as many environmentalists wanted. Small operators were exempted for about three years, and it allowed strip mining on several terrains as well as national forests and prime agricultural lands. In addition, it provided that surface owners must consent before mining was allowed on federal land. An incomplete victory, the passage of the Federal Strip Mining Control Act was another example of linking national environmental goals to energy production.

[4]Cited in James Branscome, "The TVA: It Ain't What It Used to Be," *American Heritage*, vol. 28 (February 1977), p. 76.

COAL, ELECTRIC UTILITIES, AND AIR POLLUTION

The Clean Air Amendments not only had provisions for ambient air quality standards but for emission standards from stationary sources of air pollution. The states were required to enforce the federal standards but could set more stringent ones if they desired. A unique feature of the law was the establishment of variable emission limits for existing sources of pollution and uniform national emission limits for new sources.

Air quality standards were to be based on health criteria and emission limits were to be determined, in part at least, on projected abatement costs. The EPA had substantial discretionary power, which led to endless negotiation and litigation with industry. Implementation of the law was also sidetracked by the energy crisis. In 1973, for example, the EPA suspended clean air standards so electrical utility plants could convert to coal. Ironically, many utilities had recently abandoned coal for fuel oil, to comply with the new emission standards.

By 1975—the original target date for achieving the quality standards of the Clean Air Amendments—proponents of air pollution reform were dissatisfied with the sluggish implementation of the new law. The concern over energy had supplanted environmental goals. It was not until the election of Jimmy Carter that advocates of revised air pollution standards came to believe that a presidential veto was no longer waiting for them.

About one month after the new strip-mining law was passed, a new set of Clean Air Act amendments were also passed. The most important change was the inclusion of the highly controversial "no significant deterioration" provision. No reduction of air quality was to be allowed in areas that currently had high air quality, especially national parks and wilderness areas. Coal interests, utilities, and others fought the provisions, and further extensions for meeting the standards were granted. However, in the conflict between energy and environment, no clear victor emerged.

Electric utilities faced additional environmental challenges over thermal discharges and the extension of high voltage powerlines across farmlands. In Minnesota, for instance, farmers protested the stringing of powerlines across their land. When legal means failed in 1974, they turned to more direct action. In 1978, state troopers were called in to keep the angry farmers from scaring off surveyors and construction crews. According to one source:

> A kind of guerrilla warfare broke out on the western plains and 430 miles of powerline proved difficult to defend. At night, towers were attacked by "bolt weevils" and fell to the ground; the land was littered with glass as an epidemic of "insulator disease" broke out; and high-powered rifle bullets (or was it "wire worms"?) splayed open the conducting wire. Local sentiment was with the farmers and law officers made no arrests.[5]

[5]Barry M. Casper and Paul David Wellstone, *Powerline* (Amherst, Mass., 1981), p. 5.

In one of the most highly publicized environmental cases of the late 1970s, the TVA was back in the news over the construction of the Tellico Dam and the fate of a three-inch-long fish, the snail darter. The construction of the new Tellico Dam met with disapproval from local environmentalists because it threatened to destroy one of the region's last free-flowing rivers, valuable farmland, and the homeland of the Cherokee Indian Nation. In 1973, University of Tennessee zoologist David Etnier informed the TVA that he discovered the snail darter in the Little Tennessee River above the partially completed dam. TVA thought nothing of this until 1977—with Tellico 90 percent completed—when a federal appeals court ruled that the completion of the dam would destroy the only known habitat of the snail darter and thus violate the Endangered Species Act. The Supreme Court concurred in the ruling.

The decision created a predictable storm among TVA officials and elation among environmentalists. The issue—which clouded the major questions of the need for the dam and the flooding of the valley—was only laid to rest when Congress enacted special legislation exempting Tellico from the Endangered Species Act, thus allowing the dam to be completed. TVA won this round.

NUCLEAR POWER: THE ULTIMATE ENVIRONMENTAL BATTLE

The conflict over nuclear power during the 1970s was a classic encounter between proponents of large, centralized systems and those suspicious of high technology and unrestrained economic growth. Both sides dragged out mountains of evidence; demonstrations, public debates, and myriad accusations were commonplace and recurrent. This was warfare of a special type.

The controversy developed on two levels: one centered on the nature of the energy source itself, the other, over the role of centralized power. Debate on the first level revolved around the question of safety. To advocates, nuclear power had a spotless record; reactors incorporated the latest technology and were constructed under rigorous supervision. Opponents questioned these claims, arguing that accidents had occurred in the past but were covered up, and they were likely to happen in the future if the technology proliferated. While advocates focused on reactor safety, opponents discussed the unreliability of technical safeguards and human error. They looked beyond reactors to potential problems all along the production cycle, from mining of uranium to disposing of radioactive wastes.

On the second level, broader societal and institutional issues were at stake. Advocates touted nuclear power as an answer to the energy crisis and to OPEC's control of oil. The technology of light-water reactors had already proven itself, they argued, and nuclear power could help to divert petroleum from the production of electricity to other essential needs—namely, transportation. Advocates, turning the environmental issue around, characterized dependence on coal as a greater risk than was nuclear power.

Opponents were suspicious of centralized power production as manifest in large nuclear systems. Centralized power production kept energy development in the hands of government and big business, and it left consumers vulnerable to their whims. A move toward decentralized systems, especially toward solar energy, would not only reduce the need for nuclear power, they argued, but weaken the trend toward corporate control of society.

The controversy over nuclear power soon became newsworthy in its own right. In this complex debate, citizens and their government officials were asked to choose between the scientific experts aligned with the two sides and between alternative energy futures. With the technical issues beyond almost everyone, few people knew what to believe or whom to trust.

The AEC and Calvert Cliffs

While the war of words grew more intense, environmentalists scored some important victories for the antinuclear cause. In a curious reversal of roles, proponents found themselves as nay-sayers and prophets of doom. They claimed that, by obstructing the development of nuclear power, the environmentalists were eliminating an important alternative to expensive foreign oil.

The impact of the environmental movement was felt in the changing role of the AEC and governmental participation in nuclear power development. Nuclear opponents argued that the AEC could not be promoter and watchdog at the same time. The safety review programs were nothing to be proud of; the criteria for siting plants were not sophisticated; and the regulatory structure was weakened by insufficient operating experience for the new generation of plants. Critics also assailed the AEC for not providing sufficient public input into policy decisions and limiting disclosure of information about nuclear power.

On the twenty-fifth anniversary of the AEC, a major reorganization was underway: partly to maintain federal hold over nuclear development and partly in response to the criticism. President Nixon had appointed James Schlesinger as chairman of AEC in August 1971, because he was a proven administrator and had experience in dealing with environmental issues. Hardly a product of the environmental movement, Schlesinger might temper AEC's strident promotion of nuclear power by reemphasizing its regulatory function.

The Federal Court of Appeals, rather than the new secretary, nudged the AEC toward paying greater attention to environmental costs. *Calvert Cliffs Coordinating Committee* v. *AEC* grew out of a citizen protest against the Calvert Cliffs Nuclear Generating Station near Lusby, Maryland. In July 1971, the court found AEC regulations in violation of the NEPA mandate to make a detailed assessment of costs, benefits, and the environmental impact of nuclear power plants before licensing them.

Until that time, AEC and the nuclear industry had limited citizen input in the licensing process and had interpreted NEPA narrowly. Hoping to avoid more litigation and wishing to restore AEC's faltering image, Schlesinger announced that the commission would comply with the court decision. He also boldly stated that a new policy would emphasize serving the public interest rather than simply promoting the growth of the nuclear industry.

The Calvert Cliffs decision did not make over the nuclear industry or destroy AEC's power. It did activate NEPA by establishing an important precedent and forced AEC to tone down its promotional role. To nuclear advocates, Calvert Cliffs made the licensing process more cumbersome and politically volatile, thus undermining the rapid deployment of commercial atomic power. But AEC's problems went deeper than compliance with the court's decision or filing environmental impact statements. Twenty-five years of promotion had not been matched by equal attention to safety or effective regulation. The selling job had been fairly effective, but it depended on claims too grand for the immediate future.

Safety and the Rasmussen Report

The problems of radioactivity and reactor safety acquired center stage in the early 1970s. Most environmental questions—radiation release, thermal pollution, radioactive waste, risks due to sabotage, and reactor safety—had already been raised in one form or another. Of rising importance was the development of the breeder reactor. The AEC's decision to continue development of the breeder—despite opposition by such groups as Scientists Institute for Public Information and the Union of Concerned Scientists—led to further criticism of its health and safety programs. Of special concern was the production of plutonium through the breeder and through fuel reprocessing. Plutonium, a requisite ingredient in atomic weapons, is highly toxic with a 24,000-year half-life.

Through the early 1970s, the AEC had treated safety programs as in-house matters. This was becoming more difficult to do as environmentalists demanded a public accounting. Particularly disruptive was an internal debate over the dangers of radioactivity, which erupted after the 1969 publication of a report by Dr. Ernest J. Sternglass of the University of Pittsburgh. According to Sternglass, radioactive fallout from atmospheric nuclear tests in Nevada in the 1950s could cause the deaths of 400,000 babies. In response, two staff members of the Lawrence Radiation Laboratory, Drs. Arthur R. Tamplin and John W. Gofman, were assigned the task of evaluating—and discrediting—the Sternglass report. Tamplin and Gofman disagreed with Sternglass's numbers, not his general conclusions. (They believed that 400 infants and fetuses were likely to die from radiation exposure.) In the fall of 1969, they charged the AEC with poor radiation protection standards and repeated their claims before congressional investigating committees. Pressure from the AEC to censor the findings ultimately turned Tamplin and Gofman into public critics of the AEC. Their resignations in 1976 gave the antinuclear movement a significant publicity device.

The public furor over safety put the AEC on the defensive by 1972. Schlesinger tried to meet the criticism, this time by initiating a new safety study. The Reactor Safety Study, while not conducted independently of AEC, was to have the appearance of independence. Dr. Norman C. Rasmussen, an MIT nuclear engineer, was selected to direct the study. While not on the AEC payroll, Rasmussen had links to the nuclear industry, which was almost unavoidable in this field. He possessed substantial expertise in nuclear power but had little specialized training in reactor safety per se. The task force he headed included about sixty scientists and engineers. The study, which cost between $3 and $4 million, took two years to complete and extended to nine volumes.

Rasmussen was under constant pressure to produce the report quickly. The haste indicated the degree to which AEC wanted to use the results to defend its position on safety. The draft report was published in August 1974, with a final version appearing in 1975. The Reactor Safety Study (WASH 1400) concluded that the risks from nuclear reactors were very small, and core melt-downs were particularly remote (1 in 20,000). It added that the fail-safe systems made a serious accident highly unlikely. The most vivid (and most quotable) claim was that the chance of 1 person dying from a nuclear accident was 1 in 5 billion, or about the same as the chance of being struck by a meteor. To reinforce its statistical evidence, the report included data for comparative risks, car fatalities, tornadoes, and so forth. According to the findings, if 100 nuclear reactors were in operation, the average number of deaths per year would be 2. Comparatively, 50,000 people a year die in automobile accidents, 18,000 from falls, and 6,000 from drowning.

The AEC and industry officials broadcast the report's findings widely and received favorable press attention. Criticism began almost immediately, however, challenging every aspect of the study from its methodology to its estimates. The Rasmussen team had not made a general study of all U.S. nuclear plants; it focused instead on a couple of "representative" plants. Critics claimed that the report was too theoretical and also discredited the "fault-tree" analysis as an unreliable way to acquire probability estimates.

Beyond the specific claims of the report, additional questions remained: How do you factor in human error? What about safety questions beyond the reactor? Contrary to the AEC's hopes, the Rasmussen report raised more questions than it answered. But for nuclear advocates the report and the lack of any catastrophic accident was vindication or, at least, recognition that criticism of the safety program was prematurely alarmist.

The Demise of the AEC

If the Rasmussen report proved useful to defend the safety programs of the AEC, the onset of the energy crisis offered the chance to promote nuclear power as a hedge against OPEC and the scarcity of oil. By the end of 1973, the five-fold increase in imported oil prices made nuclear power competitive again. Particularly in areas where early experiences with nuclear plants had been favorable, in the Southeast and Southern California, or where low-sulfur coal was not readily available, in New England, utilities found nuclear plants to be an attractive alternative to fossil fuel plants. By late 1974, orders for light-water reactors reached a new peak.

But almost as quickly as it rose, the nuclear power market collapsed, by the end of 1974. The drop in the consumption of electricity in the wake of the energy crisis was an ironic turn of events for the nuclear power industry. Financial problems among utility companies, induced in part by falling demand, eliminated the need for new plants. Orders for new plants of all kinds were deferred and several were cancelled.

The setback to the industry was further aggravated by the demise of the AEC. On the surface, its dismantling was part of the Nixon administration's larger effort at reorganization. But it was more precisely a response to the energy crisis and the growing criticism of government management of nuclear power. Before the reorganization, in February 1973, the President tried to mute criticism of the AEC by appointing as new head Dr. Dixie Lee Ray. A marine biologist with a strong interest in ecology, Ray also possessed an equally strong commitment to nuclear power. She faced an unenviable task in light of the problems of the energy crisis and growing criticisms from environmentalists.

Watergate disrupted Nixon's reorganization plans. It fell to his successor, Gerald Ford, to maintain the executive branch's control over federal energy policy. In response to Ford's request, Congress passed the Energy Reorganization Act of 1974. The long-standing conflict of interest within AEC between promotion and regulation was dealt with by abolishing the commission and dividing its functions between the Energy Research and Development Administration (ERDA) and the Nuclear Regulatory Commission (NRC).

The Joint Committee on Atomic Energy was likewise affected by the nuclear controversy. It had never demonstrated much sympathy for environmental issues and sustained itself only as a promotional force. Those in Congress not connected with the JCAE increasingly resented its sweeping power. House Democrats began to whittle away at that power, ultimately splitting its functions among five standing committees. The Senate supported the House action, and the JCAE was abolished by a revision of the Atomic Energy Act in 1977.

From Browns Ferry to Seabrook

As a near-future energy alternative, nuclear power should have benefited from the oil shortages of the early 1970s, or so its proponents believed. But the rise and fall in the industry's fortunes were indicative of a nation undergoing an energy transition. The persistence of nuclear critics, the long-standing uneasiness with atomic power, the rising issue of radioactive waste, and some newsworthy accidents reignited the nuclear controversy in the last half of the decade.

A bizarre, but prophetic accident occurred in 1975 at the Browns Ferry nuclear plant near Athens, Alabama. This TVA plant was the world's largest nuclear generating facility. On March 22, a fire broke out under the control room: a candle used by an employee to check for ventilation leaks ignited a sealant on electrical cables that controlled the emergency core-cooling system (ECCS). The flames burned out the ECCS cable controls, resulting in malfunctions in seven of the twelve safety systems. The fire lasted longer than it should because—through a misunderstanding—water was not used to douse it. Fortunately, no major water coolant pipe broke during the eight-hour fire, and a catastrophe was avoided.

Predictably, the NRC played down the accident while antinuclear critics played it up. Pronuclear forces pointed to the success of the redundancies built into the plant, but critics had legitimate cause for concern. Within its first year of operation (beginning in August 1974) sixty-five "abnormal occurrences" had taken place in the plant. Those who argued that the Rasmussen report failed to take into consideration "Murphy's law" (whatever can go wrong, will go wrong) had a point.

Caught between the goals of the environmental movement and the problems of the energy crisis, Americans did not speak in a single, clear voice on nuclear power during the mid-1970s. In the West, an effort to stop nuclear expansion and the operation of plants in California failed at the polls. Nuclear critics blamed the well-financed pronuclear forces (especially the Atomic Industrial Forum) and cited that the legislature undermined the initiative by passing laws partially restricting nuclear development. Still the vote was two-to-one against the proposition. In twelve other states, only one nuclear initiative passed.[6]

In the East, protests harkened back to the sixties in the form of mass demonstrations and acts of civil disobedience. Unlike the delaying tactics of environmental groups during licensing hearings, some antinuclear forces took to the streets. The best known protest took place in Seabrook, New Hampshire. In August 1976, under the leadership of the Clamshell Alliance, more than 1,200 demonstrators occupied the site of the proposed nuclear plant at Seabrook. The incident became a media event, with many of the demonstrators having been arrested and carted away.[7] Although EPA refused to approve a permit for the plant's cooling system, and the NRC suspended all but ex-

[6]In 1976, a California law initiated a moratorium on new plants until the federal government came up with a waste disposal plan. A U.S. Supreme Court decision in 1982 upheld this law as well as the right of states to regulate in the nuclear field.

[7]Prior to the demonstration, residents had tried legal channels to voice their protests. Failing this, the mass demonstration ensued.

cavation at the site, another mass demonstration took place in April 1977. The tension was greater, with Governor Meldrim Thompson taking a hard line against what he called the "terrorists."

As the sides polarized, more demonstrations followed. On the thirty-second anniversary of the bombing of Hiroshima (August 1977), several demonstrations were held throughout the country. These protests indicated the degree to which the antinuclear campaign linked commercial nuclear development with the proliferation of atomic weapons. Antinuclear activism continued to manifest itself in public demonstrations throughout the decade and into the 1980s. Whether the protests were effective in increasing support for the antinuclear cause is unclear. Certainly, they sustained the effort to delay construction of new plants—possibly at the cost of widening the gap between the pro- and antinuclear groups.

Three Mile Island

The future of nuclear power was uncertain by the late 1970s. Anxieties over the energy crisis had ebbed, if only momentarily, thus the one compelling reason to move ahead with nuclear power was slipping away. But 1979 proved to be more dramatic than anyone could have imagined: the Iranian crisis and the accident at Three Mile Island brought into sharp focus the conflict between the need for alternative energy supplies and the environmental cost of that quest.

Uncertainty about further construction of nuclear plants was aggravated by a growing number of safety problems at a variety of installations—pipe cracks in reactors, flaws in electrical systems, siting problems along earthquake faults. The whole issue of risk was put into question when, in January 1979, the NRC quietly announced that "The Commission does not regard as reliable the Reactor Safety Study's numerical estimate of overall risk of reactor accident." So much for the Rasmussen Report. What evidence was used by the NRC in determining that reactors were safe? Congressional leaders and others asked that same question.

Under the circumstances, the accident at Three Mile Island was not the departure point for a loss of faith in nuclear power—it was the climax. America's worst nuclear accident took place at a station owned by General Public Utilities and located on Three Mile Island in the Susquehanna River (about ten miles southwest of Harrisburg, Pennsylvania). The power station has two units; TMI-2 was dedicated in September 1978.

The accident occurred on March 28, during the "graveyard" shift. At 4:00 A.M., a pump on the main water-feed system malfunctioned. Within two seconds, the flow of water to cool the reactor stopped, and the plant safety system automatically shut down the steam turbine and electric generator. A relief valve popped open to reduce the pressure in the reactor and stayed in that position. Unfortunately, an indicator on the control panel led the crew to believe that the valve was shut. Instead, it drained water from the reactor for more than two hours. Believing that the reactor was adequately supplied with cooling water, the operators shut off the emergency cooling pump. The loss of cooling water caused the fuel to overheat and brought the core dangerously close to a meltdown. The top of the core became uncovered, hydrogen was generated, and an explosion in the containment building occurred. (Not until a day later did the operators learn about the explosion.)

By about 7:30 A.M., the station manager declared a general emergency. The auxiliary building had already been evacuated and soon the control room in TMI-2 was cleared. Teams of technical personnel were sent into the surrounding neighborhoods to monitor radioactivity levels, and Route 441 near the plant was closed. On Friday, March 30, the situation worsened when more radiation releases took place, although no major release occurred.

The event created great confusion. Coordination between on-site, company, NRC, and government officials proved difficult. Several possible evacuation plans were bantered about, but without notifying or consulting the plant staff. Rampant rumors of large-scale evacuation led Governor Richard Thornburgh to recommend that pregnant women and preschool children leave the area within a five-mile radius of the plant. Independently of the governor's announcement, many people had already left their homes. Chaos did not break out, but citizens were confused, scared, and uncertain. Even the site inspection by President Carter on Sunday did not assuage fears or rectify the problems in communication.

The aftermath of the accident was almost as dramatic as the event itself. As one observer noted, the accident at Three Mile Island was "red meat" for the press. Coverage was extensive and editorial responses were frequent and often strident. Public reaction ranged from relief to indignation. Antinuclear protesters held a new round of demonstrations. In May, some 70,000 protesters staged an event at the Capitol to strains of "Hell No, We Won't Glow!" In attendance was Jane Fonda—antiwar protester and star of *The China Syndrome* (a thriller about a mythical nuclear accident) which was released days before the real occurrence at Three Mile Island. A surge of black humor also surfaced, manifest in T-shirt slogans such as "I SURVIVED THREE MILE ISLAND—I THINK."

The official response was typical. Dartmouth College President John Kemeny headed a presidential commission, which placed the blame on plant builders and managers, operators, and federal regulators but fell short of recommending a moratorium on construction of new plants. Several congressional investigations, as well as NRC and industry inquiries, followed. Charges of "human error" were raised by both critics and supporters of nuclear power—the former, as a way of demonstrating that "it could happen again" and the latter, as a way of defending a "sound technology."

A DOE-sponsored study made an interesting point:

... Three Mile Island was not so much a technological event as a human and historical one. ... It was not only a mechanical breakdown but a series of human choices that crippled a nuclear reactor and threatened injury and death to the public. What escaped at Three Mile Island was not only radiation, but, more importantly for the nuclear power industry, public confidence in technology and technocracy.[8]

Yet the accident at Three Mile Island seemed to have little effect on the strongest proponents and opponents of nuclear power. Even an event as dramatic as the accident of Three Mile Island could do little more than to leave nuclear power in limbo, where it remained during the early 1980s. Controversy continued to rage over reactor safety, uranium enrichment, nuclear sabotage and terrorism, international proliferation, transportation of nuclear fuels, and especially radioactive waste. The AEC's panacea in 1970—storing wastes in abandoned salt mines near Lyon, Kansas—met local resistance and brought into question the technical feasibility and safety of such a choice. A newer plan for surface storage facilities posed its own problems. Since the late 1970s, commercial spent fuels were stored in pools of water alongside the various power reactors throughout the country in limbo.

While countries such as France committed themselves to nuclear power—risks and all—the nuclear industry in the United States was stalemated. In 1979, only seventy-two nuclear plants were operational, contributing only 14 percent of electricity production and only 4 percent of total energy consumption. The environmental movement can take only partial credit for the weakening commitment to nuclear power. Economic highs and lows made forecasting of needs difficult for utilities and inspired more cautious plans for meeting future energy needs. The array of energy choices available, although many were little more than speculation, made it difficult to choose a single source for the future.

ALTERNATIVE ENERGY FUTURES

The debate over nuclear power is in part a microcosm of the much larger controversy over energy's role in modern American society. Trying to determine what that role is and should be, led to questions about what the society is and might become. The events of the 1970s resulted in a vigorous and conscious soul-searching about "alternative energy futures." While the American public was mostly concerned with immediate energy needs, scholars, social commentators, scientists, public officials, and others produced abundant books, articles, reports, plans, scenarios, and strategies as guidelines for the passage through the third energy transition.

Alternative Fuels

On a mundane level, the search for alternative energy futures led to a search for new or little-used energy sources to replace or complement those that

---

[8]Philip L. Cantelon and Robert C. Williams, *Crisis Contained; The Department of Energy at Three Mile Island* (Carbondale, Ill., 1982), p. xi. See also Daniel F. Ford, *Three Mile Island* (New York, 1982); Daniel Martin, *Three Mile Island* (Cambridge, Mass., 1980).

were becoming scarce (or were perceived as scarce). Several untapped sources of fossil fuels were available, including the conversion of coal into gas or liquid; the liquefaction of shale in Colorado, Utah, and Wyoming to retrieve oil; the extraction of oil from tar sands in Utah (and Canada); and efforts at tertiary recovery from oil deposits. (Primary recovery derives from natural gas pressure or pumping; in secondary recovery, oil is pushed from a reservoir through the injection of water or other liquids; tertiary recovery depends on detergents and chemical agents injected into a well to release oil from sandstone.)

Various forms of solar energy attracted considerable attention, and some began to demonstrate commercial viability: solar thermal conversion; photovoltaic cells; wind power; tidal power; ocean thermal conversion; and biomass. Photovoltaic cells are usually composed on thin layers of silicon that have been "contaminated" with boron and phosphorous. When sunlight strikes the cells, an electric current is generated that can be adapted for the production of light, heating, and cooling. Biomass, such as municipal organic wastes and agricultural wastes, have solar energy stored in them. Biomass conversion to methanol or ethyl alcohol has several applications. The best known is gasohol, composed of 90 percent gasoline and 10 percent ethyl alcohol.

Geothermal energy, heat in molten rock deep within the earth, has been harnessed in special locations in Hawaii, California, and at various other sites. Sources of geothermal include crystal rocks, sediments, volcanic deposits, and various steam emissions from the ground. Controlled thermonuclear fusion, the conversion of hydrogen into liquid, and cogeneration[9] represent a range of other intriguing technologies.

The oil embargo stimulated federal action with respect to alternative fuels. In December 1973, the AEC released a report, "The Nation's Energy Future," at the request of President Nixon. The report explored various energy sources and called for the establishment of ERDA. However, Congress did not enact legislation to promote research and development among several energy alternatives until after Nixon's resignation. In September 1974, Congress passed the Geothermal Energy Research, Development, and Demonstration Act, and the Solar Heating and Cooling Demonstration Act. These were followed by the Solar Energy Research, Development and Demonstration Act, and the Federal Non-Nuclear Energy Research and Development Act. Finally in 1980, these laws were supported by additional implementing legislation and bills promoting other sources, such as synthetic fuels, biomass energy, ocean thermal energy, and wind energy. While drawing attention to various alternative fuels, these efforts were too diffuse, uncoordinated, and underfunded to have much impact.

Debate over alternative fuels has been intense, and it centers on technical feasibility. For example, fusion is theoretically possible, but the process

---

[9]Cogeneration is the simultaneous production of electricity and useful thermal energy such as hot water, steam, and hot gases.

of super-heating hydrogen atoms and then finding a medium to contain the resulting energy release poses incredible problems. Accessibility of the energy source has also been an important question. Potential locations for exploiting geothermal energy are few in the United States. Even scarcer are locations where dams could be built across the mouth of a bay to tap ocean tides for power. Some experts estimated that the United States possesses, at best, one site for developing a tidal power facility. More promising is OTEC (ocean thermal energy conversion) which takes advantage of temperature differences in the ocean to power heat engines. However, this energy source is generally restricted to tropical areas. The "sustainability" of an energy source has been yet another crucial consideration. Some experts question whether solar thermal conversion or the use of wind power has broad application, or must be restricted by climate and other physical limitations.

Cost by far has been the most significant point of debate and the most difficult to determine. All new sources of energy have been evaluated with an eye to cost. Can solar power compete with central-station electricity generation? Does it make more sense to develop additional offshore oil sites than to develop programs of energy retrieval from shale or tar sands? The debate over cost has been at its most intense when noneconomic issues are raised. A frequent question is whether cost is defined too narrowly—too much attention to short-term goals, too little attention to long-range implications.

The Debate over Growth

The debate over cost suggests that the question of energy futures goes well beyond alternative fuels. A Resources for the Future study stated: "Energy has become the testing ground for conflict over broader social choices." Energy expert Earl Cook asserted somewhat pessimistically: "The 'hidden crisis' of today is a crisis of attitudes and institutions rather than energy shortages and higher prices. It involves a shortage of planning and decision capability."[10] How different the tone of these assertions is from the optimism of the nineteenth century.

The realization that energy is, has been, and will continue to be an integral part of American life led an array of experts and commentators to evaluate future energy use and development within the larger context of the shape of the nation and the world to be. Several long-held values and traditions came under scrutiny. Issues no less monumental than individual rights and freedoms, economic equity, the preservation of the environment, the role of government, and world peace were introduced into the debate over America's energy future.

The convergence of the environmental movement and the energy crisis made economic growth a centerpiece for debate. The roots of the debate go back into history. During the 1960s, the question of worldwide population growth became a highly publicized issue—not simply in terms of anticipated

---

[10]Earl Cook, *Man, Energy, Society* (San Francisco, 1976), p. 443.

food shortages but also because of the depletion of resources and the increase in industrial pollution. Professor Kenneth Boulding criticized unrestrained growth as reckless and pioneered the concept of "spaceship earth." A "spaceship economy" (an economy of limited resources) took into account the finite nature of the world's resources, suggesting a move away from the idea of unlimited growth. This was an early form of "ecological economics," which placed emphasis on social and political equity as well as on economic growth.

With the onset of the energy crisis, the debate over growth moved beyond ecological economics to energy futures. At its most tepid, the debate concentrated on the *rate* of growth; at its most volatile, it focused on the *ends* of growth. Proponents of continued energy growth stressed past benefits—comfort, material well-being, high employment, and more leisure time. They maintained a faith in the market mechanism to adjust to scarce resources, to produce technical fixes in exploiting available energy sources, and to create or discover new sources.

Opponents of unlimited growth questioned the equity in distribution of wealth due to past economic practices. They viewed growth as leading to more material goods, rather than better services or an improved quality of life. Those holding the most extreme position—zero economic growth—were apprehensive about continued industrialization, fearing that it would lead to the exhaustion of resources and future ecological disasters. Those with more moderate views did not fear total exhaustion of resources or the reaching of absolute environmental limits but were concerned about scarcities and increased costs, which would put goods and services beyond the reach of many Americans.

Some stressed the social and political consequences of unlimited growth. More complex centralized systems that produced and sustained growth might threaten personal liberty, even the democratic process. To redress these potential and real inequities, those opposed to unlimited growth offered several major adjustments: steering growth away from resource-intensive industries, redistributing income, giving higher priority to quality of life interests. In essence, these goals required a shift in values.

Little wonder that the debate over growth tended to polarize the sides. Speaking about what he conceived as a three-pronged crisis in the 1970s—energy, environment, economy—Barry Commoner noted: ". . . each effort to solve one crisis seems to clash with the solutions of the others—pollution control reduces energy supplies; energy conservation costs jobs. Inevitably, proponents of one solution become opponents of the others."[11] This may be too simple an answer, but the debate over economic growth extended into broader considerations of alternative energy futures.

An important popularization of the no-growth or antigrowth view was expressed by E. F. Schumacher in *Small Is Beautiful: Economics as if People Mattered* (1973). Drawing ideas from Buddhist teaching, Gandhi, and decentralists such as Tolstoy, Lewis Mumford, and Theodore Roszak, Schumacher

[11]Barry Commoner, *The Poverty of Power* (London, 1976), p. 1.

criticized governmental and economic bigness and centralization and lauded communal, human-scaled, decentralized cultures. He blamed society's commitment to unlimited economic growth, high technology, and consumerism for the social and economic ills of the world:

> We shrink back from the truth if we believe that the destructive forces of the modern world can be "brought under control" simply by mobilising more resources . . . to fight pollution, to preserve wildlife, to discover new sources of energy, and to arrive at more effective agreements on peaceful coexistence. Needless to say, wealth, education, research, and many other things are needed for any civilization, but what is most needed today is a revision of the ends which these means are meant to serve. And this implies, above all else, the development of a lifestyle which accords to material things their proper, legitimate place, which is secondary and not primary.

Soft versus Hard Energy Paths

Schumacher's message captured the spirit of the counterculture of the 1960s. However, it did little more than pillory modern society in ways that it had been criticized before. Amory B. Lovins—a young American physicist living in Britain, representative of the Friends of the Earth, and ardent opponent of nuclear power—focused the antigrowth debate on the energy issue with his article, "Energy Strategy: The Road Not Taken?" published in *Foreign Affairs* in 1976. In this article and subsequent studies, Lovins presented a critique of the contemporary American energy system and offered a radical alternative.

Lovins' critique was built on the assumption that the energy question could not and should not be restricted to technical issues. Too much expertise, he argued, tended to obscure the basic questions that deal with choice based on personal values. First, much of the energy debate was "divergence about what the energy problem 'really' is." Lovins stated that the policy of sustaining growth in energy consumption and limiting imports was no answer at all. Instead, he recommended an "end-use orientation," that is, to determine "how much of what kind of energy is needed to do the task for which the energy is desired, and then supplying exactly that kind."[12]

In Lovins's eyes the energy problem was not so much tied to the source as to the society that used it. While he opposed nuclear power, he was more concerned with the possible formation of a "plutonium economy." A significant social change, he reasoned, was necessary to get off the "hard energy path" and onto the "soft energy path." Hard energy paths were "high-energy, nuclear, centralized, electric"; soft paths were "lower-energy, fission-free, decentralized, less electrified."[13] Even a scaled-down "nuclear-electric future" was still "hard" since electrical power would remain centralized. Furthermore, the giant energy facilities on the hard path were remote and unfamil-

---

[12]Amory B. Lovins, *Soft Energy Paths* (Cambridge, Mass., 1977), pp. 3ff.

[13]Lovins and John H. Price, *Non-Nuclear Futures* (Cambridge, Mass., 1975), p. xxiii.

iar, while soft energy systems, especially solar power, were closer to end-use and thus within the control of those that utilize energy. A soft path, with human-scaled, environmentally safe energy systems, reinforced individualism, participatory governance, and reduced the authoritarianism associated with centralization.

Lovins's dichotomy between hard and soft energy paths attracted considerable attention. Some energy experts refined the construct or borrowed from it in touting their own energy strategies for the future. In *Energy in America's Future* (1979)—the product of Resources for the Future's Energy Strategies Project—the polar views of energy policy are stated as "expansionist" and "limited." The expansionist view emphasized the increased availability of energy supplies to meet growing demand, while the limited view emphasized reduction in energy demands and preservation of environmental values. To reconcile these conflicting positions, the study sought to outline a "consensus" position, drawing the best approaches from all those available.

The much-publicized Energy Project of the Harvard Business School resulted in *Energy Future* (1979), under the direction of Robert Stobaugh and Daniel Yergin. It also sought a "balanced" energy program. Unwilling to call for a basic restructuring of society, *Energy Future* proposed to ease the transition from the energy crisis of the 1970s to the new century's "more balanced system of energy sources" through development of solar energy and "conservation as energy source." The Ford Foundation's Energy Policy Project produced *A Time to Choose: America's Energy Future* (1974), which advocated a slower growth than the historical patterns of previous years.

Some proposals were closer to Lovins's intention than those above. David Morris' *Self-Reliant Cities* (1982) advocated that cities move toward energy self-reliance through the development of decentralized power plants and other decentralized energy systems. The "ecological city" (and energy independence) was possible because of rising energy and material prices, as well as the role of modern science in providing effective decentralized systems.

James Ridgeway and Bettina Conner, in *New Energy* (1975), envisioned a system based on several principles akin to Lovins's view: the nation's natural resources belong to all of the people, thus citizens should expect a fair share of energy. The system must be rooted in local popular control, and access to energy information must be open. Energy prices should be as low as possible, with nonrenewable resources used only when necessary. The authors emphasized the creation of a new local governmental unit, the Public Energy District, to establish and administer energy policy.

Lewis J. Perelman, in *Energy Transitions: Long-Term Perspectives* (1981), foresaw an inevitable transformation of the United States from a society based on fossil fuel energy to one based on solar energy. The social ramifications of such a transition would be enormous. In the twenty-first century, the United States would become a feudalistic society where wealth and power would be based on land holdings, politics would be decentralized, social stratification would be by class and caste, and the economy would be a "quasi-steady-state." Perelman concluded that the soft path was "almost certain to become the dominant social paradigm of America," because fragmenting a society was easier than integrating it. But Perelman warned that the transformation needed to be done with an eye to avoiding "a stifling, inhumane society," which avoided the excesses of conflict. Perelman's view took the Lovins projection beyond advocacy to scenario building, and thus it raised questions about the manner in which such a transition could be achieved.

Advocates of the hard path—or critics of the soft path (these are not necessarily the same)—questioned Lovins's defense of "appropriate" technology and his decentralist position. It was common for critics to characterize the decentralist approach as "romantic" or simply the promotion of "a post-industrial pastoral society." Samuel C. Florman, engineer, commentator, proponent of centralization and critic of "the anti-technological backlash," responded to the decentralist argument in a chapter entitled "Small Is Dubious":

> "Smallness," after all, is a word that is neutral—technologically, socially, aesthetically, and, of course, morally. Its use as a symbol of goodness would be one more entertaining example of human folly were it not for the disturbing consequences of the arguments advanced in its cause.[14]

Soon after Lovins's piece appeared in *Foreign Affairs*, congressional interest mounted, resulting in a joint hearing of two Senate committees. This attention tended to legitimize decentralization and the soft path as potential policy alternatives. But it also heightened the criticism of Lovins's proposals—from his use of statistical evidence to his broad contentions about transforming society. Some feared that Lovins's proposals could lead to a policy effective enough to retard or even curb economic growth. Others questioned turning away from conventional sources of energy so quickly, which would lead to economic stress among energy industries and divert attention from the problems of the present. Beyond the extremists among Lovins's critics were pragmatists who tried to emphasize the differences among short-term, intermediary, and long-term energy requirements and goals. Energy issues were, in the modern era, also worldwide in scope and impact. Some critics could not reconcile a decentralization plan with that fact.

Several studies favoring a new direction for energy policy did not begin with the premise that Lovins's views offered the only hope for the nation. Instead, they argued that U.S. energy prospects were not likely to change dramatically overnight, and thus goals for the immediate future were most pressing. How much government intervention or how much of a free market approach would be necessary to continue the flow of energy supplies and avoid a repeat of the problems of the 1970s was paramount. For example, the comprehensive energy analysis conducted for the Department of Energy by the National Research Council Committee on Nuclear and Alternative En-

---

[14]Samuel C. Florman, *Blaming Technology* (New York, 1981), p. 96.

ergy Systems, *Energy in Transition, 1985–2010* (1979), made several observations that were more modest in tone than the studies cited above: (1) energy conservation was of prime importance; (2) fluid fuel supply was a critical immediate issue; (3) for the intermediate period, only coal and nuclear power were viable options; (4) the breeder option had to be kept open; and (5) investment in research and development of new energy sources was essential.

Given the vast array of views expressed by energy experts, self-proclaimed or otherwise, the nation faced confounding choices by 1980. The options were at once complex and specific, practical and revolutionary. A pessimist looked at the intensity of the energy debate and saw an insurmountable problem. An optimist saw in the energy debate the first real effort to come to grips with the nation's energy requirements, environmental concerns, and future needs. In contrast with the early nineteenth century, the place of energy in American life seemed gigantic, unwieldly, and imposing during the 1970s. But going into the third energy transition, the role of energy had not grown so much as it had changed. In an age of abundance, energy was easier to take for granted. The threat of scarcity took away that luxury.

FURTHER READING

Mary Clay Berry. *The Alaska Pipeline.* Bloomington, Ind., 1975.

Steven Ebbin and Raphael Kasper. *Citizen Groups and the Nuclear Controversy.* Cambridge, Mass., 1974.

Daniel Ford. *The Cult of the Atom.* New York, 1982.

Craig R. Humphrey and Frederick R. Buttel. *Environment, Energy and Society.* Belmont, Calif., 1982.

Donella H. Meadows and Dennis C. Meadows. *The Limits to Growth.* New York, 1972.

Marc Messing, H. Paul Friesema, and David Mosell. *Centralized Power: The Politics of Scale in Electricity Generation.* Cambridge, Mass., 1979.

Mancur Olson and Hans H. Landsberg (eds.). *The No-Growth Society.* New York, 1973.

William Ophuls. *Ecology and the Politics of Scarcity.* San Francisco, 1977.

Michael Parfit. *Last Stand at Rosebud Creek: Coal, Power, and People.* New York, 1980.

Jerome Price. *The Antinuclear Movement.* Boston, 1982.

John Quarles. *Cleaning Up America.* Boston, 1976.

Marc J. Roberts and Jeremy S. Bluhm. *The Choices of Power: Utilities Face the Environmental Challenge.* Cambridge, Mass., 1981.

Elizabeth S. Rolph. *Nuclear Power and Public Safety.* Lexington, Mass., 1979.

Walter A. Rosenbaum. *The Politics of Environmental Concern.* New York, 1973.

Allan Schnaiberg. *The Environment: From Surplus to Scarcity.* New York, 1980.

Epilogue: Into the 1980s

> By the next decade, old-timers will be trying to explain to youngsters that there was a President from the State of Georgia who believed that the energy problem was "the moral equivalent of war." When the youngsters ask "why?" I bet the old-timers won't remember.

That description was made by an environmental science professor in a 1981 *Newsweek* editorial. The optimism of the statement is remarkable, given what had transpired just two years earlier. The editorial affirmed the virtue of the market system, and declared that a positive result of declining consumption, replacement of oil with other fuels, and the loosening grip of OPEC was the potential for an energy self-sufficient North America. "Our energy costs may not go down very much," he concluded, "but the fuels we use will be home-grown and more secure. The Middle East will become a much less interesting place."[1]

During the Carter administration, the Commission for a National Agenda for the Eighties was created. In its 1980 report, it declared that "Our energy predicament remains unsolved." But it added:

> Past reliance on the rhetoric of crisis has probably harmed the nation's ability to cope with its energy problems because Americans soon discovered that predictions of imminent catastrophe did not materialize. Gas lines came and went without long-term impact, and the absence of a crisis came to be interpreted as the absence of a problem.

In the October 1980 issue of *New Age*, Amory Lovins referred to the "energy crisis" in a decidedly different tone than in the 1970s:

> The energy problem is no longer interesting. The conceptual outline of how to solve it is clear. The much tougher problem of implementation still offers a real challenge, but millions of individuals are already tackling these "insurmountable opportunities," and the tools are available for anyone to join in. We are increasingly persuaded that it is likely that our culture *can* emerge from the energy problem more or less in one piece—and thus be able to address the more interesting and challenging problems, such as water/land/food/population, ecolog-

[1]*Newsweek* (May 18, 1981), pp. 32–33.

320

ical and climatic stability, peace and social justice, which may or may not be soluble.[2]

In the aftermath of the energy crisis and in the midst of a new-found optimism about the nation's energy present—if not its future—Ronald Reagan became the 39th President of the United States. Inauguration Day, January 20, 1981, was a time of joy and apprehension. The American hostages held in Iran for 444 days were coming home, but the nation was in the throes of a recession complete with inflation and high unemployment. Self-assured before the television cameras, the new President offered the United States "the elixir of 'supply-side economics' mixed with a strong draught of military spending" to cure its economic woes.[3] Reagan's approach to government was built on faith in the productive capacity of the United States—not on a fear of future energy shortages.

Within the next few years, oil prices stabilized and even declined in the wake of an international oil glut. Experts warned about the transitory nature of the consumers' boom—and the possible financial repercussions—but it was difficult not to breathe a little easier. OPEC's imminent demise was proclaimed in newspapers and magazines as a self-fulfilling prophecy of sorts. When the American economy began to climb out of the recession, it seemed that the decade of the 1970s was eons away. The most recent National Energy Policy Plan, announced on October 4, 1983, formally abandoned the national goal of energy independence. Energy Secretary Donald Hodel asserted: "This plan does not contemplate total self-sufficiency. This contemplates working toward what I would call energy non-dependence, in which we continue to import where that makes economic sense, but not to the extent that an interruption drastically undercuts our economy or our military capability."

The return of optimism in the early 1980s may be temporary, but it suggests that historic forces have had a stronger impact on the nation's energy present than have the fading memories of the energy crisis. The United States did not move quickly toward a "postpetroleum economy" after 1979, and aside from some conservation of gasoline, electricity, and home heating fuels, Americans did not lose faith in America the Abundant. The Reagan administration tapped the long-standing commitment to progress through economic growth by focusing on energy production rather than end-use. It perpetuated the traditional concepts of abundance and the market economy.

Does the book, then, end where it began? Has nothing really changed in more than 160 years? Was the energy crisis simply a false scare or a contrivance? Did a new energy transition derail before it began? The answer to all these questions is a decided "no." Possibly the pessimism of the 1970s was

[2]Amory Lovins and Hunter Sheldon Lovins, "Good News About Energy," *New Age*, vol. 6 (October 1980), p. 30.

[3]William E. Leuchtenburg, *A Troubled Feast* (Boston, 1983), p. 283.

exaggerated, but the corresponding optimism of the early 1980s was likewise premature.

ENERGY ABUNDANCE

Scarcity in an Energy-Intensive Society

During the 1970s, the notion of scarcity challenged that of abundance. Energy experts were quick to point out, however, that the nation experienced a "fuel" scarcity rather than a full-fledged "energy" crisis. In an absolute sense, there was plenty of energy to be exploited, only oil and gas posed an immediate problem. The fuel scarcity was a serious matter, which in a positive way helped to dispel the notion that energy sources were inexhaustible. A 1981 estimate stated that the United States had only about eight years of proved recoverable reserves at the 1979 production rate, and only about ten years of natural gas. On a world scale, there were about twenty-eight years of proved recoverable reserves of oil, and fifty-one years of natural gas.

Yet the faith in abundance was not undermined even by these grim predictions. Scarcity challenged abundance but could not replace such a long-standing American tradition. Some observers suggested that the oil problem was not a question of supply per se; rather, it stemmed from limited access due to the prevailing international situation (oil as a diplomatic problem). Advocates of supply-side economics believed that more aggressive efforts at oil exploration—especially on federally held property, better recovery techniques, and greater incentives to oil companies—would increase immediate supplies and expand proven reserves (oil as a political and technical problem). Still others called for more effective conservation measures, more efficient electrical consumer goods, and more restrictive utilization of oil and gas to stretch supplies until alternatives became available (oil as an end-use problem). In all of these cases, an end to a petroleum-based economy was not envisioned.

Part of the reason for the unwillingness to look beyond the near future for oil was the degree to which energy use habits affected American culture over the years. Not only had the United States become a petroleum-based culture in the twentieth century but also the most energy-intensive society on earth. It was committed to a one-dimensional transportation system dominated by the automobile. The built environment became utterly dependent on electrical power. Industry was increasingly mechanized and much less labor intensive. The middle-class lifestyle was the envy of the world, but it trapped Americans into a society founded on massive use of energy (see Figure E.1). The flurry of interest in wood-burning stoves, better home insulation, and even the move toward smaller cars were cosmetic changes that did not alter the situation.

While oil and gas shortages challenged the notion of abundance, the

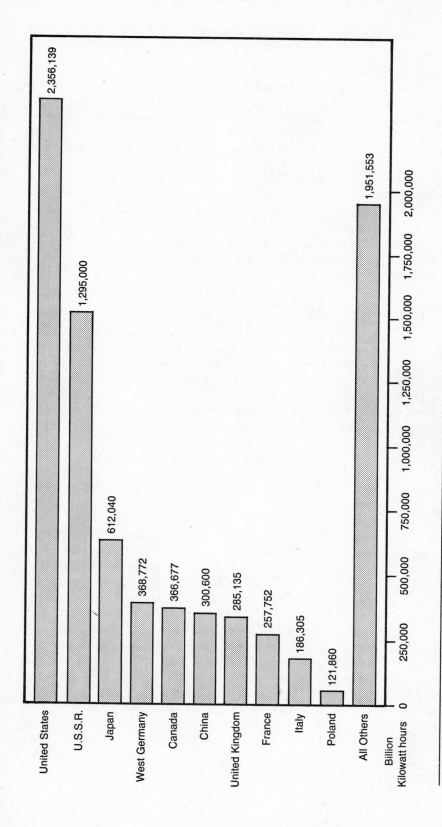

Figure E.1 World's Largest Electric Energy Producers, 1980
Source: Adapted from *Information Please Almanac, 1983* (Austin, Tex., 1983), p. 344.

definition of abundance was broadened by the energy crisis. As they calculated the statistical limits of oil and gas reserves, energy experts also evaluated alternative sources. For example, in comparison with oil and gas, the United States has more than 100 years of proven recoverable coal reserves—191,000 of the world's 693,000 million metric tons. Other alternative sources—theoretically at least—surpass oil, gas, and even coal in availability; they include various forms of solar power, atomic fusion, hydrogen utilization, and so forth. While these sources are admittedly long-range alternatives, study and evaluation of new energy sources have helped to undermine the single-source mentality of Americans. The awareness of alternatives, however, has also reinforced the faith in American know-how, American technology, American prestige and power, and America the Abundant. It would seem that a society that could put a man on the moon, as the saying goes, could solve its energy problems.

The Third Energy Transition

The energy crisis in the 1970s was, at the least, pause for reflection. It was also the beginning of the third energy transition. That the transition was just beginning is borne out by the contradictions that emerged in the wake of events in the 1970s. For example, higher fuel costs encouraged some conservation, but the United States continued to depend on foreign oil supplies. In 1980, imports dropped by 20 percent; and between April 1981, and April 1982, 36 percent. Yet imports still accounted for one-quarter of the nation's petroleum needs.

The automobile continued to be the mainstay of American transportation; there were no challengers on the scene, although during the late 1970s, there was much talk of upgrading the nation's anemic mass transit system. During the early days of the Reagan administration, discussion of federal support for mass transit all but evaporated. Officials planned to phase out federal operating subsidies to mass transit systems by 1985; those subsidies ($1.1 billion in 1981) accounted for 13 percent of the operating revenues. Drew Lewis, Reagan's first secretary of transportation, stated: "Mass transit is always going to be subsidized . . . [but] we figure that it is not an unreasonable thing for a local community and a state to pay for."[4] State legislatures and municipalities, however, were unwilling to raise taxes to establish or upgrade existing systems. Moreover, the physical layout of major American cities—sprawling, multicentered, or no-centered—posed nightmares to planners of mass transit systems. If Houston could afford a subway system, for example, (or could build one under the subsiding city) where would it go? Who would it serve?

Despite the forces nurturing the petroleum-based culture of the United States, the control of oil by OPEC and other foreign powers forced the United States at least to explore alternative energy sources. While the poten-

---

[4]*Newsweek* (June 1, 1981), p. 44.

tial was great, initial ventures proved less promising. The renewed optimism of the early 1980s worked against crash programs on the scale of the Manhattan Project and, it indicated the tentativeness with which Americans entered the third transition.[5]

The problem for the nuclear power industry was formidable. Decline in electrical consumption—an annual increase of only 2.8 percent in 1979 as compared with 7 percent in the early 1970s—while a hopeful sign for advocates of energy conservation, was deadly for the nuclear industry. Despite the enthusiastic endorsement of President Reagan, nuclear power was unlikely to be the energy panacea of the near future. Between 1972 and 1983, 102 nuclear plants were canceled with only 88 in operation. The on-again, off-again industry found itself caught between market competition with fossil fuels and strong resistance from antinuclear forces.

Other alternative energy sources also showed great potential, but they failed to enter the energy market in a major way by the early 1980s. An article in *Time* clearly stated the fate of coal: COAL MAINLY STANDS AND WAITS. While coal continued to be an important fuel for electric utilities, its environmental risks undermined its resurgence. Coal's cousin, synthetic fuel from shale, lignite, and low-sulfur coal, had a promising send-off by the Carter administration, but it quickly languished. Carter's plan, which called for federally subsidized synfuel plants ($88 billion in loan, purchase, and price guarantees), lost ground as oil prices stabilized. The sharpest blow to synfuels was the decision of Exxon and Tosco Corporation to pull out of the Colony Shale Oil Project in Colorado in May 1982. The only surviving major effort was the Great Plains Coal Gasification Project in Beulah, North Dakota. The Reagan administration also scaled down funding for the Synthetic Fuels Corporation which administered the federal program.

Solar power has been viewed by many as a promising alternative—inexhaustible in supply, essentially nonpolluting, and most frequently decentralized. While not a practical transportation fuel, solar power offered the potential for assuming many energy tasks formerly done by fossil oil and gas. But as the editor of *Sun Times* (which is the magazine of the solar lobby in Washington) asserted: "Solar energy, often praised for its simplicity, is simple only in concept. Converting sunshine into useful and economical energy requires thoughtful engineering as well as strong public support."[6] Photovoltaic cells, passive solar systems, and solar water-heating have increased in use but remain technologies still in their infancy.

Solar energy failed to attract the kind of financial and political backing enjoyed by nuclear power and the oil industry. In 1980, DOE set a goal that 10 to 15 percent of the country's electricity would derive from solar energy by the year 2000. But in 1981, the budget for solar was cut from $576 million

---

[5]The traditional American bias against long-range planning in any context has also been a factor. How to plan nationally in a nation of states and distinct regions exacerbates the dilemma.

[6]Kevin Finneran, "Solar Technology: A Whether Report," *Technology Review*, vol. 86 (April 1983), p. 48.

to $300 million, and it was in for more cuts in succeeding years. The Reagan administration stated that solar energy must rise or fall in the marketplace on the strength of private development—a pronouncement that inaccurately implies that other sources of energy have done the same.

For the Reagan administration, in particular, and for many Americans, in general, energy sources remained competitive rather than complementary in the early 1980s. Stability in price and supply of the prevailing energy source precluded much attention to future alternatives. In this sense, the early stages of the third transition were fragile—a quick rise in gasoline prices or a sudden drop in supply and the crisis could start anew.

The onset of the third transition revealed only subtle changes in values linked to energy. The debate over centralized versus decentralized energy systems was most revealing about changing attitudes. An intriguing example was the interest in local self-reliance and the generation of "neighborhood power." While advocates of self-reliance overstated their success, the activities of the Institute for Local Self-Reliance and similar groups gained national attention. Local self-reliance goes beyond energy questions, but the establishment of "humanly scaled" energy systems is an integral part of the program. Cogeneration technology is at the heart of the self-reliance approach, and it received an important boost when Congress passed the Public Utility Regulatory Act of 1978 (PURPA). To encourage the use of cogeneration and renewable resources for power production, PURPA required utility companies to purchase electricity from independent power producers and to provide backup power at low cost. Independent power producers were also exempted from state and federal regulation. Curiously, this unique movement captured the spirit of limited federal intervention advocated by the Reagan administration, but it was committed to the decentralist view, which criticized the corporate interests that the administration supported.

Like the previous transitions, the latest has been gradual and sporadic in its early stages. But it has been unique in one important respect: the sense of improvement that accompanied the change from wind/waterpower/wood to coal, and from coal to oil, has not been as intense. Because the third transition has grown out of a fear of oil scarcity, rather than through a change from one abundant energy source to another, maintaining the prevailing standard of living has been a central factor. That the scarcity of oil has been treated as a resolvable crisis and that oil has continued to be regarded as essential to maintaining the status quo, indicates that long-held views toward energy are not so readily abandoned. The contradictions of the latest transition suggest its complexity as well as its potential for becoming the most significant in American history.

ENERGY, THE ECONOMY, AND GOVERNMENT

During the energy crisis of the 1970s, policy makers were obsessed with the role of the United States as a consumer of energy. The impact of the nation as a net importer hit the nation with full force after the Arab oil embargo. In the early 1980s, the Reagan administration attempted to swing the pendulum back by focusing on energy production. The application of supply-side economics to energy was the tangible sign of that shift. As it was during the New Deal, recent energy policy was subservient to broader economic interests. Like New Dealers, Reagan officials utilized the economic hard times to justify more intense energy exploration and to deregulate private energy supplies. In the broadest sense, "Reaganomics" was a return to a market-oriented approach to energy. However, it was constrained by the perpetuation of a hybrid energy market and large institutional forces outside the control of government, namely, big oil, OPEC, and so forth.

The primary force behind the faith in private development of energy was a reaffirmation of the historic role of government as promoter of economic growth. What the Reagan administration rejected was the additional role of regulator and intervener. The separate pieces of Reagan's national energy policy were codified in *Securing America's Energy Future: The National Energy Policy Plan,* submitted to Congress in July 1981. Hardly a "plan" in the strictest sense, it broke with the Carter program, asserted the value of a free energy market, and set as the top priority the fostering of increased energy production.

Since the economic interests of the nation continued to be linked to large, powerful energy industries, the Reagan administration's market orientation did not lead to unrestrained competition. There was no attempt to tamper with the large multinationals and large oil independents, or to frustrate the largest oil companies from diversifying into other energy sources (namely, coal and nuclear power). The primary goal was to remove government impediments to corporate action in the hope of promoting economic growth. Consolidation and centralization were not regarded as essentially bad. Much like Theodore Roosevelt, Reaganites who favored or at least tolerated centralization, saw in oil company diversification the means to apply greater financial and administrative resources in the development of alternative energy sources. Diversification also meant that less governmental participation was needed in that development. Critics of centralization, however, were quick to point out that energy diversification was another example of how major companies stifled competition and assured the preeminence of oil for the near future.

Since the Reagan energy policy was based on promoting economic growth, continued federal participation in the economy sometimes took precedence over the free market approach. For example, the state of the natural gas industry was precarious in the late 1970s. The Natural Gas Policy Act of 1978 began a limited decontrol program, bringing with it inevitable price increases. The recession in the early 1980s exacerbated the problem—a sharp drop in industrial demand for natural gas put serious price pressure on residential users. Since natural gas regulation differentiated between old gas and new gas, complete decontrol would ultimately benefit those holding large supplies of cheap, old gas and would hurt those controlling artificially high-priced new gas. Since the Reagan administration was trying to bring the nation out of recession, immediate decontrol could have dire economic consequences. It, therefore, decided on a plan that fell short of that step. By 1983, revision of the 1978 act was not achieved, and the winners and losers in the natural gas controversy were not yet determined.

A decision in 1983 to raise the federal tax on gasoline by $.05 a gallon also demonstrated the cross-purposes under which the administration operated. That decision came in the wake of an international oil glut, and gasoline prices dropped below $1.00 a gallon for the first time in several years. The administration justified the tax on the grounds that the nation's roads and highways were deteriorating badly, and thus the new revenue could be used for maintenance, repairs, and new construction (which would also stimulate employment).

But there were other reasons. On the one hand, the Reagan administration favored using the tax to reverse the trend in sliding prices of crude, which encouraged more consumption. At the same time, it was looking for ways to increase revenue, without raising income taxes, to offset rising deficits due primarily to large-scale military spending. The $.05 tax, therefore, was not so much an energy measure as it was a general economic measure.

The administration's advocacy of nuclear power also fell under the category of promoting economic growth—in this case providing additional supplies of electricity for the future. To justify the federal role in the promotion and development of nuclear power, spokesmen for the administration asserted that in areas where market forces were unlikely to bring about "desirable new energy technologies and practices" within *a reasonable time,* federal involvement might be necessary. Despite the growing rejection of nuclear power in the marketplace, the administration did what it could to stimulate the industry's growth. The President lifted the 1977 ban on reprocessing uranium in spent fuel rods to produce plutonium. (Carter had originally announced the ban to check the spread of nuclear weapons.) In addition, Reagan ordered the NRC to speed up procedures for licensing nuclear plants. The administration, however, encountered foot-dragging from the NRC, continued pressure from antinuclear forces, and unsympathetic court decisions; but it plowed ahead nonetheless with its efforts to get nuclear plants back on line.

In several ways, the Reagan administration did try to make good its pledge to reduce regulatory impediments to energy production and to streamline the federal energy bureaucracy; but it paid little attention to long-range future energy needs. It clearly had an aversion to planning as a way of setting policy. And it rejected the notion, which became popular in the Nixon years and after, for a comprehensive energy plan that would incorporate short, intermediary, and long-term policies. The purest application of the market-oriented approach was Reagan's lifting of the remaining controls on gasoline, propane, and crude in January 1981.

The nonplanning of the Reagan administration was often planning in a different guise. The administration argued that the nation's energy problems were caused primarily by federal interference in the marketplace, not because of fuel scarcities. As Reagan's first Secretary of Energy, James B. Edwards, asserted: "We've got tremendous energy resources in America and all we have to do is go in and unlock them."[7] The dismantling or reorganizing of the federal energy bureaucracy, especially the Department of Energy, was an important step in fulfilling many of the administration's energy and economic goals. First, reducing the bureaucracy would fulfill the campaign promise of government austerity. Second, the expunging of regulations, the curtailment of enforcement powers, and the diffusion of agency authority would remove unpopular obstacles to private energy developers. Finally, without powerful, centralized energy agencies, the federal government would be less likely to act as a countervailing force in the energy market.

The administration's view of energy was present-oriented and essentially nationalistic. Reagan officials had great faith that the private sector would meet the nation's energy needs. This belief was based on the assumption that traditional energy supplies were relatively abundant, and future energy demand would stimulate the development of alternative fuels. The major exception was its support for nuclear power. The Reagan view was essentially nationalistic, in the sense that economic growth and energy use were usually cast in domestic terms; that is, increased production at home would bring the United States closer to self-sufficiency. (Although this view may have been losing ground by late 1983.)

Significantly, the role of OPEC was in flux during the early 1980s. Never a true cartel, it came to be viewed by many energy experts outside the administration as a source of stability in the international oil market. Richard O'Brien, chief economist of the American Express Bank in London, noted: "The only thing worse than OPEC managing the price of oil is nobody managing it."[8]

The Reagan administration appeared to be affected only marginally by the energy crisis. (An exception was the claim that too much governmental intervention distorted the energy market.) Instead, the administration reasserted the historic role of government as promoter of economic growth and private development of natural resources. Some viewed Reagan as a throwback to the pre-World War I era, when energy policy was subservient to broader economic interests. Others saw a great deal of continuity with the past, especially the faith in American abundance.

ENERGY AND ENVIRONMENT

Energy and environment were inextricably linked as issues during the 1970s. But the setting for debate changed markedly in a few short years. Environmental groups were well-entrenched within the economic and political institutions of the United States, but their power and influence were still largely

[7]Cited in Jack Holl, *The United States Department of Energy: A History* (Washington, D.C., 1982), p. 9.

[8]*Time* (February 7, 1983), p. 43.

dependent on the tone and actions of government. In the 1960s and 1970s, the federal government did not always lead in efforts at environmental protection, but the presidents, Congress, and the courts at least paid lip service to environmentalist goals. Clashes between energy priorities and environmental priorities were common, but the notion of "environmental cost" was normally included in discussions of energy policy.

The Reagan administration, however, demonstrated a cavalier attitude toward the environment, which many people characterized as antienvironmental. Environmental costs were often viewed by the administration as an incumbrance to growth, or, at best, peripheral issues. In some cases, environmental risks from energy exploration and development were dismissed or ignored. Because environmental issues had been highly politicized in the past, the administration was suspicious of environmentalists and environmental groups. Public protests against nuclear power and criticism of the energy establishment, big oil, and corporate America appeared threatening to the vision of a productive, growth-oriented America. The clash of values in the 1980s widened the chasm of the 1970s.

The Reagan administration did not try to disguise its economic goals with lip service to the environmental movement. Conquering recession and restoring American world prestige, it believed, were more important than were the desires of oversensitive preservationists. The appointment of James G. Watt as secretary of the Interior and Anne McGill Burford (formerly Gorsuch) as head of the EPA were clear reminders of where the administration's priorities stood. Watt, in particular, symbolized the commitment to economic growth at all costs. Constantly at the center of an environmental storm (until his chronic "foot-in-mouth" disease drove him from office in 1983), Watt encouraged private development of federal holdings by issuing myriad oil, gas, and coal leases and by actively lobbying for weaker environmental standards for strip mining and air and water pollution. In some ways, Watt's behavior was only an extreme version of the western brand of resource development reminiscent of several of his predecessors, and an outgrowth of the so-called Sagebrush Rebellion. But Watt's open contempt for his critics—branding some as the "spiritual left"—and the panache with which he promoted resource exploitation, made environmental groups suspicious of the whole administration.

Less strident behavior also raised criticism. Charges of nonenforcement of environmental laws were common—and several were legitimate. EPA, in particular, was in the throes of controversy during the early 1980s. Congress authorized investigations into the agency's management of the $1.6 billion "superfund" program to clean up hazardous waste sites. The inquiry created a storm in EPA, leading to many firings and resignations—and a clear loss in confidence in the ability of the administration to protect the nation's health and well-being. In response, Reagan replaced Burford with William D. Ruckelshaus, the first administrator of EPA, who was a moderate with a sound reputation for effective environmental management. Some believed the appointment was merely intended to quiet opposition to the administration's economic policies; others saw it as a sincere effort to restore confidence in the EPA. In any event, environmental policy was clearly subservient to the goals of economic recovery and growth.

The response of environmental groups to the Reagan administration ranged from apprehension to dismay. In fact, there was a correlation between the administration's stated policies on energy and the environment and the rise in membership in environmentalist groups, most notably the Sierra Club and the Nature Conservancy. There was little elaboration of long-range environmentalist goals by these groups during the early 1980s, however, that was largely because environmental lobbies in Washington fought to retain the achievements of the previous decade. Attempts were made to block government offshore oil leases, to salvage the "no significant deterioration" provisions of the Clean Air acts, and to protect wilderness areas from private development. Of broader consequence were the various problems associated with hazardous wastes, including radioactive materials.

Nuclear power remained a crucial issue during the 1980s, but protests changed significantly in the post-Three Mile Island era. Siting of plants, disposal of nuclear waste, and criticism of breeder reactors remained on the environmentalist agenda. However, the stagnation of the nuclear power industry was taken as a sign of victory by many antinuclear protesters. Attention shifted back to the arms race and the possibilities of nuclear war. Tensions between the Soviet Union and the United States, the Cold War rhetoric of the Reagan administration, the proliferation of nuclear weapons, and the sophistication in the technology created a renewed sense of vulnerability.

Protests against nuclear power plants was replaced by the "nuclear freeze." In March 1981, 18 towns in Vermont supported the idea of a mutual, verifiable freeze of nuclear weapons at current levels. Within one year, the freeze idea spread to 161 Vermont towns and hundreds of town meetings throughout New England. Organized efforts were started in 43 states, including support from groups such as American Friends Service Committee, Clergy and Laity Concerned, Council for a Livable World, Federation of American Scientists, Physicians for Social Responsibility, Union of Concerned Scientists, Women's International League for Peace and Freedom, and others.

While the freeze attracted veteran antiwar activists and environmentalists, it also attracted many first-time, grassroots volunteers. The President's response was strong; he viewed the movement as "disadvantageous—in fact, even dangerous." Reagan feared that the freeze would weaken his attempts to rebuild the nation's defense in the face of the Soviets' "definite margin of superiority." He sought to undercut the freeze movement with an arms control proposal of his own, which would incorporate a long-term, rather than an immediate, freeze.

"Ground Zero Week" in the spring of 1982 was meant to raise America's consciousness about nuclear power. Much less grand, it was vaguely reminiscent of Earth Day, which took place more than a decade before. The freeze issue mirrored protests in Europe and Japan, and it was a strong criticism of the reinstitution of the Cold War. But it also took attention away from the controversy over energy and environment raised during the 1970s. In much the same way as the Reagan administration had forgotten the energy crisis, advocates of the nuclear freeze had reduced the environmental debate over nuclear power to a lower level of discourse.

In several ways, the changing perception of energy issues during the early 1980s has been a reaffirmation of the long history of energy and environment in industrial America. While guided by powerful values embedded in such concepts as abundance, Americans have taken a short-term view of their energy needs. In part, this response is the result of the many competing interests in American society, but it is also the result of the nation's rich natural wealth and its ability to acquire the resources of others. Policy makers and citizens alike have found themselves coping with abundance throughout the nation's history. In this sense, energy is not simply a commodity to produce wealth or heat, light, and power—it is an expression of the culture in terms of how we choose to exploit it, produce it, and use it. What was most difficult about establishing a national energy policy in the past was having too many choices—not too few. Coping with abundance has been and remains a major challenge for an affluent society.

INDEX

Windfall Tax Act, 293. *See also* Jimmy
    Carter, NEP
wind power, 17, 313. *See also* alterna-
    tive fuels
Windscale Pile Number One, 237. *See
    also* nuclear power
Women's International League for
    Peace and Freedom, 331. *See also*
    nuclear freeze
wood, 18–19; and ironmaking, 22; and
    railroads, 21; and steamboats,
    20–22; as transportation fuel, 20;
    deforestation, 31–32; home heating
    and, 19, 24; shortages of, 19–20;
    transition to coal, 17–34; wood-
    based energy system, 24
Work, Hubert, 149
World War I, 11, 89–102, 127; and
    coal, 91–97; and giant power, 117,
    118; and Muscle Shoals, 122; and
    oil, 97–102; and road projects,
    109; and the expansion of govern-

ment, 90; and the postwar econ-
    omy, 103. *See also* Woodrow
    Wilson
World War II, 177–195; and coal,
    180–181; and labor, 179–180; and
    oil, 181–185; and tidelands oil,
    257; gas rationing in, 186–189; im-
    mediate aftermath of, 199; prepar-
    edness, 177–180; rubber shortage
    during, 185–187. *See also* Franklin
    D. Roosevelt
WQXBS. *See* television

Yates, Eugene, 206
Yergin, Daniel, 317
Yom Kippur War. *See* Arab-Israeli War
    (1973)

Zahedi, Fazlollah, 247
Zero Population Growth, 297
Zionism. *See* Israel

ABOUT THE AUTHOR

Martin V. Melosi is a native of San Jose, California, who received a BA and MA in history from the University of Montana and a Ph.D. in history from the University of Texas at Austin. He is currently professor of history and director of the Institute for Public History at the University of Houston-University Park. He was previously on the faculty of Texas A & M University for nine years. Among his publications are *Garbage in the Cities: Refuse, Reform, and the Environment* (1981), *Pollution and Reform in American Cities, 1870–1930* (1980), and *The Shadow of Pearl Harbor: Political Controversy over the Surprise Attack* (1977).

A Note on the Type

The text of this book is set in a face equivalent to CALEDONIA on a CRT computer composition system. CALEDONIA is a Linotype face designed by W. A. Dwiggins. It belongs to the family of printing types called "modern face" by printers — a term used to mark the change in style of type-letters that occurred about 1800. CALEDONIA borders on the general design of Scotch Modern, but is more freely drawn than that letter.

The type for this book was set by P & M TYPESETTING, INC., Waterbury, CT. The book was printed and bound by BANTA COMPANY, Harrisonburg, VA.